W9-BWS-684

1135

DISCUSSION AND GROUP METHODS

Under the advisory editorship
of J. Jeffery Auer

DISCUSSION AND GROUP METHODS

THEORY AND PRACTICE

SECOND EDITION

ERNEST G. BORMANN
University of Minnesota

Harper & Row, Publishers
New York, Evanston, San Francisco, London

Sponsoring Editor: Walter H. Lippincott, Jr.
Project Editor: Holly Detgen
Designer: Jared Pratt
Production Supervisor: Will C. Jomarrón

DISCUSSION AND GROUP METHODS: Theory and Practice
Second Edition

Copyright © 1969, 1975 by Ernest G. Bormann

All rights reserved. Printed in the United States of America. No part of this book may be used or reproduced in any manner whatsoever without written permission except in the case of brief quotations embodied in critical articles and reviews. For information address Harper & Row, Publishers, Inc., 10 East 53rd Street, New York, N.Y. 10022.

Library of Congress Cataloging in Publication Data
Bormann, Ernest G.
    Discussion and group methods.
    Includes bibliographical references.
    1. Forums (Discussion and debate) 2. Small groups.
I. Title.
LC6519.B6 1975   301.14   74-12142
ISBN 0-06-040863-4

CONTENTS

part II. theory

part III. applications

PREFACE

This second edition of *Discussion and Group Methods* benefits from the insights and research stemming from the increased study and practice of discussion and group methods. In the preface to the first edition, I predicted that the course in small-group communication was assuming a central place in the study of communication. That prediction was more than fulfilled as interest in small-group communication increased rapidly and the growing popularity of humanistic psychology resulted in a wave of sensitivity and encounter groups which swept through much of American society and helped create a strong new interest in interpersonal communication. Teachers of speech communication had long recognized the role of public discussion in the democratic dialogue, but they were now also making more and more applications to task-oriented small groups in organizations.

Discussion and Group Methods draws most of the theoretical formulations from small-group research conducted in speech communications, social psychology, industrial and educational psychology, psychiatry, and sociology. The book continues, however, to rely most heavily on the program of research in small-group communication at the University of Minnesota for its theory. In the years since the first publication of *Discussion and Group Methods,* the research program at Minnesota has expanded and almost doubled the data base of case studies upon which the theoretical conclusions in this book are founded. The scope of the research program at Minnesota has expanded to include case studies of simulated organizations as well as case studies of leaderless group discussions.

The basic theory of small-group communication presented in the first edition has been supplemented and supported, rather than modified, by new research information and conclusions. The discovery of the importance of group fantasy and organizational mythology to the tone and function of small groups has been an important addition to small-group-communication theory and supplements the core theory. The second edition also reports the discoveries stemming from the Minnesota Studies of simulated organizations and the effect of organizational context on inter- and intragroup communication.

This edition continues to view group discussion and small-group communication as involving two important sets of theory—general communication theory and small-group theory. Contemporary communication theory is relevant to a wide variety of situations and to many media, including the problems of small-group communication, providing the influence of the small-group social field on the communication variables is taken into account. Group methods are applications of small-group theory to specific communication problems. The scope of this book is the area in which communication theory and small-group theory overlap. The objective has been to provide a small-group-communication text that balances the task dimension, including decision making and problem solving, with the social dimension of interpersonal relations. The philosophy underlying the book gives equal weight to solid theoretical content and early and continous practice in group meetings.

The second edition has been recognized into three parts. Part I, Foundations, includes a completely new chapter that deals with the emergence of sensitivity and encounter groups as ways of discovering the human potential and the consciousness-raising group as a way to facilitate social and political indoctrination. The new chapter distinguishes between matters of communication style and communication science. In addition, Part I contains the material on gathering, preparing, and processing information for group use.

Part II, Theory, presents the core of the small-group-communication theory from the first edition supplemented by extensive revisions and additions to the chapters on cohesiveness and roles; two previous chapters on leadership have been integrated into one essay, and the chapter on group acculturation has been largely rewritten. The new theoretical material includes a treatment of the importance of group fantasy chains to cohesiveness, role emergence, group acculturation, and decision making; the relationship of individual personality to the assembly effect in group composition; the risky-shift phenomenon in decision making; and the changing status of women in regard to leadership.

Part III, Applications, contains practical suggestions for using the small-group-communication theory in the planning, participating, and evaluating of one-time meetings, workshops, and conferences. In addition, the final chapter suggests applications of the theory to ongoing groups in institutions, business corporations, governmental agencies, and other organizations.

I am indebted to the research of many scholars in many different disciplines, as the references at the ends of chapters indicate. Among the most useful works for this revision has been that of Robert F. Bales and his associates at Harvard in their discoveries of group fantasy chains and the relationship of individual personality to group roles. Two of my colleagues at the University of Minnesota have made important contributions to my thinking about groups in the organizational context. William S. Howell's application of the discoveries of the Tavistock group in conducting human relations workshops and George L. Shapiro's clinical insights from extensive observation and consulting work with organizations, as well as the research into organizational communication of David H. Smith, formerly a colleague, now at Ohio State University, were all important contributions to my thinking. Dennis Gouran and his associates at Indiana have done much to illuminate the nature of the task dimension in small groups.

I wish to acknowledge the expeditious and helpful advisory editorship of J. Jeffery Auer. Jean McDonald provided extensive and valuable editorial assistance. Most especially, I thank my many students over the years in the Small-Group Communication Seminar at the University of Minnesota; I am indebted to them for much knowledge and insight. Finally, I am grateful to the students of the small-group-communication course, who not only provided much participant-observer data but also suggestions, discoveries, continuous criticism, and enthusiasm.

Ernest G. Bormann

PREFACE TO THE FIRST EDITION

The first course in discussion is assuming a central place in the study of communication and public address. Group discussion owes its new prominence both to new information and to new applications. The new information has come not only from the large-scale research programs being conducted at some of the leading graduate schools in speech but also from extensive research in many other disciplines. Teachers of speech and communication have long recognized the role of discussion in the democratic dialogue, and while that application has continued to be emphasized in their courses, it has been supplemented by the discovery that in modern industry, education, and government agencies—that is, in nearly all highly developed organizations—most of the important decisions and most of the power transactions are now compromised or negotiated by small groups of people in discussion.

This book reflects the new vitality and substance in group discussion courses. It draws out the most useful principles from recent small-group research conducted in the disciplines of speech, communications, social psychology, industrial and educational psychology, and sociology. In addition, it reports the results of a program of research in small-group communication at the University of Minnesota. All of these findings are integrated into a consistent theory of group process applied to discussion; the theory provides the content for a significant course that can contribute to the liberal education of the student, as well as to the development of discussion and group leadership abilities of a more practical nature.

Group discussion is viewed as involving two important sets of theory, general communication theory and small-group theory. Contemporary communication theory is relevant to a wide variety of situations and to many media, including the problem of discussion, provided that the influence of the small-group social field on the communication variables is taken into account. Group methods are applications of small-group theory to specific communication problems. The scope of this book is the area in which communication theory and small-group theory overlap. The objective has been to provide a small-group communication text that balances the task dimension of discussion, including decision-making and problem-solving, with the social dimension of interpersonal relations.

The philosophy underlying the book gives equal weight to solid theoretical content and early and continuous practice in group meetings. A beginning student may think of discussion as a simple matter, but attempts to work with groups under guidance soon reveal the complexities of group communication. This book is designed to be used in conjunction with a series of exercises and projects in group practice.

The book is divided into two parts. Part I considers techniques of group discussion. It contains the principles of planning, conducting, and participating in public discussions, committee meetings, and conferences. In addition, this section presents a complete set of guidelines for preparing, adapting, and testing information for group discusion. Part II provides the small-group theory necessary to develop group methods for discussion. This section deals with such matters as cohesiveness, roles, leadership, norms, and group decision-making.

Since the book begins with the more basic and fundamental principles of group discussion and progresses logically into the more complex and comprehensive theoretical matters, it is easily adapted to courses that emphasize either problem-solving discussions or group methods. For the course that emphasizes critical thinking, gathering and testing information, and the various forms and techniques of discussion, Part I—supplemented by the chapters from Part II dealing with cohesiveness, group climate, and the dynamics of group problem-solving—provides the basic material. For the course that concentrates more heavily on the theoretical dimensions of group processes, Part I provides a review of basic techniques and Part II contains the core of the course.

The author is indebted to the research of many scholars in many different disciplines, as the references at the ends of chapters indicate. A few deserve special acknowledgment. The teachings and writings of A. Craig Baird first introduced me to group discussion; the writings of Robert F. Bales and his associates have been most helpful; and David K. Berlo persuaded me some years ago that small-group research was relevant to group discussion.

I wish, too, to acknowledge the expeditious and helpful advisory editorship of J. Jeffrey Auer. Most especially, I thank my many students over the years in the Small Group Communication Seminar at the University of Minnesota; I am indebted to them for much knowledge and insight into group methods.

E.G.B.

DISCUSSION AND GROUP METHODS

CHAPTER 1

NATURE AND DEVELOPMENT OF DISCUSSION AND GROUP METHODS

In a highly organized urban society, such as the one in the United States, everyone works in groups for at least several hours each day. In addition to the family and the group at work, many people attend committee meetings, discussion groups, or business conferences because they are members of various social, professional, political, educational, or religious organizations. Many citizens attend meetings, watch televised discussions, or listen to radio programs where important public-affairs topics are discussed. Many people regularly attend conferences to increase their knowledge, understanding, or skills.

Because group discussions are the heart of any sound program of communication for an organization, more and more meetings are called each year. The task-oriented meeting can inform personnel directly about important matters, in a setting where questions can be asked and comments made. No form of written or pictorial communication can make this claim. In addition, small-group meetings can build a feeling of commitment and involvement, a sense of group and organizational loyalty that increases the effectiveness of the organization and satisfactions of the participants.

In recent years, there has been a change in some of the theories and techniques of management and organizational administration. Basic to this change was the discovery of the vital importance of the small group in the functioning of organizations. As early as 1953, Rensis Likert and his associates at the Institute for Social Research at the University of Michigan made extensive studies of "what makes

1

organizations tick." Likert discovered that managers tended to emphasize the supervision of individuals. When they did this, they overlooked the important leadership methods involved in managing the unit "as a group." In addition to working with individuals, Likert and his associates suggested that supervisors must think of the unit as a team and develop teamwork and group loyalty.

According to John Kenneth Galbraith, the basis of power in America has shifted over the years from ownership of land to ownership of capital and, finally, to the possession of knowledge. When technology was limited and society predominantly rural, the ownership of land gave power and influence. In the plantation economy and society of the antebellum South, for example, land meant power. After the Civil War, land became more accessible and technology increased farm production, making land less important. The rapid postwar industrial development taxed the capital resources of the country, so power shifted from ownership of land to ownership of capital. Capital was power in the latter half of the nineteenth century.

Today's stockholder invests his capital, draws his dividends, and, perhaps, votes at the annual meeting; but the real power in the corporation resides in a managerial class largely divorced from the control of the ownership of capital. Likewise, the citizen watches his government, listens to debates over policy, and, perhaps, votes in the periodic elections; but the actual power in various branches of government resides in a managerial class largely divorced from the control of the voter. The managerial class comes to power because it commands a resource that is in short supply. That resource is the knowledge required to run the business or industrial corporation or the governmental department or agency. One important component of that knowledge is the ability to meet with a small group of people around a table and arrive at understanding and decisions. Power, today, is largely negotiated at group discussions within the context of large and powerful social units.

Clearly, group discussions are a vital and widespread form of communication in contemporary American society. Yet, many surveys of managers in many different institutions and organizations reveal two frequent negative attitudes toward meetings. Many leaders feel that they must attend too many meetings and that too much of their time is wasted by inefficient and unproductive discussion. Why do so many people feel that way? The answer is that too many meetings are badly organized, badly conducted, and serve little useful purpose. Sometimes the answer is fewer meetings, but often the solution is better meetings. Every individual who hopes to make a significant contribution to his society and his time must function close to the power transactions of the age. For such a person, understanding and skill in group discussion is one necessary component of his education no matter how technically skillful or well-trained he may be in any of the sciences or professions.

group discussion

Group discussion refers to one or more meetings of a small group of people who thereby communicate, face to face, in order to fulfill a common purpose and achieve a group goal. The key concepts in the definition are *small group* and *communication*.

THE NATURE OF SMALL GROUPS

Extensive studies by behavioral scientists reveal that the small group is an identifiable social entity. Granted, authorities differ in setting arbitrary limits to the size of a small group. Nonetheless, the communication networks and interpersonal relationships that develop during the course of discussions conducted by a few people change discernibly when the size of the group is increased, and these qualitative changes can be used to identify the small group. Since the introduction of a third person into a social field changes the nature of the working and social relationships, a small group is defined as being composed of at least three people. Group discussion, therefore, does not include the dialogue, two-person communication, or a partnership.

The upper limit of the small group is difficult to locate on qualitative grounds and must, therefore, be set in more arbitrary fashion. When the size becomes so unwieldy that a group begins to change character it is no longer small. One important way in which groups change with increase in size is in their patterns of communication. In groups of 5 or less, all participants generally speak to one another. Even those who speak very little talk to all the others. In groups of 7 or more the quiet members often cease to talk to any but the top people in the group. As groups become even larger, the talk centralizes more and more around a few people, and group interaction falls off. In groups of 13 or more, from 5 to 7 people often hold the discussion while the others watch and listen. In permanent work groups larger than 13, people tend to form smaller groups (cliques) within the larger.

The optimum size for a discussion group varies from 5 to 7, and a group of 10 or 11 is often too large. Five is an excellent number. People in groups with fewer than 5 members complain that their group is too small, their viewpoints too narrow, and their resources too limited. Groups composed of an even number of people tend to be less efficient than those containing 5 to 7 people.

An aggregation does not become a small group until the people have communicated with one another and formed an impression of each other. Small groups are structured. When the group members go to work and get to know one another they divide up, coordinate, and structure their working procedures. They also develop interpersonal relationships that are hierarchical in nature. They begin to take a position in the liking and status network that comes to link the members.

The second key concept in the definition of group discussion is *communication.* The primary modality through which the group does its job and maintains its social relationships is speech. In everyday conversation the term *discussion* can refer to talk about almost anything including the weather, foreign policy in Africa, student power, football, sex, race relations, or religion. Although discussion is often synonymous with talk, it connotes something more than conversation: Discussion is considered to be serious and systematic talk about a clearly specified topic. Discussion is task-oriented. People engaged in discussion have a common purpose and are striving for common goals. Under such circumstances, the primary purpose of much of the talk in a group discussion must be to communicate.

The practice of group discussion requires, therefore, an understanding of communication theory and an ability to communicate. Discussion requires the adaptation of general principles of communication to the social context of small, face-to-face interacting groups. It also demands skill in listening, speaking, reading, and writing.

group methods defined

Group methods are the strategies and tactics of dealing with group interpersonal relations and task functions through the application of knowledge about group process and dynamics. The rise of humanistic psychology and the human potential movement provided new insights into the psychodynamics of group process. Concepts such as trust, self-disclosure, confrontation, conflict resolution, and congruency (keeping the outer manifestations in agreement with the inner feelings) have become important ideas in the study and practice of group work. Thus, concepts from communication theory and from the human potential movement may be applied to the psychodynamics of the task-oriented small group.

For example, when a person approaches a management problem using group methods as opposed to the supervision of individuals, he analyzes the problem in terms of the immediate social context. He asks such questions as: What effect does the group have on the individual in question? Is the individual conforming to a group norm and thus causing the problem? What is the individual's status in the group? What makes the group attractive to him? The teacher who approaches an instructional problem by using group methods as opposed to teaching individuals asks similar questions about the dynamics of the learning group. A member of a work group in which several colleagues are involved in a "personality conflict" might use group methods by examining the dynamics of the group and asking if the antagonists are struggling because of their differing opinions about the group's direction or because they are contending for the same role or for influence and esteem within the group.

historical roots of discussion

Courses in group discussion are largely a development of the last 50 years. In the nineteenth-century American college the curriculum was often classically oriented and designed to give a literary education. After 1900, the rise of land-grant colleges and state universities encouraged a more pragmatic, diverse curriculum designed to meet the practical realities of making a living and participating in community affairs. By 1920, cultural changes had influenced the extent and kind of group activity to the point where learning to work with groups became an important need for the education of citizens. One result of these changes was the development of courses such as the one for which this book is designed.

GROWING PRAGMATISM OF HIGHER EDUCATION

Our grandfathers faced the challenge of the frontier and an increasingly industrial economy, and thus they admired men with know-how, who invented gadgets, developed better ways to do things, or accumulated great wealth. Many successful men were uneducated in the classical sense, yet they were effective in the world in which they lived.

Proponents of practical education attacked the study of classical languages and cultures, theology, natural philosophy, and metaphysics as the proper education for all college students. This cultural development was accompanied by a rapid expansion of knowledge, particularly in the sciences.

As knowledge accumulated, scholars had to specialize, and the professor who taught courses in science, philosophy, mathematics, theology, and rhetoric was an anachronism by the end of the century. Owing to the increasing specialization, colleges and universities began to organize into departments and the elective system emerged as a consequence. The student also began to specialize and to plan his studies with a career in mind. After 1900, most universities had professional schools, such as institutes of technology, colleges of engineering, schools of journalism and business administration, colleges of education, social work, and schools of fine arts and music.

Although educators continued to value a classical education and did not want to produce graduates who were merely trained technicians, they began to recognize as one of their objectives the meeting of society's specific needs. Sometimes, to be sure, these needs included the desire of the community for spectacle and excitement, which the university met with a semiprofessional athletic team. For the most part, however, they met basic social needs by systematic research and by the development of educational programs to disseminate the results of such research.

By 1920, the battle for practical courses was largely won. At about this time, the need for training in group discussion became apparent; and the newly formed departments of speech, now often called departments of speech communication, began to offer courses in discussion.

A complex web of factors determines the intellectual style of any age, and the need for competence in working with people is part of the changing style of American life that has characterized the twentieth century. Two features of our culture stand out, however, as being particularly important in the growth and development of public-discussion courses: the increasing urbanization of our society with its resultant corporate or bureaucratic organizations; and the impact of science on the intellectual community since the Civil War.

THE URBANIZATION OF SOCIETY

Our country began as an agricultural society, with its roots in the agricultural societies of Western Europe. Early settlers on the North American continent found an environment that encouraged agrarianism—a vast new continent only sparsely settled by the natives. Land was cheap and available. The settling of the new land coincided with the enthusiasm for nature that swept through intellectual circles in France, Germany, and England. The result was an idealization of the yeoman farmer (lately referred to as the farmer on the family farm) and the development of an agrarian myth, which presented in romantic hues the good life as essentially a rural life, close to nature, filled with hard work, thrift, and virtue. Individualism and, subsequently, rugged individualism were positive values in this agrarian myth. Individualism often found expression in our literature in stories of strong men fighting the elements. The pioneer, scout, cowboy, and homesteader fighting the wilderness, drought, or locust were all part of the mystique.

By 1900, although many popular values remained agrarian, our society was well on its way to urbanization. With the inertia typical of established value systems, agrarian values, reinforced by such giants of American history as Jefferson and Lincoln, lingered after the United States became urbanized in the 1930s. A new urban value system developed gradually but inevitably. The Progressive movement in politics and the Social Gospel in religion gave voice to the new value system. The primary targets were the practice of competition and individualism. Proponents dramatized these issues as a question of the masses against the classes and pointed to the unsavory conditions that developed from unregulated competition and the exploitation of the masses by a few ruthless predators. The Progressive orators and Social Gospel preachers expressed the new values in terms of *cooperation* and *brotherly love.* Heavy blows came to the rural value system during the Great Depression of 1929 to 1939. The clash between rural and urban interests still centered around the agrarian value of liberty or freedom (noninterference with the way a man ran his life and his farm) versus security (assurance that under no circumstances would a man lack the minimum essentials of life). Today the urban values have become predominant.

THE CHANGING STYLE OF AMERICAN LIFE

The urbanization of America brought with it a new way of living and working as well as a new set of values. The corporate or bureaucratic organization of work, community activity, and play accompanied the rise of industrialism and the growth of the cities. Twentieth-century America is largely organized into corporate structures: Colleges, high schools, businesses, churches, social clubs, service organizations, labor unions, political parties, and sports are all organized along corporate lines, as are the various branches and departments of local, state, and federal government.

The changing style of American life during the early decades of this century was reflected by personnel managers in business organizations. It became policy to try to hire employees who could "get along on the job." For many positions, a brilliant worker who disrupted the morale of his fellows and caused dissension was less desirable than a competent worker who could get along well with others. Specialized fields of study dealing with management and personnel began to flourish. Do-it-yourself courses and books designed, as one influential volume suggested, to teach the reader *How to Win Friends and Influence People* appeared in ever-increasing numbers.

The managerial class discovered that the skills and talents required for management were remarkably similar regardless of the nature of the enterprise; management in General Motors, the University of California, the Brotherhood of Teamsters, or the Internal Revenue Service required the same abilities. Primarily, all managers needed to organize people into work groups. They had to distribute the work, set goals, satisfy the workers' needs, and evaluate performance.

By 1920, if the worker could not find satisfaction in working with groups, he was doomed to a life that was, perhaps, less than he hoped for and less than it should be. This trend continues today at an accelerated pace. The nineteenth-century pioneers, homesteaders, explorers, and farmers did not need skills in working with groups. They needed to know how to shoot, how to keep alive in the wilderness, and how to plan, plant, and harvest. Citizens today, including those who farm, need to know how to work productively with others.

In the 1950s, David Riesman's perceptive and imaginative study of the changing political style of the American people in *The Lonely Crowd* described the temper of the time so accurately that its title became a cliché. Riesman and his associates theorized that the bulk of the people they interviewed adopted one of two political styles: The "inner-directed" follow a political path guided by an internal mechanism similar to a gyroscope; the "other-directed" derive their political direction by means of social antennae that, radarlike, pick up signals from their social and political environment. *The Lonely Crowd* documents the changing style of American life under the pressures of urbanization. The inner-directed man, who knew what success was and how to achieve it, and who knew what was good and bad, was well adapted to fighting the wilderness and the elements. He knew that success was the accumulation of money or land and that the right thing to do was work hard, save money, and take care of oneself and one's own. Although he frequently was a "character" and had an engaging stubbornness or strengh of will, people often found it hard to work with him.

In the 1960s, John Kenneth Galbraith's popular book, *The New Industrial State*, presented a comprehensive and thorough-going glorification of the group as the key to the technology of such highly developed countries as those of Western Europe, North America, and of Japan. Galbraith argued that the modern corporation was a pyramid of committees and that the real power in society had passed to the managerial class who used committees and business meetings to exchange and test information and make decisions. Galbraith praised group decisions as superior to most individual decisions and presented the core of industrial society as an organization that could create a "group personality" that was superior to an individual and had the added advantage of continuing on for generations.

In the 1970s, Alvin Toffler's *Future Shock*, which became a bestseller, depicted a future in which organizations would no longer be organized into divisions with lines of authority but would form ad hoc work groups to deal with projects and tasks. Toffler predicted that, in the future, people who worked productively in organizations would have to have the ability to take the social shocks inherent in starting up zero-history groups to deal with significant problems over substantial periods of time.

The writings of Riesman, Galbraith, and Toffler symbolize and represent a number of works that emphasized and glorified the group ethos in the years after World War II. By the 1970s, an ethic that saw communal, cooperative, and corporate groupness as a positive value was widespread in the United States.

THE IMPACT OF SCIENCE ON NINETEENTH-CENTURY INTELLECTUALS

During the nineteenth century, the results of scientific discoveries were applied more and more systematically. Technological advances changed the character of industry and increased its productivity. The impact of science on the intellectual community was enormous. The scientific method furnished a kind of knowledge that made it possible for man to control his environment.

Until the middle of the nineteenth century, physics was the most influential field of investigation. Newton's monumental works on mechanics revolutionized thinking. But Newton's work was largely integrated into the general theological pattern of intellectual thought. Newton himself wrote theological treatises and saw no reason to suppose that the law of gravity was not a law of God. However, Darwin's work on the origin of the species not only demonstrated that living organisms are as subject to scientific "laws" as inanimate matter, but also challenged the foundations of theological explanations of the origin of man.

The net result of these developments was considerable optimism in this country that man was on the verge of a great millennium in which the good life would be reached, thanks to the application of the scientific method to man's problems. The pattern of evolutionary development that Darwin had applied to the species was often applied to support the idea of the progress of civilization. Every change was thought of as progress that resulted in an evolution of even higher forms of civilization. Science, which had solved a good many of man's material problems and had made life longer and more comfortable, must now turn to solving the problems of human relations. The great new "science" of the late nineteenth century was sociology.

immediate sources of development

By the 1920s, American institutions of higher learning were accustomed to their role of preparing students for careers and for life along the lines suggested by the great educational philosopher John Dewey. Thus, they had reacted to meet the changing needs of the increasingly urban society.

The introduction of college training in group discussion created a need for some theoretical framework around which instruction could be structured. This need was met by an attempt to apply the scientific method to human relations and social problems. The broad historical framework of public discourse encompassed the recent changes as well as old needs and traditions, many of which still existed and influenced the newly emerging forms of public discussion.

ADULT EDUCATION

Throughout the nineteenth century, Americans vigorously supported programs in adult education. The Lyceum and the Chautauqua were two major institutions that met the public's desire for culture, enlightenment, education, and entertainment. Both depended primarily on the lecture. National lecture bureaus often supplied the local forums with prominent men. From these lecture platforms such speakers as Ralph Waldo Emerson, Henry Ward Beecher, Wendell Phillips, Robert G. Ingersoll, Theodore Parker, Mark Twain, and William Jennings Bryan spoke to thousands of Americans eager for self-improvement and for knowledge.

By 1920, adult-education programs were using the discussion group as well as the lecture as an educational tool. Church groups and YMCA groups met regularly to discuss religious questions. The Great Books discussion group is a contemporary extension of this movement. The increasing use of discussion groups for educational purposes was accompanied by the appearance of handbooks on the organization and conduct of discussions. Thus, when speech teachers began instructing students in public discussion, handbooks were already available.

THE ROLE OF DEBATE IN PUBLIC AFFAIRS

The tradition of public debate was an established and honored one. From the colonial town meeting to the great legislative debates in the Senate, the oratorical debater whose eloquence dramatically carried the day was a popular and honored figure. Indeed, in the mid–nineteenth century, honor and success were generally thought to be achieved through the power of eloquence. Chauncey Goodrich, a famous nineteenth-century teacher of rhetoric at Yale, told his students:

> It is by tongue and pen that you are enabled to win your way to influence, property, and usefulness. Eloquence, therefore, should be the object to which all your efforts are ultimately

> *aimed. And fortunately, the rewards of eloquence are probably greater in this country, than any spot on earth.*[1]

Although the lecture and the sermon were still important and political stumping was still influential in elections, by the 1920s, the style of public discourse was changing, and the role of legislative debate in decision making was on the wane. Increasingly, legislative assemblies made important decisions in committees, and the floor debate became more of a ritual. Increasingly, complex corporate organizations relied on conferences and committees for more and more decisions. Conferences became a way of life for the managerial class. Every service club had its share of councils and committees. Every church, labor union, fraternity, sorority, and college faculty had a host of standing and special committees to investigate, decide, and implement policy. And the informally organized group meeting was playing an important role in public affairs in this country.

THE IMPACT OF BROADCASTING ON PUBLIC ADDRESS

Two important technological innovations influenced public speaking in the second, third, and fourth decades of this century. One was the development of the film industry as a major entertainment medium. The entertainment function of the Lyceum and Chautauqua lecture was in part supplanted by the more graphic, effective film. But more important, the 1920s and 1930s saw an incredibly rapid proliferation of radio broadcasting. Radio was used not only as an important source of entertainment, but also for political and economic persuasion. Before radio, the flow of argument, persuasion, and information had been largely limited to the press and the platform; now the American people were inundated by such stimuli broadcast over radio waves. The first public-affairs broadcasts were public speeches delivered before the microphone. Gradually, however, public speeches gave way to programs that exploited the intimate, informal qualities of radio. Programmers sought to create an illusion· of spontaneity and informal conversation. Speeches and lectures were replaced by the round-table discussion or question-and-answer panel programs. Discussion programs such as the *Chicago Round Table of the Air* and the *Northwestern Reviewing Stand* set the style for many programs on local stations.

The advent of television continued the trend away from the speech and debate toward the public-affairs program. Even the celebrated Nixon–Kennedy debates of the 1960 presidential election campaign resembled *Meet the Press* more closely than a parliamentary or forensic

[1] Cited in John P. Hoshor, "Lectures on Rhetoric and Public Speaking by Chauncey Goodrich," *Speech Monographs*, **24** (1947), 1–37.

debate. The more common public-affairs formats on television include a group of authorities informally talking about a problem or reporting to the American people; one or two authorities being questioned by a panel of newsmen; or a political candidate being interviewed or answering questions telephoned in by his listeners.

The more informal and spontaneous discourse which was replacing oratory, debate, and eloquence was often called *discussion*. Teachers of public speaking and debating were among those most interested in the changing forms of public address, and work in *group discussion* was usually introduced into college and university curriculums in the field of speech. Often a unit on discussion was added to a course in speech fundamentals or to a course in debate.

The notion that discussion should be taught as a separate subject was rejected by many teachers of public speaking who felt that, despite having lost much influence, the older forms of public address remained the proper vehicles for training students to be citizens in a democracy. These teachers maintained that discussion was only a less formal, less organized, less careful, and less desirable form of argumentation. Others embraced the new form as the best way of preparing the student for his role as a citizen. Laverne Bane outlined this position in an article entitled, "Discussion for Public Service vs. Debate Tournaments." Some teachers considered abandoning debate entirely as no longer relevant to the twentieth century.

One approach that emphasized the importance of discussion was expressed by Wayne Thompson in his article "Discussion and Debate: A Re-examination." He suggested that discussion and debate should be considered complementary forms of investigation. Specifically, he indicated that the debater should be as cooperative as the discussant.

Thompson's position was vigorously refuted by Hugo Hellman in the same journal, in an article entitled, "Debating Is Debating—and Should Be." Hellman wrote his article to take issue with what he called "the current group of enthusiasts for group discussion." These proponents of discussion "conceive it as something basic among speech activities and before which debate must bow respectfully and retire to a seat in the back row." Hellman argued that training in debate was much more practical than what he felt was an idealistic emphasis on open-minded inquiry by the "enthusiasts" for discussion.

the emergence of public discussion

Since teachers of public speaking and debate were oriented to speaking and debating before audiences, they were preoccupied with the role of public discussion as a tool for social control. They thought of discussion as a technique for making decisions in a democracy. Discussion informed citizens in a democracy of basic problems and enabled them to hear all sides of a controversy. The first emphasis, therefore, was on what can be called *public discussion.* The first courses in discussion contained considerable material on the practical matters involved in organizing and presenting discussion programs; they also included a theoretical rationale for public discussion as a decision-making tool.

The second major component in the early courses in public discussion reflected the late nineteenth-century tendency to apply the scientific method to human affairs. Early writers suggested that the proper way to use public discussion to solve problems was to adopt the objective empirical attitude of the scientist and the techniques of scientific inquiry. The philosophy and logic of the philosopher John Dewey provided the details of a scientific process of inquiry appropriate for public discussion.

DISCUSSION AS TRAINING FOR CITIZENSHIP

The early courses stressed the use of public discussion as the best way to mold public opinion and make decisions. In this context, the term *discussion* had a considerably broader meaning than the preparation and presentation of discussion-type programs before audiences, although the practical sections of early handbooks often stressed the latter.

Discussion was contrasted with other techniques for social control. It was compared favorably with the use of decrees and orders backed by the threat of force in totalitarian societies. It was contrasted with the manipulation of public opinion by mass persuasion, and it was asserted that discussion encouraged the citizen to participate in public decisions.

In addition to citing its virtues for democratic decision making, early writers in the field stressed the relation between public discussion and freedom of speech. They used the classical formulations of John Stuart Mill in his essay, *On Liberty.* According to Mill, all opinions and arguments should be allowed a fair hearing; if all points of view are presented, the people will distinguish truth from error. He asserted that repressing unpopular ideas may be unwise because they may contain truth; if the public is searching for truth, the majority must not shut off any possible avenue to knowledge. However, Mill continued, even if the unpopular ideas are false, they should be given a hearing because the old familiar truths lose their vitality unless they are periodically challenged and defended. He contended that the continued challenge of the orthodox is sound practice because the defense of orthodoxy revitalizes the truths it contains.

The defense of public discussion as the main technique of social control rested on certain assumptions that are part of the justification of representative democracy. The first assumption is that the citizen can vote wisely if he is given an opportunity. By means of public discussion, he is given a chance to hear all sides of important public questions. Although some citizens will not act wisely, in the long run the majority of informed citizens will make wiser decisions than the most enlightened of despots. Paraphrasing Lincoln, you can fool some of the people some of the time, but you can't fool all of the people all of the time. On occasion, students in classes in discussion will express a different attitude. They will try to avoid discussing complex public questions, such as some aspect of American foreign policy, because the topic is confusing, or because they feel they cannot become well enough informed to consider the matter. If the experts in the State Department do not understand or cannot solve the question, how can they be expected to do so? Perhaps the complexities of the modern world make the above basic assumption of democracy untenable, but students should be aware of the implications of rejecting it. If the citizens cannot make broad policy decisions and support their convictions at the polls, then they must put their trust in experts. Even if experts begin to make all important decisions, public opinion must still support them. This stand implies a political situation in which an elite group of decision makers rules the country and then uses experts in mass persuasion to manipulate or (to use the term of Edward Bernays, a leading public-relations counsel) "engineer" public opinion.

A second assumption grows naturally from the first: that the individual citizen has an innate worth and dignity. The individual is important in his own right and is not a cog in the machine of the state, or a means to a more ultimate end which is the state. Therefore, he has a right to participate in determining his own destiny. He should not be manipulated and treated as though his selfhood and individuality are unimportant. He must be consulted about decisions that affect his welfare. Even though he may choose unwisely, he has the right—in Jefferson's words, an "inalienable right"—to make certain decisions. The authorities may feel that the citizen should not smoke cigarettes or read the novels of Henry Miller or spend $5000 for an automobile, but according to this assumption, the citizen should have the right to make these decisions for himself. He must, therefore, be given a mechanism by which he can obtain information and make judgments about public policy as well as his personal affairs. Thus, public opinion is not a commodity to be brought into line with public policy, but rather a sign to be considered in determining public policy.

The use of public discussion as a technique of social control also assumes that, although man frequently commits irrational acts, he also acts rationally, basing some decisions on facts. Further, it assumes that such rational decisions are the best decisions that man makes. The conclusion then follows that training in public discussion, with heavy emphasis on discovering the facts and drawing sound inferences from them, is also training for democratic citizenship.

THE APPLICATION OF SCIENCE TO HUMAN RELATIONS

For the intellectuals at the turn of the century, the ultimate tool of reason was the scientific method. Therefore, they thought that, with training in public discussion which incorporated the main features of the scientific method, the citizen should be able to solve those problems of human relations he had hitherto never successfully solved. As the engineer solved the problem of protecting man from heat and cold, so the application of the scientific method to human relations would solve the problems of juvenile delinquency, marriage and divorce, labor–management relations, race relations, and war and peace. Early training in public discussion sought to accomplish this miracle by inculcating the scientific attitude and the scientific pattern of inquiry.

The scientific attitude. In the early years of the twentieth century, the intellectuals had an image of the scientist in his laboratory as a man who was open-minded and objective. If his experiments turned out in an unexpected way the scientist did not ignore the new results, but was willing to reject old theories in favor of new and better ones. He weighed facts objectively. He purged himself of all emotional prejudices, interests, and biases. He erected elaborate safeguards to insure his objectivity. In addition, the scientist was curious. He wanted to know and would go where the facts led him. He was not committed to a position that he defended to the death. The lawyer as advocate had a much different attitude; he had a duty to defend his client to the best of his ability no matter what the facts. The scientist, on the other hand, had no duty but to the truth; he tested all evidence rigorously, and when he found evidence that withstood this rigorous testing, he accepted it and accommodated his theories to it.

Of course, the scientists working in their laboratories seldom resembled this idealized portrait, but the writers of early handbooks in public discussion adopted the idealization of the scientist as the model for the participant in public discussion. They urged students to adopt the scientific attitude, to be open-minded, to welcome differences of opinion and challenges to their own thinking, to remain objective and uninvolved when evaluating ideas and facts. They stressed the notion that public discussion was the application of the process of inquiry. The discussion group was to seek the best solution to the problem under consideration on the basis of facts; the group, like the scientist, was to follow reality to the best solution. This adaptation of the scientific approach to the discussion of social and political problems was called the *discussional attitude.*

The thinking of the prominent and popular educational philosopher John Dewey caught the temper and fancy of the early theorists in public discussion. Dewey was a pragmatist, thoroughly imbued with the basic assumptions of democracy, and one of the foremost advocates of education for the realities of life. Although he was trained as an idealistic philosopher and was a student of Hegel, he was heavily influenced by scientific methodology. He published a book in 1910, *How We Think.* The book was largely philosophical and speculative, but it did contain, in prescriptive form, an analysis of *reflective thinking.* Reflective thinking is a somewhat generalized model of scientific and rational thinking. Dewey's analysis of logic and reflective thinking was particularly well suited to the problems of teachers of public address searching for theoretical foundations for public discussion. They incorporated Dewey's notion of reflective thinking into the group context, recommending that the group should use in its search for truth precisely the form of thinking recommended by Dewey in *How We Think.* Dewey suggested that reflective thinking followed a pattern that began with a problem or a felt difficulty. The individual tries to make an indeterminate situation determinate. When he locates the source of his difficulty, his mind leaps forward to suggest possible ways to resolve his problem. At this juncture, rather than blindly trying solution after solution as one would do through trial and error, he deliberates and reflects on the solutions available to him, and, weighing the advantages and disadvantages of each, he selects the best. If his difficulty is removed, the solution has been sound, and the individual is again in a state of equilibrium with his environment. If not, he examines the remaining solutions and tries again.

Dewey's analysis of reflective thinking was translated into the *discussional pattern* or the *steps in the discussional process.* These steps varied in number and formation, but most of them contained the hard core of Dewey's pattern in the form of (1) analysis of the problem, (2) listing the possible solutions, (3) weighing the alternative solutions, (4) selecting the best solutions, and (5) taking steps to implement the solution. Quite often two additional steps were added to this core: the definition of terms and the establishment of group goals.

The basic form of group-discussion courses solidified along these lines during the decades immediately preceding World War II. By the 1940s, a great number of such courses had been developed and were offered for credit by departments of speech.

historical roots of group methods

The same historical forces that brought about the public-discussion courses in speech departments were operating to bring the small group to the attention of social scientists—including the sociologists, anthropologists, and psychologists. They began discovering the importance of the small group for a number of their concerns.

Industrial psychologists studying worker morale and productivity found that one of the important factors in industrial psychology was the nature of the worker's immediate social group and how he related to it. Sociologists began to study the group in hopes of discovering in miniature the social mechanisms that controlled larger institutions and organizations that were more difficult to study. As their study continued, however, they found the small group worthy of study in its own right. Psychologists, on the other hand, studied the small group because they hoped to find out more about individual psychology.

Social scientists did not begin large-scale research programs in the area of small groups until World War II. Students of politics and business administration, on the other hand, had long been interested in the phenomenon of leadership and had developed theories explaining the phenomenon, although they had not often used the research method of the behavioral sciences. The military, since the time of organized warfare, had developed programs to train "leaders." World War II gave the study of small groups considerable impetus because of the need for military leaders and industrial managers. Interestingly enough, the German army, even before World War II, was using the technique of leaderless group discussion to aid in selecting officer candidates.

The war put a great premium not only on leadership but also on morale and productivity. Both government and private industry mobilized many social scientists to research such diverse matters as whether a persuasive speech or a group discussion would result in persuading more housewives to buy visceral meats and the effects of stress situations on the performance of bomber crews.

The work during these years revealed the practical importance of the relationships among group interactions, morale, and productivity. The trend toward small-group research is indicated by the number of books and articles reporting research in group dynamics and small groups. A. Paul Hare's *Handbook of Small Group Research,* published in 1962, contains a bibliography of 1385 items. Hare reports that his search of the literature reveals that the number of items dealing with social interaction in small groups grew from about 5 in the decade from 1890 to 1899, to 112 in the decade from 1920 to 1929, to 210 from 1930 to 1939; and to an annual output of over 150 items per year by 1950. Today the body of research literature relating to small groups has grown to voluminous proportions.

THE DEVELOPMENT OF GROUP DYNAMICS

The *Psychological Abstracts* first indexed research articles under the term *group dynamics* in 1945. The reference was to work by the Gestalt psychologist, Kurt Lewin. Lewin developed the notion of a dynamic social field and a topological psychology he called *group dynamics*. Under Lewin's direction, the Research Center for Group Dynamics was set up at the Massachusetts Institute of Technology in 1945; another Research Center for Group Dynamics was established through his influence at the University of Michigan. Dorwin Cartwright and Alvin Zander at this center edited a collection of research articles entitled *Group Dynamics: Research and Theory* in 1953 and brought out revised collections of articles in 1960 and 1968. The work of the Michigan laboratory, as well as some of the early work of Lewin and his associates, was inventive, thorough, and impressive. Particularly useful was the portion of their work that related to investigations under controlled conditions of group process. A number of persons, from a wide variety of fields, who were interested in the practical application of group techniques also used the term *group dynamics*. Some of these new apostles of group dynamics were zealous; to some critics, they seemed to be on the way to intellectual faddism. As early as 1950, Robert Gunderson made this charge about the work of such organizations as the National Training Laboratory of Group Development at Bethel, Maine, in an article entitled "Group Dynamics—Hope or Hoax?" He was answered by Herbert Kelman, in an article entitled "Group Dynamics—Neither Hope nor Hoax."

THE DEVELOPMENT OF SMALL-GROUP RESEARCH

Partly to offset the odium attached to the term *group dynamics* by some zealots, the term *small group* has gained preferred status. It appeared in the *Psychological Abstracts* for the first time in 1950, which indexed work by Bales and Deutsch. Since 1950, *small group* has become the most popular label for serious research in the social dimension of group interaction. Much of the work in this area has been basic research which has, as yet, little practical application for the student learning to work more effectively with groups. Some of it has been poorly designed, and the results have been trivial. Yet a sound analysis of group process is gradually emerging from the mass of research.

immediate source of development

The general prestige of science and rationalism was challenged in the 1960s by the rise of a romantic impulse, which some characterized as the alternative culture or the counterculture, and which one popularizer labeled the "greening of America." The movement challenged the morality of scientific research, charging it with being a tool of militarism, capitalism, and colonialism. The impulse further challenged the validity of the scientific method by glorifying immediate experience and mystical consciousness raising. The movement created alternatives to behaviorism in human psychology such as humanistic psychology and the human potential movement.

The impulse of the romantic tradition was in its glorification of deep feeling and mysticism, its denial of rationalism, and its emphasis on authenticity, openness, sincerity, and the stripping away of manners, cultural artifacts, and social "masks." The core of the movement rested solidly on group methods for its technique and on a value system that denigrated individualism and celebrated groupness. The goals of the new romanticism were communal. Participants sought community and group mystical experiences. The group techniques varied from relatively mild sensitivity sessions borrowed from the group-dynamics tradition, to intensive marathon groups meeting continuously for several days, to group drug-taking sessions, to nude encounter groups, to living in communes and practicing group marriages.

Numerous group techniques developed, including such nonverbal exercises as trust walks, in which a blindfolded person allowed another to lead him about, or psychodramatic exercises where members of the group would flail one another with pillows, lift a member in the air, search another's eyes and seek to communicate without words. Under the pressure of the group for conformity to norms established by such techniques, members often grew emotional, some would cry, others grow angry; tension was released with laughter, and some of the intense experiences reached the mystical level of communion characteristic of religious experiences. Many who did not achieve religious experiences, nonetheless, felt part of a close and warm group in which they could risk disclosure of their innermost hopes and fears.

The group values inherent in the communication style of the movement included such things as being cooperative rather than competitive, of being open, honest, and congruent rather than manipulative, secret, or reserved. The conventional manners that typified some segments of the society were rejected as "games people play"; the alternative value system suggested that such game playing was dehumanizing, but the immersion in a rewarding, deeply personal, and intense group experience would free a person and release the human potential in the group's members.

One branch of the new romanticism took a political turn and sought to break up the political and economic system which its participants saw as racist, repressive, manipulative, and wasteful. The political romanticism was often called the "New Left," although the various communities and cultures included under that term were often almost as different from one another as they were different from those dedicated to the group approach to the religious and mystical experience or those dedicated to expanding awareness by group drug experiences.

Among the group-oriented values of the political movement were such things as participative democracy in which no formal leadership structured an organization, but rather as things evolved around certain actions or ideas people would group and collect and participate. For some, the slogan "power to the people" implied that community members would spontaneously take control of their economic, political, and educational institutions. Most important for the study of small-group communication was the use of group techniques for indoctrination. Group indoctrination for religious and political conversions has had a long history in Western civilization. Political activists, reformers, and revolutionaries in the 1960s once again made the group session an important method for building commitment to the movement. One of the more popular forms of such indoctrination was the "consciousness raising session" which was used by such groups as some branches of Women's Liberation, by Gay Liberation, and by the Weathermen, a group of political revolutionaries.

A group engaged in consciousness raising, while reflecting some of the same values as the encounter group such as intensely intimate communication, openness, self-disclosure, and trust, differs markedly in that the participants know the desired outcome of the session. Just as the frontier Methodists of the early nineteenth century knew the desired outcome of a love feast or prayer meeting where they prayed and testified to their religious experiences, so the participants in a consciousness-raising session knew the desired outcome. The purpose of the meetings was to raise the consciousness of the participants so that they would be more aware of the repressive nature of the society by which they were victimized. In direct contrast to the notion of a discussional attitude where the participant was open-minded and tentative, seeking for the solution to a problem and willing to change direction and focus during the course of the meeting, the participant in a consciousness-raising session was already a believer in the values implied in the movement, knew that the system was corrupt and repressive, knew that action must be taken to liberate the oppressed, and used the group meeting to inspire deeper commitment and stronger impetus for action.

emergence of group methods

Instructors of small-group-communication courses in departments of speech communication did not ignore the new developments relating to empirical research in other disciplines. Many scholars in speech and communication were impressed by and caught up in the impulse toward humanistic psychology and the human potential movement. By the late 1950s, several textbooks in discussion used the language and concepts of group dynamics and small-group research for the development of some of their materials, particularly those relating to role development and role-playing. Although the impact of humanistic psychology and the human potential movement was, perhaps, greatest in the area of interpersonal communication, it also was influencing small-group communication by the 1970s. Contemporary theory and practice of group methods thus combine the results of empirical research in small groups and some of the values and practices of the human potential movement. Courses in discussion and group methods, conference methods, and small-group communication thus usually continue the tradition of training students in skills relating to small-group communication, decision making, and problem solving and often include the adapting of group methods to conflict resolution, building trust, establishing cohesiveness, and a positive social climate in the task-oriented small group. The result is a course in applied small-group-communication theory that is relevant to many of the basic needs of contemporary society and promises to be of increasing significance in the future.

QUESTIONS FOR STUDY

1. How did group-discussion courses meet some of the pragmatic needs of the early decades of the twentieth century?
2. In what ways were the early discussion courses compatible with the newly developing urban value system?
3. What is the relationship between training in group discussion and training for successful corporate management?
4. In what sense can it rightly be said that group discussion is "scientific"?
5. What is the difference between discussion and debate?
6. To what extent do you think that course work in discussion can be justified as training for citizenship?
7. How valid is John Stuart Mill's defense of free speech for today's citizen in an urban corporate society?
8. Can the attitude and methods of the scientists be applied to the problems of human relations?
9. To what extent is John Dewey's notion of "reflective thinking" similar to "scientific thinking"?
10. What are the differences between a task-oriented group and an encounter group?

EXERCISES

1. Find a recent free-speech debate on your campus or another campus that was reported in the press, and write a 300-word case study suitable for class discussion based on the controversy.

2. Examine some of the early textbooks on group discussion in the reading list below, and make a comparison of the way in which they treated the topic of John Dewey's steps of "reflective thinking."
3. Write a paper of 400 words evaluating the differences and similarities between discussion and debate.
4. Observe three television public-affairs programs, and analyze the elements of discussion present in each.
5. Read Barry Collins and Harold Guetzkow, *A Social Psychology of Group Processes of Decision Making,* and then read Franklyn Haiman's review in the *Quarterly Journal of Speech,* **51** (1965), 222–223. Write a 300-word critique of Haiman's review.

References and suggested readings

For a discussion of Likert's findings see:

Likert, Rensis. *New Patterns of Management.* New York: McGraw-Hill, 1961.

Galbraith's analysis of the sources of power can be found in:

Galbraith, John Kenneth. *The New Industrial State.* Boston: Houghton Mifflin, 1967.

For a discussion of the forces at work in the development of the departmental organization of higher education with special attention given to speech departments, see:

Smith, Donald K. "Origin and Development of Departments of Speech." In Karl R. Wallace, ed. *History of Speech Education in America.* New York: Appleton-Century-Crofts, 1954, pp. 447–470.

For the changing style of American life, see:

Carnegie, Dale. *How to Win Friends and Influence People.* New York: Simon and Schuster, 1937.
Riesman, David, Nathan Glazer, and Reuel Denney. *The Lonely Crowd.* New Haven: Yale University Press, 1950.
Toffler, Alvin. *Future Shock.* New York: Random House, 1970.

For some early books on discussion method growing out of the adult-education movement, see:

Elliott, Harrison S. *The Process of Group Thinking.* New York: Association Press, 1928.
Fansler, Thomas. *Discussion Methods for Adult Groups.* New York: American Association for Adult Education, 1934.
Fansler, Thomas. *Teaching Adults by Discussion.* New York: New York Service Bureau for Adult Education, New York University, 1938.
Sheffield, Alfred D. *Joining in Public Discussion.* New York: Doran, 1922.

For representative articles reflecting various points of view regarding the role of discussion in a democracy and the relation between discussion and debating, see:

Allison, Robert. "Changing Concepts in the Meaning and Values of Group Discussion," *Quarterly Journal of Speech,* **25** (1939), 117–120.

Auer, J. Jeffrey. "Tools of Social Inquiry: Argumentation, Discussion and Debate," *Quarterly Journal of Speech,* **25** (1939), 553.

Bane, Laverne. "Discussion for Public Service vs. Debate Tournaments," *Quarterly Journal of Speech,* **27** (1941), 546–549.

Gulley, Halbert. "Debate Versus Discussion," *Quarterly Journal of Speech,* **28** (1942), 305–307.

Hellman, Hugo E. "Debating Is Debating—and Should Be," *Quarterly Journal of Speech,* **31** (1945), 295–300.

Thompson, Wayne N. "Discussion and Debate: A Re-examination," *Quarterly Journal of Speech,* **30** (1944), 288–299.

Thonssen, Lester. "The Social Values of Discussion and Debate," *Quarterly Journal of Speech,* **25** (1939), 113–117.

For books stressing discussion as training for citizenship and the application of scientific method to human affairs, see books designed for adult education above and college textbooks such as:

Baird, A. Craig. *Discussion: Principles and Types.* New York: McGraw-Hill, 1943.

McBurney, James H., and Kenneth G. Hance. *Discussion in Human Affairs.* New York: Harper & Row, 1950.

For the source of the freedom of speech argument, see:

Mill, John Stuart. *On Liberty.* London: Longmans, Green, 1867.

For the source of the application of the scientific method to group discussion, see:

Dewey, John. *How We Think.* Boston: Heath, 1910.

Dewey, John. *Logic: The Theory of Inquiry.* New York: Holt, Rinehart and Winston, 1938.

Bibliographies of research in small groups include:

Hare, A. Paul. *Handbook of Small Group Research.* New York: Free Press, 1962.

Hare, A. Paul, Edgar F. Borgatta, and Robert F. Bales, eds. *Small Groups: Studies in Social Interaction.* New York: Knopf, 1955 (rev. 2nd ed., 1965).

McGrath, Joseph E., and Irwin Altman. *Small Group Research: A Synthesis and Critique of the Field.* New York: Holt, Rinehart and Winston, 1966.

Strodtbeck, F. L., and A. Paul Hare. "Bibliography of Small Group Research: From 1900 Through 1953," *Sociometry,* **17** (1954), 107–178.

The research articles from the University of Michigan Research Center for Group Dynamics are collected in:

Cartwright, Dorwin, and Alvin Zander, eds. *Group Dynamics: Research and Theory.* New York: Harper & Row, 1953 (rev. 3rd ed., 1968).

The articles raising the issue of the validity of group dynamics are:

Gunderson, Robert G. "Group Dynamics—Hope or Hoax?" *Quarterly Journal of Speech,* **36** (1950), 34–38.

Kelman, Herbert C. "Group Dynamics—Neither Hope nor Hoax," *Quarterly Journal of Speech,* **36** (1950), 371–377.

For a discussion of some of the trivialities of small-group research see the article about Barry E. Collins and Harold Guetzkow, *A Social Psychology of Group Processes for Decision Making* (New York, Wiley, 1964) by:

Haiman, Franklyn. Book review in *Quarterly Journal of Speech,* **51** (1965), 222–223.

For a discussion of training groups, see:

Bradford, Leland P., Jack R. Gibb, and Kenneth D. Benne. *T-Groups Theory and Laboratory Method: Innovation in Re-education.* New York: Wiley, 1964.

Dunnette, Marvin D., and John P. Campbell. "Laboratory Education: Impact on People and Organizations," *Industrial Relations,* **8** (1968), 1–27.

Golembiewski, R., and A. Blumberg, eds. *Sensitivity Training and the Laboratory Approach.* Itasca, Ill.: Peacock, 1970.

For a popular survey and introduction to the romantic impulse as expressed in group practices, see:

"The Group Phenomenon," *Psychology Today,* December 1967, pp. 16–41.

A popular book in the romantic tradition was:

Reich, Charles A. *The Greening of America.* New York: Random House, 1970.

For a study of consciousness raising, see:

Chesebro, James, John F. Cragan, and Patricia McCullough. "The Small Group Technique of the Radical Revolutionary: A Synthetic Study of Consciousness Raising," *Speech Monographs,* **40** (1973), 136–146.

PART I
FOUNDATIONS

CHAPTER 2
SMALL-GROUP COMMUNICATION

The concepts and explanatory structures that provide a small-group communication theory come from two major sources: (1) the general theory that accounts for human communication in all contexts, and (2) the small-group theory that accounts for the dynamics of all aspects of group interaction. Small-group communication theory thus consists of the application of communication theory to the context defined by the small group.

the nature of communication theory

A *communicative style* is a distinctive or characteristic mode or form of verbal and nonverbal communication common to a group or community of people. Communication styles are artful creations of human beings that evolve as people go about their daily affairs talking to one another for many different reasons and for many different purposes. Although one can discover commonalities that cut across communication styles, they are creations in the sense that they represent innovation, novelty, and unpredictability. An individual's ability to participate, appreciate, and use a communication style does not come naturally, but is always a result of study and understanding. One is never born a good communicator in a given style, but must always be taught to appreciate it. A naïve person coming into a meeting of a task force in a company which produces computers may well be confused, bored, or upset by the way the participants conduct the meeting, by their use of acronyms, by their no-nonsense preoccupation with getting the job done, and by their slavish devotion to time limits. Another naïve person coming upon a sensitivity group session may well be confused and upset by the way the participants conduct the meeting, by the high emotional tone of the session, by their preoccupation with feelings, and by their willingness to spend interminable amounts of time rehashing the same materials.

People who participate in a communication style have become connoisseurs who appreciate discussions that conform to their criteria of excellence. They learn to appreciate good communication by study of theory, by practice, and by critical evaluations according to the theory of examples of communication. Part of the communication theory associated with a style consists of standards of excellence, models of exemplar communication events, and concepts to help people learn about key features of the style.

The act of communication has a scientific component as well as an artistic one. Scientists in a communication laboratory can measure the acoustic power of a sound wave. A person in a small group, no matter what the style of the meeting, will speak in such a manner that the sound wave will contain a certain amount of energy. An investigator can measure the amount of energy, and the power in the sound wave will affect its ability to stimulate the ear drum and ultimately have a bearing on whether other members hear and understand the participant. Investigators can measure the attention span of a group of people in a discussion. They can discover group pressures on new or deviant members to conform to group norms. Sometimes theoreticians fail to sort out elements of communication theory that are scientific, in the sense that they are invariably associated with small-group interaction no matter what style of communication is used, from those that are artistic, in the sense that they are idiosyncratic and artful creations which vary across styles.

Two major styles of small-group communication characterize the contemporary scene in the industrially developed countries. One style is pragmatic and views communication as instrumental to other goals of groups and individuals. Devotees of the pragmatic style judge a meeting in terms of its success in achieving goals and ends other than communication, particularly goals that are common to the entire group. The other style is less easily characterized. This style celebrates feeling, emphasizes self, and deemphasizes analytic discourse. The style is both aesthetic and consummatory in that the participants often view communication as an end in itself and judge a meeting in terms of the satisfactions they derive from deep and significant communication with one another. Of course, the pragmatic style is not without its aesthetic component, and vice versa; but the participants of one tradition strive for and appreciate a group meeting that is much different in style and tone from that appreciated by those in the other tradition.

The people who participate in the pragmatic or instrumental school of small-group communication view the sessions of a group as a work or business meeting. They often design agendas to save time and assure that the group deals with all important topics related to some clearly specified group goals. They divide up labor, allocate resources, and make step-by-step plans to achieve objectives. Such meetings are task-oriented and the participants criticize the communication in terms of its usefulness for the work of the group.

The people who participate in the theory, practice, and criticism of the human-growth-through-communication school of group practice view the sessions as an opportunity for meaningful communication which is often an end in itself. They may seek to concentrate on the "here-and now" experience of the meeting in order to raise their consciousness of communication processes. Each individual may try to increase his or her own potential by revealing a self to the group and by using the group's responses to that self as a way to change and become a better person. These people may seek to develop greater sensitivity to others and to build relationships with fellow group members. They may seek to gain insight into the nature of the human experience, to raise their consciousness about humanity, or to participate in such deep and intimate communication that the result is a mystical, almost religious, communion.

A less widespread, but nonetheless important, style of small-group communication gained adherents in the 1960s and early 1970s. Adherents refer to the style as "consciousness raising." In many respects, consciousness raising is similar to the human-growth style. The major difference is that the consciousness-raising session has a pragmatic as well as a consummatory reason for being. The participants in a consciousness-raising session have a common goal to intensify their commitment to some social or political position and to raise the consciousness of new members so that they will adopt the group's culture, political position, and life style.

the pragmatic style of small-group communication

Engineers who were applying scientific theory to practical problems of communication gave the pragmatic style much of its impetus in the years following World War II. Norbert Wiener, a pioneer in the field of transferring information from man to machine, from machine to machine, and from machine to man, focused attention on *feedback* as one of the most important features of the pragmatic style. Communication theorists learned a good deal about the process from working on the practical problems of trying to find ways to program the new thinking machines. The machines were passive, docile, and made no inferential leaps on their own. Humans had to teach the machines every grammatical rule, every part of speech, and all the principles of logic.

If a programmer wished to communicate with a computer, he had to explain every step of the program very carefully and clearly. If the machine did not understand, it would often stop. Of course, machines stop for many reasons such as running out of power, a defective part, or breakdown of some other feature of the machine. The people teaching the machine languages and trying to program it soon discovered that they could speed up the process if the machine could be taught to indicate what was wrong. Once the programmers found ways to teach the machine to indicate the source of the problem, they made a major breakthrough in developing computer technology. The machine's ability to indicate the nature of the difficulty led to the formulation of a very powerful principle, *feedback,* which encouraged the development of information-processing systems and control instruments.

Cybernetics, the study of the way humans set goals and control behavior to achieve those goals and the way in which machines can come to serve the same functions, was based on the ability of organisms and machines to provide for and use feedback. The principle of feedback is illustrated in simple terms by the thermostat. The homeowner selects a temperature level as a goal and sets the control to that temperature. The thermostat contains a sensing mechanism that measures the actual temperature level. When the actual level departs from the desired level (the goal), the thermostat sends an electrical message to the furnace which either turns it on and thus furnishes more heat to bring the level up to the setting, or cuts it off and allows the temperature to cool back down to the desired point.

The term *feedback* came to refer to the principle of continuously providing data concerning the output of a machine to an automatic control device so errors might be corrected and performance could be controlled. The principle of feedback, of course, was an important one for goal-seeking behavior of all organisms including human beings. A person reaching for an object in the dark usually uses a groping procedure to pick it up. If a person can see the object, the eye can provide continuous data concerning the relation of the object to the hand, and the individual can modify the reach to achieve the goal. Although the principle was always operating in goal-directed behavior of organisms, it had not drawn much attention and had never been provided with an explicit concept and term until the development of automation and computers elevated the principle to a key position in the theory of communication.

The communication theory that evolved out of the pragmatic school of engineers and scientists had a set of critical standards as well as a rationale for practice. One of the criterion for successful communication was *fidelity.* The concept of fidelity referred to how much of the message was transmitted through channels without distortion. *Noise* in a channel would cut down on fidelity, and to combat noise the engineers discovered the device of repeating message elements until the machine could decipher the appropriate information. They referred to repetition of message elements as *redundancy*. The pragmatic theorists discovered that redundancy was often costly in terms of time and energy. They developed two further criteria of good communication: efficiency and low cost. Communication scientists thus came to evaluate good communication in terms of balancing the relationships among noise, redundancy, and fidelity. They suggested an ideal situation as one in which noise was minimized and the redundancy level adjusted to a rate that resulted in the highest degree of fidelity with no unnecessary repetitiveness.

All communication theory includes descriptions of good communication which serve as touchstones for criticism and as models for neophytes to follow as they practice to improve their performance. The pragmatic style used the device of a *communication model,* usually depicted in graphic form, as a technique for describing the exemplar or touchstone communication event.

The philosophy of communication is concerned with the evaluation and analysis of theory in terms of basic assumptions, functions, and structure. Philosophers have puzzled a good deal about the functions of models in communication theory. One answer was that the communication model was analogous to the models that account for observations and allow for prediction and control in some of the natural sciences. Physicists, for example, used theoretical structures such as models of the molecule, the atom, and of subatomic particles and processes. Careful exploration of the analogy of the communication model with scientific models in the natural sciences, however, revealed that the former were not able to account for all observations nor to provide by mathematical deductions applications to specific situations as did the models of the scientific theories. Some disillusioned philosophers of communication decided that the schematic blueprint or model so widespread in communication theory was little more than a complex visual aid to help in the exposition of concepts and insights about communication. They saw the model merely as an organizational device to lend structure and coherence to notions relating to communication. Clearly communication models are not like the models of scientific theory, but they are more than rhetorical devices to aid a lecturer or writer in organizing and presenting ideas about communication. A communication model is important because it functions as an exemplar of the communication that serves as a touchstone for practitioners and critics within the style.

When swine fanciers develop the art of raising a particular breed, say Poland China hogs, they require an exemplar against which to judge all candidates for prizes at swine shows. The exemplar also serves as an aid for the breeder who is selecting an individual animal to prepare for the show. The communication model of the pragmatic style serves the same purpose as a series of pictures and descriptive accounts of an ideal Poland China hog. Hog breeders who compete for prizes at a state fair judge individual animals against standards developed for both aesthetic and pragmatic reasons. Thus, judges of swine may change their standards for a prize winner with changes in public taste in regard to the fatness or leanness of good bacon. But even when the change in the standards is based on pragmatic reasons, the judges of a competition will evaluate the individual hog by comparing it to the touchstone or exemplar.

All communication theories associated with a unique style require touchstones analogous to the exemplars of an ideal prize-winning swine. Communication styles that emphasize a pragmatic or practical dimension must be more sensitive to the ends for which a given culture uses communication than those styles that are primarily aesthetic or consummatory. Since people in highly developed countries use communication for such practical purposes as organizing large groups of people into institutional and corporate structures and for automating factories, processing data by machine, and so on, such practical uses influence the standards for laudatory communication. The communication model in contemporary theory is a part of the description of the exemplar or touchstone of good communication within the assumptions of the pragmatic style.

Engineers in the years following World War II tended to blueprint their plans for electronic circuitry for machines and transmission and receiving apparatus in schematic form, and one of the first important descriptions of the ideal communication of the new emerging style was a schematic model developed by Shannon and Weaver and published in their study, *The Mathematical Theory of Communication.* Schramm, who was more interested in human communication than machine application, modified the Shannon and Weaver model soon after it was published. Berlo, who studied with Schramm at the University of Illinois, developed a communication model in 1960 which continued the Shannon–Weaver–Schramm tradition. Berlo's model was complete and explicitly adapted to two-person communication and gained wide acceptance. In the decade of the 1960s, many theorists discussed, criticized, and modified Berlo's model, and many created new schematic and graphic blueprints of the process of communication.

While communication theorists in the pragmatic style have often been preoccupied with the modification of previous models or with new graphic representations of the old ones, their changes were always variations on a basic theme and the standards for evaluating communication and the touchstone of excellence have not changed appreciably.

The model presented in this chapter is a representative one that contains the basic elements and standards of excellence within the pragmatic style. Once a person learns the model, he can evaluate small-group communication, can learn to practice communicating in the style of the task-oriented small group, and can discuss and appreciate the experience.

the pragmatic model of communication

The basic touchstone of the pragmatic style comes from the model of man talking to machine. Once a person clearly understands the ideal situation for a programmer talking with a computer, then the next logical step is to add the complexity required for a model to account for human beings talking with other human beings.

Assume that a person wishes to carry on a conversation with a computer newly arrived from the assembly line. The computer is more helpless than a newborn infant in terms of communication because a baby can cry and indicate that something is disturbing it. The first step that a person must take in talking with the computer is to teach the machine a language. The programmer provides the computer with a set of rules about the proper sentences of the language, their grammatical forms, and about the vocabulary that will be used in the language. In addition, the computer contains memory storage units that can accept patterns of electrical charges. The patterns function to store coded information that can be translated or decoded into a natural language such as English. The person who wishes to talk to the machine must develop a language that includes directions on where to store information and when and how to retrieve it.

Once he has taught the computer a language and told it how to go about storing and retrieving information, the programmer can begin communicating about the work that he wants the machine to perform. If the people who talk with the machine properly encode the messages they transmit to it, the machine will always decode the information in the same way and will always understand. Although simple-minded, the computer is a severe taskmaster when it comes to grammar. The machine demands perfect syntax.

When a person has a clear purpose, understands the machine's language, encodes the program and the data in perfect grammar, and transmits the program to the computer accurately, the machine dutifully follows the directions, processes the information, and does the work that the programmer intends for it to do. The human and the machine understand one another. The programmer has succeeded in talking to the computer.

If one defines *process* as a series of progressive and interrelated steps by which some end is achieved, then the linking between a human and a machine described above can be characterized as a communication process. Notice that the programmer initiates the communication and continues without interruption in step-by-step fashion until the computer indicates trouble. At the point where the computer fails to understand, the interrelationship that characterizes a process becomes apparent. The individual will have to do things the way the computer specifies if the communication is to succeed. The programmer selected the goal of the communication. The process thus moves toward an end selected by the human. Success or failure of the process is a function of the human being's achieving his or her objective through the messages transmitted to the machine.

Figure 1 represents a model of the process of man talking to machine which contains the basic elements, the criteria for evaluation, and the standard or ideal paradigm of the pragmatic style. The elements of the model consist of a message *source,* which in this case is the person communicating with the computer, a *message* such as punch cards, *channels* through which the message reaches the central processor of the computer such as a card reader, and the *receiver* of the message, the computer.

The process or activity points in the model are the places where interchange, transaction, and give-and-take are located. These process points include the place where the source's objective or intent is encoded into symbols that the machine can understand, the place where the machine decodes the symbols, the place where the machine prints out error statements and other feedback, and the place where the programmer interprets the feedback to aid in the preparation of revised messages.

Early influential figures in the development of the pragmatic style of communication were much taken with the world view that saw the second law of thermodynamics as indicating that the universe was tending toward chaos, a sameness with no differentiation. They saw the tendency as disorganization and used the word *entropy* to refer to the process. They thought of information as fighting against the natural tendency of things to go toward disorganization. In this view, the creation and transmission of messages required energy and was sustained only by effort and skill. Left alone organization would decay under the natural entropic forces of the universe. Energy was a value to be protected, and energy for organization and communication was, therefore, to be expended carefully and sparingly.

Norbert Wiener approvingly referred to the aphorism that communication is a cooperative game by the speaker and the listener against the forces of confusion. In the game against confusion the computer was always cooperative. People talking with one another were not always willing to play the game as a joint effort to fight entropy. When people

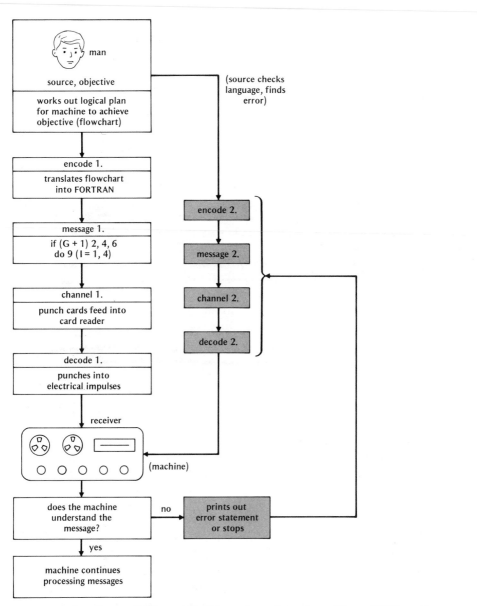

Figure 1. Paradigm of Man-to-Machine Communication. (From William S. Howell and Ernest G. Bormann, *Presentational Speaking for Business and the Professions,* Harper & Row, 1971, fig. 3.1.)

entered into a competitive communication game, into negotiations where bluff and other devices were used, the expenditure of energy was wasted in terms of fighting entropy, and, indeed, entropy might be accelerated rather than decreased. Thus, the ideal communication for humans was that exemplified by machines. Although the programmer might be frustrated and confused because the machine failed to provide adequate feedback under certain circumstances, he could be assured that the answer was there to be found and that the computer would not systematically change the problem in order to outwit the programmer.

Several features of the process of man communicating with machines are worth emphasizing. First, the machine does not have a goal and does not initiate the communication. Second, the machine always indicates when it has been unable to understand a message if it has been programmed to do so. Third, the machine will not tolerate bad grammar, faulty analysis of its vocabulary, or demands for logical computations beyond its ability. Fourth, when the computer indicates a breakdown in control, it feeds back messages to aid the programmer in debugging (correcting) the message. Complete understanding is necessary for the machine to proceed; thus, the criterion of high-fidelity communication is emphasized. Fifth, the programmer is the source of the communication; the human being works out the objective as well. The computer is the *receiver*. The machine does not have an objective of its own, which might conflict with the objective of the message source, and it would not process data except for the initiative of the message source.

Once the process is under way, however, the computer does not remain inert. The machine goes to work to decode messages and process data. When a human transmits a message that breaks the internal rules of the machine's logic, it sends back an error statement and the source's attention then shifts from the overall objective to an instrumental task of solving the error. Thus, the interdependence of the process is clear. The programmer must play the game and cooperate with the machine in a joint effort to win out against confusion.

In many respects, when people discuss with one another they exhibit the same behaviors as a computer does when processing data. Like a computer, human beings must have sentences in suitable form and encoded words within their vocabulary before they can understand messages. The grammatical rules used in small-group communication are more loosely specified than those required by computers. People will tolerate and often decode elliptical references, ambiguous statements, poetic flights, and sentences that violate the standards of good grammar. Even so, however, contemporary linguists and ordinary language philosophers have discovered and explicated a number of rules relating speech acts to context and speaker intent that indicate that meaningful expressions, even when grammatically deviate, must follow basic rules of the language game.

Like the computer, human beings as message receivers can feed back error statements and indicate difficulty in understanding messages. Indeed, although people are potentially more efficient at providing feedback than machines, they often prove much less so. One need not expect that people who dislike the pragmatic style of communication would be much interested in feedback. Ironically some who do see the pragmatic model as a standard of good communication still fail to provide feedback as the model prescribes. Man is less efficient than the computer on many occasions because, unlike the computer, which will not continue the process until it understands every bit of the message, persons often think they understand or pretend to understand messages when they do not. Hence, a person will not always ask for explanation or clarification at a point in a message where the computer inevitably would do so.

In the final analysis, however, the major difference between a person talking to a machine and people talking with one another concerns objectives. Feedback, the crucial process principle of the pragmatic style or model of communication, requires that the message source set the goals for the process. Unless someone wants a certain level of temperature to be maintained in a room, there is little point in installing a thermostat. Unless a person wants to reach for a pencil, there is little need for feedback about where the individual's hand is in relation to the pencil. The source–message–channel–receiver model of communication requires that the message source have a goal against which to test the feedback. Both fidelity of information transmission and control are associated with feedback in the pragmatic style. Feedback can indicate how complete the meeting of the minds of the participants is; that is, how successful the source is in achieving a satisfactory level of understanding. Feedback is equally important in terms of allowing the source to estimate how well the messages are succeeding in controlling the receiver's behavior. Some theorists criticize the pragmatic model because it is linear and too "source-oriented" or not really a process model. Such criticism, while couched in factual terms, is often actually a challenge to the pragmatic style itself.

The message source in the standard communication model of the pragmatic style has an objective and initiates communication with a receiver to achieve that objective. The source is preoccupied with that objective. When the receiver is a machine, the computer is compliant and accepts the source's objective for the communication without question. The computer enters into the relationship of interdependence and accepts control from the source as it is led to an understanding of what to do and how to do it. When a person initiates a communication event with another person, however, the latter often is not compliant, does not accept the source's objective without question, and does not enter into the relationship of interdependence. More important, the target for the source's message often does not accept *control* from the source. What frequently happens, therefore, is not communication according to the ideal standards of the pragmatic style; that is, much communication fails to measure up. Instead, after the initial attempt of one person to assume the role of source, a contest ensues over whose objective will be achieved, over who will control the situation, and the interdependent relationship required for understanding and control may change to the interdependent relationship of conflict.

The prescriptive nature of the communication model is clear from the fact that feedback, as the concept is used in the pragmatic style, is often not a feature of two people talking in one another's presence. If the model were "scientific," all communication events would invariably fall into the pattern described by the model. For instance, when people are placed in a leaderless group discussion and work together for a period of time, they invariably begin to specialize. The model of role specialization is thus scientific. The pragmatic model of communication is not scientific, and the theorist explaining the style will usually urge (prescribe) more and better feedback as a way to improve communication fidelity.

Figure 2 presents a model of human communication in the pragmatic style. The source begins a communication in the same fashion as the programmer begins to prepare messages for the machine. The source has an objective in mind and develops and encodes a message to achieve the objective. In the case of another person as receiver, the speaker must evaluate motives, interests, vocabulary, knowledge, habits, physical capacity, understanding of the rules governing speech acts, and so on. As complex as the programmer's analysis of the computer's language and logical capabilities may be, it is much simpler than the analysis required for human communication. Next, the source selects a channel or channels and transmits the message to the potential receiver. If the listener accepts the role of receiver and agrees to allow the speaker to play the role of source as indicated by the exemplar model, the communication can continue in a way very like the programming of a computer. The success or failure of the source in achieving his objective—whether it be the meeting of minds or the control of the listener's behavior—is primarily a function of the communication skills the two bring to the task, including the receiver's ability to provide feedback. Since the communication event closely follows the model of the pragmatic style, the skill of the participants can be evaluated in terms of fidelity of communication judged against the criteria of the source's objective and efficiency in terms of time and the allocation of resources including energy to achieve the desired results.

Often, however, the listener does not accept the role of receiver. Rather the listener develops a conflicting objective of his or her own

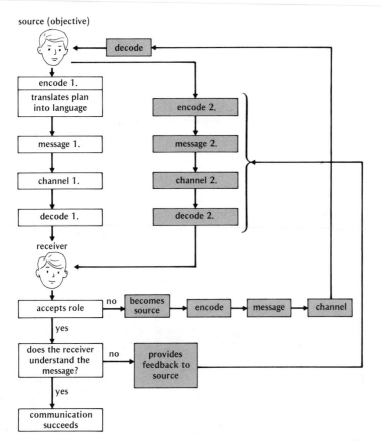

source (objective)

decode

encode 1.
translates plan
into language

encode 2.

message 1.

message 2.

channel 1.

channel 2.

decode 1.

decode 2.

receiver

| accepts role | no | becomes source | → | encode | → | message | → | channel |

yes

| does the receiver understand the message? | no | provides feedback to source |

yes

communication
succeeds

Figure 2. Paradigm of Man-to-Man Communication. (From William S. Howell and Ernest G. Bormann, *Presentational Speaking for Business and the Professions,* Harper & Row, 1971, fig. 3.2.)

and then creates a message designed to achieve that objective. The listener has initiated a new communication event in which he or she would now be playing the role of source and the other person must decide whether to become the receiver or not. In short, the listener is trying to turn the tables on the speaker and wrest the initiative away from the source.

The listener's response in this situation is not feedback as that principle is idealized in the model of the pragmatic style. The listener's message, encoded to achieve a different objective, is not designed to aid the first speaker in debugging a program to achieve understanding or control, but is a message in its own right. The original message source ought not to interpret such messages as feedback indicating misunderstanding but as a preliminary move much more of the order, "Oh, you are inviting me to participate in a joint game of communication against the forces of confusion. However, before I agree to play the game according to the ideals of the pragmatic school I will have to find out more about your goal, and only if I come to share it will I agree to play the receiver role and provide you with feedback."

If the first speaker fails to interpret the message of the second properly, he may continue to encode messages and transmit them to the other person doggedly trying to achieve his original objective and assuming that he has simply not managed to penetrate the thick skull of the other person. The second individual may follow the same pattern, and the result is the not uncommon spectacle of two people talking past one another, both functioning as sources, with neither playing the role of receiver. The critic evaluating such communication against the touchstone of the communication model of the pragmatic style would find it either bad communication or define it as no communication at all, much like a judge of swine coming across a hog with a silhouette and a size differing significantly from the exemplar or model hog might say that it is a poor specimen or that it is not really a Poland China at all.

For a student of small-group communication with an interest in discussion and task-oriented groups, the pragmatic style has much to commend it. Group meetings in the pragmatic style accomplish much of the coordination and planning for major projects by corporations, cooperatives, organizations, and institutions. Anyone who wishes to work with organizations in the developed countries would do well to become knowledgeable about and able to practice small-group communication in the pragmatic style.

application of the communication model to the small group

INTERNAL COMMUNICATION

The pragmatic model is adaptable to the small-group discussion in terms of individual participants alternating as message sources and receivers. The potential for feedback, as that principle is described in the pragmatic style, in a group discussion is both spontaneous and continuous. Thus, the ideal of high fidelity and control, of efficiency of time and energy usage, and of an ideal ratio of noise to redundancy is possible within the task-oriented small-group meeting.

The first criterion of successful communication in the pragmatic style is high-fidelity transmission of information judged against the intent of the message source. To fulfill the requirements of good communication the small-group context must allow for and encourage the participants to assume alternately the role functions of source and receiver. Some of the features of small-group dynamics encourage people to join in and to agree to play the cooperative game against confusion. A clearly stated common objective encourages members to work cooperatively to achieve it. In addition, people tend to identify with a group in which they participate, and, thus, there is a dynamic that encourages a feeling of belonging and of attraction to a group which can be called *cohesiveness*. Cohesiveness thus becomes a very important feature and a vital concept for the pragmatic school of small-group communication. Chapter 7 is dedicated to a detailed analysis of cohesiveness. A common goal and feelings of cohesiveness combine to encourage a climate of unselfish helpfulness in a group meeting. A person who willingly plays the role of receiver of messages must be unselfish enough to appear uninformed, slow to decode messages clearly, and risk some loss of status to assure group success; he must give clear and frequent feedback.

Other forces, however, arise within the dynamics of groups which inhibit members from assuming the role function of message receiver as prescribed by the pragmatic model. Members of groups suffering from role instability in which people are striving for status or control of the group are often reluctant to play the receiver role. Instead, in competitive circumstances, members tend to engage in a display of activity designed to show the others their competence and interest. When several aggressive members are displaying their ideas and competence, they often want to be message sources achieving their personal goals and intentions and are unwilling to give others the floor to act as message sources.

As members of a group interact over time they come to specialize in performing certain tasks for the group. With specialization comes a status hierarchy within the group with some roles perceived by the others as more important to the group than others. High-status members can assume the role of message source more easily and with greater compliance on the part of the others than low-status members. Thus, the ideal of the pragmatic style of maximum feedback to achieve high-fidelity transmission of messages becomes compromised by the growth of status relationships within the group.

The second criterion for successful communication according to the pragmatic model is the control function in which a message source's goal is achieved by monitoring feedback and changing the messages. If members of a group perceive an individual's trying to be a message source with intent to control the group as motivated for personal objectives, they will usually reject the attempt and will not play the role of receiver. When a member attempts to control the group in terms of some objective, that person is involved in an important kind of communication according to the pragmatic style. Certainly, one way to view leadership is in terms of control. Thus, when a person tries to assume the role of communication source with an eye to controlling the behavior of the others, the communication will often not be good according to the standards of the pragmatic style because there are no receivers. What often happens under those conditions is that others begin to encode messages as sources, and the result is a number of message sources talking past one another. Members of such groups often complain that nobody listens to anybody.

Two developments in the evolution of groups encourage members to play the role of receiver and to maximize feedback to achieve control of group members. The first is the drive for teamwork or cohesiveness discussed in connection with the transmission of information. As cohesiveness increases, the welfare of the group often encourages members to submerge their distaste for external control, and they then are willing to participate as receivers when others explain group goals, divide up work assignments, integrate plans, and give directions on how to proceed to achieve the goals. The second feature of groups that encourages the willingness to play receiver comes about with the emergence of a stable role structure in which some members come to specialize in playing message sources with intent to control group behavior to achieve group goals. When a leader emerges, the followers then perceive the communication aimed at achieving group goals not as evidence of personal aggrandizement by a power-motivated individual but as a necessary part of working cooperatively together. The leader comes to symbolize the group's common need for structure and control, and when the leader articulates a goal and proceeds to encode messages to achieve it the goal is, symbolically, viewed by those willing to be receivers in the communication as *their* common goal and not the goal of the leader.

Even when the forces of cohesiveness and role stability encourage members to play the role functions of message source and receiver alternately, to maximize feedback in order to achieve efficiency in information transmission and control, the standards of good communication in the pragmatic style are difficult to achieve. Just as a programmer discovers that the planning and writing of a computer program are difficult and that the actual programming requires much checking and rewriting of mistaken messages, so do people in a small group working hard and cooperatively at communication find the task difficult. The skill with which the source encodes messages and the ability of the receivers to decode and to provide feedback play an important part in the success of the communication according to the model.

EXTERNAL COMMUNICATION

Task-oriented groups usually function within an external context. Often the group is a creature of a larger organization. The group must process information gathered from outside sources and transmit messages to external groups and individuals. The pragmatic style provides a general model that relates to the group's efforts to communicate with outsiders. Thus, the SMCR model is general enough to provide standards for communication in which the entire group is viewed as message source and another group is viewed as receiver.

When one views the group as message source, it fulfills the assumptions of the model when all of its members understand the group's intent or goal and they work together on messages (or delegate message drafting duties to one or more members), which are then transmitted through channels to the target audience. Under ideal conditions the target audience decodes the message, accepts the role of receiver, and feeds back information about its understanding and acceptance of control to the group.

When one fits the group into the SMCR model as message source or receiver, the analysis often moves into the area of organizational communication. This book emphasizes the analysis of the internal communication within small task-oriented groups. Chapter 14, however, does deal with the organizational context and influence of other groups on the small group. A few comments are in order here pointing up how difficult it is for groups to communicate with one another and approximate good communication according to the standards of the pragmatic style.

Competition is destructive of the ideal of playing a joint game against confusion. Even groups that ought to be working cooperatively for organizational goals often come into competition and filter information, restrict the flow of messages, indulge in bluff, and hide information from other groups. Members of the Small Group Communication Seminar at Minnesota often seek out groups in ongoing organizations to study. The number of "real life" groups whose members are willing to allow their meetings to be tape recorded for study is remarkably small. Often the organizational context encourages secrecy not just from outside researchers but from other groups in the organization.

When groups are clearly in competition, the pragmatic model is often irrelevant. Talking with a machine is difficult and frustrating at times, but the programmer can rely on the fact that, once the problem is discovered and the program is debugged, the machine will communicate according to the rules that govern the transaction. When groups come into competition, however, they often willfully embark on strategies designed to surprise and mislead one another. They transmit messages filled with bluff, with misinformation, with cues designed to confuse rather than serve as feedback for high-fidelity communication. In short, the competitive communication game is not a joint effort to overcome confusion but rather a game in which each group tries to maximize the other's confusion while minimizing its own.

Engineering application of scientific theory to practical problems of communication flourished in the late 1940s and early 1950s to the point where the pragmatic style became the dominant mode of communication. During the same period, however, innovators within the dominant approach were nurturing another style. Participants in the scientific study of group dynamics, such as Kurt Lewin, were also seeking ways to make practical applications of information about groups to everyday problems. Followers of Lewin began to design workshops to train people to participate more effectively in groups. At first they continued largely in the scientific and pragmatic style, but other influences were at work in the disciplines of clinical psychology and psychiatry where therapists were using groups as a technique to help people with personal psychological or psychiatric problems. Gestalt psychologists, Freudian psychoanalysts, and Rogerian clinicians began to employ group meetings to discuss patients' problems. A training laboratory at Bethel, Maine, set up workshops in small-group dynamics designed to help people who were well adjusted and normal, that is, not in need of clinical help. The trainers called their approach *sensitivity training*, and the groups that achieved the goal of sensitizing individuals were referred to as *training groups* or *T-groups*.

Meanwhile, Moreno was using *psychodrama* as a way to help people with problems. Moreno's patients would act out their problems in a dramatic setting with other actors and properties. Many picked up the technique of role-playing situations or problems of individuals as a device to stimulate group interaction and create understanding of personal difficulties.

In the 1950s, the innovative style often contained an amalgam of the pragmatic with the new tendencies. The impulse evolved into a distinctive communication style in the 1960s, at which point it not only purged itself of most of the behavioristic features of social science, particularly of psychology, but came to take an antiscientific stance.

The rise of humanistic psychology, of the human potential movement, and of interpersonal communication discussed in Chapter 1 coalesced to form the context for the consummatory style of small-group communication.

Like the pragmatic style, the consummatory style had its descriptions of good communication, which served as touchstones for criticism and as models for neophytes to follow in becoming adept practitioners in the style. The consummatory style, however, did not use the device of a schematic *model* to depict the exemplar, as did the pragmatic. The devotees were rebelling against several elements of the pragmatic style, including the paraphernalia of the engineer and the scientists such as formulas expressed mathematically and schema for blueprints or models. Specifically, the followers of the consummatory style objected to the principle of feedback as enunciated in the pragmatic style. Feedback implied control, and they rejected the concept of one human being's controlling another. They rejected the comparison of man with machine and celebrated man's *human* potential. Interestingly enough, they continued to use the term *feedback*, but as they developed the concept, it became much more general and abstract than the principle enunciated by the pragmatists. For proponents of the consummatory style, *feedback* referred to the verbal and nonverbal responses that expressed reaction to another person, or feelings, or response to another's communication and behavior. One of the aphorisms of the style was, "You cannot not communicate." The point of the aphorism is that all responses to a participant in a communicative setting can be interpreted as meaningful in terms of relationships, feelings, and attitudes. For the pragmatists with their emphasis on high-fidelity transmission of information, the notion that one cannot not communicate was simply wrong. Observations of the world revealed many situations in which their model of good communication was not achieved. But, of course, for those in the consummatory style, the notion that something is always being communicated and that unintentional behavior should be viewed as communication was a rejection of the basic principle of a message source intentionally controlling the communication situation.

How then did the consummatory style present its exemplar of good communication? The theoreticians of the consummatory style described good communication in a way much more characteristic of the theologian and the philosopher than of the scientist. Indeed, certain theologians such as Buber and Kierkegaard, as well as philosophers such as Sartre, provided some of the sanctions as well as some of the more esoteric formulations to describe the exemplar. Ambiguous terms of high abstraction were used to characterize the exemplar communication event. The connoisseurs then drew out the ramifications of the abstract formulations in terms of further clarification and counterclarification and sharing of insights. One discovered the nature of the exemplar by participating in discussions that dealt with ambiguous abstractions and in which all participants shared openly their thoughts and cooperatively created the insights required to reach a high level of commitment. Thus, the participants came to learn the exemplar by participating in group meetings and experiencing it. Among the important characterizing terms were: *experiential, dialogistic, congruency, trust, openness, authentic,* and *self.*

To present the touchstone of the consummatory style in straightforward descriptive terms is to do it an injustice. The pragmatic style celebrated scientific forms of communication, which emphasize clarity of exposition and care to phrase messages to achieve high-fidelity transmission of information, and the resultant description of their exemplar form of communication, while inelegant and unexciting, was, nonetheless, relatively straightforward and clear. The consummatory style celebrated experience rather than linguistic descriptions of it. Feeling was a higher value than analyzing and critically evaluating ideas. (This does not mean that they did not critically evaluate communications, for the style implies strong critical sanctions for neophytes who stray from the norms of good communication.)

Having entered the disclaimer, let us try to see the main outlines, at any rate, of the ideal communication according to the newer style. People who really communicate have learned to do so by ceasing to play games with one another and have turned to being real, to being honest, to taking risks, and to revealing their authentic selves to one another. The basic attitude of a person in the exemplar mode was that of dealing with others as authentic human beings and not as things or machines to be manipulated. One no longer needed to wear the masks that made a person less human and shielded the individual from contact with others. A person could open up and disclose his or her feelings. Self-disclosure is risky, and people begin communicating about themselves with fear and trembling; but once risked, it tends to open up others, and they in turn disclose. The climate of the group meeting is warmed by such disclosing communication, and, as people take more and more risks and are accepted for themselves without their masks and without game-playing, a climate of trust evolves.

In the warm and trusting climate of a good meeting, people can open up their innermost feelings, they can discuss their hopes and fears. People can discover their authentic selves, they can express their feelings, cry, and laugh without worry of acceptance or rejection. As the climate builds to ever more intimate and significant communication, important relationships evolve among the participants. Meade's notion that a person's self-image was built up through communication encounters with others often provided a rationale for the style's strong emphasis on self-image. A strong and good self-image was a prerequisite to the good kind of communication. The recommendations for building a good self-image often included self-disclosing communication or opening up oneself to others in a group setting, receiving frank and honest feedback (i.e., response and evaluation of oneself as exposed: the others describe their reactions to the speaker so an individual can evaluate both self and worth), and then a frank accepting of the feedback, followed by honest attempts to change. In the process of disclosure, evaluation, reaction, frank acceptance, and honest attempts to change, a person discovered her or his potential and became aware of the authentic self. The process of communication raised the participants' understanding of self and of others. The end result was a stronger self-image and a greater sensitivity to others as people and a higher consciousness of how to deal with people as human beings rather than machines.

The heightened awareness also included more careful and sharper tuning of the senses. The exemplar communication was often multi-sensory. The evolving theory emphasized nonverbal communication as more authentic than verbal. Theoretical discussions took in such matters as the communication of touching and of smell as well as of gesture. Training sessions often stressed feeling, touching, smelling, and other nonverbal communication exercises. One technique, for example, was to have neophytes participate in a nonverbal group meeting where no talking was allowed but where the members *communicated* by touching, hugging, looking in one another's eyes, and so forth.

the mixing of communication styles

Some communication theorists were impressed by the attractive features of both styles and tried to integrate the two. For example, some attempts were made to begin a discussion of theory with a schematic model drawn from the pragmatic style and then go on to describe the exemplar mode of communication in terms of openness, trust, congruency, self-image, defensive communication, and other concepts drawn from the consummatory approach. The styles were, however, in many respects incompatible. The consummatory style of the 1960s was a reaction against the scientific pragmatic communication style of the 1950s.

Partisans of both styles came more often into conflict. The issues were drawn around such topics as the charge by those participating in the consummatory style that most communication models were linear in that they emphasized the message source and the source's attempt to control the receivers through intentional communication. They argued that communication was continuous, on-going, nonlinear, a process, and a joint enterprise in which both people participated to their cooperative growth rather than a situation in which one person achieved a goal or objective by strategically adjusting messages to bring the receiver's responses in line with the speaker's intent. The pragmatic school argued, on the other hand, that communication theory ought to be descriptive rather than prescriptive and claimed that their "theories" simply described the communication process and made no prescriptions about how to communicate.

The conflict between the two styles is illustrated in an interesting fashion by what happened to the concept of feedback. Theorists for both schools took the term as a key one, but each defined a very different concept to be named by the term. For the pragmatists, feedback, as was described above, was the corrective information provided by the receiver to the message source to achieve fidelity of information transmission or control over the receiver's behavior. In the consummatory style, feedback became a much more abstract and less clearly defined but equally important notion. In a growth group, a person disclosed a part of himself or herself and then received an appraisal of the exposed part. The appraisal might be subtle nonverbal cues from the others, but the members who were sophisticated in the consummatory style would, if possible, set group norms where the feedback consisted of explicit and frank evaluations of the other person and of the others' feelings about the relationship that was evolving among them. Feedback thus was directed to response to one another as people with an emphasis on the feeling dimension of the response as opposed to an analytical or thought-out evaluation.

Given the current state of communication theory, what is the best approach for the student of small-group communication? Indiscriminate mixing of the two styles is likely to cause frustration and difficulty. On occasion, students in the small-group-communication courses at Minnesota join task-oriented groups fresh from an exciting and satisfying series of consummatory-group meetings. They often begin to disclose themselves, state their feelings about other people clearly and explicitly, and try to set the norms that evolve in a good meeting conducted in the style of the T-group or encounter session. They do not create more trust, openness, and a positive social climate in the task-oriented group unless enough of the other members are participants in the consummatory style to create a group comfortable in that way of interacting. Since the groups usually contain members from the pragmatic school, the results tend to be frustrations, tensions, and disruptions.

Perhaps a future communication style will emerge that will include key elements from both of the main styles popular in the 1970s and thus will transcend the differences. Until such a time, however, a person should become sophisticated about the current styles of communication and try to insure that the expectations for any given group meeting conform to one or another of the styles. Much as a person might learn to enjoy both good French and good Japanese cuisine, a person may be able to appreciate different communication styles. But the unwary diner who enjoys beefsteak and fried potatoes and expects them will be upset to find raw squid on the plate, and even the more flexible and sophisticated gourmet may be irked to find raw squid served as part of a French dinner.

This book emphasizes the common dynamics of groups that remain constant no matter what style of communication is employed to develop the norms characteristic of a given style of communication. For example, the dynamic process of group-norm development is a constant even though norms vary widely in function and style. The process of role specialization in a small group is also an invariable development even though the role functions required for the pragmatic style differ from those required for consummatory groups. When stylistic concerns become important, the analysis will distinguish between styles and, for the most part, will emphasize the pragmatic or instrumental style of communication. On occasion, however, as in Chapter 14, Group Techniques in Interpersonal Training, the consummatory style provides the rationale.

QUESTIONS FOR STUDY

1. What is a communication style?
2. What are the differences between the scientific and the artistic components of a small-group style?
3. Why must one always learn to participate in and appreciate a communication style?
4. What is the pragmatic style of communication?
5. What is the consummatory style of communication?
6. What are the elements of the communication model presented in this chapter as typical of the exemplar of good communication in the pragmatic style?
7. How does the consummatory style describe the exemplar of good communication?
8. What is the difference in the way the pragmatic style uses the concept of feedback and the way the consummatory style uses that concept?
9. How might the pragmatic model of good communication be applied to the internal communication in a group discussion? How might the description of exemplar communication in the consummatory style be applied to a group meeting?
10. How might the pragmatic model of good communication be applied to the external communication of a group?

EXERCISES

1. Read several textbooks in speech communication, and sort out the style in which the authors are participating. Are the authors picking elements from both styles, or are they consistently pragmatic or consummatory?
2. Survey some typical group meetings in your school. These may be committees of fraternities or sororities or student government groups or meetings at student religious houses. What style of communication is popular on your campus?
3. Observe a discussion group, and evaluate it in terms of the exemplar of good communication in the pragmatic style as described in the chapter. Do people alternate the roles of source and receiver? Do they listen carefully and decode the source's messages? Do they provide feedback to allow the sources to code new messages to achieve high-fidelity communication?

4. Observe a discussion group (if you have a tape recorder you might use the same group used for exercise 3), and evaluate it in terms of the exemplar of good communication in the consummatory style as described in the chapter. Do the people take risks, disclose themselves, express their feelings, search for authentic responses, stress honest and open communication, and emphasize the relationships that develop during the meeting?
5. Observe a task-oriented group working in an organizational context, and evaluate the group as message source and receiver in terms of the model of pragmatic communication. Does viewing the group as a message source in communication with other groups in the organization give insight into the intergroup communication?

References and suggested readings

The sources of the pragmatic style as represented by models include:

Berlo, David K. *The Process of Communication: An Introduction to Theory and Practice.* New York: Holt, Rinehart and Winston, 1960.
Schramm, Wilbur. *The Process and Effects of Mass Communication.* Urbana, Ill.: University of Illinois Press, 1954, pp. 3–10.
Shannon, Claude E., and Warren Weaver. *The Mathematical Theory of Communication.* Urbana, Ill.: University of Illinois Press, 1949.

For the early definitive discussion of the concepts of entropy and feedback, see:

Weiner, Norbert. *The Human Use of Human Beings: Cybernetics and Society.* Boston: Houghton Mifflin, 1954.

For further discussions of information theory and communication, see:

Drum, Dale D. "What Is Information?" *Speech Teacher,* 5 (1956), 174–178.
Fulton, R. Barry. "Information Theory and Linguistic Structuring," *Central States Speech Journal,* 14 (1963), 247–257.
Weaver, Carl H., and Garry L. Weaver. "Information Theory and the Measurement of Meaning," *Speech Monographs,* 32 (1965), 435–447.

For a survey of some of Lewin's early research, see:

Lewin, Kurt. *Field Theory in Social Science.* New York: Harper & Row, 1951.
Shaw, Marvin E. *Group Dynamics: The Psychology of Small Group Behavior.* New York: McGraw-Hill, 1971, pp. 46–48.

For psychodrama, see:

Moreno, Jacob L. *Who Shall Survive?* Washington, D.C.: Nervous and Mental Disease Publishing, 1934.

For a book of readings in the consummatory style, see:

Stewart, John, ed. *Bridges not Walls: A Book About Interpersonal Communication.* Reading, Mass.: Addison-Wesley, 1973.

For some basic sources in the consummatory style, see:

Batchelder, Richard L., and James M. Hardy. *Using Sensitivity Training and the Laboratory Method*. New York: Association Press, 1968.

Bradford, Leland P., Jack R. Gibb, and Kenneth D. Benne, eds. *T-Group Theory and Laboratory Method*. New York: Wiley, 1964.

Burton, Arthur, ed. *Encounter: The Theory and Practice of Encounter Groups*. San Francisco: Jossey-Bass, 1969.

Egan, Gerard. *Encounter: Group Processes for Interpersonal Growth*. Belmont, Calif.: Brooks Cole, 1970.

Golembiewski, Robert T., and Arthur Blumberg, eds. *Sensitivity Training and the Laboratory Approach*. Itasca, Ill.: Peacock, 1970.

Howard, Jane. *Please Touch*. New York: McGraw-Hill, 1970.

Johnson, David W. *Reaching Out*. Englewood Cliffs, N.J.: Prentice-Hall, 1972.

Jourard, Sidney M. *The Transparent Self*. rev. ed. New York: Van Nostrand Reinhold, 1971.

Otto, Herbert A. *Fantasy Encounter Games*. Los Angeles: Nash, 1972.

Otto, Herbert A., ed. *Explorations in Human Potentialities*. Springfield, Ill.: Thomas, 1966.

Perls, Frederick S. *Gestalt Therapy Verbatim*. Lafayette, Calif.: Real People Press, 1969.

Rogers, Carl. *On Becoming a Person*. Boston: Houghton Mifflin, 1961.

Schein, Edgar H., and Warren G. Bennis. *Personal and Organizational Change Through Group Methods: The Laboratory Approach*. New York: Wiley, 1965.

Schultz, William C. *Joy: Expanding Human Awareness*. New York: Grove, 1967.

For a critical evaluation of groups in the consummatory style, see:

Back, Kurt W. *Beyond Words: The Story of Sensitivity Training and the Encounter Movement*. New York: Russell Sage, 1972.

CHAPTER 3

THE ETHICAL IMPLICATIONS OF SMALL-GROUP DISCUSSION

the nature of ethics

Many statements in this book are what a student of ethics would call *value statements*. They support and shape what we have said about the ends and uses of discussion in our society; the relationships between discussion, democracy, and science; the gathering and processing of information; the development of group cohesiveness, roles, norms; and the nature of decision making. The purpose of this chapter is to outline and explain a value system for the student of discussion and group methods.

What distinguishes the ethical from other concerns is the act of choice. The inevitable is not ethical. A person should not be held responsible for events that are beyond his control. However, an individual may be held responsible when he deliberately chooses to lie, to steal, or to blacken another's reputation with malicious half-truths, innuendoes, and suggestions. Choice is the prerequisite for praise and blame, and the most important ethical considerations reach the ultimate question of, What is praiseworthy? Choice implies both the freedom and the ability to make the praiseworthy decision. One ought not to praise or blame a person who is unable or incompetent to choose.

Participants in small task-oriented groups make ethical decisions largely about ends and means; that is, a member must sometimes choose between his personal goals and the goals of the group because the two are in conflict. He must sometimes choose between the goals of his group and those of other groups or the larger society because such goals also come into conflict. In addition to ends, purposes, and goals, an ethical scheme should give equal weight to the means used to reach the ends. Each participant must choose the personal code he will follow in dealing with his fellow group members as well as weigh the common code the group follows to achieve its goals. He may find the end praiseworthy but reject the tactics of his group as too dirty, violent, or extreme for his personal value system.

The student of discussion and group methods is thus faced with a two-step ethical problem. The group has an internal ethic that causes its members to praise ends and means that aid the preservation and success of the total group. The first major point of tension is therefore between individual and group. In addition, the participant must make choices about means and ends in terms of their impact on other groups, institutions, and society. The second major point of tension is between the goals and tactics of the particular group and those of other groups and the general welfare. Answers for the ethical problems posed by participating in a group come largely from two contexts, which roughly parallel the two points of greatest tension. First, one set of answers is contained in the specific ethical code that emerges from the study and practice of discussion and group methods. The specific code pertains to the proper, correct, and accepted information, techniques, and practices and is similar to the professional codes of medical doctors and lawyers. A second ethical system stems from the more generally accepted and widely held system of time-honored values common to the general culture.

This chapter begins with an examination of the tension points and the major ethical dilemmas they pose, summarizes the value system reflected in this book, outlines an appropriate professional code, and, finally, presents some of the ethical insights pertinent to small-group discussion, which are part of the cultural heritage upon which our society rests.

ethical problems

THE INDIVIDUAL VERSUS THE GROUP

Conformity and nonconformity. Journalists and essayists writing on contemporary American culture often berate the general public for their "conformity." They deplore mass culture, mass man, and standardization. If there is a value to which the contemporary American conforms, it seems to be nonconformity. Too frequently, critics use *conformity* as a convenient oversimplification with which to belittle actions or values that they dislike. Because conforming behavior relates so closely to the ethics of working with small groups, the student of group methods should examine this widespread tendency to deplore it.

A shepherd who lives for months without seeing another human cannot comply or fail to comply with a norm. He conducts his business as he sees fit. If the abstract artist does not adapt to the norms of the local of the Teamsters' Union or Farm Bureau chapter, it is an idle exercise to compare his behavior to the norms of these groups. The artist usually does not care what the teamsters or the farmers think of him or his work. The critic of conformity should watch the painter at work with his fellow abstract artists. He will find that the artist turns out to be a conformist. The hero of those who deplore conformity in the abstract, the mythical fellow who hears a different drummer, is not, as we are led to suppose, the only one to hear it. He hears the beat of a different group.

The point is that everyone who takes any part in any group is a conformist to some degree. Conformity is a necessary phenomenon associated with all groups. When members fail to comply with the role expectations or with the norms, they distract the group from its job. Other members become uncomfortable. Having failed their expectations once, they reason, the nonconformist might act in other unexpected ways. Will he fail to do his share of the work? Can he be counted on in the future or must the whole group reorganize itself to be sure that the jobs will be completed? Nonconformity results in role struggles, secondary tensions, and back-biting. Systematic and continuous nonconformity will result in an organization that is torn with dissension and socially punishing to its personnel. Rather than introducing new and challenging ideas, the nonconformist makes himself and others unhappy, in the most destructive and unproductive sense. He may choose to undermine a group in this way because he wishes to destroy it for some ulterior purpose.

A simple stereotype suggests that the nonconformist is the creative person. He is supposed to be the individual who introduces new ideas, great discoveries, and works of art, and he must therefore be encouraged. Again, the stereotype should be examined in terms of a relevant group. Every organization that requires creativity, or needs open and extended debate and discussion, develops norms that encourage such behavior. One goal of the university faculty, for example, is the discovery of new knowledge. The faculty members do not punch time clocks when doing research. The work norms for research teams encourage the creative process by allowing individuals to work in their own way at their own pace without close supervision. The faculty also has academic freedom in its work. Every scholar is allowed a wide latitude of investigation. He may study the nature of snails or the way bees find their way back to the hive; he may study ancient Egyptian drama or the history of the Communist party in the United States. But if a professor became a nonconformist by suggesting that this norm of academic freedom be restricted, he would cause considerable alarm in the university.

Industrial research and development groups, governmental research facilities, play casts, and advertising agencies all develop their own norms to encourage creativity and innovation on the part of their personnel. Some of the often-satirized linguistic innovations of the ad men are a function of the agency norms that encourage new and different gimmicks. Nonconformists in such groups would discourage rather than encourage creativity.

The United States Senate has developed a norm called *unlimited debate.* The code of the Senate encourages full discussion of legislation. Should a senator suggest a serious restriction of the right of debate as a permanent change of procedure, he would be a nonconformist.

Clearly, a person might still praise nonconformity, but he would logically do so because it is harmful to a group he dislikes. The critic of conformity might applaud an FBI agent who infiltrated a Communist cell or the Ku Klux Klan and failed to conform to the group norms, because he dislikes the goals and activities of these organizations. Of course, the conservative who wishes to restrict the academic freedom of a socialist professor, or the hippie who criticizes the style of life of the upper middle class are not *non*conformists. Such attacks on the outgroup do not violate the norms of their own groups. Attacking the outgroup simply increases the pressure for conformity within the group.

Some organizations have norms that are restrictive and discourage creativity. They encourage conformity to the party line. Militant action groups, which must move quickly and with firm discipline in order to win, establish such norms. Revolutionary organizations, such as some branches of the communist movement, are tightly organized and disciplined, and they follow the party line. Religious organizations, during periods of change, often punish the heretic. Conforming to the norms of such groups discourages innovation and creativity.

Many groups may have ways of doing things and may advocate goals that a person dislikes. An individual has every right to deplore an organization for its goals, but he should understand that not conformity but the norms themselves are at fault. He may not like the goals of a gang of juvenile delinquents and thus may pronounce moral judgments about their behavior. He may not like the norms of the Ku Klux Klan or the Black Panthers and may be disturbed by the way these organizations operate.

He will have most fun when he is criticizing another group's conformity within the context of colleagues, who reinforce his feeling by supporting his criticism. When he belongs to a highly cohesive group that has a norm of belittling the conformity of people in other groups, he enjoys poking fun at the mindless way other people follow the dictates of the herd.

When an individual joins a group and works for it, he must give up a certain amount of liberty. The group exacts a toll in return for the social, esteem, and security rewards it furnishes. The group may require an individual to do work that he does not enjoy, or it may demand discipline that he does not demand of himself. Membership may require a distasteful compromise of principle, or restrict individual freedom of expression. A given group may exact all these costs, and a person may find the price too high. However, if he weighs all the costs and still joins the group to work with and for it, he must then understand that conforming to norms and goals that are good for the group is a basic requirement for the group's success.

Group efficiency versus member satisfaction. In the days when rugged individualism was dying out and even the farmers were joining alliances and granges and forming political parties and cooperatives, the priests of the new urban culture were at work inculcating the new ethic. *Co-operation* and *organization* were the good words, and *competition* was bad. Since the heyday of progressive education, children have been taught to adjust to the group and to work with others. Many students of contemporary American culture, however, have discovered that co-operation—although absolutely necessary for the effective functioning of groups in an urban, corporate society—is not without its problems. Some yearn for an older, simpler individualism. The citizen today, however, lives in a society that requires cooperation or, in contemporary terms, conformity.

Groups inevitably make demands on their members that reflect the pressure of the external environment. The good of all is often at variance with each member's personal good as he sees it. The tension between the good of the unit and the rights of the individual creates an ethical dilemma for all participants. Organizations often ask members to make a personal sacrifice for the good of all.

History furnishes many examples of organizations whose norms forced their members to sacrifice personal goals for the good of the group. One was expected to die, if need be, for the efficiency of the unit. On the other hand, some groups have developed a set of norms that place member satisfaction above group efficiency. The issue is raised in many contemporary situations. If a classroom group is under pressure of time, facilities, and teaching resources, what are the rights of individuals when compared with the overall goal of providing maximum opportunity for all? What are the rights of students with little ability? What are the rights of those with extraordinary potential? Often task efficiency exacts a toll in the social dimension. Some years ago, a new kind of specialist emerged who studied the "time and motion" of workers. Called "efficiency engineers," they conducted careful studies of the ways workers do their tasks, and then developed more efficient ways of performing the jobs. However, workers often resented being taught to redo their jobs according to step-by-step directions, because they feared becoming extensions of the machinery. The result was a loss of employee morale.

One of the troublesome ethical issues facing contemporary management is balancing the profit-making goal against the employee's social and esteem needs and the belief that a man's work should contribute to the quality of his life. The question of balancing an organization's effectiveness against individual rights and needs is not unique to industry. For example, the discussion group may find that for the good of all, certain students will have to give up a prominent part in the final program. Member A may have to talk less than he wants to or feels that he should.

Authoritarianism versus democracy. To a large extent, the question of the individual versus the organization is focused on the tensions between authoritarianism and democracy. Often one defends democracy on the basis that, although it is slow, cumbersome, and inefficient, it recognizes the rights of the individual and protects them. Totalitarianism, on the other hand, is efficient, but makes its members cogs in the overall structure, subservient to the demands of the unit. The group, left to its own devices, will tend to act for the good of all and thus crush the minority that opposes it. If the goal is clear and within the grasp of the group, an authoritarian set of norms and leadership roles will increase the speed with which the group attains its objectives. Authoritarianism is characteristic of athletic teams and military units. When speed is a crucial commodity for its self-preservation, .the unit often turns to an authoritarian mode of operation.

Authoritarian groups may be healthy in terms of both task efficiency and member satisfactions. Athletic teams can be highly cohesive, and playing on such a team, even though the coach is a dictator, can be very satisfying. If the group is an elite organization, making the team can furnish a player with great prestige. It may also provide him with an opportunity to play a position that he enjoys. A team player sublimates his own desires to the goal of winning; the joy of participating in a team victory largely replaces the enjoyment he would normally get from individual achievement.

Democratic groups may also fulfill the criteria for a good group. Leaderless group discussions, which have achieved a stable role structure and in which leaders emerge who adopt a democratic style, may yet reach a level of work that results in a high-quality product. The democratic style is appropriate to policy-making and decision-making organizations. The ethical problem is not answered by the simple decision that authoritarianism is bad because it emphasizes the group and neglects the individual. The rejection of the democratic style because group decisions are complex and experts should make them is not an adequate answer either. What right does the family group have to tell its children what they should do and think? What right does the federal government have to tell its young men that they must serve in the armed services? What right, on the other hand, does an individual have to reject the decision of others if his action will jeopardize the entire group? What right does a student have to fail to appear at the planning session of his discussion group?

Freedom of dissent. Small groups often develop norms that restrict communication. Although freedom of speech is the law of the land expressed in the Bill of Rights and buttressed by the legal system, the organization will often restrict the flow of communication. Lincoln said in his first inaugural address that "perpetuity" was implied in all governments, and that no government contained within its structure the mechanism for its peaceful dissolution. To some extent, small groups fight for their lives against people who seek to destroy them. The participant who challenges the basic purpose of the group, who fights its norms and foments malingering, sabotage, and absenteeism often finds his own freedom of thought and expression within the group restricted. The question that must be faced is to what extent should participants who are perceived as destructive to the group itself be given the opportunity for free expression within the organization? Even the most authoritarian organizations require some questioning of norms and goals in order to insure adequate flexibility to deal with changing circumstances. Yet, unlimited freedom for those who challenge the group may destroy it. For example, what right does the family have to restrict the freedom of expression of the children within the home? But what right does a son have to attack the basic norms and values of the family? Both sides of the issue pose an equally difficult ethical consideration. Participants do not challenge the group's culture as often as they absorb it. What right has a college fraternity to change the pledge's norms and value systems? Students who bring a set of religious beliefs to the university may experience a crisis during their first few years. The faculty may say that it had no responsibility in the matter because it merely provided a context in which the student was exposed to knowledge, and he made up his own mind about religious matters. But the student inevitably felt the pressure of the group to conform to the norms of the college.

The cultural heritage of the United States emphasizes democratic values and institutions. The implication is that the member must be considered in any group. He is to have equal opportunity with others in the group to climb in status, power, and esteem. He is to be able to choose which of the group's goals and norms he will follow. He is to be respected as an individual, and the group is to serve him so that he will have a maximum opportunity to develop his full potential as a person of worth and dignity. Democratic values imply freedom of speech. Each person has the right to make his choices on the basis of as much information as possible. He should have the right to challenge a group's goals and norms even if he pushes the group to destruction. The group, in turn, has no right to impose its opinions and advice on the individual. He may listen to the others' arguments, but he should be free to reject or accept the group's value system on his own. Carried to its extreme, democratic values suggest that neither the family, the church, nor the university has a right to impose its norms on the individual.

Democratic values are often violated by the actual practices of institutions and organizations in the United States: The group has a dynamic that forces it to defend itself, and it destroys individuals who stand in its way. One of the large ethical problems each person will face in the last decades of the twentieth century concerns the extent of his allegiance to the group and the extent to which he will strive to protect the older democratic values.

GROUPS AND THE GENERAL WELFARE

Just as a weed might be an especially healthy specimen, so might a group be extremely efficient and cohesive. A gardener, however, might consider the healthy weed bad for his garden, just as a larger view of the public good might yield a judgment that a cohesive band of delinquents is bad because of its effectiveness in theft and vandalism. An adequate ethic for the judgment of groups requires external as well as internal criteria.

Group versus group. Many groups have a dynamism that forces them to expand. A business firm often drives to expand its share of the market and increase its size and influence, and at the same time, within its corporate structure, as within the corporate structure of most bureaucracies, empire building is rampant. One way to gain prestige is to be part of a successful unit. Within a bureaucracy, success is measured by group power and a broad base of control. As the organization grows, there are new domains for conquest. The small groups who have a chance to stake out claims move into the new territory and compete. Inevitably their goals conflict, for if one achieves dominance, the other loses its chance. The groups fight each other for new territory, and fight encroachments on the areas they already control. In this regard, the study of small groups tends to support the newly publicized territorial-drive theory of naturalists, which states that the drive to own and defend territory is basic to animals and to man. In our corporate society, this territory, or field of influence, becomes the area of contention. The more successful units build empires within the bureaucracy to the glory of their leaders and members.

Some groups are prohibited from growing in size, but are placed in direct competition with other groups. A common example is furnished by athletic teams. Many other groups compete with one another in less clear-cut ways.

Ethical tensions between the individual and his group are strong, but even stronger are problems posed by conflict among groups. A person often finds it more difficult to treat members of his group in unethical ways than strangers or enemies from competing groups. A football player may find it more difficult to trip a teammate during practice than an opponent in a close game. The support of his group may even encourage him to commit acts of violence and to harbor feelings of hatred toward the members of a competing group. Often people with the lowest status within the group will show the greatest rancor toward the enemy. Conflicts among groups thus may result in actions that are blatant violations of the ethical codes governing the internal pattern of social relationships. The issue is illuminated by the example of athletic contests; for here, the pressures are strong to adopt a win-at-any-cost ethical code, and values such as good sportsmanship conflict with success. "It does not matter if you win or lose; it is how you play the game," is answered by "Nice guys finish last!" Playing dirty to win is condoned, and blame is cast only on the member who is caught. Breaking the rules of competition, whether these are codified in a book or entrenched in the mores of the culture, gives the rule breakers a competitive advantage if the opponents are caught by surprise. Such tactics, however, increase the loser's frustration, and he often adopts similar measures in the future. Thus, competition among groups encourages participants to ignore ethical questions relating to means and to justify any action on the basis of good ends—that is, group success.

Group versus society. Often small groups develop goals and tactics that are counter to the general welfare. Extreme examples are furnished by gangs of delinquents or groups of criminals. Equally relevant ethical issues are raised by the business corporation that increases prices, indulges in deceptive advertising, or conspires to fix prices, and by the labor union that demands unproductive featherbedding or restricts its membership. Even praiseworthy goals may raise ethical issues relating to means. Civil rights movements may provoke questions concerning the use of violent versus nonviolent means. The fraternity whose goal is to improve the chapter's grade average may face the ethical issues relating to stealing examinations, cheating, and providing less able members with term papers.

In more subtle ways, group ends and means may be destructive to the general social welfare. Public discussion and freedom of speech inevitably come under attack from the new corporate values. The attack on the freedom of political expression is most dramatic and well publicized, because powerful groups have always tried to restrict the rights of expression of their opposition. From the Alien and Sedition Acts through the Know Nothing Party to the Anarchists, Bolsheviks, Communists, and Fascists, history is replete with attempts to restrict political advocates. Elaborate safeguards now exist to protect the rights of political speakers. That such rights need continual defense goes without saying, but there are more subtle erosions of free expression that are of recent development.

In an agrarian society, a citizen had three major groups with which he identified: his family, his church, and his fatherland. In an urban society, he identified with a multitude of groups. On the farm in 1800, the child absorbed the norms of his family with few outside distractions. In today's suburbs, the child becomes part of groups outside the family before he starts school. Soon the norms of the family conflict with the elementary-school peer group, and children reproach their parents with, "But Johnny doesn't have to. . . ." The more relevant attack on freedom of speech comes in the restriction of the flow of communication as a group defends itself from other groups. Information is kept confidential or secret, in order to achieve a better competitive position. The widespread practice of marking communications "secret" or "top secret," because of the danger to the group if outsiders discover the information, is a pervasive and subtle restriction of freedom of speech. In the aftermath of the incident in the Democratic Party Headquarters at the Watergate during the 1972 presidential campaign, a series of investigations, including one by a Senate Select Committee, revealed the extent to which the executive branch of the government had become addicted to marking documents secret and to clandestine meetings and to information drops reminiscent of intelligence agents in a foreign country. The restriction of the flow of information by the executive branch and its attempts to manage news are a prime, but by no means isolated, example. Finally, the development of the mystique of experts, the specialization inherent in group structure, erodes freedom of expression. Experts develop their own jargon and thus defend their status. They hoard information and typically rely on presenting judgments as conclusions, which they say are based on secret knowledge too important or too technical to reveal. Even within the group, the expert may protect his status by hoarding his information. The bureaucratic structure is so complicated, and the flow of communication so restricted by the boundaries of organizational structures, ad hoc committees, and distributed responsibility that much information is lost in transit.

Public discussions and conferences provide a mechanism by which the free flow of communication within a corporate and urban society can be encouraged. Values have inertia and often are gradually transformed rather than radically altered. Skill in public discussion continues to be an important way in which freedom of speech can serve the ends of society. Technological advances in the mass media give public discussion an added power. If the restrictions inherent in bureaucracy could be loosened and information released through public discussion on television, the democratic values of free speech and inquiry might be preserved in a viable form for an urban society.

some basic assumptions

Throughout this book are hints and implications relevant to the ethical issues raised by the relationship of the individual to the group, groups to groups, and groups to the general welfare. One of the major assumptions is that there is a close connection between discussion and a democratic society. Both share a common set of values. These include the belief that the citizen can rule wisely if he is given the opportunity; that each individual has an innate worth and dignity; that groups, institutions, and political structures must take into account, preserve, and uphold that dignity.

A second major assumption is that the discussant has a right and obligation to make up his own mind. His participation implies individual rights with their concomitant obligations. He should be allowed to decide for himself without being coerced, duped, or manipulated. This assumption further implies that every person should acquire and process information in such a way that he can make sound decisions. The channels of communication leading to the group and those within the group should be such that maximum freedom of expression is coupled with maximum feedback. When one becomes a group member, he is choosing to conform to the group's norms. The ethical standard is simply that he ought to make the choice for himself, with a full understanding of its implications for him as an individual as well as for his group.

A third major assumption is that each individual ought to have the opportunity to grow and develop his potential within the group. A praiseworthy group does not neglect the desirable (those things that meet the needs on the deficit ladder: material goods, security, social approval, prestige, and esteem), but it goes beyond the desirable to the ends and means that transcend the self. The praiseworthy group, therefore, is one in which the member's potential for achievement and self-transcendence is realized. Role struggles, hostilities, and destructive norms that are barriers to such growth should be overcome as soon as possible.

A fourth major assumption throughout this text is a faith in reason and communication. Man differs significantly from other animals in his ability to use symbols in connected discourse to reason not only about the things present in his immediate perceptual field, but also about the past (man is capable of history and tradition) and about the future (man is capable of purpose, ends, and goals). Man is able to plan and evaluate. He is the only ethical animal; only man can conceive of future ends and means and judge when they are desirable or praiseworthy. When he brings language and reason together, he exhibits some of his most unique and best human characteristics. When man sees the facts clearly and reasons about them consistently, he is knowledgeable; but when he praises intelligently, he is wise—and wisdom should be prized above knowledge.

Our final major assumption is that in the conflict Karl Menninger characterizes as *Man Against Himself* and *Love Against Hate*, the instinct for life and the capacity for love are more praiseworthy than the death wish and the ability to hate. Conflicts and aggressions among group members and among groups that result in destructive attacks on either the persons or personalities of others are bad. This book assumes that lowering the status of others, showing antagonisms, and creating social tensions are destructive to the group and to the individuals.

a code for the practitioner

THE ETHICS OF PARTICIPATION

No ethical principle emerges more clearly from the study and practice of discussion and group methods than this: The person who deliberately chooses to use his group or any of its members as means to help him achieve his personal ends is to be censured. He ought to be labeled with the term *manipulator*. He is unethical, for even if he fails to achieve his own ends, he nonetheless creates a destructive group environment. On the other hand, the person who forgets his own welfare in seeking to work for all is to be praised. Like the individual who forgets his own happiness in working for the good of others and often finds a meaning and purpose in life that makes him happy, so the person who forgets his own status in order to work for the good of the group often wins esteem. Thus, building cohesiveness by showing solidarity for the group, raising the status of others, volunteering to help, releasing social tensions, and showing affection and regard for colleagues are all praiseworthy means.

Karl R. Wallace has suggested that there is a close connection between persuading and giving advice. The participant, too, finds himself advising his colleagues. When he views the facts, examines a course of action, and contemplates means to achieve ends, he takes the role function of group adviser. An adviser has certain duties and responsibilities. He must present his information honestly, fairly, and accurately.

He should be open about his sources and cooperate with the others in testing the truth of his statements of fact. Lying is intolerable in a group. It breaks the trust members have in their information-processing norms. Lying disturbs both the task and social dimensions of group process. An adviser should be prepared to defend his advice in terms of the common good, rather than his own selfish interests.

When participants receive advice, they, in turn, have a responsibility. They must do more than say, "Tell us what to believe or do and we will believe or do it." They must test and determine for themselves. This does not mean "buyer beware," but both the giver and receiver should assume their proper responsibilities in the evaluation of the advice.

The ethical code suitable for the practitioner in small groups ought to be pertinent to the wholeness and mental health of participants. The connection between group experience and mental health is weak in brief and transitory groups and grows impelling in those basic groups to which one devotes much of his life. The discussion group that meets for only one night in a religious center may mark a person superficially, while the family group will bend him for life. The basic person-to-person ethics that govern interpersonal relations develop an individual's self-image and may result in inferiority complexes, loneliness, neuroses, depression, and even psychoses. Man's inhumanity to man has always been a source of evil. Nowhere is it more damaging than in the confines of a small group. An ethical code that views each person as significant, having dignity, and being worthy of respect, is of vital importance. Whatever the status arrangement, the human relationships ought to reflect the values of trust, respect, and honesty.

THE ETHICS OF TEACHING

As the student gains knowledge about discussion and group methods, he faces new ethical choices as a result of that knowledge. The expert on small groups must follow a more professional ethical code. In many respects his problem is similar to that of the student of persuasion whose knowledge may be put to the service of praiseworthy or evil ends.

An adequate ethical code for the small-group practitioner requires that the expert as well as the participant does not manipulate groups for his own ends or for the ends of employers who hire him to achieve their own ends. It is quite possible for group techniques to be used as persuasive devices, but when they are so used without a clear label of the intent, the practice is unethical.

An expert in discussion should not tease or use groups for his own amusement. A hypnotist is able to use his powerful skill to amuse himself and others. An expert in group methods could also arrange demonstrations and projects that make the participants look amusing or ridiculous. The indiscriminate use of either hypnotism or knowledge about groups may result in permanent damage to the subjects.

The expert should use his knowledge to develop better, healthier groups. The student of discussion ought to be dedicated to improving small-group communication, increasing cohesiveness, and developing efficient productive groups.

The expert should not pretend to have greater knowledge and understanding than he possesses or that the state of the art will support. Since the interpersonal dimension of group process is so clearly allied to mental health and has so many psychiatric implications, students of group methods are often tempted to play, if not God, at least psychiatrist. The practitioner has an ethical obligation to make clear to the layman the extent of his knowledge in the difficult area of mental and emotional health. He must be careful not to damage the personality of an individual in the course of role-playing exercises or group-evaluation sessions. If an expert in group methods criticizes a person in front of a group, he has an obligation to be objective and fair and to indicate the good as well as bad qualities of that person. He ought not to justify such behavior on the basis that the purpose of the criticism is to make the person aware of his shortcomings. When one deals with another's self-image, he should treat it with reverence and care.

Finally, the expert should not simplify the problem of learning to work productively with or lead groups. The demand for training in leadership, discussion, and group methods is so strong that unscrupulous people are often tempted to offer patent-medicine-type panaceas. An expert who cloaks his knowledge in some mystery, talks some impressive unintelligible jargon, and promises quick and easy success may develop a lucrative practice in bilking the general public. Many people have so vital a stake in working with and leading groups that they will pay considerable amounts of money to achieve success. They may be more reluctant to invest the time and effort required for genuine understanding, so the promise of painless, quick competence is tempting.

ethical guidelines for public welfare

The participant in a group must make choices relating to his allegiance to his group when he finds their norms and ends in conflict with the larger purposes and norms of his society. He must decide what goals he will suggest and fight for within the group. If his programs and tactics are not adopted, he must decide whether to support the group or not. When he can no longer subscribe to purposes or means, what should he choose to do? When does his responsibility to the group cease and his duty to the larger public welfare begin?

Irving Janis has made a perceptive study of the way group pressures can pose ethical issues in his book, *Victims of Groupthink,* where he discusses the effects of group norms and pressures for conformity on such high-level decisions as the Kennedy administration's move to invade Cuba at the Bay of Pigs and the Johnson administration's move to escalate the Vietnam War. Certainly, the same issue was posed for members of the Nixon administration who perjured themselves to cover up the Watergate burglary. In less world-shaking ways, the same issue develops whenever one works for a period of time in a small group.

Does our culture contain some general universal values suitable to aid the participant with such choices? One should not take the more general value statements as rigid and unbending principles, but they do furnish starting places to reason about a given problem. In addition to the values already summarized as the basic assumptions of this book, several other widely held and time-honored insights deserve consideration.

Small-group communication has much in common with public speaking. Some of the best minds of ancient and modern times have puzzled over the question of the ethical responsibility of the speaker. Most have come to a consensus about certain basic values. The next few paragraphs must of necessity have an old and familiar ring. The fact that wise men in succeeding generations have sought in vain for a better ethic testifies to the power and validity of these basic values.

Two important insights from the classical rhetoricians may be adapted to guide workers in groups. The first is Aristotle's imperative that rhetoric should be used to defend the truth. In an age when speech often was used for attack and defense of persons, his notion that rhetoric ought to be dedicated to truth was an ethical revolution. Thus, instead of personal aggrandizement or attack of one's enemies, Aristotle suggested that knowledge and skill be used to discover and defend truth. The second important guide from classical times is Quintilian's dictum that a praiseworthy speaker is a good man, as well as a skillful and effective technician. The orator, according to Quintilian, ought to be a good man speaking well.

The group participant should defend the truth and be a good person participating effectively and skillfully. The group itself should defend true statements of fact, praiseworthy value statements, and sound advice. It ought to be a good group when judged within the context of the larger society.

In terms of human relations, the Biblical commands to "love thy neighbor" and "to do unto others as you would have them do unto you" remain basic general values of our culture against which to judge choices in a group context. The same insight was given a slightly different twist in Kant's ethical imperative that a choice is praiseworthy insofar as it ought to be generalized to all similar situations. One might ask of a given decision: Would it be a good thing if all others who faced a similar choice made the same decision?

Finally, and of utmost importance in any consideration of the ethics of communication, is the necessity of judging means in terms of a general framework of ethics, rather than in terms of the end to be reached. History furnishes many instances when people have justified lying, cheating, aggression, hate, physical violence, and psychological destructiveness on the basis that the end was praiseworthy. One of the most frightening aspects of the propaganda and persuasion of the international communist movement under the leadership of Stalinist Russia and of the Nazi movement in Germany under the leadership of Hilter and Goebbels was the wholehearted and cynical adoption of the ethic that the triumph of that system justified the use of any means whatsoever. A similar argument is often an element in the tactic of the demagogue. Huey Long proclaimed that he was the official "thief" of Louisiana State University and on one occasion told a group of educators that the politician would always be with them and that politicians would always steal, but what the school men ought to do was to get the politicians to steal for the schools. When Joseph McCarthy of Wisconsin was a senator, he often charged individuals with being Communists or communist sympathizers on tenuous evidence, and his tactics were justified on the basis that the elimination of the communist menace required such means. Gandhi's ethical insight, "Evil means, even for a good end, produce evil results," continues to serve as a sound touchstone for the student of discussion and group methods.

QUESTIONS FOR STUDY

1. Do you believe that a good goal will justify almost any means that a group may use to achieve it effectively?
2. In what respect can it be said that a group member faces a two-step ethical problem?
3. What are some ways in which conformity to group norms can stifle individual integrity, freedom, and creativity?
4. To what extent do you think an individual should sacrifice his personal desires for the good of a group?
5. Is a democratic group style preferable to an authoritative one?
6. How important is free speech and freedom of dissent in the development of good groups and in individual fulfillment?
7. Is there a tension between specialization and the development of experts and the democratic value system?
8. What is your personal code of ethics for a group member?
9. Under what circumstances, if any, would you justify a member intentionally asserting a false statement of fact to be true to the other members of his group?

10. Do you agree that the use of group methods for persuasive intent without the knowledge of the group members is unethical?

1. With a group of your classmates, develop a case study that poses a common ethical issue faced by a group member. Use the case study to stimulate a discussion of the issue in class.
2. With a group of your classmates, develop a role-playing exercise that places the role players in a situation of ethical tension. Use the role-playing exercise to stimulate discussion of the issue in class.
3. With a group of your classmates, develop a mock-trial situation. Select members of the group to act as judge, prosecuting attorney, defense attorney, and defendant. Select one person to be a witness for the prosecution and another to be witness for the defense. Accuse the defendant of some unethical group behavior. The prosecution makes the charge, the defense attorney answers, the prosecution examines the witness, the defense cross examines; and then the defense presents its case, with each lawyer taking eight to ten minutes to sum up his side of the case. The rest of the class may serve as jurors.

References and suggested readings

For help with the general framework of the chapter and for some of the basic ethical insights, I am indebted to the editorial advice and writings of Karl Wallace. See, for example:

Wallace, Karl R. "An Ethical Basis of Communication," *Speech Teacher,* **4** (1955), 1–9.
Wallace, Karl R. "Rhetoric and Advising," *Southern Speech Journal,* **29** (1964), 278–287.
Wallace, Karl R. "The Substance of Rhetoric: Good Reasons," *Quarterly Journal of Speech,* **49** (1963), 239–249.

For other discussions of the ethics of communication, see:

Brandenburg, Earnest. "Quintilian and the Good Orator," *Quarterly Journal of Speech,* **34** (1948), 23–29.
Haiman, Franklyn S. "A Re-examination of the Ethics of Persuasion," *Central States Speech Journal,* **3** (1952), 4–9.
Jensen, J. Vernon. "An Analysis of Recent Literature on Teaching Ethics in Public Address," *Speech Teacher,* **8** (1959), 219–228.
Johannesen, Richard L. *Ethics and Persuasion.* New York: Random House, 1966.
McKeon, Richard. "Communication, Truth, and Society," *Ethics,* **67** (1957), 89–99.
Nilsen, Thomas R. *Ethics of Speech Communication.* Indianapolis: Bobbs-Merrill, 1966.

Rogge, Edward. "Evaluating the Ethics of a Speaker in a Democracy," *Quarterly Journal of Speech*, **45** (1959), 419–425.

Wieman, Henry Nelson, and Otis M. Walter. "Toward an Analysis of Ethics for Rhetoric," *Quarterly Journal of Speech*, **43** (1957), 266–270.

For a general discussion of ethics, see:

Baier, Kurt. *A Moral Point of View: A Rational Basis of Ethics*. Ithaca, N.Y.: Cornell University Press, 1958.

Brandt, Richard B. *Ethical Theory: The Problems of Normative and Critical Ethics*. Englewood Cliffs, N.J.: Prentice-Hall, 1959.

The January, 1966, issue of *The Annals of the American Academy of Political and Social Science*, **3063**, is devoted to "Ethics in America: Norms and Deviations."

For the group pressures for unethical conduct, see:

Janis, Irving L. *Victims of Groupthink*. Boston: Houghton Mifflin, 1972.

The two Menninger books mentioned are:

Menninger, Karl. *Love Against Hate*. New York: Harcourt Brace Jovanovich, 1942.

Menninger, Karl. *Man Against Himself*. New York: Harcourt Brace Jovanovich, 1938.

For discussions of Long and McCarthy as demagogues, see:

Baskerville, Barnet. "Joe McCarthy: Brief-Case Demagogue," *Today's Speech*, **2** (1954), 8–15.

Bormann, Ernest G. "Huey Long: Analysis of a Demagogue," *Today's Speech*, **2** (1954), 16–19.

CHAPTER 4

DEVELOPING INFORMATION FOR GROUP DISCUSSION

One of the strengths of the contemporary organization and industrial corporation is the ability to take trained and talented but not extraordinary people who have specialized deeply but narrowly and coordinate their skills and knowledge to develop new ideas, to make decisions, and to solve problems relating to broad and complex areas of endeavor. The modern organization can mobilize the highly specialized knowledge of many individuals to achieve, for example, the wonders of manned space flight. Indeed, one of the keys to the complicated and efficient economic systems of the highly developed nations is the ability of their people to organize and maintain corporate structures. After the saturation bombing and total defeat of World War II, the major resource remaining to the German people was the knowledge required to sustain the modern organization. When material resources became available, West Germany quickly became one of the most highly developed nations of Western Europe.

The main tool for accomplishing the pooling of expertise and arriving at decisions within the contemporary organization is the group discussion conducted in the pragmatic style described in Chapter 2. This chapter presents the critical and theoretical standards of the pragmatic style in regard to the collection and evaluation of information and the development of policies or courses of action. When a group discussion deals with its external environment in an attempt to reach a clearly specified objective, it may become both the source of and the receiver of messages from the world around it. The group gathers messages from the external environment, evaluates the soundness of the information, responds with communications of its own, and searches for feedback to estimate its success.

Participants in group discussion should make individual efforts to seek information. People are often invited to participate because of their specialized knowledge. Each participant should prepare by sifting and evaluating his information to choose the data that seem most useful to the purposes of the discussion. The discussant should then work through the best method for communicating his information to the others. During the discussion, members will both present and test messages. Thus, ideally the group finally accepts and uses information screened first by the individual who gathered it and then by the dialectic processes of the discussion itself.

Problems within the social dimension may limit the group's potential to act with a clear impression of the facts and may inhibit its ability to decide wisely among potential courses of action. The next few chapters, however, assume that the interpersonal relationships within the group are such that it can concentrate maximum attention on the task dimension.

This chapter provides a set of guidelines for analyzing and testing the content of messages. An individual criticizing the soundness of information should first describe the content of a message and then apply standards of evaluation to arrive at a judgment. A good way to describe the content of communication is by categorizing the statements within it according to important qualitative differences. Critics need, in addition to such a set of descriptive categories, a system of standards of excellence for use in evaluating the content of each category. The guidelines in this chapter consist of a system for categorizing linguistic statements into propositions of fact, of value, or of advice (policy). Each category is defined and distinguished from the others on the basis of important qualitative differences. These guidelines contain criteria for evaluating each kind of statement.

A person should apply the tests of good information both while preparing for and participating in group discussion. The tests also provide a basis for subsequent evaluations of the excellence of the discussion. We begin with an explanation of the techniques for gathering information and conclude with the description of a critical method useful in preparing for, participating in, and evaluating group discussion.

When the reader ought to be particularly alert to some specific problem of testing information *before* the meeting, the analysis views the problem from that perspective; for the most part, however, the chapter discusses the material in terms of a group's dealing with its external environment. The shifting perspective should cause no trouble in understanding if one remembers that the standards for sound information remain the same whether one is preparing for, participating in, or evaluating a discussion.

Evidence defined. As used in group discussion, *evidence* is material assembled by a member to furnish grounds for belief or to make something evident to the others. Evidence tends to prove or disprove an argumentative position. The concept of evidence is important in legal matters where it consists of material furnished by the lawyers to support a contention. In the courts, evidence may consist of the testimony of witnesses and the exhibition of facts such as documents, weapons, and so forth. *Proof* is a sufficient marshalling of evidence to achieve belief within the other discussants. *Evidence* implies, according to this definition, anything that carries weight as proof with the others in the group and includes both words (linguistic phenomena such as oral and written testimony) and things (facts such as prototypes of new products, wind tunnels, buildings).

Information defined. Information is closely related to evidence. Information may be used as evidence in support of reasons during an argument or a presentation in the discussion. The term will not, however, be considered as synonymous with *evidence;* this definition arbitrarily restricts *information* to linguistic statements. *Information* thus denotes only part of the material useful as evidence. In addition, the term *evidence* will be used to imply proof and an argumentative stance toward some proposition that is contested within the discussion. The group may use information, as here defined, to satisfy the curiosity of its members (enlightenment) or to get the "lay of the land" (orientation). Information connotes inquiry; evidence, advocacy.

Information consists of statements of fact, opinion, and advice. The grounds for accepting or rejecting each kind of statement differ as do their uses. Statements of fact describe the world. They refer to things. Opinion statements express value judgments and suggest goals or purposes. Statements of advice propose courses of action, recommend beliefs or attitudes and policies. Whenever a group deals with its environment, it needs factual descriptions of the case to orient it to current conditions. Members help the group deal with its environment by providing it with suggestions for courses of action. When the group begins to consider the wisdom of various courses of action, it usually evaluates them on the basis of agreed-upon goals, values, and purposes expressed in opinion statements. When a discussion group has an accurate description of the world and a clear statement of its common goals and values, it can better evaluate proposed courses of action.

gathering information

Most students of discussion have had previous training in seeking information, using the library, preparing bibliographies, and taking notes. However, a summary of these techniques as they relate to the general features of information gathering, with an emphasis on those items important to preparing information for the group, is in order.

SOURCES OF INFORMATION

Personal experience. One of the major sources of information will be the discussant's background and experience. The student should not rely on spur-of-the-moment inspiration, but should write down his information to discover the gaps to be filled.

On occasion, he can round out his background by direct observation of the conditions under discussion. If the group's topic deals with new teaching techniques, he might visit classes taught by closed-circuit television or observe teaching machines in use. He should record his observations by taking notes during or immediately after the field trip.

Interviews. Another excellent source of information is the interview. The student may find eyewitnesses to question about events, or he may interview authorities on a subject. Authorities may testify concerning both facts and opinions. If the group plans to interview a large sample of people, they may want to draw up a list of questions to ask each person. If only a few people are being interviewed in depth, group members will want to conduct an open-ended interview, which enables the authority to introduce directions they may not have considered. The interview should be planned to elicit as much of the desired information and opinion as possible. If several participants are interviewing, a common set of questions is important. The results of the interviews can be more easily compared if all respondents are asked the same questions. Too often, students begin an interview with a vague statement that they would like to know about communism in Latin America. If the interviewed authority asks what specific information the students want, they cannot provide an answer. Interviewing is a complex and difficult task. If the group members are to use many interviews, they should study research methods dealing with interviewing techniques.

An accurate record of the interview should be kept, by using a tape recorder if possible. If the interviewers plan to quote the person directly, they must record his statement verbatim and should inform him that they plan to use his actual words. Such statements should be carefully and clearly written at the time of the interview.

Libraries and archives. A final and important source of information consists of written documents, records, manuscripts, letters, diaries, books, journals, magazines, and newspapers. Students of discussion find the library their richest source of information. The ability to use the library effectively is part of the equipment of an educated person. One wit observed that he could become the world's *second* greatest authority on any subject in three weeks, given the resources of a good library.

BIBLIOGRAPHY

Bibliography defined. In a general way, bibliography refers to the study of writings and publications. This study includes the history, identification, description, and evaluation of published works. More specifically, the term often means a list of writings dealing with a particular subject, the writings having been read in the original by the lister. Such a bibliography may be annotated; that is, it may contain short descriptions and evaluations about the items. The term *bibliography* will be used here to refer to the discovery, evaluation, and systematic listing of writings that have been consulted by the student and deal with a particular subject.

Collecting bibliography. Soon many librarians will be using computers to search for and retrieve information. The gathering of a bibliography will then be quite simple. Until most libraries are computerized, group members will continue to use the time-honored research techniques of the scholar. They will ·collect items for study by examining indexes to books, government documents, periodicals, and newspapers.

The group should work up a list of key words before its members begin an extensive search of indexes. Of course, during the investigation, new key words will be discovered, but puzzling about key words as a group early in the investigation will cut down the drudgery of preparing a bibliography.

The next step is to find bibliographies already written on the subject. Three good general works of this sort are: (1) *A World Bibliography of Bibliographies and of Bibliographical Catalogues, Calendars, Abstracts, Digests, Indexes, and the Like;* (2) *Bibliographical Index: A Cumulative Bibliography of Bibliographies;* (3) *Bulletin of Bibliography and Magazine Notes.*

Most questions suitable for public discussion have been the subject of books and dissertations. Bibliographies at the end of such works can enlarge the group's bibliography.

Often, background information can be quickly gathered by examining reference books and encyclopedias. Library researchers should become familiar with such works as *Guide to Reference Books, Fundamental Reference Sources,* and *Reference Books: A Brief Guide for Students and Other Users of the Library.*

After bibliography cards have been made for sources that look promising, researchers should turn to the card catalogue of the library; in particular, they should become familiar with the major indexes to contemporary magazines and journals. These include the *Readers' Guide to Periodical Literature, Applied Science & Technology Index, Business Periodicals Index, The Education Index,* and the *Social Science and Humanities Index.*

Since 1851, *The New York Times* has been indexed in *The New York Times Index.* Many libraries have a file of recent issues of *The New York Times,* and discussants can quickly locate the news stories relating to their work. To check a local paper's version of a story, they can check the files for the local paper on the days surrounding the date of the story in *The New York Times.*

Students preparing for discussion should not overlook the publications of local and state governments as well as the United States Government Printing Office. An important index to local publications is the *Monthly Checklist of State Publications.* Because government publications are so diverse and voluminous, many libraries have a separate Government Document Section with librarians available to help find sources. The *Congressional Record* is carefully indexed and contains information on most questions of public policy. A good general index to federal government publications is the *Monthly Catalog of United States Government Publications.*

Bibliography cards. When a researcher finds an item that seems pertinent and useful, he should make out a bibliography card. The group should decide on the form of bibliographical notation that every member will use. If they keep a common bibliographical file, all members should use the same bibliographical form and cards.

The bibliographical notation should include: the name of the author, compiler, or editor; the exact title as it appears on the title page of the book; the place of publication; the name of the publisher; the number of the edition if it is a revised edition; the number of volumes; the date of publication; and pertinent page numbers in an edited volume or periodical.

The following examples illustrate a recommended form for bibliographical information:

(1) For a book with one author:
Hare, A. Paul. *Handbook of Small Group Research.* New York: Free Press, 1962.

(2) For a book with two or more authors:
Collins, Barry E., and Harold Guetzkow. *A Social Psychology of Group Processes for Decision Making.* New York: Wiley, 1964.

(3) *For an edited book:*
Cartwright, Dorwin, and Alvin Zander, eds. *Group Dynamics: Research and Theory.* New York: Harper & Row, 1953.

(4) *For an article in an edited collection:*
Asch, Solomon E. "Effects of Group Pressure upon the Modification and Distortion of Judgments." In Dorwin Cartwright and Alvin Zander, eds. *Group Dynamics: Research and Theory.* New York: Harper & Row, 1953, pp. 151–162.

(5) *For a book of two or more volumes:*
Lindzey, Gardner, ed. *Handbook of Social Psychology.* Springfield, Mass.: Addison-Wesley, 1954. 2 vols.

(6) *For an article in an encyclopedia:*
Raymond, Ellsworth. "Communism," *Encyclopedia Americana.* New York: Americana Corporation, 1949, VII, pp. 417–419.

(7) *For a magazine article, author given:*
Pines, Maya. "The Coming Upheaval in Psychiatry," *Harper's Magazine,* October 1965, pp. 54–60.

(8) *For a magazine article, author not given:*
"What's Wrong in Latin America," *U.S. News & World Report,* May 24, 1965, pp. 40–44.

(9) *For a newspaper story:*
The New York Times, March 8, 1965, p. 1.

In addition to the essential information about a book or article on the bibliography card, the participant should add a brief annotation concerning its value. Discussants often cite authorities such as Henry Kissinger or James Reston, but when asked for further information, they can only report that the expert has had experience in the government or that he is a newspaperman. The information on the bibliography card for an important book or article should include a brief note about the author's background, training, position, and bias. Some of this information is available on the book jacket or in the preface. One can often learn more about the author from such reference works as *Who's Who in America* and *A Dictionary of Current Biography.* Book reviews in *Book Review Digest, Saturday Review,* or *The New York Times Book Review* can be helpful.

When using magazines, it is well to learn their reputation for accuracy and the slant of their interpretations. Research that is confined to the *U.S. News & World Report* will provide a much different impression of Latin American affairs than that confined to *Ramparts* magazine. Such magazines as *Reader's Digest, National Review, The Nation, Time, Newsweek, The Atlantic Monthly, Harper's Magazine, The New Republic,* and *The Progressive* slant the news in their unsigned stories. They also tend to print signed articles that are congenial to their editorial position. A student should appraise the magazines in his bibliography so that his reading is not confined to sources with a similar bias. People tend to seek out reading materials with biases similar to their own. If discussants want the soundest information available, however, they must examine magazines and newspapers that represent a broad spectrum of opinion.

Here is a sample of an annotated bibliography card:

Skinner, B. F. "Why Teachers Fail," *Saturday Review*, October 16, 1965, pp. 80–81, 98–102.

B. F. Skinner is Edgar Pierce Professor of Psychology at Harvard University. A leading experimental psychologist, he has concentrated his research on the psychology of learning and language. His viewpoint is that of a behaviorist, and his work has evolved into a "school" of Skinnerian psychology. Skinnerian psychology is controversial and important. Skinner's "learning" theory has formed the basis for the development of teaching machines and programmed learning.

This article is useful for its thought-provoking attack on traditional teaching methods. The conclusion of the article hints at a way to improve teaching by following the principles of Skinner's operant conditioning, but an actual program is not developed. Should be read by all members of the group.

Note-taking. The discussant keeps a record of information for two primary purposes. First, he will need the record for his own use during the discussion. His system can be very personal and idiosyncratic as long as it assures adequate information, accurately transcribed and quickly found. Second, his system must be organized so that other group members or members of the audience can use it.

Recent technological improvements have facilitated record-keeping. Most libraries now have fast, inexpensive (only a few cents per page) copying machines. Despite these recent, impressive developments, group members will find that efficiency as well as economy will require note-taking for much of their recording of information.

Researchers should take the same care with their note cards that they take with their bibliography cards. Each note must have the exact citation for the material recorded from the book or article. The addition of a general heading to each note will aid in filing the material. If notes can be indexed around general headings that break the topic into logical subdivisions, the discussants will be able to find a given bit of information more rapidly.

Most of the books and articles read will contain statements about factual matters, arguments based on these statements, and value judgments. If the factual matters are particularly important to the group, their original source should be located. For example, if an article in a magazine quotes statistical information drawn from the Bureau of Labor Statistics, the members should find the report of the Bureau and use it. This is particularly crucial if the statistics differ in various books and articles. Information commonly accepted by all commentators on a question and of incidental importance to the group's work can be gathered from secondary sources.

When he finds something to record, a member must decide whether the material should be copied verbatim or outlined or paraphrased. Many students waste time copying too much material word for word. Much information can best be preserved by outlining or summarizing. A good rule of thumb is to paraphrase or outline *unless* the student can think of a good reason for taking a direct quotation. If other members of the group are going to read the note cards, they must be complete enough to be self-explanatory.

Although discussants need not make direct quotations very often, on some occasions they should do so. If a member plans to support or refute an argument he may wish to quote the argument directly. If the author is unusually authoritative, or has expressed an idea in a particularly apt or interesting way, or if he has testified to factual matters in such a way that the language he used expressed important distinctions, a direct quotation may be preferable.

When recording direct quotations, the student must use the exact wording, spelling, and punctuation of the original. If he finds an error, he should insert the Latin word *sic,* underlined, in brackets following the error. *Sic* means *thus,* and when any member of the group refers to the note later, he will know that the mistake was in the article and not in the copying. Omitted material is replaced by ellipses (. . .). Underlining indicates italics.

Group members should always take notes that reflect the general spirit and tenor of the original material. Quoting out of context often distorts the position of the authority. Indeed, one form of dishonesty is to quote out of context purposely to distort the position of the witness. If necessary, the student can add explanatory material in brackets within a direct quotation to insure that when others examine the note they will not distort the quotation by mistake.

Group members must judge the relevance, importance, and soundness of the material they read in order to take good notes. Each bit of information recorded in a note must be tested, and only the information that passes the appropriate tests should be recorded.

testing information

The first step in testing information is to examine each sentence in the message to discover whether or not it contains information. Questions seek rather than contain information. The only sentences to be categorized are statements or imperatives. The next step is to classify each declarative sentence as to whether it is a statement of fact, opinion, or advice. Imperative sentences always express opinions or advice.

STATEMENTS OF FACT

Definition of statements of fact. The major difference between statements of fact and other kinds of statements is that factual assertions are true *or* false in a special sense of the terms *true* and *false.* People quite often use the word *true* as a compliment. They say someone is a "true scholar" when they wish to compliment him. Sometimes individuals use the word *true* in another sense as an expression of some mystical and undefinable value. Then they spell the word with a capital *T,* as when they say "He is a seeker after Truth," or "The scholar searches for Truth," or "The entire Truth is never knowable." Such use of the term *Truth* can lead to deep discussion of a philosophical nature. Discussions of *Truth* are usually fun and sometimes important to a student's education. Using the term in this way can lead to some muddle-headedness, however, and can confuse a group meeting to deal with the here-and-now. A group trying to deal sanely and maturely with its environment is well advised to judge the truth of its information on much more precise and restricted grounds.

A *statement of fact* is a sentence that refers to the world in an unambiguous fashion and is clearly understood by members of the group. Every member can think of a set of *observations* that would furnish evidence for the *truth* of the statement. In addition, the statement is so clear that each person thinks of the *same* set of observations.

Take a situation in which two members of a discussion group meet shortly before class. Fred says to Harry, "Joe is absent today. Our group needs him for the discussion program. A fellow who shirks his responsibility like that is a jerk." Fred has made several kinds of statements. The first is factual; the last is a value judgment. The proper response for Harry if he wishes to check the statement of fact is to *observe* whether or not Joe is present. If he sees Joe in the classroom, he decides that Fred has asserted a *false* statement of fact, that is, Fred has said something is the case when it is not the case. If Joe is not present he decides that Fred has asserted a *true* statement of fact. The terms *true* and *false* refer to the relationships between observables and statements about them. *True* describes the relationship when the statement squares with the observations. *False* is the converse of true.

The last statement, "A fellow who shirks his responsibility like that is a jerk," is neither true nor false. No possible set of observations made by either Fred or Harry can yield a decision about the truth or falsity of such a statement. This statement implies a value judgment that meeting obligations in a responsible way is good. Reasonable men will differ in value judgments. Another member of the group might disagree and say, "Joe is in no condition to take part in a discussion program. He might go all to pieces. I think Joe should stay away and care for his mental health. After all, it is more important for Joe to care for himself than meet his responsibilities to our group." All members of the group can agree that the statement "Joe is absent today" is true; they may not all agree that "Joe is a jerk for being absent."

The most important characteristic of a statement of fact is that it asserts something about observables that can be judged true or false. There must be agreement about the observables (facts) of the statement if the participants are to make a truth judgment about it. If a discussant asserts that "The GNP is up 3 percent when compared to the first quarter of last year," he is making a statement of fact, but to function as such for the group, it must be understood. The member who asks "What is GNP?" is in no position to judge the truth or falsity of the statement. An important thing to remember, however, is that the discussion group provides an excellent environment in which to clear up misunderstandings. On occasion, group members differ as to the truth or falsity of statements of fact, but they usually can resolve these differences. The first step in resolving the differences is to make sure each person understands what is being said; that is, is everyone thinking of the same set of observations? The second step is for each individual to make suitable observations in order to check the facts for himself. Harry must first know the individual named *Joe,* and, second, he must look at the students in the classroom to see if he recognizes Joe among them.

Take another example: Fred says, "Joe is absent today." Harry is puzzled because he has observed Joe in the group for the last 30 minutes. Clearly, Joe is not absent, so he says, "But Joe is here." Fred replies with some irony in his voice, "Joe is not physically absent, but he isn't really with us." Harry now understands that Fred is asserting a different proposition than he interpreted at first. Harry now thinks he knows what Fred is saying about the facts, namely, Joe is preoccupied; and he makes another set of observations about the truth or falsity of Fred's statement.

Directly verifiable statements of fact. When Fred says to Harry, "Joe is absent today," Harry can observe the conditions that will make this statement true or false. He can look directly and personally at the facts for himself. This is the simplest of all verification situations. For the remainder of this book, the term *facts* will refer to the things that can be directly observed in order to verify the truth or falsity of statements of fact. In this sense, such things as ships, trees, houses, people, books, grain, dogs, cattle, factories, bank balances, automobiles, and credit cards are all facts. If the group decides to make a field trip to Skid Row to examine conditions, and Fred says to Harry, "Look! The windows in that hotel are broken," Harry can observe the facts (windows in the hotel) and decide whether the statement is true or false.

The group can usually resolve questions of truth or falsity at this level rather quickly. Yet differences as to truth decisions do arise. Many words that describe facts also carry a connotation of value judgment. Thus, if Fred says to Harry, "Look! The windows in that flophouse are smashed," Harry might respond by saying, "I really think that is a pretty decent place for this area. I would hardly call it a flophouse, and I see only two windows that are cracked and none that I would say are smashed." Again, the give-and-take of discussion can resolve these differences, and in the presence of the windows, Fred and Harry should be able to come to an agreement about the facts.

Indirectly verifiable statements of fact. Many statements of fact that are crucial to a group's work cannot be observed directly by all or even some of the group. Probably no members of a group discussing population growth in Argentina can go to Argentina to observe conditions directly. A group studying the extent of alcoholism in the Skid Row locale of their own city will not be able to observe all the facts directly. Yet, fact statements about these situations are either true or false. Such statements are indirectly verifiable statements of fact. Members of the group make their truth decisions on the basis of observations, but the facts they observe are of a different order. Often these facts are statements from books, magazines, or newspapers. These observations (reading) serve to furnish *evidence* for the truth or falsity of indirectly verifiable statements of fact.

A clear distinction should be made between *facts* (observables) and the *language* used in discussing facts (statements of fact). The terms *true* and *false* should be used as adjectives that modify language. Facts are not true or false; they either exist or they do not. The statements people use to discuss the world, on the other hand, may be true or false.

Evidence relating to statements of fact. Evidence for the truth or falsity of a directly verifiable statement of fact can be discovered by observation. Lawyers call this *real* evidence. If a lawyer holds a jacket up before a jury and asserts "This jacket has a hole in it, right there," the jury members may observe the jacket and decide whether or not the statement is true. Real evidence is usually easier to evaluate than the *evidence* for the truth or falsity of indirectly verifiable statements of fact.

Two examples of indirectly verifiable statements of fact arranged in order of complexity illustrate the problems in evaluating such evidence. The simplest statement is the one asserting that the hole in a jacket has been made by a .38-caliber bullet. Evidence in support of the truth of this statement consists of both facts and statements of fact. The jacket with the hole in it is available for the jurors to see (fact). They can also directly verify statements about the presence or absence of the hole, about its location, and about its size.

For the members of the jury, however, the question of whether the hole resulted from a bullet passing through the jacket, or from, say, a knife or a nail cutting through the fabric, is an indirectly verifiable matter. No person on the jury will have been present when the hole was made. The prosecution may call an eyewitness of the shooting to testify to the facts. Thus, if witness A asserts, "I saw John Harvey shoot the deceased on the evening of June 7th, and the deceased was wearing that jacket," and identifies the prosecution's exhibit, the prosecution has presented *evidence* of a second kind, namely, statements of fact asserted to be true by a witness who has been able to verify the statement directly. The introduction of a witness raises new problems for the jury because they must now evaluate the truth of the witness's testimony. Witnesses make mistakes. On occasion they willfully assert as true statements of fact that they know to be false from their own observations. The introduction of indirectly verifiable *statements of fact* as evidence poses one of the most difficult problems for those testing the truth or falsity of assertions.

The prosecution may also introduce an *expert* witness who testifies that the hole is, indeed, a bullet hole. The expert might state that the hole was of a size made by a .38-caliber bullet, that under microscopic examination he discovered traces of powder, and that the fabric was broken in a way that is characteristic of bullet holes. All of these statements *could* be verified directly by members of the jury. They, too, could measure the size of the bullet hole and examine it under a microscope. But even if they distrust the expert for some reason, they will usually rely on his or some other expert's testimony simply because they are not trained to make the observations required even when facts are present. A marketing expert may interpret the results of survey research and estimate the potential of a new product when an engineer might not be able to do so. An expert's statements of fact are accepted as true on the basis of the knowledge and integrity of the expert making the statements.

Finally, the expert could testify that all the directly verifiable statements he asserts to be true conclusively demonstrate that the hole was made by a .38-caliber bullet. The jurors will then have the following evidence for the indirectly verifiable statement that the bullet hole in the jacket was made by a .38-caliber bullet: (1) the facts—the jacket itself; (2) statements about the events at the time of the shooting—eyewitness says he saw the hole made by a .38-caliber revolver; (3) statements of fact by an expert that he has directly verified and that could be verified by others—the jacket and the hole; (4) the expert's judgment—that he is convinced the hole was made by a .38-caliber bullet.

Proving truth and falsity. Assume that when the jury enters the jury room to decide the case, nine jurors assert that they believe the hole in the jacket was made by a .38-caliber bullet. For these nine jurors, that statement has been *conclusively demonstrated* as true; that is, on the basis of the evidence presented to them, they *believe* the statement to be true. Two jurors believe the statement is false. For them, the evidence has *conclusively demonstrated* the statement to be false. One juror cannot decide. For him, the statement is *inconclusively demonstrated.*

Thus, indirectly verifiable statements may be *conclusively demonstrated* for a given individual or group, or audience, or they may be *inconclusively demonstrated.* Whether or not the demonstration is conclusive depends on (1) the amount and quality of the evidence; (2) the clarity with which it is presented; and (3) the level of proof required by the individual, group, or audience. The level of proof required depends not only on the training, temperament, and gullibility of those making the judgment, but also on the situation. If a man's life is at stake, a jury will usually demand a high level of proof. Of course, two different individuals, under similar conditions, will often require different amounts of proof before they judge that an indirectly verifiable statement of fact has been demonstrated as conclusively true. This being the case, the way is open for disagreement about factual matters; and, on occasion, the statement of fact under dispute may be vital enough to a large enough number of people, to make a public discussion program devoted to the question useful and justified.

Turn now to the more complicated statement of fact asserting that only 30 percent of the residents of Skid Row are alcoholics. The problem here is that the statement refers to such a vast and complicated set of observations that a group does not have the time, the money, or the skill to make them all and therefore must verify the statement indirectly.

Even the experts, in fact, seldom make all the possible observations required to enumerate completely the facts covered by this type of statement. Usually they generalize about the total population on the basis of observations made on a carefully drawn sample of facts. In order to decide the truth or falsity of such statements, therefore, it is necessary to judge the skill of the witnesses who made the observations and of the experts who drew the inferences. This judgment requires some knowledge about the point of view of the experts. Even natural scientists have a point of view that slants the manner in which they interpret their observations, and social scientists have a much more pronounced bias no matter how removed they may seem from vested interests. A Marxist economist will draw different conclusions from the same set of observations than a Keynesian economist. A Freudian psychoanalyst will arrive at a different interpretation of the same events than a Jungian psychoanalyst. Therefore, before accepting as true the conclusions offered by an authority such as John Kenneth Galbraith or Erich Fromm, it is necessary to consider not only the knowledge and integrity of that authority but also his point of view.

TESTING STATEMENTS OF FACT

Testing directly verifiable statements. Directly verifiable statements of fact are less difficult to test than indirectly verifiable statements. Discussion topics for public programs are usually complicated and very few of the statements of fact dealing with the topic itself can be directly verified by a discussant. He will find, however, that numerous statements of fact regarding sources of information are used by his colleagues; and, given the opportunity, he may want to verify these statements for himself. Thus, a member of the group asserts that on page 44 of the May, 1965, issue of *U.S. News & World Report*, it is stated that there was an increase of 3,400,000 people in Argentina from 1954 to 1964. If another discussant thinks the first member is mistaken, he can check the magazine to verify the statement. The accuracy of such directly verifiable statements should be checked. If the group gets misinformation through carelessness or mistakes at this level of investigation, there can be little hope of intelligent discussion.

Although they are important, statements of fact about what is said by authorities or eyewitnesses are really only tools to help the group orient itself to facts relating to the problem at hand. Accuracy in quotation is indeed important, but, in the final analysis, it is only a means to the basic end of gaining understanding about an historical event. Each discussant may verify directly the linguistic content of documents, surveys, statistical compilations, and so on, but the direct verification of such statements of fact is useful only insofar as it provides evidence of actual situations. In order to understand actual conditions, it is often necessary to know how to evaluate indirectly verifiable statements.

Testing indirectly verifiable statements. Statements of fact are made, orally or in writing, by people who may or may not have been eyewitnesses to the things they report. When no member of a group can directly observe the reported facts, the report, for the group, becomes an indirectly verifiable statement, and its source must be tested. When the source of the information is an eyewitness, he is a *primary source*. When a source makes statements on the basis of what others have told him, and he has not personally observed the facts, those statements are hearsay, and the source is a *secondary source*. If a writer testifies that "On the banks of the Ganges I watched . . . ," he may be considered a primary source for the statements of fact that follow. However, should he say, "Usually authoritative sources high in the Indian Government admitted . . . ," he would be a secondary source for the statements that follow. The same book or article or newspaper story, therefore, may contain statements of fact for which the author is a primary source and statements for which he is a secondary source.

Evaluations of factual information should distinguish between eyewitness and hearsay statements. As a general rule, *the primary source for statements of fact is the best source for the information*. Our legal system considers this point so important that hearsay evidence is inadmissible in litigation.

It is sometimes difficult to tell whether or not a statement is based on a primary or secondary source. Because they know of the persuasive power of firsthand accounts, some writers consciously avoid distinguishing between firsthand and secondhand information. Their writing thus suggests greater firsthand knowledge than they possess. Obviously, such articles should be treated with greater skepticism than those in which the author clearly distinguishes between personal observation and secondhand information. Of course, an unscrupulous author may assert that he has directly observed facts when he has not and yet carefully identify other statements as secondhand. Even authentic eyewitness reports must be tested because eyewitnesses may make honest mistakes and even, on occasion, lie.

The first step in testing statements by primary sources is to decide exactly what the maker of the statement intended to say. The earlier example of Fred's ironically asserting that "Joe is not with us today" illustrates this point. Taking Fred's words literally results in a misinterpretation of the statement. Therefore, after the literal meaning has been deciphered as carefully as possible, the intention of a statement must be considered. That is, first, What does it say? and next, Was it intended to be a literal statement, or ironic, or figurative, or guarded?

The next step is to test the competence of the primary source to make an accurate report. Was the statement made by an expert or a layman? Could a layman make competent observations regarding the matter in hand? A professional soldier should report the progress of a battle more accurately than a pediatrician, and the pediatrician should do better than the soldier in describing the symptoms of a sick child.

Was the primary source of the statement in a position to observe the relevant facts, and was he motivated to make adequate observations? Even a highly competent observer must have actually observed the facts if his account is to be accurate. A newspaperman who files his story from a hotel room, without going into the jungle to observe the guerrilla warfare he reports, is liable to err in his statements. If the renowned surgeon has not examined the patient and the laboratory findings himself, his description of the symptoms may be wrong.

It is also necessary to know whether or not the source of the statement was both willing and able to tell the truth. Does the reporter work for a newspaper or periodical that typically slants its news reports? Was the witness an enemy of any of the people involved in the events? Were any of the witness's friends injured? Was he personally frustrated, or was he rewarded by any of the events he discussed? An observer from the United States will see things differently than a Russian or Communist Chinese representative. A Democrat may report events differently from a Republican if the facts have political implications. Quite often, the people most directly concerned and in the best position to report the facts have such deep personal involvement that they are tempted to distort the facts or assert false statements to be true. Sometimes, of course, distortions are not deliberate, but are unconscious reflections of such deep personal involvement.

Topics suitable for public discussion such as labor strife, political campaigns, religious beliefs, race relations, war and peace, economic theories and dislocations, and morality are often charged with emotion. In such matters, few observers are objective. Even the most dispassionate tend to become emotionally involved in such questions. When a person has a position to defend, he reports his observations in a way that does not contradict his views.

The eyewitness may misrepresent the facts for many other reasons. He may understate or overstate the facts in order to please his audience. All material gathered from speeches should be evaluated in this light. Newspapermen and book authors who aim their works at a given audience may select and distort information because of their target audience. Certain occasions follow traditional forms, and statements of fact that appear after such occasions are often inaccurate. Diplomatic communiques and reports from political candidates, football coaches, and boxers fall into this category. Sometimes the reporter is circumspect to avoid being sued for slander or libel or because he feels a blunt statement of fact would be in poor taste, impolite, or unkind. His report may consist of true statements, so selected that they compose a systematic distortion of what he actually observed.

Even if the observer's only purpose, in addition to making a factual report, is to write an exciting and lively account, he may distort the story to heighten its dramatic impact. Finally, the observer may subconsciously use false statements of fact because he has strong preconceived ideas of what he will see under the circumstances.

At this point, the student may feel that it is impossible to find an ideal primary source. He might wish to give up the entire project because finding conclusive evidence for indirectly verifiable statements of fact is so unlikely. He must always remember that although the ideal source may never be found, he should work to discover the most reliable statements he can.

The student should evaluate each specific statement of fact within the entire report of a primary source regardless of his overall evaluation of the report. Highly biased accounts may contain true statements of fact. If the facts are common knowledge, the witness may have to admit them for fear of prejudicing all his testimony, particularly if the report is published while other witnesses are alive to refute it. If none of the other witnesses refute a generally unreliable account, the silence can be taken as evidence that this part of the report was truthful. If the witness remains silent until the other witnesses are dead and unable to challenge his account, this fact prejudices the testimony. In the words of an old proverb, "He who remained silent when duty commandeth him to speak must henceforth not speak for duty commandeth him to remain silent."

If the witness includes in his report statements of fact that are against his best interest and prejudices, he gains strong evidence of their truthfulness.

The agreement of two or more independent reports is good evidence of their accuracy. It is, therefore, desirable to compare statements made independently by several observers of the same facts. It should be determined that the reports are *independent*. Although the same statement appears in seven different books and articles, analysis may reveal that six authors got the statement from *one* original source or from *one another*.

The topic, the time for preparation, and the importance of the discussion will determine how much evidence for statements of fact the group seeks in primary sources. Usually, the topic is of such magnitude and time is so limited that discussants must rely to some extent on secondary sources, written by authorities who claim to have used primary materials for their evidence. Group members can evaluate a secondary source by examining the primary sources he allegedly used in his article or book. A scholarly authority uses footnotes to indicate origins of his evidence. An author who does not use footnotes may still discuss and evaluate his sources in the text, preface, or appendix.

A secondary source may present an argument for the truth of statements of fact that are for him indirectly verifiable. An astronomer may present a series of statements about observations he has made by telescope and observations he has made of pictures taken by space probes. He uses these statements that are directly verifiable for him and *for other astronomers* to form an *argument* to support his judgment that there is life on Mars. The astronomer cannot verify the latter statement directly, and he is, therefore, a secondary source although an expert one. He is, of course, a primary source for the report about his own observations.

Kinds of statements of opinion. Many extremely important statements used in the decision-making process of group discussion are statements of opinion. Unlike statements of fact, statements of opinion cannot be proved to be either true or false. Statements of this kind may simply express matters of taste, as in, "I adore Chanel No. 5," or "Rock-and-roll music is terrible"; or, more importantly, that they may be value statements, or express goals and purposes of individuals or groups.

If the reader resists the notion that a cherished value statement is not true, he should recall that the terms *true* and *false* have been given carefully specified meanings, by which a statement is considered true only on the basis of *observed* evidence. It should not be assumed that because statements expressing ethical values and moral judgments are not true or false as are statements of fact they are not as good or as important. In my opinion, such statements are more important in decision making than statements of fact. Note the phrase, "In my opinion." The assertion that "such statements are more important in decision making than statements of fact" is not true or false. It expresses my value system and my commitment to the importance of the study of values in the humanities as opposed to the study of facts in the sciences. The ultimate evidence for science comes from observation. The scientist studied the atom and ways to split it. The decision to make an atomic bomb, to test it, and to drop it was made on the basis of value judgments. Statements of ethics and morality can usually be distinguished from statements of fact because they translate into commands. One old and important set of ethical statements is embodied in the Ten Commandments. The statement, "Murder is a sin," can be recast as an imperative sentence, "Thou shalt not kill." "We should always treat other people as we would like to have them treat us," becomes the imperative Golden Rule.

Examples of opinion statements are many.

> *Human life is the most precious and sacred thing on this earth.*
>
> *Some things are worth fighting and dying for.*
>
> *Every man has an inalienable right to life, liberty, and the pursuit of happiness.*

When you come right down to it, the only thing in life that counts is money.

Greater love hath no man than this, that a man lay down his life for his friends.

All I want is a few precious and beautiful things, some good books, and the leisure to enjoy them.

So live your life that when you die, the world is a better place for your having lived.

Give me a husband, healthy children, and enough to live comfortably.

Eat, drink, and be merry, for tomorrow we die.

Honor and courage and death if necessary for God and fatherland.

Every man should have an equal opportunity regardless of race, color, or creed.

These statements are neither true nor false. But an expert's acceptance of, and commitment to, such statements furnishes yet another measure of the value of his advice.

Individual decision making is guided by a process of intrapersonal opinion argument that differs from person to person; sometimes major decisions are even made on the subconscious level without conscious expression of the opinion statements involved.

Testing statements of opinion. Unexamined opinions are seldom wise guides for an individual or a group. Statements of opinion cannot be tested as to their truth or falsity, but they can be examined for *consistency.* If the group accepts contradictory opinion statements as guidelines for action, they may well find themselves working at cross purposes.

Statements of opinion are tested in three ways: (1) by examining the source of the opinion; (2) by examining the true statements of fact that contain, at least in part, the supporting reasons used to justify such statements; and (3) by developing the implications of the statement to show what decisions and further statements of taste, value, ethics, goals, or purposes flow from the statement.

Some opinion statements are accepted because of their source rather than their substance. One may decide what pictures to buy, what wine to serve, or what music to listen to on the basis of an authority's opinion. Ethical statements or rules may be accepted because the Buddha, Jesus, the Bible, or the Koran is the authority.

Testing the implications of opinions. Most important opinion statements are attacked by those who hold the opposite opinion, and the resulting conflict generates arguments in support of both opinion statements. The argument that supports a value statement may be tested by examining the truthfulness of the statements of fact it contains and by examining the implications and consistency of the opinions.

The opinion statement that civil disobedience is justified by a higher moral law has a number of implications. It implies that when man-made laws conflict with what is right, they can justifiably be disregarded and disobeyed; it further implies that breaking the law is a good thing. The higher moral law, however, is not codified by community opinion into institutional law. Ultimately, each man must discover the higher moral law for himself, since there are no legal codes to consult. Thus, two men may perceive two different moral laws. The statement that civil disobedience is sometimes justified implies, therefore, that each man may disregard those laws he personally finds bad, wrong, or distasteful. The group may still accept the statement as a guide to action, but determining its implications will allow them to make their decision, fully aware of its ramifications.

The group might accept the contrary opinion that our country should have a government of law not of men; this is, what constitutes antisocial behavior will be decided on the basis of legal codes developed by governmental bodies, rather than on the basis of individual men searching their consciences and judging each case on its merits. Legal codes, however, always reflect the past struggles of powerful groups for control of governmental machinery and incorporate old prejudices and values. Thus, in the eyes of the majority of contemporary society, government by law will always result in some substantial injustices. Again, the group might accept the statement that we should have a government of law not of men, but understanding its implications will allow them to make wiser decisions.

Determining the implications of opinion statements often indicates their inconsistency. The group that says the Federal Voting Registration law that works to their advantage should be obeyed, but that southern segregation laws must be disobeyed, will discover the contradiction in their position when they consider the implications of their stand. So will the group that asserts that the Federal Civil Rights laws that work to their disadvantage should be disobeyed, while the local laws that they like should be obeyed. Inconsistency in these matters can, of course, be resolved by dropping the contradictory position, but achieving consistency in this way is often unrealistic. An order of value statements must be established so that one takes precedence over the other when they conflict.

The importance of opinion in discussion. In making decisions, a group must not only orient itself to the world as it is to deal with its environment successfully, but it must also find some common ground acceptable to the majority concerning statements of values and purpose. If it cannot agree on such statements, the group cannot reach a decision on rational grounds. Members may be coerced, duped, or manipulated into a decision and into action, but they cannot arrive at a reasonable consensus unless they agree on some set of value statements of the order. "We must minimize the loss of human life through violence, but we must achieve equality of education through integration within the next ten years." Once discussants have agreed on such value statements, they can test advice in terms of these values as well as in terms of statements of fact. Thus, they might decide that although a suggested solution would achieve integration of public schools in ten years, the resulting violence and loss of life would be prohibitive.

The implications of the value statement that "Human life is the most precious thing on this earth" are soon indicated in a discussion of the question "Is mercy killing justified?" The discussant who believes that certain circumstances justify mercy killing may be challenged by another, who asks if he does not believe that human life is given by God and is precious. The first participant replies that he does. Does it not follow, continues the challenger, that we can never justify taking a human life? But, the first replies, unnecessary suffering is evil, and if the case is hopeless, it is more humane to end a person's suffering. You think, then, the questioner might ask, that suffering is a greater evil than killing a human being? So the testing and drawing out of the implications of value statements proceeds in discussion. If the two participants present one another with arguments designed to change the other's value systems, and both parties maintain their value systems, which is likely, further discussion is fruitless.

TESTING ADVICE

Statements such as "Go to college" are not factual and cannot be characterized as true or false. Since questions of policy are often the topics for discussion groups, statements of advice need to be tested as carefully as do statements of fact.

Testing the authority for the advice. The source of advice is an important test of the substance of advice. When dealing with extremely complex problems, people often accept without question the advice of an authority they trust. Authoritative statements are used both to support statements of fact and to give sanction to advice. Thus, if a person has faith in a lawyer, doctor, dentist, or butcher, he may enter into a lawsuit, submit to surgery, have a tooth pulled, or buy a steak when advised to do so. The complexity of decision making in our urban culture forces people to base more and more decisions on the advice of experts. A considerable body of research has examined the question of the persuasive power of authority figures. These studies indicate that the habit of picking an authority figure to consult about crucial decisions can be generalized as a willingness to accept advice from recognized authorities more readily than from unknown sources.

When evaluating the source of advice, individuals often consult friends or acquaintances who have had to make similar decisions. Thus, they may consult friends in a new community before selecting a family doctor, dentist, or real-estate agent. Statements from satisfied customers that the advice they received had been good furnish evidence for faith in a given expert's advice.

If more evidence than the testimonials of satisfied clients is required, the group may examine the evaluations of the authority's fellow experts. Has the authority been honored by his profession? Is he rated highly by his peers? Does he have a field of specialization and is it appropriate to the group's problem? Even if he is a highly regarded authority, the group may ask if he has studied the facts on the specific question before giving his advice. Finally, and most importantly, individuals analyze the authority as a human being. Is he given to rash, thoughtless statements? Is he emotionally unbalanced? Is he highly biased or likely to accept bribes? Will he talk frankly? Sometimes the advice of a highly regarded authority is not accepted simply because he is not liked as a person.

The general preoccupation of our times with a man's "image" is understandable. Citizens may not feel competent to judge a man's ability in his profession, but they do feel competent to judge him as a man. If advice comes from a man people like, admire, and trust, whose competence is established, it is likely to be accepted on these grounds.

Testing the content of the advice. After the source of the advice has been examined and each authority's competence, knowledge of the facts, bias, and personal characteristics have been probed, the substance of the advice should be tested. Policy recommendations are seldom made without an accompanying argument (advice systematically developed to guide action). This argument purports to be a conclusive demonstration, or proof, analogous to the demonstration of the truth of an indirectly verifiable statement of fact. Of course, the nature of the advice statement makes such a demonstration impossible, but criticism of the argument is nonetheless useful in making decisions related to the world as it is rather than as the group wishes it to be. Reasons for accepting advice are largely grounded in statements of fact asserted by the advocate to be true, and on statements of value that serve as criteria to judge the recommended policy.

One of the best tests of the substance of advice is to check the truth of the factual statements in the supporting argument. For example, in discussing the policy of limiting exhaust emissions from automobiles, authorities have asserted that the emissions are dangerous to health. The argument is based on statements of fact describing the effect of automobile exhausts on the human organism. One important check on the advice, therefore, would be to examine the truth of statements of fact about the health hazard.

summary

The discussant's main sources of information include his personal experience, interviews, and search for library material. The first step in gathering material from the library is to develop a bibliography. Once the discussant finds useful items, he should begin recording information.

Information consists of statements of fact, of advice, and of opinion. Statements of fact may be judged true or false on the basis of observations and may be directly or indirectly verified. If the group can make a truth decision on the basis of indirect verification, the statement may be conclusively demonstrated. If not, the statement is inconclusive for the group.

To test indirectly verifiable statements of fact, eyewitness accounts should be sought out. These primary sources must be evaluated carefully for accuracy and truthfulness. Not all statements of fact require support from primary sources. Some background information may be so widely established that secondary sources are sufficient.

Advice and opinion cannot be tested as to truth or falsity by observations. The group can, however, make a thorough examination of the source of the information. In addition, the group may wish to examine the substance of the advice for consistency and to see if the statements of fact used in the arguments to support it are true.

Opinion, like advice, cannot be tested for truth or falsity. Opinion consists of statements of taste, value, and purpose. The source of the opinion should be examined. In addition, opinion should be tested by drawing out the implications of a given position and searching for contradictions. Finally, opinions are supported by argument, and the statements of fact within such arguments should be evaluated for their truthfulness.

QUESTIONS FOR STUDY

1. How does the pragmatic style of communication relate to the analysis of developing information outlined in this chapter?
2. In what situations should a person preparing to take part in a discussion copy information verbatim from a written source?

3. What distinguishes statements of fact from statements of opinion?
4. What is the relationship between observations and the concept of truth as defined in this chapter?
5. What is the difference between directly and indirectly verifiable statements of fact?
6. What is the difference between evidence and proof?
7. What is the difference between primary and secondary sources?
8. What is the difference between testing authoritative statements of fact and authoritative staements of advice?
9. What are the advantages and disadvantages of group discussion as a technique for testing opinion?
10. What is the role of opinion statements in rational decision making?

EXERCISES

1. Make a list of 30 statements, 10 of fact, 10 of opinion, and 10 of advice.
2. Record a group meeting, and listen carefully to the first 15 minutes. List the statements of fact, and evaluate the truthfulness of each one.
3. Select an article arguing for a controversial policy. Count the number of statements of fact, opinion, and advice. Evaluate the author's truthfulness, decide if you agree with his opinion statements, and criticize his advice.
4. Record a group meeting, and listen to the comments of the most talkative member. Transcribe this person's opinion statements, and write an evaluation of the value system they imply.
5. Record a group meeting, and listen to the advice statements. Count the number of advice statements that are supported with an argument, and contrast that number with the advice statements that are not supported with an argument. Write a short paper in which you discuss the proportion of both supported and unsupported advice statements that are disregarded, that are followed by the group, and that are contended by others.
6. With a group of your classmates, select a topic for discussion. Search the library for sources relating to the topic, and prepare 20 bibliography cards in proper form to bring back to your group.
7. With a group of your classmates, select a topic for group discussion. Survey 20 sources for useful information relating to the topic. Prepare 10 note cards in proper form to bring back to your group.

References and suggested readings

The complete references for the guides to bibliography are:

Besterman, Theodore. *A World Bibliography of Bibliographies and of Bibliographical Catalogues, Calendars, Abstracts, Digests, Indexes,* and *the Like.* 4th ed. Lausanne: Societas Bibliographica, 1965. 5 vols.

Bibliographic Index: A Cumulative Bibliography of Bibliographies, 1937–. New York: Wilson, 1938 (semiannual).

Bulletin of Bibliography and Magazine Notes. Boston: Faxon, 1897–(quarterly).

For guides to reference works, see:

Enoch Pratt Free Library, Baltimore. *Reference Books: A Brief Guide.* Comp. by Mary Barton. 7th ed. 1970.

Cheney, Frances Neal. *Fundamental Reference Sources.* Chicago: American Library Association, 1971.

Winchell, Constance Mabel. *Guide to Reference Books.* 7th ed. Chicago: American Library Association, 1967. Suppl. 1–3, 1968–1972.

For guides to periodicals, see:

Applied Science & Technology Index: A Cumulative Subject Index to Periodicals in the Fields of Aeronautics, Automation, Chemistry, Construction, Electricity & Electrical Communication, Engineering, Geology & Metallurgy, Industrial & Mechanical Arts, Machinery, Physics, Transportation and Related Subjects. New York: Wilson, 1958–. (Supersedes *The Industrial Arts Index,* which was published in 45 volumes from 1913–1957.)

Business Periodicals Index: A Cumulative Subject Index to Periodicals in the Fields of Accounting, Advertising, Banking & Finance, General Business, Insurance, Labor & Management, Marketing & Purchasing, Office Management, Public Administration, Taxation, Specific Businesses, Industries & Trades. New York: Wilson, 1958–. (Also supersedes *The Industrial Arts Index.*)

The Education Index: A Cumulative Author and Subject Index to a Selected List of Educational Periodicals, Proceedings and Yearbooks. New York: Wilson, 1929–.

Social Sciences and Humanities Index: Formerly International Index. New York: Wilson, 1916–.

Readers' Guide to Periodical Literature: Author and Subject Index. New York: Wilson, 1901–.

The best index to newspapers in this country is:

The New York Times Index. New York: The New York Times, Sept. 1851–1906, 1913–.

For publications by various state governments, see:

Monthly Checklist of State Publications. Washington, D.C.: Government Printing Office, 1910–.

For publications of the federal government, see:

Monthly Catalog of United States Government Publications. Washington, D.C.: Government Printing Office, 1895–.

For a more detailed treatment of bibliography and footnote citations, see:

Turabian, Kate L. *A Manual for Writers of Term Papers, Theses, and Dissertations.* 3rd ed. Chicago: University of Chicago Press, 1967.

For bibliographical information about authorities, see:

American Men and Women of Science: The Social and Behavioral Sciences. 12th ed. Tempe, Ariz.: Jacques Cattell Press, 1973.

Directory of American Scholars: A Bibliographical Directory. 5th ed. New York: Bowker, 1969.

Who's Who in America: A Bibliographical Dictionary of Notable Living Men and Women. Chicago: Marquis, 1899– (biennial).

For book reviews, see:

Book Review Digest. New York: Wilson, 1905–.

For a discussion of the fallibility of witnesses, see:

Allport, Gordon W., and Leo Postman. *The Psychology of Rumor.* New York: Holt, Rinehart and Winston, 1947.

For a survey of research relating to the persuasive power of authoritative sources, see:

Anderson, Kenneth, and Theodore Clevenger, Jr. "A Summary of Experimental Research in Ethos," *Speech Monographs,* **30** (1963), 59–78.

For a more detailed analysis of factual and nonfactual statements, see:

Bormann, Ernest G. "An Empirical Approach to Certain Concepts of Logical Proof," *Central States Speech Journal,* **12** (1961), 85–91.

Bormann, Ernest G. *Theory and Research in the Communicative Arts.* New York: Holt, Rinehart and Winston, 1965, chaps. 4, 5.

For an analysis of several weekly news magazines and their slanted treatment of the facts, see:

Newman, Robert P. "The Weekly Fiction Magazines," *Central States Speech Journal,* **17** (1966), 118–124.

CHAPTER 5
ADAPTING INFORMATION FOR GROUP DISCUSSION

statistics

Applied arithmetic and statistics are two branches of matematics that provide numerical descriptions of facts. This chapter considers statistics in detail because members of discussion groups in the pragmatic style find them particularly useful and because they pose special problems of interpretation and evaluation.

USES OF STATISTICS

Statistical statements are quantified descriptions of a number of facts. Discussion groups often use statistics to provide a general description of features of the external environment. Precise statistical statements regarding the population in Argentina cover facts of great number and complexity. Yet a paragraph or two of such statistical descriptions can convey much highly compressed information. To know that the enrollment of a given college has greatly decreased over last year is helpful, but to know that the decrease has been 100 students, that this is a 10 percent decrease over the enrollment last year, and the largest percentage of decrease since 1941–1942, is even more helpful.

SHORTCOMINGS OF STATISTICS

In spite of all their power and precision, statistical statements have some shortcomings. Since they are often abstractions drawn from a complicated set of facts, they may focus on a single aspect and neglect other important information. For example, the statistic that 312 persons were killed as a result of automobile accidents on a holiday weekend may prove useful to a discussion group; but this statistic, of necessity, omits much important material—it does not reveal such things as the mental condition of the drivers involved, how many victims were in love or neurotic or in good health, how many were drunk, or how many were killed instantly. Nor does it provide information on the mechanical condition of the automobiles or the road conditions. Although other features of automobile accidents can be described with further statistical statements—for example, how many drivers had alcohol in the bloodstream and how many had children—many important questions cannot be answered with statistics because only depth studies of individual cases could provide the necessary information. Statements about the physical and mental health of the victims, for example, would require extensive research.

Statistics take on greater meaning when supplemented with case-study material or real examples. Without such interpretation, statistics can, in a sense, distort the facts because of the very abstractness and precision which is their greatest virtue. They can become cold and meaningless.

DANGERS IN STATISTICS

The precision usually associated with numbers poses a danger to accurate interpretation of statistics. Most students are conditioned to accept numerical descriptions as accurate and scientific. They find it difficult to counter the statement, say, that "10 percent of the college students are emotionally disturbed" unless they have statistical information of their own. A group member may say, "I didn't know it was that high," or, "My experience certainly wouldn't indicate that"; but if another member repeats the statement, the precision of the number, *10 percent,* is a kind of word magic that is persuasive and difficult to refute.

Everyone has used numbers expressing measurements of height, weight, and temperature and knows how accurate and useful such measurements can be. Unless discussants are careful, they will regard other less accurate numerical descriptions as though they were as precise and unanswerable as the statement that Joe is 6 feet tall and weighs 182.5 pounds. If a member adds that Joe has an estimated vocabulary of 8000 words, a reading rate of 600 words per minute, and an IQ of 140, these last statements seem as accurate and precise as the statements about his height and weight. They are not as accurate, however, and must be evaluated very carefully when used in counseling Joe about matters such as his future career.

Finally, statistical statements can be selected in such a way that they systematically distort the reality they appear to describe. Statistics on unemployment are important in public discussions relating to social-welfare measures. Generally, the larger the number of unemployed, the more imperative the need for action. To make their unemployment statistics sound more impressive, advocates often count college students leaving summer jobs to return to school, women who have left their jobs to marry, or working wives who quit to have babies. On the other hand, advocates who need small estimates do not include these individuals and often do not include the people actively seeking full-time work who can get only part-time employment.

Because of these dangers in the use of statistical statements of fact, one often hears such warnings as, "Figures don't lie, but liars figure." Members of discussion groups sometimes use humorous remarks to discredit impressive statistical arguments by laughing at them. A humorous belittling will serve to refute statistical information for some audiences. The discussion group, however, should understand how the statistics were gathered and computed so they can discover the nature and extent of distortions. Such an understanding requires a grasp of the way investigators gather and interpret statistics.

kinds of statistics

Statistics are used in two ways. Investigators may observe all the individuals or facts in question and describe certain general features of the total population numerically. Statistics compiled in this way are called *descriptive statistics*. On other occasions, compilers of statistical information observe a sampling of individuals or facts and estimate the character of the total population based on the sample. Statistics compiled in this way are called *inferential statistics*. Descriptive statistics are generally more accurate than inferential statistics; the latter *always* have a margin of error in their conclusions.

DESCRIPTIVE STATISTICS

Descriptions of central tendency. Descriptive statistics are particularly useful in providing a quick, overall survey of many facts. One important kind of statistical generalization is a number indicating the central tendency of facts. A number indicating central tendency is an index of what is a typical, common, usual, normal, or ordinary characteristic or property of the facts. For example, the health service could weigh all male students. First, a statistician could add all the weights together and divide by the number of students to get an average weight of,

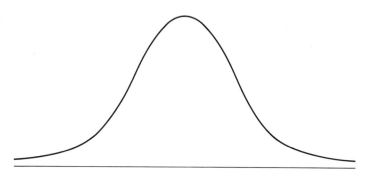

Figure 3. A Normal Distribution.

say, 168 pounds. The technical term for this arithmetic average is the *mean*. For some investigations, this arithmetic average may not be as useful in indicating the typical or usual as either the *mode* or the *median*. The mode is the most frequent value. The median is the middle value. The health service might weigh 5000 men and discover that the most frequent weight is 170 pounds and that exactly half of the men weigh more than 169 pounds. The mode for this distribution of weights would be 170 and the median, 169.

The best overall picture of the weight of the male students is some statistical indication of central position such as an average weight. If a group tries to make generalizations about typicality on the basis of a selection of individual cases, they may be misled. The selection might include a disproportionate number of atypical students: a dozen men who weigh less than 140 pounds, or 12 who weigh more than 200 pounds. Often, such emphasis on atypical cases will be discovered in a study of discussion questions. Extreme examples are more graphic than more usual cases and can make the problem seem much more severe than it is. Discussants studying juvenile delinquency may find the case of a very wealthy and intelligent boy who commits a brutal murder emphasized in a number of sources, while more mundane cases of juveniles arrested for possessing beer are seldom mentioned. Only a statistical distribution based on a numerical description of severity of juvenile crimes will provide an index of the usual or typical act of delinquency.

The distribution of values such as the weights of 5000 male students will tend to fall into a pattern that is called the *normal* curve. (This is the same notorious pattern used by instructors who grade on the curve.) Many facts will show this pattern when they are quantified. Figure 3 indicates the characteristic shape of this curve. A distribution of this kind is such that few values are on the extreme ends of the distribution, and the number of instances increases as the values approach the center of the curve. For normal distributions, indicators of

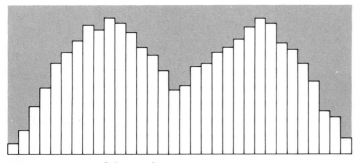

Figure 4. A Bimodal Distribution.

central tendency are often similar. Thus, whether the group uses the average weight (168), the mode (170), or the median (169), in the example of 5000 male students, makes little difference; all three figures supply roughly the same information about the usual or normal weight of the male students.

Some distributions do not fall along a bell-shaped curve; in these cases the arithmetic average can be misleading. The health service might also weigh 5000 coeds and discover that these weights fall along a normal curve with an arithmetic average of 130 pounds. If a statistician combines 10,000 weights of male and female students, he will obtain an average weight of 149 pounds. Yet, fewer students weigh in the neighborhood of 149 pounds than weigh around 130 and 170 pounds. These 10,000 weights when plotted would present a bimodal (having two modes) distribution such as the one indicated in Figure 4.

Sometimes a group will find the mode the most useful score. The fact that the average student at Abraham Lincoln elementary school is in the third grade might not be as good an index of the central tendency as the fact that the largest class is the first grade and the second largest is the second grade.

Finally, some statistical distributions contain very large scores at one end of the distribution, so that averages are misleading. A developing nation might comprise an extremely wealthy class of few people, a middle class, and many poor people. Average per capita income figures for this country might lead to the conclusion that the majority of people are more affluent than they are. The extremely large incomes of a few people inflate the average. In this case, the median income would be a better indication of the typical income.

The problem with the arithmetic mean as an index of central tendency is illustrated by such reports as: The average citizen has two and one-half children, one and one-third television sets, one and one-fourth cars, and a little over two radios.

Descriptions of variability. A second important statistical generalization is a numerical description of how facts vary about the central tendency. Statistical generalizations can indicate the range of the facts. It may be important to know that a student body ranges in age from 14 to 68 years. The student in a class of 100 students can better interpret his grade of B if he knows that the entire class received grades of either B or C. The group studying tax assessments needs to know that although the average assessment of houses in the Golden Lane suburb was $7,000, the range was from $2,000 to $10,000.

The degree of variability around the central tendency may also be ascertained. If, for example, a student discovers that the grades in his class of 100 were distributed rather widely with 10 A's, 20 B's, 40 C's, 20 D's, and 10 F's, he will interpret his grade of A much differently than if he discovers that the distribution was 2 A's, 18 B's, 60 C's, 19 D's and 2 F's.

A numerical description of variability often has practical applications. For example, a teacher preparing to instruct a class of 40 fifth-grade students for the first time gives a battery of achievement tests. He discovers that the averages of their reading and arithmetic scores fall in the fifth-grade level. As a class, they are typical of other fifth grades tested, *on the average.* However, their scores indicate that they range in reading ability from first-grade to ninth-grade level, and their achievement in arithmetic ranges from the third to the seventh grade. He now has a clearer understanding of the problems involved in teaching the class. If he further examines the variability and discovers that two-thirds of the class is reading at the fifth-grade level and 36 are reading at either the fourth-, fifth-, or sixth-grade level, he will approach the class differently than if 5 students read at first-grade level, 2 at second-grade, 1 at third-grade, 2 at fourth-grade, 15 at fifth-grade, 5 at sixth-grade, 3 at seventh-grade, 5 at eighth-grade, and 2 at ninth-grade level.

The less variability in the scores, the more homogeneous the facts covered by the statistics. The more homogeneous or similar the events under study, the fewer the surprises for the user of the statistic. If the students cluster rather closely around the central tendency, a generalized program will deal with most of them.

Percentiles furnish a statistical summary of the range and variability of scores related to the median. When a statistician divides a set of scores into 100 parts, he calls each part a percentile. The median is the fiftieth percentile. The statistician computes the other 99 percentiles in similar fashion. He finds a point on the distribution where 1 percent of the cases have smaller values (99 percent have larger values) and calls that point the *first percentile.* He calls the value that falls on a point where 75 percent of the cases have smaller values (25 percent have larger values), the *seventy-fifth percentile.* If a student takes an achievement test as an entering freshman, his raw score is often compared to raw scores made by some group of students. Perhaps records have been kept for a number of years of the scores made by other freshmen. A percentile rank of 81 may be assigned on the basis of this comparison. This means that the student did better than 81 percent of those in the comparison group.

The *range* of a series of values is obtained by subtracting the lowest from the highest. Thus, if two large sections of a psychology class take an objective examination and the lowest score for the test in one section is 43 and the highest is 94, the range is 51 ($94 - 43 = 51$). If the equivalent scores for the other section are 45 and 90, the range is 45 ($90 - 45 = 45$).

The range is sometimes useful, but it is often unstable. Because a few extreme scores can cause wide fluctuations in the range, an *interpercentile range* is a better index of variability than the total range. For example, the instructor of the psychology classes could find the range for the middle half of the scores by subtracting the twenty-fifth percentile score from the seventy-fifth. If this yielded a range of 10 test points for the first section and of 15 for the other, he would know that although the first section had a larger total range (greater distance between best and worst test scores) than the second, the middle half of the first class was clustered more closely around the median (only 10 points separate them) than the middle half of the second (15 point spread). The interpercentile range can be calculated between any two percentiles.

Another measure of variability is related to the way values differ from the average (mean). One way to compute this difference is to find how far each value is from the average, add these differences together, and find their average. The result is the *average deviation* from the mean of all scores. Another way to get similar information is to square the deviations from the mean, add them together and divide by the total number of values. This figure is called the *variance*. Neither the variance nor the average deviation from the mean is widely used in reporting descriptive statistics. The more common measure is the *standard deviation*. The standard deviation is simply the square root of the variance. It provides an index to the dispersion of values similar to that furnished by the interpercentile range and is another good guide to variability. The middle two-thirds of the distribution will fall in a range one standard deviation above and one standard deviation below the mean. Approximately the middle 95 percent of the range will fall between two standard deviations either side of the mean.

Uses of descriptive statistics. Descriptive statistics are based on an examination of all facts or individuals in a given population. The Census

Bureau uses descriptive statistics to generalize about information gathered each ten years by a complete enumeration of all United States citizens. Of course, the census takers miss some people, and other errors creep into the compilation, but theoretically the census counts each person. State and local governments compile *vital statistics* in a similar fashion. Officials record such things as each birth, death, and marriage, thus furnishing raw data for statistical generalizations. Although, generally, descriptive statistics are compiled and interpreted with care, they should be checked—did the compilers collect accurately? Were the statistical computations made correctly? Inferential statistics, which often appear exactly the same as descriptive statistics, must be examined with much more care.

INFERENTIAL STATISTICS

Investigators often want information about extremely complex events and do not have the time or money to compile descriptive statistics. A reporter may want student opinions concerning coeducational dormitories; pollsters may be interested in a candidate's popularity; sociologists may wish to know the extent of alcoholism on Skid Row; businessmen may want to know the potential market for a new product. A survey might include every member of the population concerned with the question; however, such surveys are costly. More often, the researchers draw a sample from the population, observe this sample, and estimate what the values would have been if the survey had included the entire population. Such estimates are based on *inferential statistics*.

Sampling procedure. Sampling is quite common in everyday affairs. A person may receive a sample product. The assumption is that if he likes the sample, he will like the product. A prospective buyer may take a sample by removing a small plug from a watermelon and tasting it. Although a sample can be misleading, decisions based on a sample tend to be better than those made without any observations.

A group studying a homogeneous population can make a wise decision on the basis of a small and arbitrary sample. If a product is of uniform quality, a very small amount of it will reveal its basic characteristics. However, discussion groups often study populations that are not highly homogeneous. In this case, the members must carefully evaluate survey results based on sampling. If the sample is biased, the survey may not support the reported conclusions.

If the investigator picks one black marble from a large container filled with colored marbles, he knows only that some of the marbles are black. If he takes a handful that contains six black and four white marbles, he knows that the container holds both black and white marbles. He may infer that, although some marbles are different colors, most are black and white. If he continues to pick samples that contain only black and white marbles, he may conclude that all the marbles are either black or white.

He may next try to determine the proportion of black marbles in the container. If the top layer contains a heavy concentration of white marbles and he confines his sampling to the top of the vessel, he will be misled about the real proportion in the container. The same principle applies to an investigator who takes a sample of the population to determine the proportion of unemployed people. If his sample contains a high proportion of coal miners from southern Illinois or West Virginia, he will get a different impression than if it includes mainly residents of the suburbs of Washington, D.C., or Minneapolis, Minnesota.

Random sample. A random sample results when every individual in the total population has an equal opportunity to be selected. For example, an excellent way to estimate the proportion of white marbles to black in a container is to pick one marble at a time, shaking the container thoroughly between each selection. An investigator using a random sample can draw rather precise inferences about the parent population. The random sample is of great theoretical importance, therefore, in any analysis of statistical inferences. However, a random sample is often impractical, and another sampling procedure, such as selecting every hundredth name from a telephone list, may be used. Such a sample is *systematic* and may introduce important biases in the results of the survey. If the original list is random, the systematic selection of names from it would also be random. Most name lists are not random, but are arranged alphabetically or geographically. Once a pollster selects an individual for a random sample, that individual must be included. Substituting someone easier to contact may introduce a systematic bias into the results.

If a student reporter investigates campus opinion by stopping 20 students on the campus to ask for their opinions, his sample is systematic, not random. If a paper prints a ballot and asks students to fill in their opinions and return the ballot, the sample will again be systematic. In the first instance, the reporter may get more engineering, medical, or art students, depending on the time and place he chooses to collect his opinions. In the second instance, students who are motivated to fill in a ballot may differ systematically from the students who are not. Some critics of the Kinsey studies of sexual behavior have argued that the sampling procedure selected only people willing to talk over such matters and that no inferences about sexual behavior in the United States could be drawn from such a sample.

Statistical inference and confidence level. The technical meaning of *population* is the total universe of the sampling procedure. The population of the Kinsey studies in a statistical sense would be the totality of people interviewed if the studies were repeated over and over again. If a large number of people in the United States would never be interviewed even in an infinite replication of the studies, then the results cannot be generalized to the entire population of this country with much statistical accuracy.

Given a random sample, statisticians can draw inferences about the results of surveying the entire population. Group members need not be concerned with the technical details of such inferences, but they should understand three important considerations that have a bearing on these inferences: the confidence level, the confidence limits, and the law of large numbers. These three features of statistical inference are interrelated; they cannot be separated, because a change in one of them affects the other two.

Statistics can be thought of as the mathematics of gambling. They provide a sophisticated estimate of the odds. Statistics work best with games of chance. Statistical inference requires that the sampling procedure be random or according to luck or chance.

The notion of *confidence* is closely related to the odds of something being right according to chance; that is, the higher the odds in a gambler's favor, the closer the bet is to a sure thing, the more confident he is of winning. The *confidence level* is simply a precise numerical description of the odds. Perhaps a timid gambler will not bet unless the odds are 9 to 1 in his favor; that is, he will win 90 percent of the time. The confidence level he requires before betting is thus 0.90. Sometimes this expression of the odds is reversed, and a study reports that its findings are significant at the 10 percent level of confidence. If a study reports that the results were significant at the 5 percent level of confidence, for example, it simply means that the odds are 95 to 5 that they did not happen by luck or chance.

A gambler may figure the odds and realize that he has a better chance of winning if he bets a horse will finish first, second, or third than if he bets only that the horse will win. In order to improve the odds, he increases the range of outcomes that will enable him to win. An investigator may use the same procedure in drawing statistical inferences. Assume that he has been given a carload of marbles and wants to draw a sample to investigate the color of the marbles. He picks 100 marbles at random and discovers that 50 are white and the remaining 50 are black. What are the odds that the proportion of white marbles is exactly 50 percent in the entire carload? The odds are very much against that being the case. However, he could lower the odds by reasoning that the entire carload contained *between* 36 percent and 64 percent white marbles. If he decides that he does not need to be this confident—that is, he will settle for odds of 9 to 1, or 2 to 1—the range of his estimate could be narrowed. The points he selects as the limits of his estimate are the *confidence limits*. The wider these limits, all other things being equal, the more confident he can be that the estimate will hold for the parent population.

The *law of large numbers* explains why all other things are not always equal. The investigator may keep the odds the same and narrow the confidence limits by increasing the size of his sample. The law of large numbers simply expresses the common-sense notion that the more closely the sample size approximates the size of the total population, the more closely the distribution of the sample approximates the distribution of the population from which it was drawn. If he randomly samples half the marbles, the percentage of white marbles will come closer to the actual percentage than if he samples one-fourth of them. He can observe the law of large numbers in operation by keeping the odds constant, namely 95 to 5, varying the size of the sample, and noting the theoretical effect on the size of the confidence limits. The limits for a sample of 50 were from 36 percent to 64 percent; for a sample of 100 they were 40 percent to 60 percent; for a sample of 1000 they were 47 percent to 53 percent. Thus, if he had selected a sample of 1000 marbles and discovered that 500 of them were white, he could infer with 95 percent confidence that the actual percentage of white marbles in the entire carload was between 47 and 53 percent. In other words, the larger the sample, the more confident he can be of his inferences. Interestingly enough, however, when he increased his sample by 150 from 100 to 250, he raised the lower confidence limit from 40 percent to 44 percent, but when he increased the sample by 750 from 250 to 1000, he only narrowed the lower confidence limit from 44 percent to 47 percent. Obviously, after a sample has reached a size of several thousand, any appreciable increase in confidence requires much time and effort. This feature demonstrates the tremendous power of inferential statistics. A statistician can make inferences with considerable confidence on the basis of samples of several thousand. Public-opinion polls and television-audience surveys make estimates of the entire population on the basis of samples of several thousand people.

The discussion group should be aware of the importance of sample size, but they should not automatically reject results based on samples of several thousand or even 500 or 600. If the study has been carefully done and the sample is random, statistical inference will indicate how confident the group should be of the conclusions.

Oversimplification. The results of inferential statistics are often published for public consumption in oversimplified form. The pollster seldom reports in the newspapers that his survey indicates that, at a confidence level of 95 percent between 32 percent and 36 percent of the voters prefer candidate Y and between 30 percent and 34 percent prefer candidate X. Members of a discussion group, however, should become aware of these additional facts as they interpret statistical inferences.

On occasion, only the conclusions of a survey are published. A writer may assert that juvenile crime is up 8 percent in the suburbs, or that 9 out of 10 doctors prescribe aspirin B, and the reader may be unable to tell if these conclusions are based on descriptive statistics or inferential statistics. When possible, the source of such statements should be investigated. How large was the sample? How was it selected? If juvenile crime (or anything else) is "up 8 percent," it must be *up* in relation to some base figure. How was the base figure determined? Was it determined for statistics compiled for the year 1890? 1960? 1970? Just as there must be some base year for reports of increases, so there must be some terminal point. Are the statistics based on the latest reported statistics, last year's, or were they gathered in 1969? If more information about how they were compiled is not available, it would be wise to disregard such oversimplified presentations.

Comparing statistics. Comparisons make figures meaningful and significant. Since statistics are statements of fact containing numerical descriptions, advocates often use them to make comparisons of more or less. When a group has statistics on juvenile delinquency in their city's suburbs for 10 years ago and for the past year, it is possible to compare the two statistics and decide whether or not juvenile delinquency had gone up or down in that period. A discussion group may be interested in a comparison of current doctors' salaries with those of 10 or 50 years ago; or it may be concerned with the cost of nursing services 10 years ago, compared to today's cost.

Unless the basis for assigning these numbers is examined, the group may be misled. Investigators are most justified in describing facts with numbers when they can count some recurring feature of the facts. Counting requires an individual or a unit to be counted. When a person assigns a number to the length of tables, he refers to a unit such as an inch or centimeter. He may count the number of units required to cover the length of the table and assert that the table is 50 inches long. He could pick any unit he wished. He might use centimeters and count the number of units in the length of a second table and assert that this table is 75 centimeters long. However, he should not assert that the first table is 50 units and the second is 75 units long, and that, therefore, the second table is longer than the first, because *the units are not the same.* He does not have much difficulty when he compares inches with centimeters because these two units are standardized, called by a different name, and commonly understood. Groups often have trouble with units that are not the same, are *not* standardized, but yet have the same name. If an interior decorator has a ruler that is continually expanding or contracting like a rubber band, under varying degrees of tension he will continually make mistakes. The table that measured 50 inches yesterday may measure 70 inches today. If he compares these numbers, he might assert that the table is growing and that it is much larger today than it was yesterday. He may even project the figures into the future and predict that if the rate of growth continues, the table will soon be too large for the dining room. However, when the hostess comes to seat people at the table, she discovers that it accommodates no more today than it did yesterday.

Some units commonly used to discuss economic and other facts expand and contract like the decorator's ruler. One of the most common expanding and contracting units of measure is the dollar. Although people sometimes fail to do so, the 1960 dollar should be distinguished from the 1970 dollar, or the January 1970 dollar, because monetary units are continually fluctuating. If the gross national product in 1932 is compared with the gross national product in 1952 in terms of dollars, the increase in goods and services seems larger than it actually was, because the 1932 dollar was bigger than the 1952 dollar. The assertion that a single room in a first-class hospital in 1932 cost $5 and the same quality room in 1952 cost $25 does not indicate that hospital costs increased five times during that period.

Frequently, statistics are used to interpret data that result from counting. Here again, the decision as to what to count and what to ignore can distort the facts. Perhaps a compiler of unemployment statistics counts the man who is 45 years old, supporting a family of six, unemployed because of technological changes in his plant, and trying very hard but unsuccessfully to get work. He may also count the girl who stayed at her job temporarily after marriage, intending to quit when she became pregnant. The total number of unemployed counted in this manner will distort the facts. Similarly, a pollster might count as equal the person who has a slight preference for a candidate and the person who is strongly committed to the man. Military analysts might count the number of soldiers in each country and conclude that the country with the greatest number has the strongest military potential. Such comparisons were made shortly before the outbreak of World War II, and since France had more men in the army than Germany, some observers concluded that the French army behind the Maginot Line could defend the country against any German attack.

Finally, sometimes statistical interpretations present the information in a fallacious way. Perhaps the most common example of this is the practice of comparing recent statistics with those from the past. The latest figures regarding marriages, divorces, juvenile delinquency, drug addiction, automobile accidents, or shoplifting show that the number of each of these has increased over the last decade. Indeed, since the population has increased, these increases would be expected. But, although there were many more fatal automobile accidents in the United States in 1970 compared to 1920, automobile travel may actually have been safer in 1970 than in 1920. If the number of deaths per 1000 automobiles for each year were compared, it might show that there were more deaths per 1000 cars in 1920 than in 1970, and this comparison might be more relevant and significant than the comparison of raw values. If the number of traffic fatalities in 1920 and 1970 were compared in terms of deaths per each 100,000 car-miles traveled—that is, in terms of the number of cars times the number of miles each car traveled—still more significant index to trends in traffic fatalities would be obtained.

Statistical statements of fact have a power and conciseness that makes them indispensable to the rapid assimilation of important information. The impressiveness of numbers in an argument is such that oversimplified or mistaken interpretations of statistics can lead a discussion group astray. Therefore, group members must examine the way in which statistical information has been compiled and decide whether inferences drawn from the statistics are justified in terms of the sampling procedure, the confidence levels, and the comparisons that were made.

examples

USE OF EXAMPLES

The discussion group can use examples in two ways: (1) as *explanation* of arguments, ideas, factual situations, and definitions; and (2) as *evidence* to support an argument.

Example defined. An *example* is one of a group of things taken to show the character of the group, an individual fact selected as representative of a type or class of facts. Quite often this example (single fact) is covered along with a whole population of such facts by statistical descriptions. Throughout this chapter and this book, explanatory material has been introduced with the phrase *for example.* In discussing the problem of determining if individuals counted in statistical comparisons were really comparable, this analysis used the examples of trying to count the unemployed, of trying to count soldiers, or a citizen's preference for a political candidate. Each *example* illustrates the general notion of the difficulty of counting in concrete terms.

Hypothetical examples. When a group discusses a problem, statements of fact may be used in all seriousness as descriptions of reality. The rules of the game specify that all must try to assert as true only those statements of fact that they believe to be true. When a member willfully asserts as true something he knows is false, he exploits the expectation of his fellow members and may fool or mislead them. Such behavior damages the entire context of communication—discussants grow suspicious of all statements and can hardly talk to each other.

On occasion, however, the group may use different rules that establish a different set of expectations. Factual statements may be used, not as descriptions of what is the case, but as fanciful descriptions of what might be the case. All members understand, however, that no observations have been made to verify that a given statement is, or ever was, the case. The group assumes that something is the case in order to discuss what it would mean, or what might be done or inferred from such a situation. This kind of statement comprises a large part of fiction. Group members may develop examples in a similar fashion by prefacing their example with words such as *let us assume*, or *suppose that*, or *take the example of somebody who.* . . . They need not observe the world to dream up such examples, but can use a good imagination and fluency of expression to tailor fanciful stories to their need. Many of the examples in this chapter are hypothetical or fictitious. The man of 45 with his family of six and no job is fictitious, used to make the point about the importance of comparing similar cases. Records of such a man could be found, but the point would not be made with any greater clarity, and whatever is gained from finding an actual case is so small that it does not justify the time spent.

Hypothetical examples are useful as clarifying devices and can increase group understanding of generalizations, principles, laws, processes, and definitions. Take the case of a group analyzing the idea that appeasement of aggressor nations leads to war (this sentence is the preface to a hypothetical example). If a member says let us take the case of country A and country B, with country A making demands on small country C. Country B has a treaty with small country C to defend it in case of aggression, but when the leader of country A promises no more aggression if several provinces of country C are given to country A, country B agrees. This only assures the leader of country A that country B will never fight, and he grows bolder in his aggression against country D, and then country E. Finally country B recognizes that it must take a stand or be next, and the leader of country A is by now so convinced that country B lacks the will or means to fight that he rejects country B's ultimatum and moves in on country F, whereupon country B declares war. Such a hypothetical example is a perfectly legitimate device to help the member clarify his argument, *but it is no evidence in support of that argument.* Another member might counter with the hypothetical example of country X and country Y. When the leader of country X makes demands against country Z, country X and country Y negotiate an agreement, the leader of country X is content to live on in peace, and this successful negotiation leads to a new climate of good will in the world.

Real examples. Hypothetical examples are not useful when a group is trying to orient itself to its environment and discover what is the case. When *evidence* is necessary to the purposes of a group, examples must be used that are true statements of fact. Such examples describe factual situations and are called *real* examples. Some questions do not lend themselves to statistical analysis, and real examples may be the best evidence available.

With regard to the hypothetical example of the consequences of appeasement, if the first member wishes to support his argument with evidence from example, he must use a real example. He might use the appeasement by France and England of Nazi Germany at Munich before World War II as support for his argument.

Real examples can also supplement statistical generalizations by providing a detail of color as well as understanding of the motivations, principles, or laws that explain the statistics. Real examples must be weighed carefully and must be expressed as true statements of fact. It is also necessary to determine if the examples fall near the central tendency of all similar instances. If members of a group accept a number of real examples that fall one or two standard deviations from the mean of all similar instances, they will be misled—like the European who, seeing the United States basketball team at the Olympic games, infers that men from this country are all extremely tall and thin.

summary

This chapter considers in detail two special kinds of information: statistics and examples. The two forms supplement one another. Statistical descriptions furnish a general description of large numbers of facts. Examples clothe such general description with meaningful detail.

Descriptive statistics are compiled by a complete enumeration of the population. They are generally more reliable than statistics inferred from a sample of a population. Both descriptive and inferential procedures can furnish descriptions of the central tendencies of the facts as well as information about the range and variability of the data. In evaluating inferential procedures, however, it is necessary to know whether the sampling procedure was random (each member of the parent population had an equal opportunity to be selected) or systematic. It is also desirable to know the confidence level (what are the odds that this estimate is right?), and the confidence limits (for what range of estimates do these odds hold?).

Among the more common statistical fallacies are the oversimplified presentation of statistical results, the comparison of statistics that result from counting units that are not really comparable, and the presentation of uninterpreted statistics in a way that does not give the group an index of what it wants to know.

The second special case in handling information for group discussion is the example. An example is one of a group of things taken to represent or show the character of the group from which it came. Hypothetical examples function largely as explanatory devices. Real examples can be used as explanatory devices, but they can also supply much informative detail that is missing in statistical information. In addition, real examples can be used as evidence.

QUESTIONS FOR STUDY

1. What are some of the major problems faced by a group trying to orient itself to its external environment by means of statistical information?
2. What are the differences between descriptive statistics and inferential statistics?
3. What is meant by "central tendency"?
4. What are some typical numerical descriptions of variability and how do they work?
5. What is a random sample?
6. In what ways is it proper to call statistics the "mathematics of chance"?
7. What is the relationship between confidence level and confidence limits?
8. What are the dangers inherent in comparing statistical information?
9. What is the difference between hypothetical and real examples?
10. What are some typical fallacies in using examples as evidence for the truthfulness of generalized statements of fact?

EXERCISES

1. Gather some statistical data from your class—such as the height, age, shoe size, and so forth—and compute the mode, mean, and median of each set of data as well as the interpercentile range, variance, and standard deviation. How useful is such information in characterizing your class?
2. Develop some real examples from your class. How useful is such information in characterizing your class?
3. Read an article advocating a controversial position, and classify the statistical statements in terms of their being descriptive or inferential. Evaluate the usefulness of the statistics as evidence for the author's conclusions.
4. Read an article advocating a controversial position, and classify the examples as real or hypothetical. Evaluate the usefulness of the examples as evidence for the author's conclusions.

5. Select some public-opinion poll, audience-analysis service, or marketing survey, and make a study of the sampling procedures, the technique used for asking questions, and the presentation of conclusions in terms of central tendencies, variability, and inferential statistical procedures. Evaluate the data in terms of their usefulness as an index to public opinion or audience preference for broadcasting, advertising, or marketing purposes.

References and suggested readings

Bormann, Ernest G. *Theory and Research in the Communicative Arts*. New York: Holt, Rinehart and Winston, 1965, chap. 13.

Huff, Darrell. *How to Lie with Statistics*. New York: Norton, 1954.

Smith, G. Milton. *A Simplified Guide to Statistics for Psychology and Education*. 3rd ed. New York: Holt, Rinehart and Winston, 1962.

Walker, Helen M., and Joseph Lev. *Elementary Statistical Methods*. New York: Holt, Rinehart and Winston, 1958.

CHAPTER 6
PROCESSING INFORMATION

understanding the topic

The task-oriented group typically goes through three phases in processing information. According to research reported by Bales and Strodtbeck, groups begin by orienting themselves to the situation, move to evaluating the situation and possible courses of action, and conclude by attempting to control both the group and the external environment. In the last phase, they make decisions, mobilize group resources, and implement plans for action.

The first section of this chapter deals with understanding the topic. *Understanding*, in this context, refers to discovering the relationships among key concepts, categories, symbols, and facts. An individual in the process of coming to an understanding makes an *analysis* of the discussion question. Analysis involves discovering, explaining, and evaluating important and relevant facts. It includes the examination of possible solutions and some tentative decision as to which solution seems most likely to achieve the group's goals. Understanding thus requires that discussants study and test information bit by bit, discarding some as unsound or irrelevant, and structuring what remains into a coherent pattern.

The second section of this chapter deals with *deductive reasoning*, the dialectical process of handling the relationships furnished by understanding. It includes the combining and recombining of statements and generalizations, and the drawing out of implications from definitions, value statements, probability generalizations, and laws during the give-and-take of discussion. Typically, group members accept an inference of facts as true or a statement of opinion as wise and then proceed to draw out the implications of such positions. If this process brings them to a conclusion they cannot accept, they return to the original position and reconsider its truth or wisdom.

In this chapter, the fundamentals of straight thinking are discussed as they apply to the group as a message-processing system. These fundamentals are useful to both the individual preparing information for the group and the group, as a guideline to evaluate the communication within a meeting. The student preparing for the meeting should analyze available information according to these suggestions. This chapter, therefore, furnishes criteria with which to evaluate the communication that occurs within task-oriented small groups in the pragmatic style. Such evaluations may be made by a non-participating observer during the meeting or by the participants later on the basis of tape recordings.

ANALYZING THE TOPIC

A creative analysis is basic to understanding a topic. Analysis is the process of dividing the information into parts, examining and evaluating the parts, and discovering the important questions that relate to understanding the subject. The general features of the creative process apply to the analysis of a discussion topic much as they do to the writing of a poem. The student of discussion will profit by a brief summary of the creative process and some advice about encouraging his own creativity when he works to understand a topic.

The creative nature of analysis. An organized description of creativity often seems straightforward and mechanical. Indeed, some practical handbooks seek a programmed approach to creativity and analysis. Both have routine aspects, but the individual's preliminary groping and searching are not comparable to the step-by-step programming of a computer. A discussant begins with false starts, running into dead ends without a clear sense of direction. He has much raw material, but does not know what to do with it. If he has this feeling, he is in the first stage of the creative process, the *preparation stage.* This preparatory stage is a warm-up period; it consists of working with the material and striving for understanding. The time may seem wasted, but it is not, for the discussant must immerse himself in the subject matter to make a synthesis of the information. This stage of the creative process may so frustrate the individual that he tries to put the problem out of his mind.

The second stage is the *incubation phase.* Although a person is not actually working on the task, his subconscious is mulling over the information. During this period, one may be doing a routine job and find himself thinking about the topic in an unstructured way. He associates ideas freely, combining and recombining them in a haphazard fashion.

Later, he may be thinking of something else, when quickly and unexpectedly he sees a way through the material. This is the third stage in the creative process—the moment of *illumination*. This step usually brings pleasure and excitement.

The final stage requires critical judgment and systematic evaluation to check the wisdom of the insight. The individual must order and structure the information to see if the solution suggested by the illumination is a sound one. This is the *verification stage*.

The discussant cannot make his own *personal* analysis of the subject unless he reaches an understanding of the topic by means of several cycles of the creative process. He can always memorize the argument of an expert, but this is not the same thing.

Encouraging creative analysis. Although creativity is often groping and unstructured in the preparation phase, it requires disciplined work habits. The individual who waits for inspiration to strike before he works is rarely inspired. One common theme in articles, lectures, and books by professionals about writing is that in order to be a writer one must *write*. Likewise, the group member preparing for a discussion must systematically work on the analysis of the subject. Successfully creative people repeat this obvious bit of advice endlessly, *because it is very difficult to discipline the creative impulse.* The more creative the student, the more difficult it is to begin the preparation phase. The very talent that makes him creative dreams up ingenious reasons for not going to work. One of the most difficult problems a student preparing for discussion faces is to make a creative analysis of the topic before the group meeting. Too often members do not begin to analyze the topic until the meetings force them to do so.

A creative person can discipline his talent by systematic work habits. He should set aside a certain time every day and try to work at that time, preferably at the same table in the library or in the same place at home. Gradually, he will begin work after a shorter warm-up period. He must, however, be faithful to his schedule even when he seems to be doing very little.

The creative process requires enough time for analysis to mature through all four stages to understanding. A creative analysis cannot be done all at once, as can cramming for an examination. Preparation should begin early, and time should be allowed for the incubation phase. An hour or so should be set aside each day for contemplation. The member should take a walk or drive. Reading is *not* a substitute for contemplation because it does not leave the mind free to work on ideas.

Finally, a member should welcome farfetched ideas and expand on them. He should imagine as many solutions as possible for the problem; he should modify, change, or combine the ones already suggested. Ideas and suggestions should not be rejected immediately. Some people can develop well organized arguments against every proposal, but such people seldom achieve a creative analysis of the problem.

When an individual recognizes that the most appropriate analysis is a personal and creative matter, he can safely use some of the more mechanical techniques for analyzing information. These standard ways of approaching the processing of information are like standard opening moves in chess. Chess openings are used to set strategy, and over the years experts have devised openings that have become standards and are used over and over again. However, few chess games move to their conclusions along the lines suggested by the opening moves. Likewise, the standard ways of opening a question for discussion can help speed the analysis, assure that it is complete, and prime the creative talent during the preparatory stage. However, a creative analysis usually leaves the opening pattern behind as it reveals the unique issues of a particular question.

ORIENTATION: THE OPENING MOVES

The initial attack on a problem is often called the *orientation phase.* Of course, discussion groups do not neatly divide their deliberations and devote one phase solely to examining the problem. Neither, for that matter, do individuals preparing for the meeting confine themselves to such a mechanical approach. The guidelines that follow apply to groups in process and individuals preparing for discussion. Early in the search for understanding, the participant preparing for the meeting should orient himself to the facts as they relate to the problem under discussion. Orientation begins with the questions: Is something wrong? Is there a problem? and, Is a change necessary? If individuals or groups discover that things are going well and little is to be gained from a change, they should answer the questions negatively. Most discussion topics result from a feeling that something is certainly wrong. Thus begins a more detailed examination of the question: What are the facts that constitute the problem?

Understanding the facts. The student will find that some of the information he collects is held to be true by all observers and authorities. For example, the wording of the income-tax laws of a given state can be found in the legal code, and once the wording is known to the group that fact need not be investigated further. The question of how the wording has, in fact, been interpreted is more open to dispute. Many statements of fact become the subject of dispute. Some observers and authorities maintain that firm X in the last taxable year trucked large quantities of their merchandise across the state line just before the tax assessment time. Others maintain this statement is false. If the truthfulness of an important statement of fact is disputed, a question that isolates the disputed point should be asked. For example: Did firm X truck large quantities of merchandise across the state line last year? Such questions point up the factual controversies unique to the particular topic.

Describing the problem. When a discussant has resolved the factual controversies, he should begin to fit the statements together. The result will be a coherent description that serves as his answer to the question: What are the facts that constitute the problem? Examples of such statements might be: The state debt as of the last fiscal year was $256,562,000; state mental institutions have four psychiatrists on their staff; the governor's committee to study mental-health facilities observed rats in the kitchens of all mental hospitals; the rate of recovery and discharge at all state hospitals for the last 10 years has averaged 30 percent.

Explaining the problem. When the problem has been described, the method of explaining the facts should be determined. Usually the group assumes that these facts can be accounted for in terms of (1) prior facts, and (2) human motives. The common-sense label for this complex of forces is *causes.* Thus, the question can be phrased: What causes the problem?

ORIENTATION: ANALYSIS IN DEPTH

Explanation by causal analysis. Causal analysis is difficult because common-sense definitions of *cause* are often ambiguous and confused. Discussants must define the various uses of the term to make successful communication possible.

Consider the relatively simple case of a patient who is not feeling well. The doctor can easily describe his symptoms in factual terms: The patient has a temperature of 103 degrees, has difficulty in breathing, and coughs frequently. The doctor can also describe blood count, blood pressure, and pulse rate. The doctor must make a *diagnosis* in order to *account* for the patient's symptoms. The doctor might account for the symptoms on the basis of a bacterial infection in the lungs and say the patient is suffering from pneumonia. If he treats the bacterial infection with penicillin and his diagnosis is correct, the temperature will be lowered, and the other symptoms will disappear. In this instance, the doctor might say that the pneumonia was *caused* by an infection and that the infection was *caused* by bacteria. Such a causal analysis is adequate for his purposes.

A more complex case might be the factual statements relating to the tax situation of a given state. The governor discovers that the kitchens at the state hospitals are infested with rats. He tells the superintendent to clean the kitchens and exterminate the rats. The superintendent says he cannot afford to hire exterminators, but if given more money, he would be delighted to clean up the hospital buildings. The governor says that more money is not available because the state is heavily in debt. The superintendent asks why the state is in debt, and the governor answers that the tax structure does not collect enough money to provide the services authorized by the legislature. When asked about the tax structure, the governor says that the legislators are not willing to change the tax base or to raise the tax rates. When asked about their unwillingness, the legislators reply that they will not be reelected if they raise taxes. They indicate that the voters are unaware of conditions in the state hospitals and are, therefore, unwilling to pay more taxes to correct them. If this is so, the best solution is to inform the public about the problem in the state hospitals. If people do not want taxes to be raised so that the conditions can be improved because they do not care about the rats in the kitchens and want to keep their money for themselves, a campaign should be started to appeal to their consciences.

The analysis might proceed in another way. If the superintendent said that he does not have enough people or money for the job, the governor might reply that the budget is much larger this year, so that the superintendent can hire more staff; however, further investigation may reveal inefficient administration. In this case, firing the superintendent may be a wise solution. Clearly, an investigating group must account for the facts in a realistic way in order to take wise action.

When a group has determined the underlying causes, it can then develop an effective policy of action to eliminate a problem. Discovering underlying causes of public policy is very difficult, however. The symptom–diagnosis–treatment–cure pattern works almost every time in situations governed by the laws of the natural sciences. If an automobile stops running, the cause may be that the car needs gas. The treatment is to add fuel, which makes the car start. If the car still does not work, however, the driver seeks further causes, assuming that several things are wrong. He may discover that the carburetor is stuck and the motor flooded. When all the causes for the stopped car are taken care of, the car *inevitably will run.*

A *causal analysis* is one that isolates and organizes the relevant factors or variables relating to a problem in such a way that the problem is explained or accounted for, and dealing with the factors *invariably* results in a solution. A group will usually be successful in solving problems for which causes in this sense of the term can be isolated.

Explanation by probabilities. Often problems cannot be subjected to the causal analysis of the type just defined. Sometimes diagnosis of a problem serves to isolate factors that are not invariably associated with the symptoms. If the car is out of gas, the motor invariably stops; but if bacteria are present in the system, body temperature is not invariably elevated.

Consider the problem of bright students who flunk out of college. Do they lack interest in their work, and if so, why? Perhaps they are emotionally disturbed, lack a clear purpose in life, or are rebelling against their parents, who pressure them to get a degree. Perhaps they lack funds. All these factors may be involved, but a bright student who is emotionally disturbed, has no clear purpose in life, is under great pressure from his parents to succeed, and lacks funds may still graduate with honors.

When a group explains such situations, they move into the difficult region of probabilities. The failure of the student can be explained by asserting that under such conditions and given these motivations, the results were highly likely or probable. One meaning of the term *probability* is synonymous with the assumption of pure chance, that is, that the events have no discernible pattern and each event happens purely by chance. Using probability in this sense a statistician can ask: What is the probability that a coin will turn up heads, or that the next throw of a pair of dice will total 6? When the assumptions of chance do account for the numbers selected by a roulette wheel or the hands dealt in a poker game, the wise gambler makes decisions based on the probabilities in this mathematical sense of the term. The traditional use of the term *probability* in the study of discussion is in the sense of discovering highly likely patterns in events even if they are not as clearly discerned and invariable as patterns described by the laws of science. If a man has frequently cheated to make money, even at the expense of his health and family, will he be likely to react to a new opportunity to make a large amount of money in the same way? Based on previous observations of this man, a group may project his behavior into the future and assume that he will continue to act as he has in the past.

Since probabilities do not always come true, and the ability to predict what will happen in the future is vital to the decision making of a group, the student of group discussion must understand the basis for reasonable prediction. The process of induction furnishes the basis for reasonable prediction.

ORIENTATION: THE PROCESS OF INDUCTION

The nature of induction. Induction is the process of observing facts and making general statements about them. Man has well-developed powers of generalization. In order to generalize, man must perceive a similarity in some selected aspect of his experience so that he can refer to two or more of his perceptions by the same name. He may realize that they are not completely similar, but similar enough on some crucial dimension that under certain conditions they can be treated as the same. Having made such a generalization, man tends to treat subsequent observations that are similar to them in the same way. A child learning language goes through this process. He may become aware of a moving, four-legged, furry object that barks. He has discovered a similarity in his observations, and his parents provide the name of Rover for them. The word *Rover* is simply a convenient label for the entire class of such percepts.

One day the child becomes aware of a larger, moving, four-legged, furry object that barks, and he refers to it as *Rover.* His parents tell him that this is not Rover but another *dog.* Gradually, he learns that four-legged, moving, furry objects that bark, but are not Rover, are all named *dog.* Basic to such generalization is the notion of analogy.

Analogy is the inductive process that assumes that if two or more facts agree in some respects, they will agree in others. Ultimately, rational thinking is based on the finding of similarities and contrasts. The core of a discussion group's intellectual activity is the discovery of similarities and the drawing of distinctions. When the child learns the general name for the class of canines (dogs), he may mistakingly apply it to a cow. If he treats the cow as he would treat a dog, he may have his expectations rudely frustrated. He must notice not only the similarities that cause him to generalize from past to present and future, but also the differences. If he treats Fido as he does Rover, he may get bitten. Man draws analogies in several ways. He may find analogies in a limited class of events much as the statistician uses descriptive statistics to describe a population after a complete census. This is generalizing by complete enumeration of a class (whole).

Induction by complete enumeration of a class. If a generalization asserts that a characteristic is uniform, such as that all members of a group are male, an investigator can then infer about every individual in the group that the person is male. However, a generalization by complete enumeration might assert that half of the students in a class received a grade C. In this case, flipping a coin will be as helpful as the generalization in deciding whether or not a given student received a grade of C. The generalization that most students received a C would imply that a given student received a C on the basis that it is *probable* that one person did. Such an estimate will fail sometimes, but not as often as the decision based purely on chance. If an investigator wanted a more careful estimate, he would welcome a generalization that 80 percent of the students received a C. He would then know that a given student probably received a C, and he would also know how probable it was that the student had received a C. His estimate about the grade could be made with a precise level of confidence.

Induction to all similar instances. A second type of induction is based on a sample of observations and projected to *all similar events.* Such generalizations cover future as well as past events. This kind of generalization can serve as a basis for prediction of future happenings. With prediction comes control. If members of a group can predict that certain conditions will produce a given set of results, they can often arrange to get the results they desire.

When we find a similarity is so stable that our expectations are always fulfilled, we have discovered a *law of nature.* Laws of nature may be expressed in two linguistic forms: as a concept or as a process. A concept law takes the same linguistic form as the concept of dog. The facts covered by the concept are much different, however. Dogs may act in unexpected ways, but the facts named by the concept law *iron* will not. If a chemist takes a sample of iron, he can predict what will invariably happen when he heats it or combines it with certain elements, or tries to deflect a magnetic needle with it.

The discovery of concept law leads to inductions that assert dynamic relations among these concepts. Thus, the concepts of water, iron, and rust form the process law that iron combined with water (which contains oxygen) will always form rust (oxidize). If the relationship is invariable, the generalization is a law of nature. Obviously, a generalization that covers all similar conditions whether past, present, or future points up a very stubborn pattern in man's experience. He ignores such a generalization at his peril. If he leaves a precious iron object in the rain, it rusts. If he ignores the law of gravity by stepping off a cliff, he falls. However, he can employ such generalizations intelligently and thereby control his environment. He builds machines according to the laws of mechanics, and they perform as he predicted they would. Of course, machines break or do not perform as the inventor hoped, but, when a machine is built to dig ditches, it does not produce automobile fenders.

The group may make a similar inductive leap from relationships that they have observed frequently but not invariably and project these *probabilities* to all similar situations.

Predictions about future observations based on probability generalizations do not *always* come true. If the generalization is quite probable, predictions usually come true; if the generalizations are only slightly probable, predictions come true a little more often than if they were based on the flipping of a coin.

Induction and causal analysis. In everyday discourse, the term *cause* implies necessity. To say that the causes of the problem are such and such implies that whenever the causes are present, the problem must necessarily be present. *Cause in this sense implies laws of nature.* The group can test a causal analysis by examining the laws of nature that explain the causes. To assert that the oxygen in water caused the iron to rust implies the law of nature that whenever iron is exposed to moisturized oxygen it will rust. When an important causal analysis is found, it should be determined whether the *generalizations* underlying the analysis are laws of nature or probability generalizations. Consider the assertion that the growth of the Communist party in Chile is caused by the extreme poverty of the majority of the people. This suggests a law of nature that wherever there is extreme poverty in a country, there will invariably be a growth in the Communist party. Another example is the causal analysis that a campus student demonstration was caused by the long, hard winter and preparation for spring examinations. Such a statement implies that whenever there is a long, hard winter, student demonstrations will occur after the spring examinations. An asserted causal relationship is weak if the underlying generalizations are not laws of nature, but probability generalizations.

Induction on nonrational grounds. Since laws of nature must have perfect records for accurate prophecy, they require precisely formulated statements of fact that are verified with great care. Implications from laws of nature are often drawn mathematically. These stringent qualifications require rational thinking and truthfulness. By contrast, probability generalizations are useful if their predictions are fulfilled *most* of the time. Since probability generalizations do not require invariable success for predictions based on them, emotional, prejudiced, neurotic, or psychotic attachment to probability generalizations that are divorced from observation can result.

When a man who is sure that women are "lousy" drivers observes a woman driving a car, he immediately guards against dangerous, unpredictable moves. When a driver fails to signal properly, he assumes that the driver is a women. If he discovers that the driver is a man, he asserts that the man drives like a woman. If a female driver turns off without making an error, he sighs in relief and considers himself lucky. Every instance of bad driving by a woman reinforces his obsession. The fact that a probability generalization need only apply to a majority of instances allows the man to gratify his obsession.

Because obsessions sometimes serve nonrational psychological needs, probability generalizations are much more liable to be wrong than are laws of nature. People often cling to such generalizations in the face of contradictory facts. When the generalizations are obviously of little use in estimating developments, they may be called *superstitions.* Probability generalizations that do not describe the observed facts may be so clearly anchored in psychological mechanisms that they are called *prejudices*. The man with the obsession was *prejudiced* against female drivers.

Neither laws of nature nor probability statements can ever be completely verified, because they assert predictions about future events. Since a law of chemistry asserts that the same chemical reactions will hold tomorrow as held yesterday and as hold today, the facts cannot even theoretically all be observed. Laws of nature can, however, be judged false when one single negative instance is observed. Laws of nature are always held provisionally and retain their status only until a negative instance refutes them. Thus, in theory, laws of nature can be rendered false. Probability generalizations, however, cannot be disproved so neatly. If observations indicate that more than half of the female drivers in this country are good drivers, the generalization that a woman is probably a bad driver would be false. However, the man with the obsession could argue that the observations have not been extensive enough and results from tomorrow's observations will support his generalization. In this case, tomorrow never comes. Everyone has the practical problem of judging the probable effect of today's actions and the probability of success in solving individual and group problems. Discussants have greater success when they assume that the patterns of probability observed in the past will hold for the future. When they do this, they reconsider the probability of a woman being a bad driver on the basis of the observed facts.

Statistical estimates of probability. Estimating the result of completely enumerating a class from a sample is not the only possible use of inferential statistics. One of the more exciting and useful areas of inferential statistics concerns ways to make a precise estimate of probabilities. For instance, a university admissions officer discovers that good grades in high school indicate that a student will probably make good grades at the university. This knowledge enables him to evaluate potential students more effectively. He could make a still more intelligent estimate of the probable success of a given student if he could use inferential statistics which furnish formulas that quantify the degree of probability in a case such as this. The statistical model may be based on comparing the degree to which two sets of behavior vary together. In this case, high-school grade average might be compared to college grade average. The statistician can compute a *correlation coefficient* that will describe in numerical terms the amount of correlation between the two scores. The correlation coefficient is an estimate of how probable it is that knowing one score aids in predicting the other. The statistician may compute a correlation coefficient of 0.87 between the two sets of scores. The admissions officer will do about 50 percent better than he would by flipping a coin if his prediction is based on such a correlation and if future distributions of the two sets of scores are similar to those on which the computations are based. Discussion groups will find probability estimates derived from statistical computations an accurate source of probability generalizations to be used in accounting for the facts.

ORIENTATION: HUMAN AGENTS

Some part of most problems may be attributed to human action and motivations. One group may say that students riot in the spring because they want to rebel against authority. Another group might say that the inefficient administration of the university results from red tape created by bureaucrats who are power-hungry empire builders.

A discussion group must take into account human attitudes, motives, and emotions. However, the problems posed by motive analysis are great and must be approached most carefully. The same action may be appraised by a man's friends as resulting from high motives and by his enemies as stemming from base motives.

ORIENTATION: EXPLAINING THE SITUATION

Often experts disagree about the nature of the causes, probabilities, or human purposes that account for the facts. The discussant should isolate these points of disagreement with a question. To what extent are conditions in the mental hospitals the result of inadequate funds or of poor administration? Why are more funds not provided? Is the governor's political ambition a factor? Questions that point up specific controversies relating to a given inquiry are most useful. At this point, the student should leave the general opening moves and make a creative analysis of unique disagreements that relate to a given topic.

EVALUATION: THE IMPORTANCE OF THE PROBLEM

The second phase of a discussion group's deliberations is characterized by opinion and evaluation. The group turns to the opening question: How do we evaluate the problem? To answer this question, all members must agree on certain statements of value and their arrangement in some order of priority. How does this question compare with other problems of a similar nature? Is the support of mental hospitals to be placed ahead of the support of state universities?

Assume that a student and his parents discuss a common problem facing the family group, namely, the student's falling grade average. A few statements of fact describe the problem. The grade in chemistry is F, in psychology D, in English C, and in German D. Accounting for the problem takes a bit more time. The family group agrees that the grades cannot be explained by a lack of ability. High-school grades, passing grades for the fall semester at the university, and high test scores on the entrance examinations all discount this explanation. At first, the parents feel the student has not been working hard enough, but the student persuades them that he has been working very hard; he has carried 16 credits and has been working 30 hours a week at a downtown department store. Finally the family group decides that the problem results from trying to do too many things. The parents perceive that their son is more interested in his car (which he holds down a job to maintain) than in his degree. The parents judge the problem to be severe and large. The student feels that one term on probation will not jeopardize his college career. He wants to continue for a time and see how things work out. His parents discuss from a set of value statements that place top priority on gaining the degree and rather low priority on keeping the car. The student, on the other hand, places considerable value on the university diploma, but would sacrifice the degree if necessary to keep the car.

EVALUATION: CONFLICTING OPINIONS

Once the group is oriented to the facts, the discussants should organize the statements of opinion relating to the topic. Are statements expressing ethical rules pertinent to this topic? What are the contending positions? What group purposes and goals relate to this question? One good way to organize these statements is in terms of consistency. Statements that are logically consistent are placed together. If the topic relates to tax reform for the state, the arrangement might be as follows.

CONSISTENT SET OF PROPOSITIONS A

The tax structure of our state must provide an ever-increasing source of funds for the social services our state should provide.

The tax structure should be based on the ability to pay. Wealthy people should pay a larger share in proportion to their wealth.

The state must always put human values above property values.

Only the intervention of the state can protect the public welfare against the evil designs of vested interests.

Poor people are the unfortunate victims of circumstances and the state must take the responsibility of caring for them.

CONSISTENT SET OF PROPOSITIONS B

Taxes in our state must be kept at an absolute minimum.

The tax structure in our state must encourage the development of industry.

The primary purpose of government is to protect property rights.

> *Capital must be allowed to accumulate to encourage initiative and enterprise.*
>
> *Poor people must take the responsibility for their position in life.*

An alternative method of organizing opinion statements is to place the contradictory propositions in juxtaposition. For example:

> *The tax structure should be based on the ability to pay, versus, the tax structure of our state must encourage the development of industry.*

Pairing will reveal a conflict that can be phrased as a question:

> *Should the tax structure of our state encourage the development of industry even if it must be regressive to do so?*

EVALUATION: PROPOSED SOLUTIONS

The next major question that can be used to begin an analysis is: What policy might be followed to solve, the problem? Statements of advice are discussed and evaluated in terms of opinions that reflect values, priorities of purpose, and goals. The advice is also tested in terms of the causes, factors, and motives that account for the problem. The discussants can then decide if a given policy will achieve their goals, and if the action suggested is consonant with their ethical norms.

THE DECISION PHASE

The final phase of a discussion group's work is the decision period. All alternative courses of action must be weighed against the best estimates of their probable outcomes. And those outcomes must be examined in terms of acceptable statements of value and purposes. Finally, the group will make a decision as to its course of action.

The description of what must be done in this phase is simple, but the actual process by which the group reaches wise decisions is far from simple. Unfortunately, there are no fixed procedures to guide a group in this task.

Although a discussant may wish to make a tentative decision about a policy during his preparatory study, unless the circumstances are unusual, he is well advised not to close his mind to other proposals until he has deliberated with the other members of the group.

reasoning about the topic

DEDUCTION AND REASONING

Deduction is the process of drawing out, according to clearly specified rules, the implications contained in a set of premises. The disciplines that develop and study deductive systems are mathematics and logic. Discussion-group members are most likely to use deductive logic in the form of arithmetic or mathematical statistics. Formal logic as expressed in either the syllogism of Aristotle or in the recent symbolic logic is not useful for discussion groups. However, a somewhat similar way of combining and recombining concepts and drawing out the implications of definitions and premises is a common feature of group deliberations. Synthetic (factual) conclusions derived from observations should be distinguished from analytic conclusions derived by combining and recombining concepts. The latter activity, when rigorously systematized, is the province of logic. In this process, no new factual information is contributed to the argument. Chains of logic simply indicate permissible combinations of concepts—they do not add to the information already in the premises. When analytic conclusions are derived in a looser and less rigorous way in practical discourse, the process can be called reasoning.

Scientific discourse is dependent upon observation, induction, and deduction. Practical discussion is analogous to scientific discourse as it, too, is ultimately dependent on observation for its contact with the world. In addition, the process of understanding a discussion topic is similar to scientific induction, and the process of forming conclusions from premises is similar to deduction.

REASONING EXPLAINED

Reasoning may be defined as the process of concluding, judging, or inferring from facts or premises. It thus includes both induction (drawing of inferences from observations) and deduction (drawing conclusions from premises). This section of the chapter considers the process of reasoning deductively, that is, from premises to conclusions. Deductive reasoning in group discussion is a clear, plausible, and consistent drawing out of implications from definitions, value statements, probability generalizations, and laws of nature. Like pure deduction in logic or mathematics, reasoning is primarily a linguistic matter. When reasoning about information, a person manipulates symbols and fits them into plausible patterns to reach conclusions that were not apparent on first examination. Logicians and mathematicians can always check the proof (implications) that leads from one set of assumptions (axioms) to a new conclusion (theorem) and can always decide if the proof is correct or incorrect. The rules of discussion are so ambiguous that the correctness or incorrectness of a given line of reasoning is more difficult to determine. Well-trained and reasonable men will differ when checking a proof developed in the course of practical argument, but they would not when checking the solution to a problem in arithmetic or symbolic logic.

Deductive reasoning draws out the implications of definitions and assumptions. Members of a discussion group are often unaware of all that is implied by a given definition or position. When they discover all the implications, they may dislike some and change their basic assumptions. Reasoning can also reveal the vagueness of definitions, a vagueness that lends an illusion of rationality to an irrational action or position. Group members can challenge one another for clearer definitions and more comparisons and distinctions. Such dialectic clarifies value systems and helps the group come to a greater understanding of purposes and goals.

Reasoning can also be used to lend a veneer of rationality to unreasonable action. In our culture, the individual often needs to rationalize and justify the pleasurable release of emotional tensions. Most people want an argument that lends the illusion of reason to their behavior; for example, when they vent frustrations on a scapegoat, or indulge in any psychological mechanisms that enable them to ignore reality and act in immature ways. Statements of fact are difficult to manipulate into rationalizations because they are based on observations. But deductive reasoning is not dependent on observations and can therefore be used to justify what an individual or group of individuals wants to do. For this reason, members of a discussion group must make certain of the adequacy of their definitions and must be alert to the slightest shifting of meaning from term to term as they reason from one assumption to another.

GOOD REASONING

Clarity. To be effective, reasoning must be clear, plausible, and consistent. Clarity in everyday discourse, oddly enough, is dependent on a certain amount of ambiguity. Too much precision is confusing. The step-by-step demonstrations of formal symbolic logic are too intricate for group discussion. Clear reasoning in discussion skips the self-evident parts of an argument and presents an abbreviated sketch. Following are two examples from a logic textbook.

> *Lions and tigers are carnivorous mammals. Some lions are dangerous. All tigers have stripes. Some tigers are ferocious. No lions have stripes. Some mammals are neither ferocious nor dangerous. Therefore, some carnivores are neither lions nor tigers.*

> *If all drugs are contaminated, then all negligent technicians are scoundrels. If there are any drugs which are contaminated, then all of them are contaminated and unsafe. All germicides*

are drugs. Only the negligent are absent-minded. Therefore if any technician is absent-minded then if some germicides are contaminated then he is a scroundel.[1]

When properly translated into the symbols of formal logic, the first argument is invalid, and the second is valid. Clearly, the group cannot examine complicated questions by casting their arguments into syllogistic or symbolic form and clarifying the terms to such an extent that the step-by-step demonstrations of logic are useful to their deliberations.

On the other hand, if a participant omits too many steps in a chain of reasons, other members will find the reasoning paradoxical. For example, member A may confuse others by asserting member B is inconsistent because he claims to be both a liberal and a nonconformist. Before his reasoning becomes clear, member A must supply more intervening steps in his argument. He could argue that modern liberalism is a product of the Depression, that it emphasized human values over property values, and that this emphasis became a quest for security. Liberalism developed the Social Security programs and similar measures to guarantee economic security for life. He might argue that if security is emphasized, conformity will increase. Notice that this process of outlining a conclusion linguistically depends on various meanings of key words—in this case, *liberalism, security,* and *nonconformity.* The conclusion of member A might be challenged by member C who defines liberalism in a different way. He suggests that although modern liberalism developed during the Depression and placed an emphasis on human values, its entire spirit has been one of bold inventiveness. The liberals were the nonconformists who tried new approaches to old problems; they were willing to challenge old traditions and myths. Member C contends that therefore liberalism and nonconformity are not incompatible, but synonymous. This line of reasoning consists of deriving various implied meanings from the key terms *liberalism* and *nonconformity.* Since these terms are used without clear referents in conversation, intelligent men may *reason* to different conclusions during the course of a public discussion.

Clarity of reasoning requires, therefore, a judicious selection of intervening steps leading from the original premise to the conclusion. These bridging statements must be phrased so that the group members understand how they are implied by the original premise and can follow the transition easily from one point to the next, and then to the conclusion.

Plausibility. The listener who finds a line of reasoning plausible believes that it is based on acceptable assumptions and on a series of steps that seem possible and probable. The reasoning he accepts is not too

[1] Both examples are from Irving M. Copi, *Symbolic Logic.* New York: Macmillan, 1954.

far from the reality of sense perceptions. For example, a group might accept the reasoning that whoever controls Berlin controls West Germany. They may accept the next statement that whoever controls West Germany controls the heartland of Eurasia. However, the following statements become implausible: Whoever controls the heartland of Eurasia controls Europe and Asia; whoever controls Europe and Asia controls the world; therefore, whoever controls Berlin controls the world. The so-called domino line of reasoning in international affairs—which argues that if region Y falls, region X is next, and if X falls, can Z be far behind?—is only plausible if the line of dominoes is not too long.

Consistency. One way to test for consistency is to look for a contradiction. If no contradiction is discovered, a line of reasoning is judged to be consistent. Consistency is the core of symbolic logic and mathematics, and in using these ideal systems as models a group should strive for consistency in its practical arguments.

In the Lincoln–Douglas debates of 1858 in Illinois, Lincoln maintained that Senator Douglas was inconsistent in advocating popular sovereignty at the same time that he supported the Dred Scott decision of the Supreme Court. Lincoln maintained that popular sovereignty implied that the residents of a territory could decide whether the territory would be free or slave, but that the Dred Scott decision implied that it was impossible legally to deny slavery in a territory.

TESTING REASONING

Clarifying definitions. If one member uses the word *true* as specified in Chapter 4 and another uses the word to mean a mystical or intuitive apperception of a higher reality, they will certainly confuse one another when they discuss questions related to *truth.* Reasoning so often depends on moving from one term to another, and upon the assumptions implied by definitions, that examining the manner in which important terms are used can often settle misunderstandings or reveal weaknesses in the reasoning. When the reasoning of discussants is unclear or in conflict, discussion should be halted while definitions for key terms are clarified.

Terms may be defined in three ways. First, a term may be defined arbitrarily. A given word can be made to mean different things in different groups. A group may agree to use a given term, such as *lobbyist* or *communist* or *nonconformity,* in clearly specified arbitrary ways. Most definitions in this book have been of this sort. In Chapter 4, the definitions of *statements of fact, truth,* and *falsity,* of *facts,* and of *directly verifiable statements of fact* are all conventional arbitrary definitions. Such definitions aid a group immeasurably in their reasoning. When important terms have the same clearly specified meanings for all members of a group, time will not be spent in needless argument unrelated to a real difference of opinion.

Discussants should decide what particular definition will prove most useful to the group and should not be concerned about whether that is the *real* meaning of the word. It does little good to argue that a given definition is not really what the word *truth* means because words like *truth* are symbols that may be assigned in conventional fashion to any concept. To be sure, unusual and bizarre definitions of common words will be troublesome because old language habits carry over, and the immediate response may be to the more usual meaning of a term. For this reason, terms should be used as they are defined in everyday discourse, with whatever arbitrary restrictions and clarifications are useful.

The second way in which definition may be used is to describe the facts. Although it seems like the procedure of arbitrarily specifying the use of a word, it is much different. Descriptive definitions relate not to words but to facts indicated by the words. A member may define communism as a political force in countries that are militantly and aggressively colonizing other countries in the name of world revolution. What he asserts is not that he wants only to use the word *communism* when he talks about such countries (whether they exist or not) but that he is describing a group of countries (facts) and these countries are militant, aggressive, and are colonizing other countries in the name of world revolution. This definition should be checked as any other statement of fact would be. What countries is he talking about? What evidence does he have that they are colonizing other countries? If one member of the group uses the term in an arbitrary way while another is talking about actual countries, they may misunderstand one another.

The third way in which the process of definition may be used is to present opinions in a disguised form. A member may define the discussional attitude as an open-minded cooperative attitude in which the discussant does not become an advocate. In using this definition he is prescribing a course of action or expressing a value judgment. This is the prescriptive use of definitions. Obviously, the definition is not descriptive, since many discussants do not have this attitude. He might be presenting a conventional definition, in which case the group might agree to this meaning of the term in their future deliberations. But if he means this is the attitude they *ought* to have, his definition can be challenged. Another member might argue that such an attitude would achieve nothing, and that everyone should argue for a definite position. Only in the give-and-take of the arena will the best answer be pounded out, he argues.

The prescriptive definition is often used to hide assumptions that are later drawn out by reasoning. For example, *leadership* can be defined as any behavior (verbal or nonverbal) by any member that aids the group in achieving its goal. This may seem like a descriptive definition, but it actually presents the opinion that leadership should facilitate the group's movement toward its goal. This definition could be the basis for the following argument: If leadership is any behavior as defined, then every member will do something during the group's life, either by accident or design, that helps the group in this way; therefore, all members share in the leadership, and each can be thought of as a leader. This chain of reasoning is dependent on a prescriptive definition of leadership which seems plausible enough, but the implications (assumptions hidden in the definition) lead to a rather unexpected and implausible conclusion. If the discussants understand that the reasoning is based on a prescriptive definition, they can deal with it properly.

Such reasoning can be found in small-group research studies that are seemingly scientific. Prescriptive definitions are often used to support an investigator's bias that totalitarianism, tyranny, authoritarianism, and so forth, are undesirable and that democracy, equality, and a classless society are desirable. These opinions will find wide acceptance in our society, but they should be presented on their merits as opinions and not be confused with scientific conclusions.

Testing the premises. The reasoning process always begins with premises either explicitly stated or implied or both. These may be statements of fact. The premise might be that Communist China is militantly aggressive, will colonize other nations in the name of world communism, and that the Communist parties in India, Indonesia, Malaysia, Vietnam, Cambodia, and Laos are controlled by the Chinese. The conclusion could be drawn that a political vacuum in the Indian peninsula or anywhere in Southeast Asia would result in aggression by Communist China. If the reasoning process begins with statements of fact, the first step in testing the conclusion is to be certain that the premises are true. If one or more premises are false, the conclusion is unacceptable.

Often, the premises that underlie a chain of reasoning are statements of opinion. The premise of an argument might be that the basic purpose of speechmaking is to communicate with an audience. In this case, anything a speaker does to interfere with successful communication is undesirable; therefore, the speaker will not try to use language to confuse his audience. However, the basic purpose of speechmaking is not, in fact, always communication. Many speakers have other purposes. This basic premise is a statement of opinion that speakers *ought* to have as their basic purpose the desire to communicate. In general, if the group accepts the opinions that serve as the premises for a line of reasoning, they are more likely to accept the conclusion. In any case, a group testing any line of reasoning should find the asserted or implied opinions that are the basis for chains of reasoning and decide if they are acceptable. Reasoning that starts with opinion statements which the group supports or with true statements of fact and reaches a conclusion by clear, plausible, and consistent steps is most likely to lead to a constructive conclusion.

summary

If a student recognizes that his study is a personal and creative matter that requires disciplined preparation, some leisure for thinking, and a creative mental set, he can safely use the customary techniques for beginning the study of a question.

The group's work on a given decision can be divided into three major phases: (1) orientation to the problem, (2) evaluation phase, and (3) the decision phase. During the orientation phase, the discussants discover those statements of fact that describe the problem and find an explanation for these facts. In the evaluation phase, the severity and importance of the problem are decided and it is compared with other problems that demand attention. Various representative solutions are examined and evaluated. The final phase is the one in which a decision is made.

The discussant preparing for a program should understand the topic. He can do this by describing, accounting for, evaluating the problem, and analyzing representative solutions as he himself sees them.

The facts can be accounted for in terms of inductively determined generalizations and human motives and purposes. Inductions may be made on the basis of a complete enumeration of a class or on a more general basis of all similar events whether observed or not. The latter kind of inductive leap results in laws of nature or in probability generalizations. If a law of nature can be found to account for a set of facts, the generalization will always be associated with the facts. Laws of nature furnish a causal analysis of a problem situation. Probability generalizations are not always associated with the facts, and they do not furnish a causal explanation.

Deductive reasoning is the clear, plausible, and consistent drawing out of implications from definitions, value statements, laws, and probability generalizations. The soundness of the reasoning is associated with the definitions on which it may be based. Definitions are of three types. Conventional definitions specify an arbitrary way in which the group agrees to use a word or phrase. Descriptive definitions are statements of fact purporting to describe actual conditions. Prescriptive definitions imply statements of opinion.

The premises underlying a chain of reasoning may be implied or expressed. One test of reasoning is to examine the truthfulness of the factual premises and the nature of the generalizations that have an inductive basis to see if they are laws of nature or probability generalizations. A second test of reasoning is to examine the premises that are statements of opinion to see if the group accepts these opinions.

QUESTIONS FOR STUDY

1. What is the difference between understanding and analysis?
2. What is the relationship between creativity and analysis?
3. What is meant by a causal analysis?
4. What is the difference between a causal analysis and an explanation by probabilities?
5. What is the difference between induction by a complete enumeration of a class and induction to all similar instances?
6. What is a law of nature?
7. What is the relationship between induction and causal analysis?
8. What are some ways in which nonrational inductions may be drawn?
9. In what way may a correlation coefficient serve as a statistical estimate of probabilities?
10. What is the difference between deduction and reasoning?
11. How may clarifying definitions aid in the testing of the adequacy of reasoning?
12. What distinguishes the conventional definition from the descriptive definition?
13. What distinguishes the prescriptive definition from the descriptive definition?
14. How may the premises of a chain of reasoning be tested?
15. What role does consistency have in the development of a line of reasoning?

EXERCISES

1. With a group of your classmates, select a question of policy to serve as the basis for several discussions. After a thorough search for information, make a careful analysis of the topic. Prepare an outline that includes: (a) a description of the problem, (b) an explanation of the problem, (c) an evaluation of the importance of the problem, (d) a list of possible solutions with their advantages and disadvantages considered, and (e) your candidate for the best solution. The outline should follow accepted outlining procedure and be carried to the final statements of fact, opinion, and advice that justified each section. Note the sources of your information in the margin.
2. In connection with the same topic as in exercise 1, list a set of opinion statements your group is likely to accept. From these opinions derive the policy that you think best, and construct a consistent, clear, and plausible line of reasoning justifying that policy.

3. Select an article advocating a controversial policy, and describe the author's analysis. Test the adequacy of his causal analysis and his probability arguments.
4. Tape record a group meeting, and listen to the reasoning of the participants. Find a sample of a chain of reasoning and transcribe it. Evaluate its consistency, plausibility, and clarity. What opinion statements does it assume as uncontested?

References and suggested readings

The three-phase pattern of processing information is discussed in:

Bales, Robert F., and F. L. Strodtbeck. "Phases in Group Problem Solving," *Journal of Abnormal and Social Psychology,* **46** (1951), 485–495.

For more discussion of the creative process, see:

Anderson, Harold H., ed. *Creativity and Its Cultivation.* New York: Harper & Row, 1959.
Bormann, Ernest G. *Theory and Research in the Communicative Arts.* New York: Holt, Rinehart and Winston, 1965, chap. 7.
Dewey, John. *How We Think.* Boston: Heath, 1910.
Ghiselin, Brewster, ed. *The Creative Process.* Berkeley: University of California Press, 1952.
Wallas, Graham. *The Art of Thought.* London: Cape, 1926.

PART II
THEORY

CHAPTER 7

COHESIVENESS AND THE TASK-ORIENTED GROUP

The fundamentals of developing, adapting, and processing information have been presented. A student who learns and respects the fundamentals is ready to take part in group discussions. Yet, well prepared as he may be, he will discover that groups resist his information, ideas, and best-laid plans. When they do, he may find he can increase his effectiveness by learning about the dynamics of small groups.

The task-oriented small group is a group of three or more people gathered to do, in concert, a clearly specified job in which face-to-face communication, both gestural and verbal, structures the group's work and social expectations.

two aspects of the task-oriented group

Research workers have discovered a useful distinction between the functions related to the social structuring of small groups and those functions devoted to the group task. These two features are relevant to both the description and the evaluation of what takes place in a group. To be sure, social and task functions are closely intertwined, but their general tendencies are distinguishable and different in important ways.

THE SOCIAL DIMENSION OF GROUP PROCESS

To dramatize the difference between the social and task areas, consider these extremes: a group of five people gathered together for no purpose other than to enjoy each other's company, and a group of robots or computers programmed to do a particular task. The five people who assembled for a social evening get to know one another. Their talk is aimed at this purpose and at entertainment and diversion. The members of this group will grow to like or dislike one another. What joy or despair each finds in the group will depend on how he relates to the others. The rewards of this group are uniquely social.

Five carefully programmed computers, their memory storages filled with information, can be connected with one another so that information is fed back and forth among them. This information can be processed and its output transferred to another machine. Certain sophisticated hook-ups in the space program have reached this stage of complexity. The computers in this small group can be programmed so that they are completely task-oriented. Such a group has no social dimension. One of the computers will not short circuit communication because he feels a loss of status within the group, nor will one computer resist instructions transferred from another because it dislikes the bossy attitude of that computer.

Most task-oriented groups fall on a continuum somewhere between these two extremes. They have both a social and a task dimension. However, *in no case where human beings are involved will the social dimension be unimportant.*

The social dimension includes the way members perceive, relate, and interact with one another. Much communication within the group will relate to the social–emotional needs of the participants. They must spend some time talking about their hobbies, their love lives, their problems, their reading habits, their children, their parents, and their travels. Such talk helps identify each individual as a person. If he finds that the other members enjoy his company and respect his judgment, he can relax and turn his attention to the job.

Few members are completely sure about how they stand in the group. If they perceive some task-related comment as a threat to their status, they then become preoccupied with social matters rather than task considerations. Inevitably, the items of a social nature on the group's agenda make it difficult for several people to concentrate their entire attention on the group's work.

THE TASK DIMENSION OF GROUP PROCESS

Task-oriented groups devote most of their time and effort to the work at hand. The problems posed by working together rather than alone complicate the group's effort. Coordinating several people for a job requires messages that are clear, adequate, and not redundant. The communication networks established within the group are crucial to this process. Through these networks flow the messages that the group uses to transmit information; test the soundness of statements of fact, opinion, and advice; create and combine concepts; and give directions. The group's ability to concentrate all its talents and energy on the task may be hampered by misunderstanding, faulty reasoning, inadequate conceptualizing, and by the way directions and orders are given and received. If two groups have ideal human relations and can thus concentrate maximum attention on the task, the group containing members with greater task skills will be most productive. Perhaps this fact is obvious, but sometimes students of group methods become so intrigued with the importance of the social dimension that they consider it exclusively.

While the next few chapters are related to the social dimension, the emphasis remains on the task-oriented group. Group work should be socially rewarding, but the student of discussion and group methods must understand all group functions. He must have task skills as well as human-relations skills.

cohesiveness

Man has been aware of one of the major features of groups at least since he began to record his history. Military commanders and athletic coaches long ago discovered the importance of teamwork, group loyalty, and morale. The troop or team that coordinated its activity and acted quickly as a unit was effective, and sometimes its members would be stimulated to extraordinary effort. They would catch fire and sustain one another in a maximum attempt at victory. Members of a group develop loyalty, a feeling of belonging, and a willingness to work for the good of everyone. Students of group methods refer to this feeling of loyalty and *esprit de corps* as *cohesiveness*.

A SYMPTOM OF GROUP HEALTH

The level of cohesiveness depends on the extent to which each individual has made the group's goals his own. If a fraternity member must get up at 6 A.M. to clean the bathroom, how willing is he to make this sacrifice? If a basketball player has intercepted a pass and is driving toward the basket, does he pass to a teammate for a sure goal, or does he himself shoot in the hope of increasing his own point total? The answers to such questions provide a partial index to the group's cohesiveness.

Cohesiveness is one dimension of small groups that applies successfully to large organizations. It is an important feature of such groups as the PTA, the business corporation, the teaching faculty, the student body, the Loyal Order of the Old Buffaloes, and Tri Zeta; and this discussion will include information useful to large as well as small groups.

In general, the more cohesive the group, the more uninhibited and unruly the work meetings will be. Each member feels sure of himself and his place. He can relax. He need not be continually on his guard. Matters of importance are attended to. The participants are interested and involved. They disagree. Bales and his associates at Harvard studied a number of different kinds of groups and discovered the most disagreements in husband-and-wife teams. The family group is often highly cohesive, and members feel free to disagree because they know the family will not break up as a result. The PTA or Lions Club, the League of Women Voters, or even men working together in the same office, often are not as cohesive; and the personnel of such organizations do not disagree as much as do the members of a family. People are nicer and more polite in groups composed of acquaintances than in their family group.

In addition to being polite, the members of a group with little cohesiveness seem bored and disinterested. Their conversation is desultory and punctuated by pauses, yawns, and sighs. They seem to want to finish the meeting quickly. When they disagree, they use gestures rather than words. They shake their heads, frown, or look away from the speaker.

Cohesive groups spend much time in social interplay. People make comments about family, friends, and other interests. They may take off their coats, loosen their ties, put their feet up on the desk, and are likely to use first names or nicknames. They make many comments about the excellence of the group. They mention its glorious past, its present achievements, and its future potential. Individuals are complimented when they do a good job. Members offer to help each other. They disagree and argue about decisions affecting the group. They show deference to high-status members.

Members of cohesive groups have come to share a common social reality. They have developed a group subculture that includes a common set of heroes, villains, saints, and enemies. They have similar attitudes, values, and emotions in regard to certain key human actions. They often have "in jokes" which consist of allusions to dramatizations of their common history or of their common fantasies.

The interactions of groups with little cohesiveness are the converse of these. Such groups talk about their work rather than about social matters. Much of this talk is devoted to procedures to be followed rather than to the work itself. When they do talk of irrelevancies, they pick safe topics like the weather. They seldom coin nicknames for each other and seem uncomfortable when using first names. Members seldom disagree and rarely argue. At a point where someone in a cohesive group would say, 'You're wrong!" or "I disagree!" an individual in a less cohesive group will say, "I don't understand," or "I'm confused." Members of groups with little cohesion have yet to create much of a common social reality. They have few common heroes, villains, saints, or enemies. They have few "in jokes" and are not sure that they share many common values, attitudes, or motives.

Cohesiveness is an easily misunderstood concept. Often students in small-group-communication classes will say that they did not do as well on the task as they should have because their group was "so cohesive." They go on to suggest that they did not want to thresh out issues related to task decisions which would bring about conflict because they were afraid such conflict would hurt their cohesiveness. Members of such groups confuse the flight-taking tendency of groups with cohesiveness. When groups are, indeed, cohesive, they do not fear the effects that disagreement and conflict in the task dimension can have on their social fabric. *Cohesive groups have strong enough social bonds to tolerate conflict.* The members of cohesive groups are so dedicated to the group's welfare that they must raise the thorny task-area issues and resolve them through productive conflict.

What often happens is that group members find in their early interaction in a new group that the social chit-chat is pleasant and rewarding. They like one another and get on well until they try to work cooperatively on a common task. Then they come into conflict which produces tension. They rationalize the good time they have socializing as cohesiveness (a good end in itself) and take flight into small talk whenever the task discussion threatens to get too uncomfortable.

Interestingly enough, some groups have the converse problem. They discover that trying to get acquainted and socializing is difficult because of emerging norms of social shyness or awkwardness. Such groups often take flight into the task dimension, usually with unsatisfactory results. Almost all communication in such groups is devoted to task matters, and yet they do not do well. In these instances, group members rationalize their flight-taking as being too task-oriented to do a good job.

COHESIVENESS AND GROUP EVALUATION

The cohesive group may seem to be simply a *good* group. However, groups in the pragmatic style should be judged on both their productivity and the soundness of their social dimension. Work groups should be judged by the quantity and quality of their work. Some find this criterion sufficient; but our democratic traditions emphasize the importance of the individual and stress that groups exist for the individual to some extent, rather than the opposite. Groups should be judged on the social satisfactions members receive from them as well as on their efficiency.

Of course, groups in the consummatory style are largely judged on the basis of member satisfaction.

Some people question the necessity of judging a pragmatic group on social grounds. However, the social dimension of task-oriented groups can be an end in itself. Member satisfaction with the group is related to its productivity. *But for certain kinds of work, a group may not be as efficient and productive as the same people working individually.* In these cases, the main virtue in doing the job through group effort comes from the by-products of the social dimension.

Much early small-group research was concerned with whether or not a group was more efficient than individuals. The question was relevant to the argument that if the citizens discussed all sides of a dispute, they would make the right decision. If a group could do a better job than an expert, this argument would be supported. The research results indicated that groups often made better decisions than most individuals, but that for many tasks, one or two of the most talented members could do a better job alone. One authority on organizational meetings, Norman Maier, suggests that management decisions be divided into two types: first, the problems that require a high-quality technical decision and, second, the problems that require a high level of group acceptance. For the situations that require a high-quality solution, he recommends an individual decision made after consultation with technical experts. For problems that require a high level of group acceptance, he suggests a group decision. Judging a group solely on the quality of its work leaves out the important dimension of group commitment to the decision.

More important, if the members of an organization believe that the individual should not be exploited by the group, the social dimension must be considered. Even in business and industrial organizations there is growing acceptance of the idea that employees must find satisfaction in their work, and that this is important over and above whatever effect morale may have on productivity and profits.

In general a highly cohesive group will be productive and its members will be pleased and happy. People can become very upset and disturbed in a highly cohesive group, however. To fail, to lose status, or to be unable to gain a prestige position is more painful than in a less cohesive group. The man who belongs to an important and tightly knit business organization may dedicate his life to it. He worries less about his success or failure in a loosely knit community organization like the PTA. The coed is more interested in her place in a highly cohesive sorority than in the loosely knit departmental club. The criterion that members be happy with the group adds another dimension to the notion of cohesiveness.

The highly cohesive group is more likely to be productive, and the overall social satisfactions of *most* members are likely to be greater than in a group that is not cohesive. Rensis Likert, a leading management consultant, and his associates at the Institute for Social Research at the University of Michigan as early as the 1950s discovered that cohesiveness was a vital concept to management. Likert discovered that "group loyalty" was related to productivity, employee morale, and communication efficiency. Highly cohesive groups have workers who cooperate and help one another. Work flows back and forth among the workers depending on the load, and they show more initiative in distributing and handling the overload in a crisis.

The highly cohesive group has a climate that maximizes feedback and therefore encourages more effective communication. Members of cohesive groups will ask for information they need because they have little fear of appearing ignorant and thereby losing status. They also, as indicated before, will disagree more. The member who feels a given decision is bad will raise questions. He cannot sit quietly and watch the group make a mistake. In organizations with low cohesiveness, people often allow the group to take unwise action rather than strain the social fabric with disagreements.

Cohesiveness is not static. A highly cohesive organization will change membership, the nature of the internal structure and interactions will change, and over a period of time the group may lose cohesiveness until it dies. The fraternity that has been a top organization for three or four years may degenerate until it becomes inactive. Indeed, group loyalty will fluctuate slightly from day to day.

Cohesiveness is a function of group composition plus interaction. The basic factor consists of the individual characteristics of the members such as age, sex, intelligence, and psychological and social needs. Added to this factor is the element of compatibility. How do individuals who join the group mesh with one another in terms of the overall composition of the group? Are they compatible or incompatible? Is the group homogeneous or heterogeneous with respect to such factors as dominance, intelligence, authoritarianism, and the need for structure in a social environment? Both of these factors relate to group composition. The final factor of interaction has to do with the way the group develops, and this incorporates the message content and communication patterns that dynamically create relationships among the members and create a common social reality, a common group culture.

member characteristics and cohesiveness

Each member brings to a new group his or her personal characteristics which influence the way the individual behaves and the way the others respond to that behavior. An individual's style of communication, typical reaction to others, and skills and abilities provide the basic raw material for group interaction and are thus of considerable importance in the dynamics of the group.

The biographical characteristics of members include such things as age, sex, physical features, intelligence, and communication ability. A good deal of research has been aimed at discovering the influence of individual characteristics on group process. Much of the research is difficult to compare because the investigators did not use similar scoring techniques to assign numbers to the various indexes and rating systems that they used to quantify individual characteristics. Thus, a short summary is sufficient to present the conclusions that have emerged from the research to date.

Age has an influence on member participation in groups in that social participation increases with age until the teenage years. Individuals tend to increase in their conformity to group norms from a young age until about 12, and then the conformity behavior tends to decrease with age.

Most researchers have assumed that sex differences affect small-group interaction and often tried to control their studies to rule out the effect of that variable, but few studies have been directed to specific questions relating to male–female behavior in small groups. Not only are there few studies relating to sex differences, but the few results that have accumulated over the years may well have been a function of cultural norms about women's roles in society. These norms are in the process of change with the recent growth of the women's liberation movement and the general change in society's norms in regard to role expectations for both sexes.

In a recent survey of research on sex differences, Shaw concluded that women are less self-assertive and less competitive in groups than men, use eye contact as a form of communication more frequently than men, and conform more to majority opinion than males do.

In recent years, students in the small-group-communication seminar at Minnesota have made a number of case studies and written a number of seminar papers which focused on the effect of the sexual composition of groups on group process.[1] Certainly the case studies at Minnesota do not reveal that women in general are less self-assertive or less competitive in groups than men. Quite typically, groups of five to seven members that contain three or four female members will also have at least one

---

[1] The conclusions about discussion groups were drawn from a large-scale program of research conducted by the author and his associates in the small-group-communication seminar at the University of Minnesota. Some of the work has been reported in unpublished doctoral dissertations, master's theses, convention papers, and journal articles, but the rest of this book reports in comprehensive fashion the results of this continuing research program. Frequent references will be made to the research results of these studies. They will subsequently be referred to in the text as the Minnesota Studies. See the Appendix for a more detailed description of the research program.

and often several women who are very self-assertive and competitive with males in the group. The tendency to find assertive and competitive females in groups in classes in discussion and small-group communication at Minnesota has accelerated with the growing popularity of ideas relating to female equality.

The Minnesota Studies also indicate that physical attractiveness and sexual interest have an effect on the communication and the interaction patterns in small groups and may affect the formation of coalitions and cliques and the emergence of group structure.

The case studies also reveal that age and sex interact in those groups where there is a considerable disparity of age; that is, if a group is composed of five individuals, four in their twenties and a fifth person who is forty or fifty years of age, the oldest person will have considerable difficulty finding a role as a peer in the group. A number of groups in the Minnesota Studies had one older woman as a member, and these women often became a preoccupation of the group. Frequently, the older women were intelligent, dependable, and efficient. Women who return to the university after raising a family and being influential in the community are often capable and assertive, and they frequently have extensive experience in managing important projects. The younger members typically expressed their resentment of capable older women by saying they did not want to be "mothered." The older women, in turn, were often intensely frustrated because they felt that the group could be much more effective, and they often worked very hard to make it so, only to have their ideas and efforts rejected as being too bossy, pushy, or aggressive.

The research also indicates that intelligence is correlated slightly with leadership, a bit more with activity, and with popularity, and the more intelligent person tends to be less conforming to group norms than the less intelligent. These correlations, while interesting, are not very strong and do not explain much about the development of group processes. Once again, the difficulty with past research lies with the use of testing procedures to score intelligence and then trying to correlate test scores with individual behavior in a social field as complex and powerful as that found in a small group.

member needs and cohesiveness

Each member brings to a new group his or her dreams, desires, and needs. While the group may modify or drastically convert the dreams and the expression of the needs, the latter do provide the energy that compels an individual to act in support of or counter to the achievement of group goals. Thus, an analysis of the way individual needs can be satisfied in a group provides a partial account of group cohesiveness.

An exchange theory is one that explains interpersonal behavior in terms of the exchange of costs and rewards on the part of the participants. Thibaut and Kelly formulated one important exchange explanation to account for *The Social Psychology of Groups.*[2]

The level of cohesiveness at any instant is a function of the forces affecting each member. There are always some centripetal forces pulling an individual into and some centrifugal forces pushing him out of the group. The centripetal forces consist of the material and psychological rewards that the group provides. The centrifugal forces consist of the costs that the group extracts from the individual. The rewards and costs cannot be assessed in isolation. An investigator determining the pull of a group on its members must provide a context of competing or *comparison* groups for each member. For example, if one of the rewards is a salary of $10,000 per year, he must examine the pull of this reward against the next best salary the person could make. If the next best salary is $7000, the monetary reward of the first group is stronger than if the next best offer is $9500. The comparison group is always the next *best* group.

REWARDS DEFINED

A typical dictionary definition suggests that a *reward* is a "recompense" that is "given for some service or attainment." In order to examine group attractiveness, however, the concept must be limited to those recompenses that the member finds attractive. The person who is offered a reward of $5 when he is expecting $100 may reject the offer in disgust. Psychologists studying the learning behavior of rats often use the term *reinforcement.* By this they mean a reward that makes the animal learn the behavior that brings the recompense. A *reward,* then, is a material or psychological recompense provided by the group, which is sufficient to reinforce individual behavior in the direction of group loyalty. Cost is the converse of this. A *cost* is a material or psychological punishment provided by the group, which is sufficient to extinguish an individual's group loyalty or reinforce his withdrawal behavior.

In the realm of human behavior, conventional definitions such as these can lead into circular reasoning. For example, the definition of reinforcement can result in explaining any bizarre behavior of an individual rat by saying he was reinforced to act in this way. But sometimes no explanation can be given for what served as the reinforcement or

---

[2] The exchange account of cohesiveness that follows is based on the Thibaut and Kelly framework; but it has been considerably modified by the Minnesota Studies and by the author's experience in teaching classes in small-group communication, working in adult continuing education, and consulting for commercial, industrial, religious, and governmental groups.

why it worked. The conventional definition of *reward* could lead in the same direction. If a member often has a temper tantrum and upsets the rest of the group, his behavior can be explained by saying that the group rewards him for his temper tantrums. If the group responds to the temper tantrums in a way that observers perceive to be punishing, the explanation can still be that it was not punishing to the person who had the tantrum. What reward does a man get from pounding his head against a stone wall? The circular answer is that nobody knows, but he must get some or he would not do it.

This circle can be broken by an explanation of how a given reward works. It is not enough to say that what the group does for member A is a reward because he acts as though it is a reward. An adequate explanation provides reasons for his behavior. An explanation of the rewards and costs that the group furnishes its members is given by an analysis of human needs.

MATERIAL REWARDS

Groups have the power to furnish their members with material rewards. In some cases this is as obvious as a $10,000 per year salary. Groups can also give an individual less obvious material rewards. Joining a certain country club may give an insurance salesman contacts that increase his commissions. Groups may encourage their members to do business with one another.

On the other hand, membership in a group may cost an individual money. He may have an opportunity to make $12,000 a year with another group. If he decides to stay despite the cost, he must gratify other needs. Even so, the fact that membership costs him money weakens the pull of the group on him. The group's dues may go up to the point where it is an extravagance for the member. Some groups may hurt his business. His association may bring him notoriety and economic retaliation.

Money may serve as a means to satisfy a number of human needs. If the member is physiologically deprived, he can buy food, clothing, drink, or medical care to satisfy his needs. Money can provide security and may even buy entrance into organizations that gratify social needs. For some individuals, material rewards can enhance the status within an organization, and even satisfy some self-esteem needs.

Perhaps the most obvious way in which a group can increase its cohesiveness is to increase the material rewards it furnishes its members. Raising salaries or paying bonuses will often increase the cohesiveness of the group. If the organization gives monetary rewards on the basis of group success rather than to individuals, the effect will be increased. An important study by Deutsch indicates that a spirit of competition *within* the group strains the bonds that hold it together. If the instructor sets up discussion groups and suggests that only one student will receive an A, that only one student will receive a B, a C, a D, and an F, the group will not develop much cohesiveness. Such a setting encourages each member to work for himself. Should the instructor evaluate the discussion as a whole and give each student a common group grade, cohesiveness would be encouraged.

Competition within the group is disruptive; competition among groups often increases cooperation. One of the strong forces for developing cohesiveness in athletic teams is the fact that they are competing with other teams. For many years, particularly after World War II, forensic contests in high school and college often included competition in public discussion. Students participated in discussions and received a rating.

Although the judges watched to see if a contestant was open-minded and cooperative, clever contestants soon found ways to make others in the group look bad. For example, the clever competitor waited until a knowledgeable member was rearranging his note cards to ask him for specific information. The member frequently became so flustered that he could not find the suitable card, and the judge would get the impression he was not as knowledgeable as he seemed. The bitterness that developed in these discussions disturbed many forensic directors, and the practice of having competitive tournaments waned in popularity. As the forensic tournament waned, contests arose in which discussion teams from various schools would compete with one another. The judges evaluated the quality of each team's work, and the group won or lost as a team. Such conditions were more hospitable to the development of cohesiveness. The same principles of cooperation and competition can be applied to the distribution of monetary rewards.

On occasion, an organization will want to use individual rewards. If managers wish to stimulate ingenuity to improve or increase productivity, individual incentives may be useful. If cohesiveness is a relatively minor feature of a loosely knit group in which most of the work is done by individuals in isolation, such as a group of writers, painters, or teachers, the rewards of individual incentives might be advisable.

SOCIAL REWARDS

The rewards that the group is uniquely able to provide are social in nature. The group furnishes refuge from loneliness. It provides man with friends and enemies, either within his own or within competing groups. He gains a sense of belonging from the group. He learns to know other people and to find that they like and respect him.

Any group has, ostensibly, every reason to be highly cohesive. The group furnishes its members with many rewards, both material and psychological. Yet a group can be torn with dissension, full of back-biting, rancor, and cliques. In such a social climate, members spend their time and energy feuding among themselves. For example, the Minnesota Studies of task-oriented groups of college students working together for 12 weeks on similar tasks and under comparable conditions reveal that roughly one of every four such groups was highly successful and cohesive, two were moderately so, and one was socially punishing. The major differences among these groups were the amount of social rewards they furnished their members. The greater the amount of social rewards, the greater the cohesiveness.

The importance of the social dimension of group work stems largely from the fact that man's basic social needs can only be met within a group context. To some extent, a group may satisfy an individual's security needs; that is, man needs not only a secure physical environment, but he requires some security within his social environment. He needs to know that his friends will remain friendly and that the people he trusts today will be trustworthy tomorrow. Groups can provide their members with a secure social environment.

Since groups can furnish such rewards, they can also deprive their members of these basic needs. Individuals can be rejected by the group. They may not receive affection but, rather, hostility and antagonism. The social climate of the group can be in a constant state of flux and thus deny the members a feeling of security in their social relationships.

The one dimension of groups that can be changed radically and consciously through an understanding of group methods is the social dimension, and fortunately so, since social satisfactions are important. This is true in small task-oriented discussion groups like those in discussion courses. Students can apply their knowledge about group methods to the practical problem of generating greater cohesiveness within their classroom discussion. Often they have no such freedom to structure material rewards or the other incentives to cohesiveness that are available to managers and supervisors in other organizations.

The student who wants a list of formulas with which to improve the social rewards and cohesiveness of his group will be disappointed. The social dynamics of a group are too complex to allow for simple principles that will cover a wide variety of situations. The next few chapters will discuss the social functioning of groups. The student who understands the basic process will be able to make wise choices and develop creative and comprehensive plans of action designed to increase the social rewards and cohesiveness of a particular organization.

ESTEEM AND PRESTIGE REWARDS

People strive for prestige largely because of their esteem needs, so the two concepts are closely related. However, prestige differs from esteem in one important respect. Prestige rewards can be conferred on an individual by an organization, but esteem must be earned. Since receiving prestige from an organization is often easier than earning esteem, the power of a group to confer prestige is one of its attractive features.

In a given community, similar groups will develop reputations of varying excellence. A sorority, for example, may develop a reputation of being the best sorority on campus. Any group has a spongelike ability to absorb the prestige of its members. Fraternities gain luster from members who are star athletes or leaders in student government. Of course, the group also suffers if its members have a bad reputation. It may try to protect itself by putting pressure on members not to bring disgrace on the organization.

In addition to absorbing the prestige of its members, the group develops a public image in its own right, by doing a good job. The business organization that shows a profit and gives a large dividend increases its prestige. In this regard, as in others relating to the development of cohesiveness, groups often undergo cyclical changes. Success increases the prestige. Increased prestige exerts a stronger pull on the members and develops greater cohesiveness, which in turn contributes to more success. If the cycle is broken by a change in personnel or by accident, the same cyclical development can occur in the opposite direction. Failure reduces the prestige, thus reducing the cohesiveness and contributing to future failures. Organizations often go through periods of boom and bust. A college gridiron power may have a series of national championships followed by a number of losing seasons. The saying that "Nothing succeeds like success" applies to the prestige of an organization.

Another factor that contributes to prestige is a high standard of membership. Open groups have more difficulty establishing a reputation than do those that restrict their membership. Many state universities and colleges must accept any qualified high-school graduate, while private schools restrict their enrollments. A parent may be proud of a daughter accepted at Wellesley or Smith or a son enrolled at Dartmouth or Princeton because such acceptance indicates that he and his family are "better" people.

Of course, open groups may have a good reputation because they are productive and are composed in part of important people, and an exclusive group may get a bad reputation. An exclusive prep school may restrict membership with a high tuition fee, and yet, because of poor curriculum, poor instructors, and because its students are reputed to be flunk-outs from other schools, the school may have little prestige.

On rare occasions, organizations with extremely bad reputations exert a strong pull on their members because they are all outcasts. For example, an organization composed of a persecuted minority group might be highly cohesive because it is a haven from discrimination and a bulwark against society.

Not only does the group absorb the prestige that the members bring to it, but *the group's prestige is transferable to each and every member.* By being publicly associated with an elite organization, an individual gains status within the community. He is rewarded because some of his important esteem needs have been fulfilled. The group's prestige may improve his self-image as well as his reputation and the amount of respect he receives from chance acquaintances. Prestige conferred by an organization is often less satisfying than esteem earned by the individual, but it is much easier to achieve. All one has to do to gain these rewards is to gain membership. To *earn* esteem, however, requires more work and talent.

An organization furnishes a context in which esteem rewards can be earned. In every organization, some people become important and well liked. Other members listen to the esteemed person's comments, weigh his suggestions carefully, seek and follow his advice. Such direct and personal esteem rewards are among the most powerful factors drawing a person into a group.

Prestige rewards are also provided internally by the high-status positions within an organization. They explain the increased feeling of cohesiveness that often accompanies election to a position of formal leadership. Often a member who is only moderately committed will, upon election to an office, work very hard for the organization.

The members of an organization with a bad reputation experience some deprivation of their esteem needs. The last-place team is less attractive to its members than the championship team. The most important deprivation of an individual's esteem needs, however, usually results from his lack of standing *within* the organization. A low-status member finds the group socially punishing. If the others fail to pay attention to him as a person and ignore his opinions and feelings, the group deprives his esteem needs.

An organization may increase its cohesiveness by establishing a good reputation within the community. Ultimately the group's reputation rests on the quality of its membership and the effectiveness of its work, but these qualities must be communicated to the public. The group should pay some attention to public relations. A judicious use of the mass media is advisable. Members should work out informal communication channels so that the right people hear about the good works of the organization. The organization may encourage and organize this grapevine systematically to assure its success.

Organizations often attach the prestige of the group firmly to each individual by the use of some publicly displayed, clearly identified symbol. If the group does not wish to adopt a crest or a coat of arms, the members may get the same effect from a common mode of dress. The members of a high-school clique may all wear dirty buckskin shoes, or a similar hair style, or leather jackets. The group may adopt certain slang words that identify them to the general public. The difficulty with informal modes of identification is that outsiders may adopt them. Thus, the ruling clique of the high school may have to discard dirty buckskins because everybody is wearing them.

Influential members should take the time and effort to help a member gain esteem. Even the new recruit in the last rank can be assured by word and deed that he is an important part of the group. The group often tells him that "No group is stronger than its weakest member [no chain is . . .] and we are strong because every man is a good man. Everyone is vital to the workings of this organization." The group should support their words with actions. One problem in dealing with the social maintenance of groups is that insincerity and attempts to manipulate the group by correct behavior only work for a short time. When people work together for more than a few hours, they soon recognize the person who is insincere, and his attempt to manipulate them fails.

Individuals tend to be more strongly committed to a group if they have had to overcome a number of barriers to achieve membership. If a person must be invited to become a member or must in some way prove himself before he is selected, the prestige of the organization is likely to be increased.

In addition, if the new member must go through a testing period before he becomes a full-fledged member and if each test is more difficult than the last, the cohesiveness of those who survive will be increased. Some research by social psychologists suggests that the old practice of hazing may be more than sadism and may, indeed, increase *esprit de corps* for some organizations. The pledge class that goes through hell week together is often welded into a cohesive unit.

The loyalty that develops in members that "have been through hell together" helps account for low-prestige groups that are highly cohesive. Although the combat infantry was the least prestigeful branch of the service, the infantryman who had survived a number of battles developed a feeling of commitment to the infantry and to his comrades that was one of his strongest sources of support and one of the major reasons for the success of the infantry squads as fighting units.

ACHIEVEMENT REWARDS

In addition to furnishing rewards that satisfy all the basic needs, groups are attractive because they offer their members opportunities for personal growth. They may provide a chance for both self-actualization and self-transcendence. The two main achievement rewards furnished by organizations are those of work satisfaction and the opportunity to fight for a cause.

The task-oriented group requires that each member do a certain amount of work. It may enable someone to do the kind of work he or she likes. The teacher who enjoys teaching drama and directing plays will be attracted to a high school with such a job available. This organization provides the member with an opportunity for self-actualization. A person may sacrifice some material rewards, particularly if his physiological and security needs are gratified, in order to gain work satisfactions.

If the organization requires an individual to do jobs that he dislikes, it loses some of its attraction. It may require him to ring doorbells and ask for donations. Insofar as he dislikes the work the group asks him to do, the member will feel less committed to it.

The desire to do a good job, to make a contribution to other people, to feel that life has meaning over and above the satisfying of one's deficit needs are all met by work satisfactions that an organization can sometimes provide. If the member does important and difficult tasks and sees opportunities for additional training and competence, he can gratify some of his desire for self-actualization.

A number of organizations are dedicated to religious or spiritual objectives. Closely related to these are the groups organized to fight for a cause or a world view. Such groups exert a considerable pull on their membership because they provide an opportunity to transcend the self and find a larger meaning in life.

Joining an organization with a cause that the individual considers important is positive action. He may feel that he is having a positive effect on the course of history. Such a group can help assuage his guilt feelings. The Puritan religious heritage stresses that everyone is sinful and guilty and must be saved, and that once an individual is saved, he must work actively to save others. If he does not do so, he partakes of their guilt. Rewards of this type often create a level of commitment that exceeds any that can be generated by rewarding the needs on the deficit ladder. History is filled with examples of individuals who chose to give their lives fighting for a cause.

A widely used rule for increasing group commitment is that a new member must be given a job. If every person has work that fulfills his growth needs, cohesiveness will increase. Various people will, all other things being equal, enjoy some jobs more than others. Insofar as the group finds congenial work for the maximum number of members, to that extent the work satisfactions will increase.

The group can provide additional rewards by appreciating the end product. The part-time potter shows her vase to friends and they admire it; the hobbyist shows off his end table. Seldom do either of them find enough satisfaction in solitary contemplation of their work. They enjoy the vase or end table much more if others are aware of the work and appreciate it. Thus, the organization that gives all members worthwhile tasks to perform and then appreciates the work when well done will increase its cohesiveness.

Some organizations that work for causes or that are dedicated to a specific religious view cannot change their goals to increase cohesiveness. On the other hand, some organizations have ostensible spiritual purposes or stated world views, but their real purposes are different. In that case, they may be able to manipulate the "platform" or the "dogma" to make it more palatable to the membership.

Even when the goals cannot be changed, some attention to this factor can improve the cohesiveness of the group. The organization can clearly spell out its benefits and reiterate them to the membership. If the stand is unequivocal and radical, the cohesiveness of the group will be increased. The number of people drawn to the group will be smaller, but those who are attracted will be more dedicated. The group with clear goals that the members perceive as realistic is likely to be cohesive.

If the cause can be changed, the group often can draft a more attractive platform. If the political party's main purpose is to get candidates elected rather than to fight for certain programs, its platform may be abstract and ambiguous in order to avoid discouraging potential supporters. This strategy, however, will reduce the pull of the cause or spiritual satisfaction, and the group must increase other rewards to achieve high cohesiveness.

group composition and member needs

This discussion of the way groups reward or punish members has been in general terms. Like much of the early laboratory research in groups, it is an "input–output" account of group attractiveness; that is, the framework suggests that members with certain needs enter a group, interact, and emerge rewarded or punished. A complete account of group cohesiveness should include a process analysis of what happens within the group to reward or punish the members and to create a common social reality and a group identity. The first step in such an account is to examine the *assembly effect* resulting from the particular composition of a given group. The *assembly effect* is the idiosyncratic behavior of a group which stems from the particular combination of individuals that comprise it. Much of the research aimed at discovering the effects of such characteristics as age, sex, and intelligence on group process foundered because of the complexity of factors contributing to the assembly effect in groups. Groups of four or more allow for a bewildering variety of combinations and permutations of traits, which are usually too complex to explain in terms of one or two characteristics. For instance, in a group with only four members and considering only the two characteristics of age and sex, member A could be young and female, old and female, young and male, or old and male. Each of the three remaining members could be one of the four combinations. Thus, there are 16 possible combinations of the two characteristics. With five-person groups, these two characteristics furnish 32 possible combinations.

Thus, while the student of small-group communication should be aware of past efforts to account for group outcomes on the basis of the personality of members, the investigators usually posed research questions that were too general and limited to too few characteristics to yield results of more than academic interest.

Investigators studying the assembly effect have often based their research on the assumption that some ideal combination of member characteristics would result in highly compatible groups. The researchers assumed that if they could isolate the key personal characteristics and scale them in some way, then they could discover the most compatible combinations as indicated by evaluations of group productivity and member satisfaction. If such research discovered the factors contributing to compatible groups, then the practical results would be substantial. People who had to form task-oriented groups could then give some paper-and-pencil tests to a pool of possible group members and select individuals on the basis of the best combinations and assure compatible, productive, and satisfying groups. Common-sense experience in working with groups provided some hope for the success of such projects. Experienced administrators often have the notion that certain people would work more effectively than others in committees, task forces, and work projects. The notion that, as members in the case studies at Minnesota often put it, "We just seemed to get along well together," reflects a common experience and makes the search for the factors that make for compatibility plausible.

One body of research fits in with the exchange framework of costs and rewards developed above in that it was based on the concept of need compatibility. The assumption of much of the research was that when the needs of two or more members could be mutually satisfied through interaction and communication in the group, then the group would be more cohesive. The research in need compatibility is illustrated by the work of Schutz, who isolated three individual needs that he felt were important to compatible or incompatible group composition. Schutz and his associates called the approach the "Fundamental Interpersonal Relations Orientation," or FIRO. The needs consisted of *inclu-*

sion (the need to be noticed and to have esteem and prestige), *control* (the need to dominate and have power over others), and *affection* (the need for friendship and close personal ties). Schutz developed a general account of compatibility that suggested that certain combinations of needs among members of a group would result in greater productivity and cohesiveness.

Although confined to only three needs, FIRO was nonetheless an extremely complex system. Schutz expanded the approach to include three different types of compatibility, and, thus, he could compute compatibility indexes for each of the three types within each of the three need areas, which resulted in 16 different compatibility indexes. Schutz and his associates conducted a number of studies to test the FIRO assumptions, and their findings generally supported the hypotheses. Other studies, however, failed to discover the effects of compatibility anticipated by the FIRO account. Although Schutz's approach was more complex and sophisticated, his research questions may have been too complex to be answered by the scaling devices currently available to the small-group researcher.

In addition to research into compatibility of needs, some further work dealt with compatibility of displayed role functions. A group of investigators studied the behavior of group members as anticipated from tests of personality characteristics. The investigations into member behavior have been largely confined to studies of dominance and authoritarianism. The studies tend to indicate that different combinations of dominant–submissive individuals do yield more or less compatible groups. The work on authoritarianism has not produced unequivocal results. Again the dynamic interplay of five or more people within a small group is so complex that whatever features of behavior a pencil-and-paper test can distinguish among research subjects, they are often washed out among the powerful forces within the social field.

A final group of studies deals with the compatibility implied by creating homogeneous or heterogeneous groups according to some member characteristic such as intelligence, sex, or personality profile. The results of such investigations are of interest in a suggestive rather than definitive way. Generally the research suggests that groups with heterogeneous membership as to ability perform better than groups that are homogeneous, that members of groups composed of males and females conform more than all-female or all-male groups, and that groups heterogeneous as to personality profiles of members are more effective in the task area than groups with homogeneous membership.

To this point, the Minnesota Studies have isolated only one member characteristic that seems related to interaction and communication within the group meetings strongly enough to be discernible. Members of natural groups in the discussion classes at Minnesota appear to vary as to their need for group structure. Some members of most groups need a defined structure which includes clearly stated goals for meetings and termination dates for larger projects. They need an agenda or a plan of action that is relatively specific and clear. They need to know what they are to do for the group and what they can anticipate others will do at certain clearly specified times. At the other end of the continuum, some members of most groups dislike structure. They feel restricted and hemmed in by an agenda. They prefer a free-wheeling discussion and like to "kick ideas around." They want to enjoy the play of ideas and the discussion itself and dislike a preoccupation with time pressures and deadlines.

In the early phases of a group's development, those members who need structure are often frustrated by what they perceive to be the group's aimless wallowing around. They often suggest plans that would structure the group more clearly. They prepare agendas or, if sufficiently frustrated, grow angry and demand that the group pay attention to the passage of time and the need to get something done. On the other hand, should the group develop ways of working that are highly structured, particularly if the norms result from a dominant individual's aggressive efforts, the members who dislike structure will be frustrated. They will frequently withdraw from participation after several attempts to inject what they perceive to be exciting or important ideas are met by group communications about time pressures, deadlines, or to the effect that the comment is off the topic. They will often report in their journals of group experience that they dislike the group and that it is being run by a dictator and that the group seems eager to get something, anything, accomplished even if the work is worthless.

Homogeneity of structure needs tends to make for an easier time in getting the group under way. Group work norms emerge more easily, and members tend to be more satisfied earlier in a leaderless group discussion that is relatively homogeneous as to members' needs for structure. Homogeneity of low structure needs tends to make for a boisterous and stimulating conversation. On occasion, groups may spend an entire meeting on tangents unrelated to their task.

Heterogeneity of structure needs makes it more difficult for groups to evolve norms and roles. Quite often, members with widely varying needs for structure will develop "personality conflicts," and, if several members have strong needs for structure and several others have a distaste for it, the group may divide into coalitions that work counter to one another. On the other hand, some good groups in the Minnesota Studies were composed of members with high and low structure needs. These groups developed work norms that exploited the contributions that both structured and unstructured members gave to the task dimension. The structured members learned to tolerate periods of unstructured brainstorming or "mulling things over" at appropriate points in the group's grappling with a task. At those points where the group had to get the "lay of the land" and find out what various members thought of the situation or where the group needed a different angle on a problem that was proving difficult to solve, the structured people went along with the creative, free-associative, elliptical communicative give-and-take that the unstructured members enjoyed. Often the seemingly unstructured periods of group meetings produced new perspectives and creative solutions. On the other hand, once the group made a decision, the unstructured members learned to tolerate and even appreciate the way the other members would swing into action to lay plans, set deadlines, and mobilize the group's resources.

Unfortunately there is, as yet, no easy scale or test for assessing a person's need for structure while working in a small task-oriented group. Investigators at Minnesota used the case-study procedure to identify the characteristic. The case study involves both participant and nonparticipant observers listening to tape recordings and watching videotapes of group meetings to identify communication associated with the characteristic, as well as group and individual interviews to discover participant perceptions in regard to the need for structure. Most of the groups at Minnesota that worked out ways to accommodate both high and low structure needs in members did so through group discussions of their work procedures and of the various individuals' need for structure. Often individuals will discover that they desire structure in a group when they previously thought of themselves as more comfortable in an unstructured situation and vice versa. Conceivably, the need for structure is not a consistent characteristic which an individual takes from group to group, but it may be, to some extent, a function of the group's social field.

The concept of need for group structure is most useful for those groups that have been interacting for some time and that find themselves dissatisfied with their work procedures. Often members of such groups can discuss their group process and use the concept of individual needs for structure to discover some of their difficulties. If they discover they have a heterogeneous group as to needs for structure, that might account for some of their troubles, and they could then go on to try to change their procedures so that the group would be rewarding for all members.

group process and cohesiveness

Although individual characteristics and group composition are important to cohesiveness, in the final analysis what happens once the members meet and begin working together is of overriding concern. The communication networks and the messages that flow through them ultimately determine the attractiveness of the group for its members. The chapters on small-group-communication theory that follow present many of the dynamics that account for how individual needs are met or frustrated in a group. The dynamic process of role emergence is important to an understanding of the attractiveness of a group for an individual as is the process of group acculturation. The student of small-group communication will find much in the subsequent chapters that relates back to the way the unfolding communication within a small group contributes to the group's cohesiveness. The remainder of this chapter only anticipates the more detailed treatment to follow and concentrates on the way that group communication creates a common social reality which may contribute to or detract from the group cohesiveness.

GROUP FANTASIZING

For a number of years, the small-group-communication seminar at Minnesota has studied the decision-making process in group discussion. The seminar began in 1959 with two major lines of inquiry. One consisted of content analysis of group meetings and the other of extended case studies of natural groups either in the classroom or in the community. Careful case studies conducted over a period of several months provided an understanding of group process and communication that was often much more complete and useful than much of the quantitative data generated by various category systems. In an attempt to develop a method of process analysis that would capture some of the richness of case studies and still allow for generalization, the seminar attempted to make a rhetorical analysis of the communication in group discussions by studying the transcripts of group meetings, much as a critic might analyze the text of a public speech.

The attempts to make a rhetorical criticism of small-group communication were given direction and impetus in 1970 when Bales published *Personality and Interpersonal Behavior*. Bales presented one of the most elaborate analyses of the relationship between personality characteristics and group roles in the research literature. However, the book also reported that Bales and his associates had discovered something very like what had intrigued the seminar at Minnesota while working with natural groups in the classroom. Bales developed a dramatistic approach to aid in the study of small-group dynamics and provided a key part to the puzzle of how group communication creates cohesion when he discovered the dynamic process of group fantasizing. Bales provided the student of small-group communication with an account of how dramatizing communication creates a social reality for a group of people and a way to examine the dramatizing for insights into the group's culture, motivation, emotional style, and cohesion.

Bales and his associates originally developed 12 categories to use in making a content analysis of the communication in small groups. One of the categories was to "show tension release," but over the years the investigators changed the category to "dramatizes." Continued work with the communication coded into the category of dramatizes led to the discovery of "group fantasy events." Some, but not all, of the communication coded as dramatizes was chained out through the group. The tempo of the conversation picked up. People grew excited, interrupted one another, blushed, laughed, forgot their self-consciousness. The tone of the meeting, which was often quiet and tense immediately prior to the dramatizing, became lively, animated, and boisterous. The chaining process involved both verbal and nonverbal communication indicating participation in the drama.

The intriguing question, of course, is why do some dramas chain out and not others? Bales provided a psychoanalytical accounting that was heavily Freudian. One can accept the importance of the chaining out of dramas to the group's culture without the Freudian explanation; a rhetorician, for instance, might account for the chaining out on the basis of the skill with which the original drama was presented.

Bales distinguished three important dimensions to the communication events coded into the dramatizes category. The first dimension related to the manifest content of the messages. What do the group members say? The answer is that the content consisted of characters, real or fictitious, playing out a dramatic situation in a setting removed in time and space from the here-and-now transactions of the group. (The "here-and-now" is a concept borrowed from sensitivity and encounter-group practice and refers to what is immediately happening in the group. Thus, a recollection of something that happened to the group in the past or a dream of what the group might do in the future could be considered a fantasy theme.)

The second dimension of a fantasy chain was the drama as a mirror of the group's here-and-now and its relationship to the external environment. The drama played out somewhere else or in some other time often symbolized a role collision or ambiguity, a leadership conflict, or a problem related to the task-dimension of the group. Just as an individual's repressed problems might surface in dream fantasies, so a group's hidden agenda might surface in a fantasy chain, and a critic might interpret the manifest content with an eye to discovering the hidden agenda.

The third dimension of the drama was sometimes an expression in a given social field of the individual psychodynamics of the participants.

Bales argued that the past history of each individual affected the personality of the participants, and, thus, a given theme might cut more closely to the personal problems of some participants than others. Since psychodynamic problems are often repressed, some members might be more resistant to participating in discussion of a theme than others. When a member introduces a dramatic theme, either by telling a story or a personal experience, there will be differing amounts of resistance among the members to chaining into the drama. Some would find it relatively easy to mention the theme and pick it up. Others would resist the theme because it would cut too deeply and personally and make them uncomfortable. Under group pressure, however, once the theme was picked up and embroidered and reinforced by several members, a person's resistance might be overcome by the group pressure; when such people join in the chain, they contribute considerable emotional tone to the discussion. When the chaining goes so far that it cuts too deeply for some members of the group, it will be dropped as abruptly as it began.

Because of the differing composition of needs and problems of members, the dramatic themes that are chained out in one group are likely to be different from those that catch on in another. Each group will develop its interpersonal dimension somewhat differently. The struggles for roles and status will be dependent on situational elements as well as on the talent of the others in the group. The details of the group's here-and-now problems will often be somewhat idiosyncratic. Some important and universal themes such as those dealing with power, authority, and leadership may, however, chain through many different groups.

To what purpose, then, might an investigator study a group's communication to discover, describe, and evaluate their moments of dramatization? Bales suggested that such study could reveal basic here-and-now problems of the group, give insight into the personal psychodynamics of individuals in the group, and reveal important features of the group's culture.

Future chapters deal with the chaining fantasies as they relate to role emergence, leadership styles, decision making, and group acculturation. Here the discussion deals with the way the group members come to perceive the group as an entity and to participate publicly in celebrating certain common values and attitudes by the process of chaining fantasies.

During the course of a meeting, members will usually make a number of comments that observers will code as dramatizations. Not all of the dramatizations will result in the chaining process. The group tends to ignore dramas that are not related to either its here-and-now problems or to the individual psychodynamics of the members. Those situations and characters that do get the members of the group to empathize, to improvise on the same theme, or to respond emotionally not only reflect common preoccupations of the members, but serve to make those commonalities public.

When group members respond emotionally to a dramatic situation, they publicly proclaim some commitment to an attitude. Indeed, improvising in a spontaneous group dramatization is a powerful force for changing member attitudes. Dramas also imply motives, and, by chaining into the fantasy, members gain motivations. Since some of the characters in the fantasies are presented as sympathetic people doing laudable things, the group collectively identifies, in symbolic terms, proper codes of conduct. A comparison with the more direct here-and-now methods of establishing common ground can clarify the function of fantasy chains. One way to discover common values and attitudes in a zero-history group with a job to do is to confront the question directly. A member in a discussion group in a class may say, "I think we all want to do a good job, and we should all go to the library and do a lot of work. I know I'm willing to do that." If the others enthusiastically respond with comments like, "Yes, that is a good idea." "Good. Let's go to work," the problem is dealt with directly. The fantasy discovers the same ground symbolically by having members chain out in, for instance, the following fashion:

> "Last semester my roommate took this course, and he never worked so hard for a class in his life."
> "Really?"
> "Yeah, it was really great though. He took field trips to hospital labs and everything."
> "Yeah, I know this girl who took the course, and she said the same thing. She said you wouldn't believe how hard they worked. But she said she really got something out of it."
> "You know I don't mind working if you get something out of it."
> "I'm really looking forward to it."

Other values and attitudes are similarly tested and legitimatized as common to the group by the fantasy chains. Religious and political dramas are tested. If someone dramatizes a situation in which a leading political figure is a laughing stock and the story falls flat, that particular political attitude and value has been exhibited to the group but they have failed to legitimatize it. However, should the group chain out on that drama and improvise other laughable situations in which the politician has appeared as a buffoon, the group will have created a common character which they can allude to in subsequent meetings and elicit a smiling or laughing response. (They have created an inside joke, but they have also created an attitude toward a given political figure and the position that the character symbolizes.)

By participating in chaining fantasies the group gradually evolves a group culture. Bales points out that:

> As the individual person creates and maintains a system of symbols with other persons in a group, he enters a realm of reality, which he knows does or can surpass him, survive him; which may inspire or organize him, and which may threaten to dominate him as well. He "comes alive" in the specifically human sense as a person in communication with others, in the symbolic reality which they create together, in the drama of their action. It is presumably this feeling that is referred to when people talk about "becoming a group," or "the time we became a group." . . . One may feel exalted, fascinated, perhaps horrified or threatened, or powerfully impelled to action, but in any case, involved. One's feelings fuse with the symbols and images which carry the feeling in communication and sustain it over time. One is psychologically taken into a psychodramatic fantasy world, in which others in the group are also involved. Then one is attached also to those other members.[3]

In the final analysis, group cohesion is not something that results from member characteristics or from the composition of the group, but rather it is created by the communication of the group members. By their communication they create new meanings, new attitudes, and new emotions and motives as symbolized in the personalities and actions they dramatize. Cohesion and interaction do not have a reality outside of the communication of the group. Members do not communicate about their cohesiveness and their interaction, they create the meanings and motives associated with their group in the process of communicating with one another.

The case studies of group fantasizing at Minnesota reveal that groups vary greatly as to the amount of fantasizing they do. Some groups seldom dramatize their past or their future; members rarely tell jokes or stories or personal experiences; the group seldom chains into current events. They stick doggedly to the here-and-now problems facing the group, and their communication is largely discursive. They discuss the facts related to their problem and the best way of proceeding. Some groups in the Minnesota Studies have had only three or four fantasies that chained out in as many as 20 or 30 hours of meetings. Other groups set norms of fantasizing and may spend several hours in one meeting participating in loud boisterous fashion in a series of narratives.

[3] Robert F. Bales, *Personality and Interpersonal Behavior.* New York: Holt, Rinehart and Winston, 1970, pp. 151–152.

Groups that do little fantasizing are seldom highly attractive and cohesive. Such groups tend to be boring and ordinary. The cohesive groups have usually done considerable fantasizing, but not all groups that fantasize a lot are rewarding and cohesive. The fantasies that chain may contribute to creating a social reality that is warm, friendly, and hard working, that provides the group with a strong identity and self-image, and that gives the members a sense of purpose and meaning for their group's work. On the other hand, the fantasies may develop a group climate that is punishing, fascinating, but frustrating.

Some case studies at Minnesota discovered groups torn by dissension in which members were so frustrated by the group that they were aroused to hate other members and the group itself. Yet the group not only continued to meet, but the members would schedule extra meetings which would go on for hours. Fantasy-theme analysis provides a partial explanation for the apparent masochism of the members in frustrating groups. The members of the fascinating groups did a great deal of chaining into fantasy themes either in coalitions or in the entire group. The themes of the group's common fantasies, however, tended to be conflict-ridden and highly emotional. The humor associated with the dramas tended to be ridicule, sarcasm, or satire. The emotions aroused by the dramas tended to be scorn or hate. The dramatic action lines tended to be destructive or sado-masochistic. Participating in the groups came to have a fascination for their members something like that of attending a compelling horror film or observing an unpleasant accident. The members often reported in their diaries that they were ambivalent about attending the meetings, yet they could not get the group off their mind and in the end they could not stay away. One group, for example, was unable to stabilize roles or assign leadership because of a strong female contender in conflict with a strong but lazy male who felt that woman's place was in the home. As the group continued and the woman remained active and adamant, the lazy male began to miss meetings; and, although the group failed to follow the woman, no male emerged to lead the group. Another male who was in early contention became ill and could not attend some of the crucial meetings. The group created a culture that was filled with dramas of conflict and cutting one another down. One of the continuing fantasies was the castration drama. The group was discussing population problems, and, in the course of discussing methods of control, one member jokingly said the group "could send a man around with a meat cleaver." The group laughed, and a male member chained in with "Ah, I have to go." Later in the discussion the group returned to the theme.

MEMBER A: We'll just have to start breeding smaller people, lighter people who don't weigh as much, don't eat as much.

MEMBER B: How can you do that . . . kind of regulated by genes . . .

MEMBER A: All small people are getting bred out anyway.

MEMBER C: (*male*) I'd volunteer to be a breeder, but I'm too big to breed little people.

MEMBER B: (*female leader contender*) Get the meat cleaver.

The castration drama became a major theme of their discussions, and all that was necessary for a strong emotional response was for a member to allude to it.

FANTASY CHAINS AND THE DEVELOPMENT OF A HISTORY AND TRADITION

Group fantasy chains are the mechanism by which the members develop a group history and group traditions. No collection of individuals can become a group until the group has an identity. A zero-history group begins with a collection of individuals. After the members have met for a time and chained into several fantasies, someone may mention "our group." At this point the group has been identified. Cohesive groups strengthen the identification and come eventually to characterize their group as a "lively group" or a "quiet group" or an "efficient group." They have identified a collective personality, and that collective personality comes to play a leading role in some of their fantasies. The group is still composed of individuals, but it is somewhat different from the sum of the individuals. Not only are individuals playing parts in the group dramas, but now a new character, the group's corporate personality, begins to appear in their pantheon of heroes, villains, saints, and sinners.

Students of group methods have argued at great length about whether or not there actually is such a thing as a group, above and beyond the sum of the individuals composing the group, but that philosophical question need not be raised here. The fact is that people perceive groups as though they had an identity. When members begin to characterize the group as an entity in its own right, they have made an important step in the direction of group cohesiveness.

The perception of something new called *our group*, however, poses difficult problems. The group, as a concept, is extremely abstract and ephemeral. One can see the members sitting about talking with one another, but the entity of *the group* that is more than the sum of these parts is difficult to visualize. The group succeeds in identifying the entity by the process of fantasy chains in which the group is personalized in the form of a character, usually the protagonist, in a series of dramatic actions. The group members use two main rhetorical devices to create the group character. One way for members to visualize their group is to create a character of a certain sex, size, costume, and aspect that symbolizes the group. Much as a political cartoonist will create a character who is male, small, bewildered looking, and wearing a mustache and call him "John Q. Public" or a character with a tall hat and a beard called "Uncle Sam," so may group members create a character to symbolize the group. Athletic teams frequently use the device of a cartoonlike mascot to symbolize the group. The Minnesota Vikings have a character with a long drooping mustache and a helmet outfitted with horns that symbolizes their team. They often have an actor dressed as a Viking on the sidelines at their games. A more common way to visualize the group is by the device of personification. The members give the group the characteristics of an individual and talk of the way their group thinks, works, and plays.

When a series of fantasies have chained through a group dramatizing events that happened to the members because of their common activities and communications, the group begins to develop a collective memory. Once a group memory has been systematically developed, one finds it easy to perceive the group as unique and as something more than the people who compose it. The group history provides the old members with a sense of purpose and direction for the future. New members can learn of the group's past and become indoctrinated into the group's culture. Old and large organizations often have their history carefully researched by a professional historian. Many fraternity manuals contain a history, which each new member must read.

Groups often recall their history in a less systematic and formal (and less authentic) way. From time to time members will reminisce about something that happened to them as they worked together. Such reminiscenses inevitably fall into dramatic form with group members or the group itself as characters in the drama. When the reminiscenses chain out, they create the group's history. When members of a group participate in a fantasy of what has happened to them in the past, what the group has done, and how it was done, the abstract notion of a *group* takes on an added social reality. A member may well perceive the group as an entity with a life of its own. The group may seem much like an individual with the members functioning in the way the cells function in the human body. Just as cells die and are replaced while the basic physical structure and personal characteristics of the human remain, so may a person come to believe that, while the membership in the group may change, the group itself can endure.

When the group develops a collective memory, certain key and salient fantasy chains may be reenacted as traditions. Initiation rituals furnish an example of traditions that serve to recall the group's identity and history. Groups often develop traditional ways of observing important occasions in the group's life.

The member, surrounded by the traditions of the group, reminded of its history, reenacting important fantasy chains from the past, often feels that the group is more important than he is and that it existed before he did and will continue to exist after he leaves. When an individual commits time and effort to such a group and makes sacrifices for it, he gets a chance for self-transcendence.

summary

The task-oriented group has two basic dimensions: social and task. The social dimension includes the way in which members perceive, relate, and interact with one another. The task dimension consists of the communication and behavior directed toward achieving the work objectives.

The task-oriented group should be judged on both of its dimensions. First, the good group is productive. It does its work efficiently and well. Second, the good group rewards its members socially. They are committed to the group and enjoy working with the other members.

Cohesiveness is a function of both group composition and interaction. The first important factor is comprised of the individual characteristics of the members; the second is the way the individuals mesh with one another; the third is the way the group develops dynamically.

The level of cohesiveness at any given instant is the sum of forces affecting each member. The centripetal forces consist of the rewards the group provides; the centrifugal, of the costs it extracts. These cannot be assessed in isolation, but must be determined in the context of a comparison, which is the next best group a member could join.

Groups can provide their members with a wide range of rewards of varying attractiveness depending on how frustrated an individual's deficit needs may be. Among the important rewards that groups provide are money and other material goods; a feeling of security, of belonging, of being well liked, and of self-esteem and importance; groups can provide an opportunity to grow as a productive person. One important form of self-transcendence is to lose oneself in a group battling for a good cause.

The assembly effect is the behavior of the group which stems from the particular combination of individuals that comprise it. Most of the research into the assembly effect has been directed to discovering compatibility of needs or responses in a group.

Although individual characteristics and group composition are important, the way the members communicate with one another is of overriding concern.

The dynamic process of group fantasizing is an important way the group creates cohesion. By participating in chaining fantasies, the group gradually evolves a culture. Group fantasy chains are the mechanism by which the members develop a group history and group traditions. The group history provides the old members with a sense of purpose and direction for the future. The member, surrounded by the traditions of the group, reminded of its history, and reenacting important fantasy chains from the past, is often strongly attracted to the group.

QUESTIONS FOR STUDY

1. What is the difference between the social and the task dimension of group process?
2. What criteria would you use to evaluate a group?
3. Why has much of the research on member characteristics and cohesiveness failed to yield useful results?
4. What mechanism may a group use to provide its members with achievement rewards?
5. What mechanism may a group use to provide its members with esteem and prestige rewards?
6. Why might a group with little prestige in the community nonetheless develop a great deal of cohesiveness?
7. What is the "assembly effect"? How has it been studied?
8. How do the members' needs for structure affect group interaction?
9. What is the dynamic process of group fantasizing?
10. How do group fantasy chains contribute to group cohesiveness?

EXERCISES

1. Select a group that you have worked with for a period of months, and describe its cohesiveness. List the steps that you might take to increase the group's cohesiveness.
2. Select a group that will allow you to tape record their meetings. Listen to the tapes, and discover the fantasy themes that chain out. Make an analysis of the group's culture, and estimate its attractive and unattractive features for the members on the basis of the fantasy themes.
3. Select a group that you are working with, and give the members Schutz's FIRO-B test (Fundamental Interpersonal Relations Orientation—Behavior). Analyze how well your experience supports the FIRO account of compatibility and cohesiveness.
4. Select a group that you have worked with for some time and that in your opinion is highly cohesive. Write a 300-word paper in which you discuss the group's history and traditions.
5. Form a group with some of your classmates, and work out and implement a systematic program to develop the group's cohesiveness.

References and suggested readings

For a summary of the typical definitions of the concept of *group*, see:

Bass, Bernard M. *Leadership, Psychology and Organizational Behavior.* New York: Harper & Row, 1960, pp. 39–42.

Bass also reflects the criteria for evaluating groups as suggested in this chapter. His third chapter is entitled "Group Effectiveness," and his fourth chapter, "Group Attractiveness." For the student who wishes to read an extensive survey of the research, these two chapters contain many references to journal articles.

Shaw, Marvin E. *Group Dynamics: The Psychology of Small Group Behavior.* New York: McGraw-Hill, 1971, pp. 5–10.

For syntheses of research dealing with the relative efficiency and productivity of groups as compared to individuals, see Shaw, above, pp. 60–73. See also:

Collins, Barry E., and Harold Guetzkow. *A Social Psychology of Group Processes for Decision Making.* New York: Wiley, 1964.
Hare, A. Paul. *Handbook of Small Group Research.* New York: Free Press, 1962, Chap. 12.

Bales's method for counting disagreements and the reports of some early research using his method are found in:

Bales, Robert F. *Interaction Process Analysis: A Method for the Study of Small Groups.* Reading, Mass.: Addison-Wesley, 1950.

For a survey of early research on cohesiveness, see:

Cartwright, Dorwin, and Alvin Zander, eds. *Group Dynamics: Research and Theory,* 3rd ed. New York: Harper & Row, 1968.

For a study of stability of structure and cohesiveness, see:

Shelley, Harry P. "Status, Consensus, Leadership and Satisfaction with the Group," *Journal of Social Psychology,* **51** (1960), 157–164.

For a comprehensive survey of cohesiveness, see:

Lott, Albert J., and Bernice E. Lott. "Group Cohesiveness as Interpersonal Attraction: A Review of Relationships with Antecedent and Consequent Variables," *Psychological Bulletin,* **64** (1965), 259–309.

For other representative studies in cohesiveness, see:

Crowell, Laura, and Thomas M. Scheidel. "A Study of Discussant Satisfaction in Group Problem Solving," *Speech Monographs,* **30** (1963), 56–58.
Fiedler, Fred E. "Leader Attitude, Group Climate, and Group Creativity," *Journal of Abnormal and Social Psychology,* **65** (1962), 308–318.
Fiedler, Fred E., and W. A. T. Meuwese. "Leader's Contribution to Task Performance in Cohesive and Uncohesive Groups," *Journal of Abnormal and Social Psychology,* **67** (1963), 83–87.
Goldberg, Alvin. "An Experimental Study of the Effects of Evaluation upon Group Behavior," *Quarterly Journal of Speech,* **46** (1960), 274–283.
Gruen, Walter. "A Contribution Toward Understanding of Cohesiveness in Small Groups," *Psychological Reports,* **17** (1965), 311–322.
Heslin, R., and D. Dunphy. "Three Dimensions of Member Satisfaction in Small Groups," *Human Relations,* **17** (1964), 99–112.

Management theories can be found in:

Likert, Rensis. *New Patterns in Management.* New York: McGraw-Hill, 1961.
McGregor, Douglas. *The Human Side of Enterprise.* New York: McGraw-Hill, 1960.

For a synthesis of research dealing with member characteristics and cohesiveness, see Shaw, above, pp. 155–180.
For studies related to sex and cohesiveness, see:

Exline, R. V. "Explorations in the Process of Person Perception: Visual Interaction in Relation to Competition, Sex, and the Need for Affiliation," *Journal of Personality,* **31** (1963), 1–20.
Reitan, H. T., and Marvin E. Shaw. "Group Membership, Sex-Composition of the Group, and Conformity Behavior," *Journal of Social Psychology,* **64** (1964), 45–51.
Uesugi, T. T., and W. E. Vinacke. "Strategy in a Feminine Game," *Sociometry,* **26** (1963), 75–88.

An early study of individual needs for structure is:

Stotland, E., and D. M. Wolfe. "An Experimental Investigation of Need for Cognition," *Journal of Abnormal and Social Psychology,* **51** (1955), 291–294.

The exchange account of interpersonal relations is from:

Thibaut, John W., and Harold H. Kelley. *The Social Psychology of Groups.* New York: Wiley, 1959.

For a survey of research results relating to the effects of cooperation and competition on groups, see Hare, above, pp. 254–263. See also:

Dunn, Robert E., and Morton Goldman. "Competition and Noncompetition in Relationship to Satisfaction and Feelings Toward Owngroup and Nongroup Members," *Journal of Social Psychology,* **68** (1966), 299–311.

For studies relating status, prestige, and esteem to cohesiveness, see:

Medow, Herman, and Alvin Zander. "Aspirations for the Group Chosen by Central and Peripheral Members," *Journal of Personality and Social Psychology,* **1** (1965), 224–228.
Snoek, J. D. "Some Effects of Rejection upon Attraction to a Group," *Journal of Abnormal and Social Psychology,* **64** (1962), 175–182.
Watson, David, and Barbara Bromberg. "Power, Communication, and Position Satisfaction in Task-Oriented Groups," *Journal of Personality and Social Psychology,* **2** (1965), 859–864.

For the effect of initiations on group commitment, see:

Aronson, Elliot, and Judson Mills. "The Effect of Severity of Initiation on Liking for a Group," *Journal of Abnormal and Social Psychology,* **59** (1959), 177–181.
Gerard, Harold B., and Grover C. Mathewson. "The Effect of Severity of Initiation on Liking for a Group: A Replication," *Journal of Experimental Social Psychology,* **2** (1966), 278–287.

For syntheses of research dealing with group composition, compatibility, and cohesiveness, see Shaw, above, pp. 189–232.

See also:

Haythorn, W. W. "The Composition of Groups: A Review of the Literature," *Acta Psychologica*, **28** (1968), 97–128.

For a theoretical account of FIRO and reports of research supporting the assumptions of it, see:

Schutz, William G. *FIRO: A Three Dimensional Theory of Interpersonal Behavior*. New York: Holt, Rinehart and Winston, 1958.
Schutz, William G. "On Group Composition," *Journal of Abnormal and Social Psychology*, **62** (1961), 275–281.
Schutz, William G. "What Makes Groups Productive?" *Human Relations*, **8** (1955), 429–435.

For a study that failed to support FIRO, see:

Altman, I., and W. W. Haythorn. "The Effects of Social Isolation and Group Composition on Performance," *Human Relations*, **20** (1967), 313–340.

For a study that partially supported FIRO, see:

Rosenfeld, Lawrence B., and P. A. Jessen. "Compatibility and Interaction in the Small Group: Validation of Schutz's FIRO-B Using a Modified Version of Lashbrook's PROANAS," *Western Speech*, **36** (1972), 31–40.

For studies relating to personality, group composition, and cohesiveness, see:

Bouchard, T. J., Jr., "Personality, Problem-Solving Procedure, and Performance in Small Groups," *Journal of Applied Psychology*, **53** (1969), 1–29.
Goldman, M. "A Comparison of Individual and Group Performance for Varying Combinations of Initial Ability," *Journal of Personality and Social Psychology*, **1** (1965), 210–216.
Meunier, C., and B. G. Rule. "Anxiety, Confidence, and Conformity," *Journal of Personality*, **35** (1967), 498–504.

For a full account of fantasy themes and their analysis, see:

Bales, Robert F. *Personality and Interpersonal Behavior*. New York: Holt, Rinehart and Winston, 1970.

For a discussion of the question of whether or not a collection of individuals can become a "superorganic" group, see Bass, above, pp. 11–12.

CHAPTER 8
THE SOCIAL CLIMATE OF GROUPS

In what way do groups furnish their members with social rewards and how do they give social punishments? It will require the next few chapters to give an adequate answer. This chapter examines rewards offered by the social climate of the group. The following chapters make a depth analysis of the underlying structure and dynamic which account for the more powerful reinforcement effects and punishment inherent in group process.

The empirical study of task-oriented groups by investigators making a systematic content analysis of what goes on in meetings has contributed much to the theoretical understanding of the workings of small groups. These studies also have practical implications for the student interested in working with groups.

content analysis

There are two major steps in a successful content-analysis study. First, the investigator must develop a set of categories that describe the content he is interested in. They must be clear enough so that he can determine if a given item fits into one or another of his categories. In addition, when he finishes counting the items in each category he should be able to make useful inferences from the data. For example, a category system based on the parts of speech does not yield many useful inferences. The discovery that 25 percent of the words in a speech are nouns tells little about the speech's clarity.

The second requirement is that the investigator be able to define clearly the units he will count. If he selects words as his units, he will be able to count them quite easily. If long words are more important to his results than short words, he should select a different unit to count. The technical difficulties in this method of research are sometimes very great. They relate to the development of suitable categories and units and the training of observers so that they agree on the way items should be classified.

When investigators develop category systems that yield useful information, the categories themselves are often discoveries that have practical implications for the student of group discussion. This description of the social climate of groups is largely based on the significant features of group process discovered during the development of one such category system.

Bales' categories for interaction process analysis

Robert F. Bales and his associates at Harvard University have developed one of the most widely acclaimed and useful category systems for the study of small groups. Bales began his study of groups with a large number of categories which were gradually reduced to 12. These proved to be sufficient to account for all verbal and gestural communication within small-group meetings. The 12 categories are evenly divided between task-related responses and social responses.

The purpose of this chapter is to describe the social climate that makes an attractive or unattractive group. The analysis is organized around six categories of the Bales system that are useful in describing the social climate of groups. The discussion that follows is organized around the category system developed by Bales, but the material relating to the various concepts is only partially an interpretation of his work. The analysis has a different emphasis and includes additional material relating to social tensions and group solidarity. The concepts come from the Bales' categories, but the empirical amplification as well as some key concepts such as primary and secondary tensions come from the Minnesota Studies and from modifications as a result of using the concepts to teach group discussion. In 1970, Bales published a revision of his original category system which included changing the category of Shows Solidarity to Seems Friendly and the category of Shows Antagonism to Seems Unfriendly. The original category called Shows Tension Release was revised to Dramatizes. Changing shows of solidarity and antagonism to being friendly or unfriendly was useful to researchers who found they seldom used the older categories when they were making observations of groups. For pedagogical purposes, however, the categories remain very useful, for, while shows of group solidarity and antagonism are relatively rare, they are very important when they do appear. The tension analysis in this chapter remains useful and has not been changed. The important new concepts of group fantasy chains and dramatizes are dealt with at appropriate places in the chapters on group cohesiveness, role emergence, acculturation, and the task dimension.

When people participate in a group they perceive social cues not only from what is said but also from the way it is said: the pauses, pitch inflections, rate, and voice quality. A skillful actor can say a line so that the audience believes he means precisely the opposite. Such lines as "She's a great date" can be read in such a way that they communicate "I wouldn't go out with her on a bet." In addition, members get social cues from the language of gesture. If a person is expounding on his idea to a member who sits slumped in a chair looking away, he gets a much different social cue than if the other person sits erect, nods in agreement, and appears to listen to every word. Both verbal and nonverbal cues are important in developing the social climate of a group.

SHOWS OF GROUP SOLIDARITY AND ANTAGONISM

The first category of positive social response is *solidarity*. Each positive category is related to an opposite negative category—the opposite of solidarity is *antagonism*.

A show of group solidarity is any statement, comment, gesture, or cue indicating that the member feels the group is important and that he will help the group collectively and the other members individually. In larger groups, the pep talk plays much the same part as the less formal shows of group solidarity in smaller groups.

The shows of solidarity that are effective in small groups differ in quality from those that are useful for large organizations. In general, they are less formal and less inclined to be sentimental. They appeal to the more practical motives, rather than the idealistic or altruistic motives that are appropriate for shows of solidarity in larger groups. Appeals to patriotism and nationalism are essentially shows of solidarity and often reach such high levels of appeal as "Greater love hath no man than this, that a man lay down his life for his friends."

The small groups in a discussion class use appeals of a different order to build group solidarity. Even a group set up in class to meet for only an hour will probably exhibit some signs of solidarity. The following example is from a small task-oriented discussion group composed of junior and senior students in the College of Liberal Arts at the University of Minnesota. The group was to meet for several months, but the following exchange took place toward the end of their first meeting.

MEMBER A: Why don't we just agree to look this thing over here, and any of us that are ambitious enough (*growing tentative*) to go to the library and read up some more do that . . .

MEMBER B: (*in agreement*) Hmmmhummm.

MEMBER A: . . . and then bring . . . bring your suggestions for organizing our report next Monday.

MEMBER B: I know one thing . . . there won't be anybody standing up . . . at least I know I won't be standing up and cussing anybody who does any research.

> [*General agreement and considerable laughter from the other members of the group. The group is noticeably less tense after this laughter.*]

We gotta do research . . .

MEMBER A: Just the Alliance for Progress is so important that we have to do research on it . . .

> [*Member A's first statement about research was phrased and said tentatively—". . . any of us that are ambitious enough to go to the library and read up some more do that. . . ." This statement is now said with much more force and conviction. It receives general agreement and "sure," "sure" from the other members of the group.*]

MEMBER D: Everything is important . . .

> [*General agreement: "yeah," "hmmmhummm."*]

MEMBER D: . . . the whole . . . the class is important . . . our group is important . . .

> [*Another member of the group reinforces member D by saying "yes." For the last several minutes the members of the group have been using collective pronouns and saying such things as "We gotta do research . . . ," but this is the first definite mention of "our group." At this point the group has come to take on some identity of its own in the perceptions of its members.*]

MEMBER A: (*interrupting*) And the three credits of . . .

MEMBER E: (*riding over A*) Well, the thing that is probably most important to each of us individually is the interaction between all of us . . . because of the fact that . . .

MEMBER C: Right.

MEMBER E: All we're interested . . . I'm not saying all we're interested . . . our major interest . . . one of our major interests should be the grade that we get in this course . . .

MEMBER C: Right.

MEMBER E: And as we said earlier . . . what we . . . the grade we get depends on all of us acting as a unit . . .

MEMBER C: Ummmhummm.

MEMBER A: It depends on how well we achieve our objective . . .

MEMBER C: And I . . . I personally would really like an atmosphere for myself where you would just bluntly come out and tell me something . . . I mean . . . maybe not in class or something but

I won't be offended by anything and I mean I think we know each other well enough . . .

MEMBER E: Right . . .

MEMBER C: That we can do this . . .

MEMBER E: Right . . .

MEMBER C: I mean this . . .

MEMBER E: Right . . .

MEMBER C: (*interrupting*) I mean that . . .

MEMBER E: (*interrupting*) Why don't you carry matches?

> [*General laughter and cries of "right," "right." This bout of laughter dispels most of the remaining primary tension, and the social climate of the group exemplifies considerable warmth and rapport.*]

MEMBER C: I mean something like that. It doesn't do any good for a group to go carrying . . .

> [*Several members of the group say "no," "no," with inflections that suggest they agree with C: that it doesn't do any good for a group to be that way.*]

MEMBER C: . . . a chip on our shoulder.

MEMBER B: Let's face it if we can . . . if we can sit around like . . . like we are right now the first day . . .

> [*General agreement including "yeah."*]

MEMBER B: We're going to get pretty informal . . .

MEMBER C: No, I think we should have that policy . . . you know . . . just tell each other what we think . . . I mean . . . in a nice way of course . . . you know . . . you can tell what other people mean . . .

MEMBER A: Oh, sure. I think we've already started off on a sort of free and easy . . .

MEMBER C: Right . . .

MEMBER A: Way of doing it . . .

MEMBER D: I think it's a fine group . . .

This transcript exemplifies several important principles of group processes. The first show of solidarity was tentative, but when it was reinforced by agreement, other members began to assert group solidarity. All the participants became more enthusiastic and made firmer shows of solidarity. The group atmosphere warmed up perceptibly within minutes, and the spiral effect of increased cohesiveness resulted in further shows of solidarity. The group went on to become an effective and cohesive group. If the group had rejected the first tentative show of group solidarity or responded in a half-hearted or ambiguous fashion, strong and positive shows of solidarity would not have followed. For these reasons, the group stood at one of the many crossroads relating to its social climate and took, on this occasion, a path that led to a more rewarding social environment.

Why did the group choose this path rather than the other? Research on this question at the University of Minnesota has not yet led to a definite answer. Apparently, this interaction took place by chance. But, when students of discussion recognize the importance of such turning points in the life of a group, they can reinforce the tentative show of group solidarity or initiate signs of solidarity themselves. They will avoid cynical attempts to manipulate the group or insincere attempts to show group solidarity. They will remember that an individual who honestly wants the group to be a good one can express sincerely his desire to work for the group and can help or reward others when feasible. Such concerns build a more socially rewarding and cohesive group.

Why must the group's time be occupied with shows of solidarity when it could be spent working on the discussion question? Even though the members know that everyone is interested in the welfare of the group, it must be said from time to time. Expressions of interest reassure the members; the group is identified again as an entity. Even a tightly knit family suffers if its members do not tell each other that it is a good family and that they love one another. A husband may truthfully say that his wife knows that he loves her, but he makes a mistake if he does not often tell her so, and vice versa. The cohesiveness of the family unit requires it. The same is true for less cohesive and more temporary groups such as discussion groups in speech classes.

The negative social interaction that corresponds to shows of solidarity is a show of antagonism. Antagonism may be directed to the group or to individual members. If a person punishes or lowers the status of another or indicates hostility, he creates social tension. Preschool children show antagonism by hitting other children on the head with a toy truck. Members of Ph.D. seminars and college discussion groups reveal antagonisms in more subtle ways, but the effect is the same.

SOCIAL TENSIONS

The second category of positive social response that Bales discovered was labeled *shows tension release*, and the corresponding negative category was *shows tension*. Smiles, chuckles, laughter, or other indications of pleasure serve to release tension. Members show tension in a variety of ways, which can be classified into two main categories: primary and secondary tension.

Primary tension. Primary tension is the social unease and stiffness that accompanies getting acquainted. Students placed in a discussion group with strangers will experience these tensions most strongly during the opening minutes of their first meetings. The earmarks of primary tensions are extreme politeness, apparent boredom or tiredness, and considerable sighing or yawning. When members show primary tension, they speak softly and tentatively. Frequently they can think of nothing to say, and many long pauses result. The following transcript is from the opening minutes of a group that experienced an unusual amount of primary tension. This group was plagued throughout its life by its inability to release primary tensions.

MEMBER A: (*softly*) Well, see now here we got several topics that I can see that we aren't going to arrive at a definite conclusion on this nuclear testing . . . this ah policy in Berlin . . . (*dropping his voice*) what's that other one?

MEMBER B: (*more strongly*) Well, I think policy in Berlin . . . we could . . . we could arrive at a pretty fair solution to the problem (*pause*) don't you (*pause*) really?

> [*There is a pause of five seconds which seems longer because it is preceded by a question.*]

MEMBER C: (*so softly that she is almost unintelligible*) Well, I think there are solutions to be arrived at . . . probably . . . probably we could (*dropping voice even more*) couldn't contemplate them now probably . . .

MEMBER D: A lot of editorials . . . you know . . . in different papers . . . one way and another but (*pause*) common market is (*pause*) a nice one (*pause and dropping his voice*) interesting . . .

MEMBER B: (*yawns*) I like these two . . . one of these . . . nuclear testing and farm problem, but I don't want to throw any of them out either if anybody else likes them.

> [*Pause of four seconds.*]

MEMBER D: I thought you had this one at first . . .

MEMBER B: (*interrupting*) Oh, yeah, no that's (*strained laugh, but no one joins in*) that's ah (*pause of five seconds*) policy in Berlin (*noticeable sigh*), but you see the trouble is our discussion and our outline . . . you know he said after we find a problem and discuss all our solutions . . .

A person who experiences a severe amount of primary tension (similar to stage fright) will often withdraw from the group and pretend to be disinterested in the meeting. He may pull his chair back, look out the window, or look over his notes for another class.

The Minnesota Studies included interviews with such members.

They often reported that they were not sure why they did not take a more active part. They suggested that the reason was that they found the subject uninteresting. More extensive investigation revealed that a case of genuine disinterest in the work of a group as it gets under way is extremely rare. The member who seemed disinterested or who withdrew was really very tense and was exhibiting a high level of primary tension.

What is taking place that causes a high level of tension, interest, and worry? Five students meeting together for the first time have an item on their agenda that is so important to all concerned that it must be 'dealt with to some extent before any other business whatsoever. That item is the social relationships that will develop. These relationships raise questions that relate to each person's basic social and esteem needs. A student who sits in on a discussion group, even if it meets for only an hour, is offered an opportunity to enter in and develop social relations with the other people in the group. He can take a chance, enter in, and win approval. Such approval is necessary and important to him. He feels primary tension until he begins to see evidence that his social and esteem needs will be gratified. When it becomes apparent that the group will accept him as a person, he can relax and attend to business. There is the possibility of failure. He may be rejected, despised, or belittled. If this happens, he will respond with a feeling of unpleasantness and, perhaps, with frustration and anger. If he has participated in similar groups and similar situations before and has been accepted and liked as a person, he is more likely to participate. If the situation is novel, his feeling of primary tension is increased, and he is less likely to take part. In addition, in unusual situations he may lack necessary information. If the situation is like previous ones in which he has been rejected or hurt, he will have even more primary tension. If it seems likely that he will be rejected, he may not risk taking part. Of course, he also has no chance to win social approval. But, if he thinks that punishment is the more likely outcome, he may escape by pretending to be uninterested.

Feelings of primary tension are common to all collections of individuals. Primary tension accounts for uncertain behavior of people, when they begin working together. They speak softly, tentatively, and with great politeness. They all want to make a good impression and are therefore very polite. They do not insult other members, tell jokes, or express strong opinions. They are quick to laugh, although the laughter is always a bit strained. They will discuss almost any topic, such as the weather, in order to start getting acquainted. The group will listen to every word of the member who makes a statement about the weather and may devote several minutes of polite talk to the subject. Thirty minutes later, if the primary tension has been released, the group would

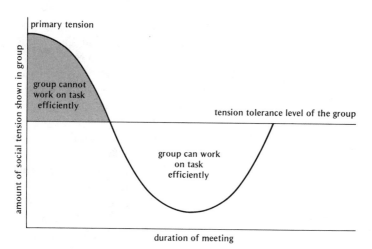

Figure 5. Primary Tension Curve.

not consider talking about the weather, because they have more important things to talk about.

Oddly enough, the group will experience a similar primary tension at the beginning of each meeting. Usually these periods of tension grow shorter as the group members settle into relatively stable relationships, but at the beginning of each meeting the participants feel the need to "warm up." They must find out if the others will treat them as they have in the past and if the group expects the same sort of behavior that it has in the past. Primary tension accounts for the universal phenomenon of small talk first and business later that characterizes interviews, conferences, and business meetings. The young man calling a girl for a date seldom begins with "Would you like to go to a movie with me this Saturday?" He usually starts with some small talk or tension-breaking conversation. Obviously this small talk at the beginning of a meeting meets a real and universal need. If it did not, it would be omitted in the hectic pace of modern living where so much time is spent in conference.

Figure 5 indicates a hypothetical construct that is useful in dealing with social tensions in a group. The horizontal line on the figure indicates the amount of tension that a given group can tolerate and still work on the task. When tensions rise above this level, the group cannot function on the task. Although many groups continue to go through the motions of discussing the problem at hand when the tensions rise above this level, the real item under discussion will be the problems causing the tensions. As the tension curve on Figure 5 indicates, the typical group finds the primary tension above the tolerance level at first, and they must release it before they can work.

The groups investigated by the Minnesota Studies have handled the problems of primary tension quite well. A small percentage of them, however, have worked together for as long as two months without ever meeting the problems posed by social shyness and tension. They were plagued by apparent member disinterest and boredom, by considerable absenteeism, and a lack of cohesiveness. These groups usually talked of nothing but the question they were discussing. They never got acquainted.

On occasion, when the tension level is high, a group should stop talking about the discussion question and consider the social problem. Some irrelevant talk at the beginning of the meeting may save time later. The good group, however, begins work as soon as the primary tension has been released. Some groups in the Minnesota Studies continued the socializing well beyond this point and wasted time. They had a lot of fun, but they did not get much done.

As a general rule, direct recognition of social tensions is a good way to release them. Primary tension is like the dog that distracts an audience by coming into the auditorium, walking up the aisle, and curling up beside the speaker on the platform. The audience will be distracted by the dog and unable to listen with undivided attention to the speaker. If the speaker ignores the dog and pretends he is not there, the audience grows more and more distracted. When the dog stretches, the audiences watches and smiles. When the dog yawns, the audience may snicker, and the speaker soon finds himself with an embarrassing and unbearable situation on his hands. The speaker can meet the problem by recognizing the dog the moment he enters the auditorium and calling the audience's attention directly and explicitly to him. Discussing the dog discharges whatever attention the audience may pay to the dog and having considered the dog for a moment they can return to the speech without distraction. In the same fashion, if the primary tension is discharged by paying attention to it directly, the group can go to work. If the tension is ignored, however, it will build up and become a larger and larger burden for the group.

Secondary tension. Most groups manage to release primary tensions within a matter of minutes and can comfortably get down to work. As the group goes about its job, two kinds of group structuring take place simultaneously. First, the group works out a social structure and a network of social relationships. Second, the group establishes a pattern of work. Structuring generates tensions of another kind. Two persons may compete for the social approval of a third. They experience social tensions during their arguments and the others grow tense because of the emotion and antagonism of the two members. A similar sort of tension can result from working on the task. Two members may have

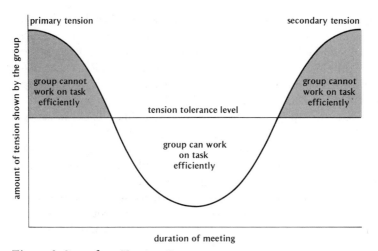

Figure 6. Secondary Tension Curve.

different positions on a matter of policy and may try to secure adherents. In either instance, they have what is called a "personality conflict." Such conflicts lead to *secondary tension*. Secondary tension creates a different group climate than primary tension does. It is noisier and more dynamic. Voices are louder and more strained. Long pauses may appear, but often two or three people speak at a time. Everyone is highly interested in the proceedings. No one seems bored or tired. Members may fidget in their chairs, half rise, pound the table, get up and pace the room, run their hands through their hair, gesture excitedly, and exhibit a much higher level of excitement and involvement.

Figure 6 continues the curve of a group that has experienced primary tension above the tolerance level, has released the tension, and has gone to work. Often such a group will experience a rise in secondary tension until it goes above the tolerance level. When this happens, the group's task effectiveness is again in jeopardy.

Secondary tensions are much more difficult to deal with than primary tensions. The members most vitally involved are not as eager to have the tensions brought into the open and released. The group can seldom diagnose the problem clinically. Usually an analysis of the roots of these tensions results in the group blaming one or two people for creating them. Casting blame in this way hurts the status of the person, strains the bonds holding the group together, and creates frustration and anger.

Despite the difficulty of releasing secondary tensions, good groups develop mechanisms to handle such problems. Unfortunately these mechanisms are not easily developed, nor are they universally applicable. Each group must work out its own salvation. To be successful, the technique adopted must have the support of the members. Faith and support come from trying several different approaches and settling on the one that works best for this particular group. Some groups will rely on one or two members to take the burden of releasing these tensions. They may joke about the problem or use irony or satire to cause laughter, deflate the tension, and *correct* the behavior that has caused the tension. They may engage in direct conciliation and negotiate a compromise. Some groups depend on a member who is a friend of both contenders to see each person outside the meeting and discuss the problem privately. Finally, if all else fails, groups may consider the matter directly. The following transcription is such a case. It is also a good example of secondary tension.

> [*The group had been meeting for several weeks. It was composed of upper-division students in a discussion course at the University of Minnesota. The instructor had not assigned a leader or moderator or chairman. At the time of the incident the group had no leader. Several members had successfully led the group and then lost support. This exchange took place when members A and B were contending for the leadership of the group. B was very aggressive and fluent and defended his position by talking over and through objections. Member A perceived the problem to be member B's inflexibility and his domineering manner; so he brought the problem up for direct consideration by the other members. Member A did not feel that he could bluntly confront B, so his tactic was to read to the group from the textbook.*]

MEMBER A: I think there is absolutely *no* doubt about that. The procedures we've been using have not' been those that are . . . uh . . . for *good* discussion and I think each one of us ought to analyze this fact and . . .

> [*At this point member B begins a side conversation with member C.*]

MEMBER A: (*continuing but bothered by the fact that member B is not paying attention to him*) . . . see if we can't . . . see if we can't do something about it. I think that if I just read the heads of these particular paragraphs here just . . . just so you can think about the fact . . .

> [*Member B is now listening carefully to member A, and he gets up from his chair and begins to pace the room.*]

MEMBER A: (*continuing*) . . . and uh . . . and uh just remember that these things are uh . . . essential to uh group discussion. (*reading*) "Good discussants, we believe, do not merely tolerate the fact that other discussants who hold that . . . who hold to opinions and attitudes different from their own. They welcome this fact." We *welcome* differences of opinion . . . we . . . we . . .

MEMBER B: You look at me when you say that . . .

[*Member A and member B begin to speak simultaneously.*]

MEMBER A: I'm not looking at you. . . .   MEMBER B: . . . for my benefit?
Or anyone else's?

MEMBER B: Just read it then.

MEMBER A: I *am* reading it. "We sense the uh presence of an attitude uh of welcoming differences in groups . . . discussion groups in which the leaders and members seem genuinely eager to hear the opinions of all members of the group—even minority opinions." *Eager* to hear minority opinions.

[*There is a pause. All the members of the group are tense, and they are watching and listening intently.*]

MEMBER B: Uh (*pause*) You giving a speech or you reading . . .

MEMBER A: (*interrupting*) No.

MEMBER B: (*ignoring the interruption*) You emphasizing any particular points?

MEMBER A: (*interrupting*) No, I just . . .

MEMBER B: (*ignoring the interruption*) . . . read . . . just read it then . . .

MEMBER A: Well, I'm . . . I don't wish to read the whole book I just . . . you know . . . I thought that it might . . . if we . . . if we seek to hear the minority. . . .

MEMBER B: (*riding over the words "the minority"*) You're not reading now. You're commenting on it. Why don't you just read it like you said you were going to without going back over it two or three times?

[*There is a three-second pause. The secondary tension has reached an uncomfortable level.*]

MEMBER B: (*in a tense voice*) If you're going to harass me, I'll harass you a little bit.

MEMBER A: I'm not harassing anybody . . .

MEMBER B: Yes, you are.

MEMBER A: I'm not.

[*The tension level has now reached a point that is so high that neither member A nor member B can tolerate it. The amount of tension that a group can bear is related to the level of cohesiveness in the group. Highly cohesive groups can stand more secondary tensions, and, therefore, the most bitter fights take place in highly cohesive groups such as the family. Member A and member B both break out in strained laughter at this point to release the tension. The rest of the group does not laugh.*]

MEMBER A: I'm sorry you're taking this attitude because . . .

[*Member B gives a half-laugh–half-snort of derision.*]

MEMBER A: I sincerely believe the discussion we held last time was ah . . .

MEMBER B: (*interrupting*) I do, too.

MEMBER A: Didn't get us anywhere.

MEMBER B: I do, too.

MEMBER A: And I think that uh . . . unless we analyze these things and uh everyone . . . particular individual has . . . and I thought . . . you know . . .

MEMBER B: Well, right now we're not analyzing that discussion. We're talking about what's in the book there that someone (*member A tries to interrupt, but member B talks over the interruption and keeps the floor*) . . . everyone in the group is supposed to have read. You're reading it for . . . you're trying to relearn us here . . . what are . . . what are . . . (*member A tries to interrupt again—he says "Yes, positive . . . positi . . . " but member B keeps talking over him*) . . . you're wasting time on the discussion of the problem when you're reading the book which we all already assume we've read . . .

MEMBER A: (*giving up*) Your point is well taken.

MEMBER B: All right then, let's forget the book. (*pause*) Thank you.

A good deal of the atmosphere of the meeting is lost in a transcription such as this one. The playscript is very different from a performance of a play. One reason these protocols are written in playscript form is to stimulate the reader's imagination to provide some of the important details of atmosphere.

In this case, direct confrontation did not succeed. The group was never able to mobilize even a majority of its members behind a move to solve its social and emotional problems. Member A received no active support from any other member of the group. The entire exchange took place between A and B. If one other person had supported A, the outcome would have been different. Member A's tactic of using the book backfired as well. It gave B an opportunity to bypass the issue by suggesting that he was "relearning" the group and "wasting time" by "reading the book which we all already assume we've read."

Secondary tensions are inevitable in groups that have released their primary tensions sufficiently to engage seriously in the task. When they arise, the good groups included in the Minnesota Studies worked out ways to handle them. Groups that ignore or withdraw from tensions develop a social climate that is uncomfortable and punishing. Groups try to ignore secondary tensions because dealing with them realistically is extremely painful. Groups are, if anything, more neurotic than individuals in their tendency to pretend that the social tensions do not exist. If they do admit that there is a problem, they often blame it on a member who is inherently "stupid" or "domineering." They dodge the problem. Often a group makes preliminary moves to deal with secondary tensions, but retreats, when the climate becomes difficult, by taking action that does not deal with the real problem. They leave the touchy area of human relations and return to the safe area of doing the job. The problem, however, never goes away and if ignored or dodged will continue to plague and impede their progress. Facing up to secondary tensions realistically is the best way to release them.

AGREEMENT AND DISAGREEMENT

The third set of climate-building interactions that Bales discovered he called *agrees* and *disagrees*. The group cannot come to a consensus about policy, problem solving, or action without the liberal use of shows of agreement and disagreement. Ideas and suggestions are tested by disagreements. Even the highly task-oriented activity of processing information, of testing the truth or falsity of factual statements, requires shows of agreement and disagreement. Agreements and disagreements are double-edged. They serve a task function and simultaneously have strong social implications. Disagreements help criticize and process information, but they damage the social fabric of a group.

Brainstorming. Some years ago a member of a large advertising firm, Batten, Barton, Durstine & Osborn, became interested in the problem of encouraging creativity; his name was Alex T. Osborn. In his work with creating advertising themes and programs, he found a method of using a group of people to encourage each other to suggest good ideas.

Osborn labeled his method *brainstorming*. He turned some of his promotional talents to publicizing his scheme for encouraging group creativity and imagination. The name itself, *brainstorming*, is something of a promotional triumph. In a short time, brainstorming became popular with some branches of the military services and with some industries.

The rules for brainstorming are relatively simple. A group of people are assembled and presented with a problem or a creative task. They are instructed to throw out as many ideas as possible in a short period of time. The core of the technique, however, is that *under no circumstances is anyone in any fashion to indicate disagreement* with a suggested idea. The wilder the idea, the better. The quantity rather than the quality of ideas is emphasized. Osborn had discovered the facilitating effect of agreement on the social climate of a group. One of the best ways to break primary tension is to have a high level of agreement. If a member feels unsure of himself and makes a tentative comment and receives agreement, he makes the next statement more easily and with greater conviction. If this too is met with general agreement, he grows enthusiastic and soon finds he has forgotten himself and his shyness. He no longer feels tense about how he will be accepted. By their agreement, the others have indicated their acceptance and liking for him. In a few minutes, a brainstorming group can develop a highly permissive and pleasant social climate simply by arbitrarily ruling out disagreement.

Agreement as reinforcement. Meanwhile, psychologists have been discovering experimental evidence in support of agreement as social reinforcement. The argument that underlies this research is behavioristic and suggests that the response of an organism can be shaped by the judicious utilization of rewards and punishments. Thus, in training a dog to "heel," the animal is conditioned to the command by the punishment involved in tightening the choke collar and the reward of praise when he obeys. Many laboratory experiments with rats, pigeons, cats, and monkeys indicate that a clever researcher can train these creatures to carry out complicated routines by the use of conditioning rewards and punishments. A number of psychological investigations of human verbal behavior have studied the changes resulting from the use of agreement as reinforcement. Sometimes the agreement was expressed verbally and sometimes in gestural terms such as nodding the head. Verbal behavior changed significantly when reinforced with agreement. Although most of these studies had a different purpose, they definitely establish the fact that perceived agreement is a social reward or reinforcement.

The role of agreement. Agreement serves as a powerful social reward for many reasons. It is the currency of social approval. When a person makes a statement and others all express agreement, he has received overt evidence that he is a person of value and that his contribution was a good one. If the members of the group agree and *act according* to one member's suggestions, he is given the social reinforcement that comes from *influencing* other people. Most people are gratified when they know that their ideas and their suggestions have been accepted. Shows of agreement are the most definite signs of approval for a person's ideas.

Agreement is also the outward evidence of status or esteem. High-status people travel in an aura of agreement. If the people surrounding an individual listen to every statement and express their agreement, he is undoubtedly a high-status individual. The same treatment will be accorded a highly esteemed individual within a small group.

Agreement also serves a valuable task function. By means of agreements, the group discovers its consensus. Group members accept factual information as true or false on the basis of shows of agreement. They accept or reject inferences from facts in the same way. Suggestions are made, plans laid, and action steps agreed upon by the same signs. There is a social edge to every task-oriented agreement. If the members agree that the factual information provided by member A is true and pertinent, they imply that he is knowledgeable and that he has done a good job. If they agree that his reasoning is valid and helpful, they imply that he is intelligent. If they follow his plan of action, they imply that he is *their leader*. The esteem needs of many persons are most gratified by acknowledged leadership.

The need for disagreement. Despite attempts such as brainstorming to eliminate disagreements, every group comes to some point when information must be tested for its truth or falsity. The discussion group that proceeds on the basis of false statements of fact will be misled.

The group must also test the inferences that are drawn from the information. If group members have accepted a fallacious line of reasoning, they may be rudely shocked. If their proposals have been tried and have failed, and if the undesirable effects of these proposals would outweigh the beneficial results, the group must reconsider those proposals. All such testing of evidence, reasoning, and policy require shows of disagreement. Disagreement is vital to the task efficiency of the group.

Disagreement and secondary tension. The task requires disagreements, and yet disagreements cause the social climate to deteriorate. Disagreements strain the social bonds and are among the prime generators of secondary tensions. Where agreement reinforces behavior, disagreement extinguishes it. Disagreement, therefore, functions as social punishment.

Disagreement and cohesiveness. Disagreements contribute to the stiffness of the social climate of the discussion. When group members disagree with an individual, they lower his status and hurt his esteem. He finds the group socially punishing, and he must have compensating rewards from the other dimension of group attraction to keep him a part of the group.

Paradoxically, disagreements are a function of cohesiveness. The more highly cohesive a group, the greater the number of shows of disagreement that can be expected in its meetings.

The handling of disagreements. Good groups develop ways to allow for disagreements without unduly disrupting cohesiveness. A plausible and often-repeated bit of advice is to preface the disagreement with a compliment or an agreement. Statements such as "I agree with you there, Bill. I think you are right about the need to take the military effect into account but . . ." are often recommended. Tact seldom hurts the social climate, but it wears off very quickly in a small group. Before the first hour of discussion is over the members will begin to cringe when Joe starts to agree with them. They know that agreement is a cue from Joe for the inevitable "but we must also look at the other side."

A member cannot keep a disagreement from hurting. If the disagreement is to do its work *it must be perceived as a disagreement*. If it is not, it does not do the job. If it is, it exacts its social toll. Members simply cannot have the best of both worlds in this regard. What happens when a person carefully words each disagreement as tactfully as possible or prefaces the disagreement with an agreement? At best he cushions the blow, and at worst he is gradually perceived as a person who is hard to pin down, slick, not to be trusted. Some groups, indeed, adopt a style that accepts the blunt, direct, and forceful disagreement as normal operating procedure and their members tolerate such disagreement as well as or better than the tactful kind. Other groups adopt as norms the "I think you have a good point, Bill, but . . ." sort of disagreement, because the blunt disagreement would be more disruptive.

The proper attitude toward disagreements is one of open-minded testing of the truth of factual statements and evaluating the advisability of action. Therefore, discussants should be objective, scientific, and uninvolved in the process of working out ideas.

Although participants in a public discussion can adopt such a discussion attitude, members of small task-oriented groups working on significant problems cannot do so. Even if the topic under discussion is not important, the group itself may be so important that members cannot remain scientific and objective. Even with the help of a status relationship, an age differential, and a context that establishes such activity as the expected sort of behavior, a student often feels considerable resentment and frustration (secondary tension) when a teacher criticizes the ideas and information in his speech or theme. Although the student reminds himself that he has paid his fees for this service and that he needs such criticism, he still feels some irritation when the instructor disagrees with him. Disagreements in speech-class discussion groups generate such social strains.

If disagreements inevitably cause social strains, is the situation beyond remedy? Not if the members are aware of the necessity for disagreements and of the social costs extracted by disagreements. The Minnesota Studies discovered a number of moderately successful and unsuccessful groups that did not maintain an atmosphere that would sustain honest disagreement. Members agreed for the sake of agreement or remained quiet when they honestly felt they should disagree. Aware of the social toll, they would rather do a poor job than risk secondary tension. The task did not mean that much to them. They report that "We get along very well. But I don't know, I guess we just aren't very interested in the topic." The successful groups were those that had enough cohesiveness to disagree. Even in these highly cohesive groups, the disagreements caused trouble, but these groups worked out ways to mend their social fabric. One of the most common methods of repair was a great show of group cohesiveness and tension release after a period of disagreement. Quite often these disagreements were concentrated just prior to moments of decision. When these moments of decision are followed by activity in the three positive social categories discovered by Bales, the damage done by disagreements can be repaired.

An example of how groups work in this regard is furnished by one of the highly cohesive and successful groups studied at Minnesota. This excerpt from the diary of one of the members illustrates how the group handled disagreements. He reported in part,

> One nite [sic] . . . I had a long talk with the group attempting to narrow the scope of the problem . . . [the leader] finally decided we were too far along to change now and so we went along as previously planned. I agreed and received much concern and consolation. I'm not bitter. I wanted to do what I considered right and so stated my desire. . . .

The key phrase in this report is "much concern and consolation." The group allowed the disagreement, and when the decision went against one of the members they hastened to assure him that he remained an important member of the group. They also closed ranks and showed solidarity by agreeing that since the decision had been made, everyone should support it.

Some groups solve the problem by settling the burden of disagreeing on one person. He is expected to disagree with anything and everything. When he does so, the group finds it easier to release the secondary tension his disagreements generate. They may say to a new member who is disturbed by disagreements, "Don't mind old Jack. That's the way he is. He disagrees with everything, but he's all right." If the group comes to *expect* disagreements from Jack, then when he provides them, they do not find them as irritating as if they had not expected them. Members discover that the habitual critic does not necessarily hurt their status.

summary

The purpose of this chapter is to provide an overview of the social climates of groups that create attractive or unattractive social fields.

The socially facilitating interactions discovered by Robert F. Bales and his associates include shows of solidarity, tension release, and agreements. The socially punishing interactions include shows of antagonism, tension, and disagreements.

Shows of solidarity are verbal and nonverbal communications that raise the status of members, offer to help a member of the group, or show commitment to the group. Tensions are generally released by laughter, smiling, chuckling, or other genuine expressions of mirth or amusement.

Shows of tension often change quality during the course of a group meeting. The early shows, primary tension, are generally more quiet and less obtrusive than the later secondary tensions generated by role conflict and task differences. In general, primary tensions are easier to release because most group members welcome the relaxed social atmosphere that results. Secondary tensions are more difficult to handle. Nonetheless, good groups develop mechanisms that work for them in releasing secondary tensions.

Disagreements are extremely important to the successful functioning of a task-oriented group. By means of disagreement, the group tests information and reasoning. Disagreement, however, exacts a social toll and tends to stiffen the social climate. Successful groups develop ways of handling the inevitable secondary tensions that develop from disagreements.

QUESTIONS FOR STUDY

1. What is meant by nonverbal communication?
2. What is the importance of nonverbal communication to the social climate of the task-oriented small group?
3. What is meant by shows of solidarity?
4. What is the difference between primary and secondary tension?
5. How might the concept of a "tension tolerance level" be used to increase a group's productivity?
6. Why is agreement often rewarding to a group member?
7. In what ways do disagreements both facilitate and inhibit group success?
8. How may groups assure sufficient disagreement?
9. What is the relationship between disagreements and cohesiveness?
10. What is the role of nonverbal communication in attempts to manipulate the group?

EXERCISES

1. Select a group that you have been working with for several months, and write a 300-word paper analyzing the way they disagree. Evaluate the effectiveness of the group's mechanism for handling the social tensions produced by disagreements.

2. Select an acquaintance who is expert at releasing social tensions. Write a brief analysis of his techniques and evaluate their success.
3. Tape record a meeting of your class discussion group. Play back the tape, and count the shows of group solidarity. Determine points where shows of solidarity were appropriate and could have been inserted. Write a 300-word paper discussing why more shows of solidarity did not occur.
4. Set up a role-playing exercise in which each member prefaces every disagreement with a compliment or an agreement. Perform a panel-discussion program of 20 minutes before the class with these roles. Discuss the effect of such disagreements on the program.
5. Set up a role-playing exercise in which each member disagrees very directly and bluntly. Perform a panel-discussion program of 20 minutes before the class with these roles. Discuss the effect of such disagreements on the program.

References and suggested readings

For a bibliography of category systems developed for the study of a wide variety of groups, see:

Hare, A. Paul. *Handbook of Small Group Research.* New York: Free Press, 1962, pp. 398–407.

Bales' category system is explained in detail in:

Bales, Robert F. *Interaction Process Analysis: A Method for the Study of Small Groups.* Cambridge, Mass.: Addison-Wesley, 1950.
Bales, Robert F. *Personality and Interpersonal Behavior.* New York: Holt, Rinehart and Winston, 1970.

The tendency of groups to turn their attention from task matters to attempts to mend the social fabric of the group by attending to group maintenance and individual needs is illustrated in:

Bales, Robert F. "The Equilibrium Problem in Small Groups." In T. Parsons, R. F. Bales, and E. Shils, eds. *Working Papers in the Theory of Action.* New York: Free Press, 1953, pp. 111–161.

This tendency supports the construct of a tension-tolerance level that leads groups to swing from working on the task to considering group maintenance and back to the task again.

The case study of secondary tension was part of a doctoral dissertation by:

Geier, John. "A Descriptive Analysis of an Interaction Pattern Resulting in Leadership Emergence in Leaderless Group Discussion." Ph.D. dissertation, University of Minnesota, 1963.

The literature on the reinforcement of verbal behavior is extensive. For a survey of some early studies, see:

Krasner, Leonard A. "Studies of the Conditioning of Verbal Behavior," *Psychological Bulletin,* **55** (1958), 148–170.

For some typical studies see:

Aiken, Edwin G. "Interaction Process Analysis Changes Accompanying Operant Conditioning of Verbal Frequency in Small Groups," *Perceptual and Motor Skills*, **21** (1965), 52–54.

Endler, Norman S. "Conformity as a Function of Different Reinforcement Schedules," *Journal of Personality and Social Psychology*, **4** (1966), 175–180.

Endler, Norman S. "The Effects of Verbal Reinforcement on Conformity and Deviant Behavior," *Journal of Social Psychology*, **66** (1965), 147–154.

Shapiro, David. "Group Learning of Speech Sequences Without Awareness," *Science*, **144** (1964), 74–76.

CHAPTER 9
ROLES

A popular psychological concept is that of individual personality. Usually personality is thought of as the sum of an individual's physical, mental, emotional, and social characteristics. One might account for personality in this sense in several ways. Personality might be regarded as the stable behavior patterns exhibited by a person in a wide variety of situations. A more detailed explanation of individual characteristics is furnished by dividing up the distinguishing features and labeling each part as a *trait* such as intelligence, extroversion, dominance, verbal fluency, flexibility, and so forth. The trait approach furnishes a theoretical basis for describing a person as having a bright, vivacious, and charming personality.

This way of describing personality is useful because it allows psychologists to name an individual's dominant traits or dominant behavior. An individual can be described as usually acting intelligently even though on occasion he has been observed to do stupid things. He could be characterized as frequently dominant and verbal even if on occasion he is quiet and submissive. Given the theory of personality traits, attempts can be made to measure the amount of various personality traits within a given person by standardized testing procedures. A clinical psychologist can, therefore, describe an individual in terms of his intelligence test scores, his critical thinking test scores, and his scores on the Minnesota Multiphasic Personality Inventory, or some other personality index. Such descriptions are particularly helpful if they enable the tester to predict how an individual will perform in a given situation. When a psychologist can discover traits that allow him to predict that a particular student can graduate from college or that Mr. S should be a successful business manager, the definition of personality as stable behavior patterns is useful.

The concept of individual personality may also be defined in social psychological terms—that is, personality is the individual's predisposition toward certain stable behavior patterns *as actualized within a given social field*. The variables that affect an individual's behavior within the group comprise the *social field.* Some personality traits remain stable, that is, do not change appreciably, as a person moves from group to group (changes social fields)—these traits are termed *field invariant*. But a number of behaviors are *determined* by the social field—that is, whether or not a person is talkative, charming, dominant, aggressive, submissive, funny, serious, solemn, stupid, and so forth. The young woman, for example, who is charming and pleasant on a double date may be shrill, unpleasant, and bossy at home with her mother and her sisters. What kind of person is she really? The second way of defining personality implies that what sort of person she is depends on both her stable personality traits (field-invariant behavior) *and* her role within a given group (field-variant behavior). The first approach to defining personality can only note and disregard the exceptions to otherwise stable behavior patterns. The second approach is more useful for the student of group methods because it provides a more complete explanation for the behavior of individuals within groups and organizations.

Bales and his associates have worked out an elaborate framework to account for individual personality in social–psychological terms. Bales developed his system using data from his Interaction Process Analysis technique (described in Chapter 8), but he also used data from a number of personality tests such as the Minnesota Multiphasic Personality Inventory and from a procedure for studying value statements in small-group communication. The system is based on the technique of factor analysis, which is a statistical procedure designed to take a complex set of relationships and boil them down to a few basic "factors" on the assumption that, if a number of relationships seem to vary together, they may reflect a more powerful underlying feature in the data.

Bales developed an account of group roles that explained behavior in terms of three basic dimensions. He interprets role positions by presenting them geometrically. He defines group space in terms of upward–downward, forward–backward, and positive–negative dimensions. One can, theoretically, observe a person in a group and plot that individual's place in group space. The account contains 26 types of group roles and their value-directions. The group role types include such positions as in the upward dimension of group space (U), in the upward–positive dimensions (UP), in the upward, positive, forward dimension (UPF), and so on, until 26 different positions are described.

A final important outcome of the framework of analysis is a paper-and-pencil "Interpersonal Rating Form." Participants in a group can use the form to rate fellow members after they have worked together for a period of time. The rating form also resulted from a factor-analysis procedure and consists of 26 items that are loaded with one, two, or three of the factors. Each question is typical of one of the positions in group space, so that a "yes" answer to one question is loaded on the upward dimension (U), one on the upward–positive (UP), one on the upward–positive–forward position (UPF), and so forth. One person can evaluate another's role by answering "yes" or "no" to such questions as "Is his (or her) *rate of participation* generally high?" A "yes" answer is loaded on the upward dimension of group space, and a "no" is loaded on the downward dimension.

Group members or nonparticipant observers may use the Interpersonal Rating Form to get an index of perceived roles in a group with little expenditure of time and effort. Assume that member A rates member B after several hours of group meetings, and the summed index of answers to the 26 questions yields an upward–positive–forward (UPF) position in group space. Participant or nonparticipant observers can use the rating to diagnose role ambiguity, conflict, stability, and structure. Bales further presents a relatively detailed analysis of each of the roles which includes such things as how the person in a type such as UPF sees himself, how others see him, how he tends to participate in the communication process and networks, and what values he expresses. The role analysis also includes an account of the way a person in a certain position tends to participate in coalitions or comes into conflict with other role types.

Bales takes the position that the way members perceive an individual's interpersonal behavior is a function of both personality and group role. Bales sees a *group role* as consisting of all of the group members' perceptions, evaluations, and expectations of an individual. He views *personality* as the relatively enduring characteristics of the member. Bales argues that a member's personality is not the same as his role in a group since his behavior in any given group reflects only a side of his personality which is elicited by that particular group. Interestingly enough, Bales suggests that the line of inference ought not to go from the analysis of individual personality to conclusions about role behavior, but rather that one can, on the basis of observed and perceived behavior, place an individual into group space and then make inferences about the kind of personality traits usually associated with that position. Thus, one studies group behavior both to discover an individual's personality and to assess the influence of the group on the individual's role.

Bales' framework of analysis of role and individual personality plus the empirical verification for it essentially agrees with the results of the Minnesota Studies as described in this chapter. Whenever independent investigators arrive at essentially similar findings, they provide corroboration for one another. By contrast with other research efforts such as Schutz's FIRO (discussed in Chapter 7) or the attempts to estimate group behavior on the basis of personality profiles, Bales' account provides a much more detailed and complete explanation that includes data from personality tests, value scales, and the process analysis of group communication.

the concept of role

The process by which roles emerge in a leaderless group discussion furnishes a detailed explanation of the way an individual, who already has a set of field-invariant personality traits, learns the additional (field-variant) behavior unique to a particular group.

In the theater, *role* means assuming or being assigned a part in a play. In group discussion, a member is assigned a role, or he assumes one. In this regard the discussant is much like the actor. However, he differs from the actor in an important way; his part is not written for him.

Role, in the small group, is defined as that set of common perceptions and expectations shared by the members about the behavior of an individual in both the task and social dimensions of group interaction. *Role* is not used in this context to refer to a formal position within an organizational structure. Quite often role is defined as a set of behaviors appropriate to a specific position within some formal organization, but here the term is used to indicate the *informal* group norms that place an individual within the group. The part an individual plays within a task-oriented small group may continue for weeks, months, or even years. When the other members know what part he will play and he knows what part they expect of him, he has assumed a role. If he works with a wide variety of groups, he may find that he plays a diversity of roles. Students in small-group-communication classes often participate in many other groups. Some are active in church groups. Some are members of athletic teams. Some are active in campus politics. One of the case studies at Minnesota included a student who played the role of a quiet, interested worker. This same student was quarterback on the football team and played the role of a field leader—a take-charge player. Was he really a field leader and take-charge guy? Or was he really a quiet, interested follower? The answer is that his personality was dependent, to some extent, on the group.

Another case study contained a handsome, fast-talking young man and an equally fast-talking attractive coed. Before the end of the first meeting they had a severe and disagreeable personality clash. Within a week the coed left the group. When interviewed about her experiences, she reported that after one acrimonious session the fellow had invited her to a campus coffee shop. They had spent several hours over coffee, and she was puzzled by how much nicer he really was outside the group. But the minute they returned to the group the fighting began again. The point is that a number of socially important behaviors are field variant. Individuals change their personality in important ways depending on the role they play in a particular group. Think of yourself in various groups, and see if you are not serious in some groups, joking and laughing and clowning in others, taking charge and leading the way in some groups, and quietly going along in others.

The role a member takes in a group is, to the objective observer (that is, someone watching, but not part of the group), what the member says and does as the group interacts, while for the group members, it also includes what they *expect* him to say and do. If they expect him to disagree, they will turn to him for such disagreement when it seems appropriate. If they expect him to crack a joke when the group feels primary tension, they will turn to him when they feel primary tension. The role a member takes includes what he thinks the group expects from him in terms of interactions and work. There are two sides to the concept of role as it applies to small groups. One side is the objective and overt behavior. Several independent observers can verify directly and can agree about the truth or falsity of statements describing this behavior; for example, observers might agree that a person got up from his chair and wrote "Time remaining—15 minutes" on the blackboard. The other side is the subjective perception of the individual members of the group. One may perceive writing "time" on the blackboard as getting the group to work and increase its efficiency. Another may consider the same action as an attempt to wrest the leadership of the group from the assigned chairman. And another may perceive the action as an attempt to show off. The Minnesota Studies indicate that each member perceives a slightly different group than does every other member. At the same time, the subjective perceptions of the participants will exhibit some commonality. They often share a consensus of what has happened and what is *expected* from the various members in the future. When these expectations stabilize, the roles within the group are stable. For the group member, the subjective side of role perception is more important than the objective side. Once common expectations about what the person will do and say have been reached, he has his *role* in the group. He knows what he is to say and do while working with the group. And like some actors, he is happier if, in effect, he knows his lines and the way the action should go.

the mechanism of role emergence
in newly formed groups

THE BASIC MODEL

The Minnesota Studies used the zero-history *leaderless group discussion* (to be referred to as the LGD) as the basis of test-tube groups for the study of the mechanism of role emergence and specialization. The basic model of group functioning is that of a generalized process typical of the LGD. Quite often, idealized models that describe basic processes can be used to predict and explain phenomena. For example, investigators began the study of the acceleration of a freely falling body by positing a simplified condition in which the object fell in a vacuum. They first determined this basic rate and then applied the model to more realistic conditions by adding such complicating factors as the effect of the resistance of the atmosphere and the force and direction of wind currents. With these additions, they were able to apply their theory to such practical problems as aiming cannons. Much the same procedure can be followed with the theory in this chapter, although the knowledge about the LGD is not as exact as the knowledge a ballistics expert has about the firing of the cannon. The model will be applied to the small task-oriented group operating in the organizational setting in Chapter 14. The model is, thus, scientific rather than a touchstone as was the model of the pragmatic style discussed in Chapter 2. One does not find groups in which the process of role specialization described by the model does not take place. The model has been successfully adapted and accommodated to the functioning of such groups within formal organizations. Roger Mosvick of Macalester College, St. Paul, Minnesota, has applied the model to the specific case of project-organized groups in his capacity as communication consultant for Minneapolis Honeywell. The author has made the same use of the theoretical model as consultant to the Rochester, Minnesota, branch of IBM, the Control Data Corporation, and the Minneapolis Honeywell Ordnance Division.

The test-tube groups used in the Minnesota Studies were composed of strangers and had no formal structure. Every member was a peer. Many of the groups were set up in discussion classes and had a clear objective and a specified time limit. The groups were newly formed and, thus, had no history.

The first important discovery in these studies was that, after several hours of discussion, the members began to specialize, and some people gained status and esteem. The case studies of many discussions indicated that specialization of function and its resultant status arrangement occurred in the majority of groups.

The second important discovery was that the discussants did not take roles, but rather each worked out his role jointly with the others. The process by which a given individual came to specialize within the LGD was a dynamic set of transactions in which the person tried out various role functions and was encouraged or discouraged to continue by the responses of the group. The dynamics of the give-and-take by which members of a group work out their roles are intricate and complicated, but the basic model emerges from the study of these test-tube

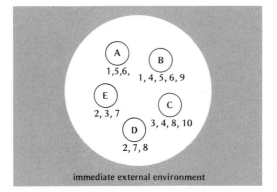

immediate external environment

Figure 7. Model of the LGD. Members have native or acquired abilities to do the following tasks better than other tasks: (1) initiating action, (2) doing routine chores, (3) being funny and releasing tension, (4) testing soundness of information, (5) dividing up group work and assigning jobs, (6) gathering information, (7) following orders carefully and doing job assigned, (8) giving suggestions as to possible ways to go about doing a job, (9) drawing inferences, and (10) evaluating inferences and plans of action.

groups. That model assumes the conditions of the leaderless group discussion. The theoretical explanation of the mechanism by which roles emerge in newly formed groups consists of two parts. The first is a list of components of the LGD including the requisite social and task functions matched against the talents, skills, and abilities of the people assembled to participate in the discussion. The second part of the model diagrams the basic transactions used by the group to test and develop specialization.

Turning to the first part of the model, Figure 7 presents some of the behaviors required for group discussion and supplies a hypothetical breakdown of how the various skills might be distributed. Thus, member A is good at initiating action, dividing a group's work, assigning tasks, and gathering information. Member B is best at initiating action, testing the soundness of information, dividing the group's work, assigning jobs, gathering information, and drawing inferences. Member C is talented in being funny and releasing tensions, testing soundness of information, suggesting possible ways to do a job, and evaluating inferences and plans. Member A could do all these things, but as an individual he is best at the activities listed.

The personnel of the LGD, of course, must do many other things than the items listed in Figure 7. These 10 role functions are among the most important, however, and the same basic model of reward and punishment is used by the group to teach additional role functions to the members.

The second part of the model of the basic process of role specializa-

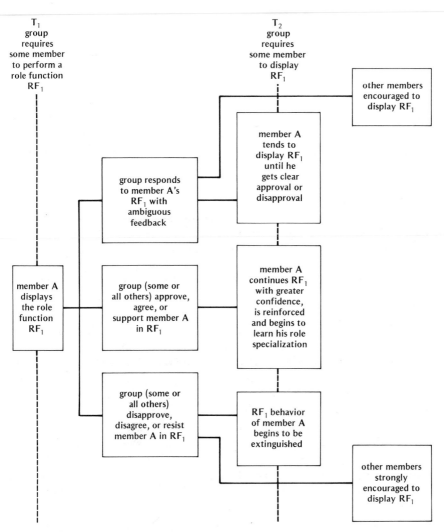

T₁ — T_1
group requires some member to perform a role function RF_1

T₂ — T_2
group requires some member to display RF_1

other members encouraged to display RF_1

member A tends to display RF_1 until he gets clear approval or disapproval

group responds to member A's RF_1 with ambiguous feedback

member A displays the role function RF_1

group (some or all others) approve, agree, or support member A in RF_1

member A continues RF_1 with greater confidence, is reinforced and begins to learn his role specialization

group (some or all others) disapprove, disagree, or resist member A in RF_1

RF_1 behavior of member A begins to be extinguished

other members strongly encouraged to display RF_1

Figure 8. The Dynamics of Role Specialization.

tion is an application of psychological learning theory to the group context as indicated by Figure 8. At a given point in time, T_1, the group requires that certain social or task functions be performed. The social field exerts pressure on the discussants to do what is needed. A given individual, member A, is stimulated to display the required behavior, role function RF_1. The group responds to A's behavior with ambiguous feedback, or with approval, or with disapproval. At the next point in time, T_2, that the group requires someone to perform RF_1, the social system already has some history which affects the response of all members to the pressure of the social field. If the original response to A's display of RF_1 was ambiguous and if member A has a strong drive to assume that role function, he will tend to repeat the RF_1 activity at T_2. However, another member with similar drives will also be encouraged to display RF_1 at T_2. If some or all of the others approved, agreed, or accepted A's behavior, he was reinforced at T_1 and will tend to display RF_1 with greater confidence at T_2. If the group again reinforces the behavior at T_2, member A will continue to perform RF_1 as the need arises. In this fashion, RF_1 becomes part of member A's repertoire of behavior within the group. He is, in a sense, taught his specialization by the reinforcement the group provides him. To be sure, each person tends to try out first for those parts that they have played successfully in other groups and for those role functions that they most enjoy and find most rewarding; but the dynamics of the process move individuals into roles that they work out with the approval of the others. When member A has been reinforced at T_1, others who may wish to perform that role function will tend not to do so at T_2.

Disapproval, disagreement, and resistance at T_1 are punishing to the individual, and he will be more reluctant to exhibit the RF_1 behavior again at T_2. If he tries and continues to receive disapproval from the others, the RF_1 behavior is extinguished, and the individual will begin to try other role functions in order to find his place in the group. Sometimes, a person has an extremely strong drive to assume a set of role functions and continues RF_1 behavior in the face of strong and continued resistance. When the individual fails to learn his role from the usual group feedback of reinforcement and resistance, he may be characterized as inflexible and insensitive. The group often finds such a person frustrating to work with, and members wonder how to deal with him.

The operation of the basic model is well illustrated by the typical first meeting of an LGD. The first task facing the LGD is to release primary tension. Referring back to Figure 7, both member C and member E have a capacity to be funny (skill 3). Having had some experience, they are sensitive to primary tensions and make attempts at releasing them. Member C has a characteristic style of being funny. He makes small talk and watches for the response. When he thinks another member will respond favorably, he makes a mildly insulting personal comment about the member and laughs to indicate that it is all in fun. He then waits for the reaction of the others. If his attempt at humor fails, he is less likely to try again. Early in the meeting, however, the typical responses are ambiguous; that is, some people smile or laugh a little, but C cannot decide whether they like his little jibe or not. Probably the members themselves are not yet sure. The primary tension remains, and E takes the opportunity to try to break the tension. He, too, has a unique way of being funny. He is clever at impersonations, a good pantomimist, and he relies to some extent on visual gags for his humor.

Member E comments that he is feeling ill at ease. He shrugs his shoulders into his coat and pantomimes to show the coldness of the group atmosphere. His grimaces and shakes are tentative, but indicate what he could do if he really let himself go. He, too, waits for the group's response. There are many other styles of being funny demonstrated by contenders for the "best-liked" role. They may be gracious, smiling, and agreeable. They may have a stock of funny stories memorized and handy for most occasions. They may kid themselves. The student can supply from his own experiences the kinds of behavior that act to release group tensions and contribute to an individual assuming the most popular role.

Typically, member E will also receive ambiguous responses to his attempts at humor, unless he is clearly much better in the eyes of the group than member C. The stage is now set for a competition between C and E as to who will do this particular job.

The competition between E and C will continue for a time until the group decides that E will be their tension releaser, or that C is more to their liking and that he will be their joker, or that E and C will share in doing this job. This sharing may involve a relatively equal balance, or one may do most of the tension releasing with the other supporting and adding to the clowning.

The group reaches the decision about member E and member C in the following way. They watch the two demonstrating their wares for a time and then vote for either E or C or the two together. The voting is done by cues that are interpreted as reinforcement or resistance. As long as E and C perceive the response to their kidding and cutting up as unclear or ambiguous, the issue is in doubt, and they will continue the contest. When A begins to relax and laugh with what E perceives as genuine delight at E, and when A groans or frowns or remains disapproving of C's attempts at humor, then A has cast his vote for E. Should B now begin to support C's attempts at humor the group would still be evenly divided, and the issue could only be resolved by D clearly indicating which contender he will support. When a clear consensus has been reached, the question is decided. The votes cannot be forced and, with the exceptions of such duties as secretary, chairman, or moderator, are seldom dealt with directly.

With the release of primary tension, the group often feels pressure to begin work. Members A and B have in their repertoire of skills the initiation of action. Member A suggests to the group that they get down to business. He is met by silence. Member B suggests that before they begin work they should consider the best procedure for working. Member D is now confused. Member E does a little pantomime about how really confused he is and the group laughs, this time not with primary tension but releasing some secondary tension because A and B are marked men.

They have both made *leadership* moves, and each member of the group is directly concerned with the question of whether A or B will initiate the group's action. A contest now ensues between A and B as to who will get this job. Again, the decision may be that either A or B will be responsible primarily for this function or that they will share it. And again, the consensus comes from social interactions that are perceived by the contenders and the others as supporting one of the two members.

In the same fashion, all other tasks that the group must perform are delegated after a period of interaction during which the members try their hand at the various chores. Some functions may become almost the exclusive specialization of a particularly adept person. For example, the function of disagreeing may become the special duty of one member. Many functions, however, will be shared by several members and sometimes by everyone. All might gather information and bring it to the group for processing. Nonetheless, one or two members would spend more of their time in the activity, and the group would expect them to furnish the bulk of the information. After working together for some time, the LGD makes assignments in this indirect way by reinforcing or resisting the interactions of the participants. When a consensus is reached on the assignment of jobs, the *roles* have clearly emerged, and members know what the group expects them to do. At this point, the roles in the group have stabilized. The stabilization of roles releases both primary and secondary tensions. People know where they fit in. The question of what the group will think of them is now answered. When the participants know what to expect and what others expect of them, there are fewer indeterminate situations, fewer rude shocks, fewer punishing and surprising social interactions. They can relax and concentrate on the job without having to wonder how people will react socially. With a few exceptions, the group's cohesiveness increases rather dramatically when roles are stabilized.

THE IDIOSYNCRATIC NATURE OF INDIVIDUAL ROLES

To clarify the diversity of functions that go into role development, one might label the typical role patterns as clarifier, initiator, information giver, tension releaser, and information tester. More dramatically, students of LGD might label such roles as Mr. Pessimist, Mr. Egoist, Miss Vivacious, Mr. Best Liked, Miss America, and Mr. Joker. Such labels are oversimplifications of the roles that actually develop in groups and should be considered as illustrative rather than descriptive. Actually, an objective description of the behavior and interactions of the members of a particular LGD would reveal that all members at one time or another function in all 10 of the categories listed in Figure 7. If an investigator made an analysis using the Bales category system or any other system, he would find that all participants had some interactions coded in every category. However, some individuals would have a larger percentage of their total interactions clustered in one or several categories.

Obviously, the concept of role cannot be limited exclusively to several categories of behavior. The 10 items of the illustrative (and also somewhat oversimplified) list in Figure 7 may divide as follows: Member A largely does 1, 6; member B does 1, 4, 5, 9; member C does 4, 8; member D does 2, 6, 7; member E does 3, 7. All the members participate in doing 6, although A and D are looked to by the group to gather most of the information.

This particular clustering of chores associated with each role and the amount of sharing of functions (A, 1, 6; B, 1, 4, 5, 9; C, 4, 8; D, 2, 6, 7; E, 3, 7) is unique to the hypothetical group. For example, if 25 students are placed by random selection in five LGDs and work until the basic process is completed and a role structure is stabilized, observers can describe their roles. If five new LGDs are set up using the same 25 students, and the process is repeated, observers will agree that an individual does not perform the same functions for the second group that he did for the first. Member B, who did functions 1, 4, 5, 9 in his first group, would not have an identical cluster in his second group, although his role may be very similar, say 1, 5, 10, and he might be perceived as the leader by both groups. (But he would not be quite the same kind of leader in the second group as he was in the first.) On the other hand, his role might be composed of quite a different set of functions, such as being funny and releasing tension. In the latter case, he would be perceived as leader in the first group, but not in the second.

Students often bring to a group meeting a simple trait framework for stereotyping the others in the group. The unstructured social field of a zero-history group is tension producing, and a trait stereotype provides an immediate short-term reward because it allows one to structure the group quickly. Unfortunately, the trait framework does not anticipate the way the group develops, and the person who persists in using a stereotyped-trait approach to get his bearings in the group finds himself continually frustrated, disturbed, and confused by the way people act in what he considers uncharacteristic ways. A person with a trait viewpoint may join a zero-history group and soon come to the conclusion that member A is quiet and unassuming, that member B is a loud extrovert, that member C is frivolous, and so forth. Once he labels any member as being a certain kind of person with one or two distinguishing personality traits, he may assume that these members will not change their personalities. When member A grows more and more active and assertive in the meetings, the individual who has stereotyped A as quiet and unassuming will often write in his diary response to a group meeting that A is changing in surprising and unexplainable ways and that he was wrong to judge A as being quiet and unassuming. Actually, he will add, A is a much more talkative and pushy person than he at first thought; he has been misled, and now A's "true" personality traits are emerging.

Students at Minnesota have found it difficult to transcend the simple stereotyping of traits and adopt the more complex and adequate framework for interpreting roles such as is presented in this chapter. Once they move from a simple trait viewpoint, they often adopt an oversimplified set of role stereotypes. They evaluate the roles of group members in static terms according to one salient role function such as: member A was an information seeker, member B was a leader contender, and member C was the socio–emotional leader. This is still too narrow a view for a realistic evaluation and for the ongoing adjustments needed for effective group endeavor.

To better understand the dynamism and complexity of group roles, one must move past the tendency to make static stereotypes that assume that every group will contain a limited number of roles and that these will consist of one or two kinds of salient communication and behavior. People act in extremely complex ways, and no static labeling of one or two salient role functions for each member can do justice to human behavior in a small group. What is required is a concept that sees each role in a group as a dynamic set of expectations and behaviors that are part of a complex communication system and are thus sensitive to changes in others' roles and to external pressures on the group. Despite the dynamic complexity of the small group as a social system, particularly as the group is beginning work and structuring itself, clusters of expectations and behaviors do emerge in time to form discernible patterns, and these profiles, as they stabilize, make up the roles of the group members.

FIELD VARIANCE OF ROLES

The mechanism of role emergence accounts for the *field-variant* portion of an individual's personality. It works like the "operant conditioning" model of the behavioral psychologists. By offering social rewards and punishments, the LGD sets up operant conditioning schedules that teach each person his role. When he behaves properly, the group members reward him; and when he behaves in a different fashion, they punish him. In successful groups, each member's behavior is, to some extent, shaped by the social reinforcements, such as shows of agreement and of tension release, that he receives. A person has a history of success and failure at doing the chores demanded of him, but never knows if a particular group will decide that he should continue to do what he has done successfully before.

Reasons for field variance of roles. Why does a group reinforce one sort of behavior rather than another for a given member? This explanation is somewhat speculative and is based largely on clinical insights of case studies rather than on systematic empirical study. Quite often the decisions seem to come fortuitously. A chance remark, an interaction that is perceived as a slight or an insult, a mistake that causes laughter, or a sudden group crisis may play a determining part in role emergence. However, groups often exhibit several tendencies that play a part in the role specializations. Although individuals may selectively resist or reinforce behaviors of other members for personal reasons, the vector of the group's reinforcement tends to support the behavior of each that is best for the entire group. When an individual does things that the others perceive as attempts to manipulate the group for his own personal satisfactions, they resist vigorously. After a time, group members seem to make some decisions as to the skill with which each functions in a given task, and they tend to reinforce fellow members in their area of greatest competence.

To return to the illustration in Figure 7, assume B is perceived by the other members to be the most competent in functions 1, 4, 5, 6, and 9. The star is B who does almost everything well and better than anyone else in the group. However, he does not do everything. The LGD conditions his behavior into certain special channels. The members perceive these as being the most vital for the group; they then turn to the second- and third-best choice for the other important chores. In this situation, something analogous to the law of comparative costs in economics seems to be operating. For example, California soil can produce oranges for 3¢ apiece and corn for 50¢ a bushel, and South Dakota soil can produce oranges for $1 apiece and corn for 75¢ a bushel. According to this principle, it is to the advantage of each state to produce its best product and trade with the other even though California can produce both crops more efficiently than South Dakota. California should use its soil to raise oranges and trade oranges for the corn they need, rather than raise oranges and corn. Thus, although B is best at gathering information, the group allows him to specialize in other things and turns to the next best members, C and D, for the gathering of information. Member A, who has been the leader of a number of similar groups, finds himself at a disadvantage because of B's greater skills and does not emerge as leader of this group. Should the group contain very little talent for releasing tension, they might call on someone to do these things who has seldom played this role. A student may discover that although he is normally task oriented, industrious, and serious, in one group he is the "life of the party."

Despite tendencies to structure the roles within a group to make maximum use of resources, there is considerable waste in the way most groups arrive at role structures, and sometimes they make mistakes. A person with ability to perform a certain function may be rejected because of his "style," and group members may assign the task to someone with a more pleasing style but with less competence. Group members have considerable difficulty describing what "style" involves. They report that there was "something" about the individual that they "did not like." Sometimes they focus on slight cues such as tics or mannerisms or facial expression or vocal inflection. Sometimes such things as verbalism, language usage, or sentence structure cause the group to reject a member in his bid for certain functions.

Many role functions are assigned gratuitously during the course of group interactions. Sometimes a person is inadvertently qualified as an authority by another participant. A member may ask "Who is the political science major?" Joe responds that he is, and another member says, "Well, I guess we know now who is the authority." The group begins to treat him as an authority, and he begins to act like one. Although Joe is a political science major, he may not be the member best equipped to do the job for the group; however, because he mentioned his political science major and because a member who was trying to break the tension asked who the political science major was, Joe assumed a certain task function. Other such chance occurrences in the early meetings can influence the way role clusters develop. Usually, if the groups develop sufficient cohesiveness and continue for a long enough time, they recognize their mistakes and reshuffle the roles.

fantasy theme analysis of roles

One important reason for a fantasy theme to chain through a group is that it can reflect a common problem for the members. If the problem is one that is likely to arouse social tensions if the members attempt to discuss it openly, they may repress it, and it then tends to surface in symbolic form as a fantasy chain. Often, when a group is in the process of discovering its role structure and status arrangements, people come into conflict with one another or feel resentment and frustration because the group seems to be pushing them into roles they find unrewarding and unattractive. On occasion, the group members feel that they cannot teach a particularly inflexible member a suitable role because, despite all of their verbal and nonverbal resistance to the unwanted behavior, the individual continues to act in the same way. Many times group members find the problems of power, leadership, and authority particularly tension producing. They may feel one of the participants is too domineering, too bossy, too pig-headed, and yet have difficulty confronting that person directly about the frustrating behavior.

Freud argued that individuals often repressed needs or problems that the conscious mind found embarrassing or painful and that these difficulties then tended to surface in distorted symbolic terms in the person's dreams. A trained person could thus use dream analysis to discover the repressed difficulty. Freud used the analogy of a country under heavy censorship so open discussion of problems was repressed. The people would, under such circumstances, express their criticism of the repressive regime and their political problems in the form of jokes, parables, and fables which could not be censored because their manifest content was not closely and clearly related to the realities of the situation; but, for someone who understood the context, the application to the immediate situation would be clear. In much the same way a group may bring its difficulties concerning the emergence of suitable roles for its members to the surface in the form of a fantasy chain on a theme that has a double meaning. The overt meaning would relate to other people in other contexts, but the covert meaning would relate to the interpretation of the story by finding applications to the group's role problems.

One of the case studies at Minnesota was of a task force investigating curriculum changes in secondary education. All of the members of the group were in their thirties and forties, and most were secondary school teachers or administrators. Very early in the group's life, a basic conflict over the role of leadership developed between two inflexible and aggressive males. The meetings often became debates between the two members over procedural matters. As a result of the bickering, the group's progress on the task was very slow, and the meetings dragged on for several hours each session. After several meetings, a new member joined the group and soon became aware of the basic conflict. Very tactfully the new member began to try to compromise differences and to give the group structure and direction. The remaining members began to support the new member's efforts at leadership, but the two antagonists continued to bicker and to monopolize the discussion, and the group remained at an impasse despite the fact that all the members were dedicated, hard working, and conscientious.

One of the female members had been working particularly hard at collecting information and preparing materials for curriculum revision. In the course of discussing the problem, she began to dramatize the difficulty of getting innovation into a school system. She noted that it was "particularly true of new teachers going into a system where everything is cut and dried already, and no one wants to rock the boat."

The group began to chain into the drama of the difficulty of innovation. One member asked, "Does the system tend to just perpetuate itself?" and a bit later asked again, "Where does change come from then?" To which the woman who began the chain replied, "As people die off, leave, or move and new ones come in. Then as new administrators come in it's much easier. For example at Olson Junior High—they have administrators who are very flexible." The group grew more excited about the drama of the hopelessness of trying to get anything accepted by the typical secondary school administration, and the plight of a "new young teacher" who was "on the ball," but had a hard time. She was characterized as spending "more energy in fighting for what she knows is right than in teaching." The woman who began the chain then noted, "I've even had trouble introducing ideas I know have worked into a traditional speech program. . . . When I make a recommendation to the team teacher he feels defensive as if I'm criticizing what he's done in the past." The chain continued for a few minutes longer and the woman finally said, "A teacher can't reach the administrator 'til she's allowed to know him honestly as a person . . . and not as someone who's supervising the system. Out of three administrators, only one I would feel confident to go confide in because he's personable, he's human . . . he's a person. The others are on cloud nine, and we see them only at faculty meetings." The fantasy was now cutting very close to the here-and-now problems of the group, and another member broke it off by saying, "Getting back to the paper now. . . ."

Clearly the drama of the inflexible and unheeding school administrators versus the flexible and willing-to-listen principal was a drama with a double meaning, and the analogy of the school administrators to the administration of the group was a useful starting place to analyze the group's problems.

An observer, facilitator, or instructor can thus use fantasy theme analysis as a diagnostic tool to help the group bring to the surface the hidden agenda items relating to role emergence which may impede their progress. Group members may listen to the tapes of their meetings and discover the fantasy themes that relate to their problems as well. Not all fantasy themes that chain through a group will relate to role problems, of course, and one must always be careful not to overinterpret a group's fantasies.

status and roles

STATUS ASSIGNMENT OF ROLES

Once roles have clearly emerged and stabilized, members arrange the roles in order of importance—the most important, the next most important, and so forth. An observer can arrange the roles in order of importance on the basis of certain behaviors exhibited by the group members.

For example, group members tend to direct more talk to the people they consider important (playing an important role). The members in the more important roles tend to talk more to the whole group. The person in the most important role receives the most consideration from the others. Members of the group perceive this ordering of roles; and in groups with stable role structures, there is considerable consensus about the status of various roles. This is particularly true of the more important roles. *Status* is the importance of a role in the group. A status ladder organizes the roles that have emerged in order of their importance. Each group with stable roles has a "pecking" order.

The functions that the group will consider important depend to some extent on the kind of group. If the group clearly succeeds or fails, such as a basketball team that wins or loses, and if the individual's contribution to victory can be clearly measured, then the task specialist (highest scorer) may have high status. In organizations where success or failure is not so easily measured, the best-liked person may be of higher status. In college discussion classes, the leader often holds the high-status role.

No common pattern of status describes groups of similar composition and functions. Some individuals may be so skillful that they are perceived as having higher status than another less skillful person whose role may be more important. Sometimes, for example, a leader emerges because he is the best of the contenders, although the others are not too happy with him. If the best-liked person is extremely talented, he may have a higher place on the status ladder than his role implies.

STATUS AND NEED GRATIFICATION

The social esteem and material rewards that a member receives are closely associated with his status. High-status positions are pleasant. The group makes a high-status person feel important and influential. They show him deference, listen to him, ask his advice, and often reward him with a greater share of the group's goods. He gets a bigger office, more secretaries, better furniture, more salary, a bigger car, and so forth. Even in communication-class discussion groups, the high-status members receive considerable gratification of their social and esteem needs. One of the most powerful forces drawing people into groups is the attraction of high status.

Since the high-status positions in the group offer such substantial rewards there is always a considerable struggle for them. Indeed, primary tensions in newly formed groups result from the uncertainty about who will become the "important" people in the group. The resulting struggles generate a considerable portion of the secondary tensions that a group experiences.

group structure and cohesiveness

As stated previously, when a role structure emerges in a leaderless group discussion, the cohesiveness of the group generally rises rather dramatically. There are, however, some exceptions to this general tendency. When a person does not like the role he receives, he finds the group less attractive. He might not like his role because it is of little importance, and the others treat him like a recruit in the rear rank. Of the roles in the hypothetical group, for example, member D, whose tasks include gathering information, doing routine chores, following orders carefully, and doing the job assigned, is the one most likely to feel this way.

When members of the group do not like the way someone performs the functions assigned to him—whether they were fooled by his early behavior or had accidentally given him an important role that he could not handle—they will depose him from his position. Such reshuffling extracts a high toll on the group's cohesiveness. It creates secondary tension and upsets the role structure to the point where the group must examine not only the two changing roles but the other roles as well.

summary

For the purpose of examining the roles assumed by individual members in small groups, personality is defined as the field-invariant potential for behavior plus the field-variant conditions that actuate that potential. The actuated behavior results from the conditioning of the individual by the group.

A nonparticipating observer may describe the role a member has in a group in terms of what the person says and does as he interacts with the group. For the participants, however, the roles are often defined in terms of their expectations. When these expectations stabilize for all or most members of a group, the role structure has stabilized.

Each group has certain tasks that must be done if the group is to succeed. Each individual brings to the group native or acquired potentials to perform some of these functions. During the course of their early interactions, members try one and then another of these functions, and the group then reinforces or punishes the attempts. Gradually the reinforced behavior is learned by each member and they expect to perform these functions and be rewarded for doing so.

Some of the assignment of role functions seems to be gratuitous, yet there are two general tendencies within the dynamics of most groups: (1) the behavior perceived by the members as most beneficial to the entire group is reinforced, and (2) the behavior of each member is channeled into the functions that he performs most efficiently. Fantasy chains often provide a useful diagnostic tool to discover problems relating to role emergence.

With the assignment of roles, the group also awards status. The group rewards valuable roles with shows of deference and other social reinforcements. Because of the status factor, most groups experience considerable struggle among at least some of the participants for the high-status positions.

General role stability usually results in a higher level of cohesiveness. However, if a number of members are disgruntled by their roles, they become inactive and actually reduce the cohesiveness of the group.

QUESTIONS FOR STUDY

1. How does the personality-trait theory account for individual behavior?
2. How does the social-field theory of group roles account for individual behavior?
3. What is the difference between the field-variant and the field-invariant dimensions of personality?
4. What is meant by "role" in the small group?
5. What is the mechanism by which the group encourages role specialization among its members?
6. What is meant by role emergence in a leaderless group discussion?
7. What is the relationship between role stability and group cohesiveness? Why are they related?
8. How does the theoretical model of role emergence account for the field-variant portion of individual personality?
9. What is the basis on which the group assigns status to individual roles?
10. Why do members often come into conflict over roles?

EXERCISES

1. Form a leaderless group discussion with a specific task and objective. Tape record the meetings. Keep a diary of your experiences in the group. Record your impressions of the role specialization, struggle, and stabilization. Listen to the tape recordings, and check your perceptions. Hold a group postmortem session in which you discuss one another's perceptions of the role structure. Isolate the group's fantasies, and see if they relate to the role emergence in the group.
2. Form a small task-oriented group with a specific task and objectives. Assign each member certain set role functions. One member may be assigned the tension-release duties, another the task of initiating action, a third may control the channels of communication, a fourth might disagree and test ideas, and so forth. Tape record the meetings. Hold a postmortem session in which you discuss the effect of assigning role functions on the development of the group structure.
3. Select a group that you have worked with for several months that is characterized by considerable tension, conflict, and lack of productivity. How much of the group's difficulties can be accounted for by role struggles and lack of role stability? Map out a course of group therapy designed to deal with the role problems in the group.

4. Form a zero-history leaderless group discussion with a specific task and a clear goal. After each session, have all of the members rate one another on one of the forms of the "Interpersonal Ratings" test found in Robert F. Bales, *Personality and Interpersonal Behavior*. New York: Holt, Rinehart and Winston, 1970, pp. 6, 12, 13. Each member also fills out one form as he estimates the others will rate him. After a number of sessions, tabulate the results, and discover if members' perceptions of one another's position in group space grow more compatible as the group continues. Read the descriptions of the role types and value directions in Bales, above, and see how they agree with the members' anecdotal reports of their perceptions of the roles in the group.

References and suggested readings

The basic model describing group process as it relates to the emergence of roles is drawn largely from the results of the Minnesota Studies. These results are in substantial agreement with the discoveries of other investigators of small groups in speech, psychology, and sociology. Many of the relevant studies that support the model are summarized in chapters 4–11 of:

Collins, Barry E., and Harold Guetzkow. *A Social Psychology of Group Processes for Decision-Making*. New York: Wiley, 1964.

The Minnesota Studies provide a particularly relevant theoretical structure for the study of discussion and group methods, since they investigated many groups composed of students enrolled in discussion and group methods courses.

Bales' framework of analysis of position in group space and the interpersonal rating system are found in:

Bales, Robert F. *Personality and Interpersonal Behavior*. New York: Holt, Rinehart and Winston, 1970.

For studies bearing on the relationship of the field-variant and -invariant behaviors of individuals in small groups, see:

Baron, Reuben M. "Social Reinforcement Effects as a Function of Social Reinforcement History," *Psychological Review*, 73 (1966), 527–539.

Borg, Walter. "Prediction of Small Group Role Behavior from Personality Variables," *Journal of Abnormal and Social Psychology*, 60 (1960), 112–116.

Mann, Richard D. "A Review of the Relationships Between Personality and Performance in Small Groups," *Psychological Bulletin*, 56 (1959), 241–270.

Stager, Paul. "Conceptual Level as a Composition Variable in Small-Group Decision Making," *Journal of Personality and Social Psychology*, 5 (1967), 152–161.

For studies relating to the process of role emergence, see the excellent summary of a large number of studies in:

Tuckman, Bruce W. "Developmental Sequence in Small Groups," *Psychological Bulletin*, 63 (1965), 384–399.

See also:

Burnstein, Eugene, and Robert B. Zajonc. "The Effect of Group Success on the Reduction of Status Incongruence in Task Oriented Groups," *Sociometry*, **28** (1965), 349–362.

Cloyd, Jerry. "Patterns of Role Behavior in Informal Interaction," *Sociometry*, **27** (1964), 160–173.

Goodchilds, Jacqueline D., and Ewart D. Smith. "The Wit and His Group," *Human Relations*, **17** (1964), 23–31.

Guetzkow, Harold. "Differentiation of Roles in Task Oriented Groups." In Dorwin Cartwright and Alvin Zander, eds. *Group Dynamics: Research and Theory*. New York: Harper & Row, 1960, pp. 683–704.

Haiman, Franklyn S. "The Specialization of Roles and Functions in a Group," *Quarterly Journal of Speech*, **43** (1957), 165–174.

Heinicke, C., and Robert F. Bales. "Developmental Trends in the Structure of Small Groups," *Sociometry*, **16** (1953), 7–38.

Sarbin, Theodore R., and Vernon L. Allen. "Role Theory." In Gardner Lindzey and Elliot Aronson, eds. *The Handbook of Social Psychology*, 2nd ed. Reading, Mass.: Addison-Wesley, 1968, vol. 1, pp. 488–567.

Simkins, Lawrence, and Jack West. "Reinforcement of Duration of Talking in Triad Groups," *Psychological Reports*, **18** (1966), 231–236.

Youngs, Richard D., and Margaret Frye. "Some Are Laughing: Some Are Not: Why?" *Psychological Reports*, **18** (1966), 747–754.

CHAPTER 10
THE PROCESS OF GROUP ACCULTURATION

If the members of an LGD work together for several weeks, they begin to share expectations about social interaction, values, styles of manner and expression, and a group tradition with its associated rituals and myths. These characteristics will be similar to those of other LGDs in similar environments, but the details of behavior and language will usually be unique to that group. These unique details comprise a group's subculture.

the development of group norms

A *norm* is a shared expectation of right action that binds members of a group and results in guiding and regulating their behavior. A stable role structure is a complex pattern of differentiating norms that are binding on each member and regulate his behavior according to his assigned role; that is, each person is expected to specialize and thus exhibit a somewhat unique set of behaviors during the course of group interactions. Shared behaviors comprise another important set of norms. For example, all members may express themselves in blunt, crude, direct language, regardless of their roles.

In Chapter 9, the basic model for role emergence furnished an explanation for the differentiating norms and how they developed. The concern here is to describe and explain the way shared norms develop as a group discovers, agrees on, and teaches members its subculture.

THE SHAKEDOWN CRUISE

Before a ship or an aircraft is put into regular service, the officers and crew test it under operating conditions in order to become acquainted with the craft and with one another. Whenever a task-oriented small group begins its work, it must undergo a similar testing under operating conditions. The members must become familiar with the group's purposes, resources, and personnel. Also, when the role structure is disrupted in established organizations, members must reorient themselves in order to stabilize roles and norms. During this preliminary period of testing, the group develops norms related to its task of dealing with the external environment. By interacting with its environment, the group will learn if its control measures (norms) are successful; the group may need to modify its norms in order to deal more successfully with the environment. Norms such as these are clearly related to statements of fact. Observations serve to correct faulty norms; thus, if the group is systematically misled, it will learn about its mistake directly—the environment will punish the group.

Another set of norms relates primarily to the social interactions among the members. This behavior is often idiosyncratic and tied to the external environment by tenuous connections, if at all. The participants may adopt a low-key or high-pressure style of work. They may function in a continual atmosphere of crisis and disorder, or they may work quietly and compulsively. They may adopt a common mode of dress or strive for as much individuality as possible. While conforming to norms developed during their social interaction, members may exhibit unusual and bizarre behavior, because these norms are largely divorced from external feedback. The same freedom to develop a similar diversity of norms relating to the task does not exist. Norms grounded largely in task requirements are limited to those that prove successful as the group interacts with the environment.

Several features of the first few meetings are important in forming the context in which normative behavior develops. First, the primary tensions in the shakedown period often are a factor. Behavior typical of people experiencing primary tension may become the norm if these tensions are not released early. In the Minnesota Studies, several groups adopted a style of politeness, apathy, boredom, and sighing. The case study used to exemplify primary tension in Chapter 8, for example, continued to exhibit the same style for the rest of its meetings. Participants slouched in their chairs; they spoke softly, seemed apathetic; when they spoke they were polite, but not involved with the group or the topic.

Second, the primary tensions typical of first meetings emphasize the sensitivity of people to social interactions. During this period, participants are alert to the social implications of all interactions, even those that are ostensibly task-related. Comments that are perceived as personal slights are more impressive in this period. Members may report subsequently that another person made a cutting comment in the first meeting;

they may indicate that they have forgotton what it was, but that they still resent it. At this point in a group's development, antagonisms may develop that establish the tone for a long period.

When a person enters the delicate social field of the first meetings with blunt statements and flat assertions, he often creates norms that remain part of the group's culture. One group in the Minnesota Studies developed a style that was extremely noisy and unruly. Often two or three people would talk at the same time, each trying to override the others. It was not unusual for everybody to be talking at once. There were few pauses in their meetings, and people stood up, pounded on the tables, and paced the floor. During the first meeting, one member ignored the primary tension by leaping into a consideration of the problem at hand. He talked at length, loudly and aggressively. Soon others were imitating his manner. Early in the second meeting, they were discussing the goals of American foreign policy when a key exchange took place that set the norm for subsequent discussion.

MEMBER A: Just how might the United States bolster . . . ?

MEMBER B: In what ways . . .

MEMBER A: In what ways . . .

MEMBER B: Because we're going to come up with several ways when I'm finished ramming them through the committee . . .

> [*The primary tension is still quite high, and the group does not react to member B's amazing declaration immediately. Rather, they continue on as though nothing unusual has been said.*]

MEMBER C: We're going to have many ways after . . .

MEMBER D: So this is the goal we set upon as our group: In what ways can we strengthen U.S. prestige around the world?

MEMBER A: Uhhuh.

MEMBER B: And by prestige . . .

MEMBER D: And by prestige we mean the influence and respect . . .

MEMBER B: Uhhuh . . .

> [*The tension is building up as the group absorbs the implications of member B's declaration of intent to ram his program through the committee.*]

MEMBER D: (*self-consciously and jokingly*) That is defining of a term.

MEMBER A: OK.

> [*The group now does a collective double-take and begins to react vigorously to member B.*]

MEMBER E: Well, I just put down a couple of goals myself here . . .

MEMBER B: Uhhuh.

MEMBER D: I think we all did as a matter of fact . . .

MEMBER E: And ah . . .
MEMBER B: We all . . . we all . . .

> [*Member B is interrupted by both members D and E who try to override him. He does not yield the floor, and all three speak at once.*]

In the subsequent battle to prevent the aggressive member from ramming his plan through the committee, the norm of active, unruly participation was firmly established.

Another person immediately emerged as a central person in one case by glibly attacking the other members' value systems. He felt college was a waste of time. He was primarily interested in gambling and in having a good time. He had already dropped out of school several times for periods of several years. In the early meetings, whenever others suggested that more information was needed to make a wise decision, this member systematically ridiculed the idea. They had selected a problem relating to gambling, and he indicated by word and manner that he knew all there was to know about the subject. Soon the group adopted his attitude towards work. They established a cynical "inside-dopester" style of belittling all published information and confined themselves to exchanging ignorances, as though they had privileged information unavailable in print. Associated with this no-work norm was another relating to a characteristic mode of expression. Since the group had little factual information and little authoritative opinion or advice, the discourse was largely filled with fantasy themes composed of figurative analogies and hypothetical examples. One person adopted the role of a hypothetical evangelist he called the Reverend Ham and then delivered long satirical diatribes against the sinfulness of gambling. As these norms remained characteristic of the group, it continued to be unproductive.

The third way in which normative behavior develops is through traumatic experiences. In one case study, a member emerged as leader during the early meetings by exhibiting a congenial discussion-moderator technique and by doing extensive preparation for the project. He prepared voluminous notes and was the most informed member. After the first meeting, one of the participants was absent for several meetings. During his absence, the other participants began to perceive their leader as a soft-sell manipulator. When the absentee returned, he began to challenge the leader's directives. The leader was caught off guard and off balance. He responded with the behavior that had resulted in his originally emerging as leader. He began to refer to his research notes. The challenger then got up and walked around the table to the leader's side. He picked up the sheaf of papers and asked the other members to look at all that research. "Isn't it ridiculous?" he asked. The others agreed and laughed and reinforced the challenge. For the next 15 or

20 minutes, the challenger continued to ridicule the leader. The leader tried to reply with factual information, but the challenger simply ridiculed "research" as belittling the intelligence of the others and as unnecessary. After some minutes, the leader was deposed, and he sat quietly for the rest of the meeting. From then on, no one indicated in any way that he had done any "research." This interchange was sufficient to set the norm that no member would use the claim of gathering information as a means of establishing status.

THE BASIC MODEL

Roles can be included as a special kind of norm. The group develops its norms and roles by the same process. The basic model needs only slight modification to account for the way an LGD develops a culture. One important norm concerns the way the group deals with the primary tensions of its early meetings. If members do not release the primary tensions, the climate common to such tension may be incorporated as normative behavior. However, if several people begin to break the primary tensions and a majority begins to reinforce this behavior, a norm will gradually be established. Often the person who successfully breaks the tension will set another norm. People are emotionally involved in the problem posed by primary tensions. When a certain type of tension release is used successfully, the group tends to adopt that style as a norm. For example, if primary tensions are released by shows of sarcasm and personal insult, the participants develop a norm of treating one another in a friendly, but insulting and sarcastic way. Nicknames may be insulting—meathead, stupid, fatty, lame brain—and even shows of solidarity, indicating affection, or raising another's status may be accomplished with sarcasm. Often such norms develop to release tensions in all-male organizations engaged in difficult work. Groups of football players, heavy-construction workers, or infantrymen may adopt such norms. If people release their original tension by gossip, they may adopt a norm of gossipy small talk and interlace their work meetings with such digressions.

Norms of this sort are established simply by behavior that indicates support for one way of proceeding. Since most people exhibit primary tensions at the beginning of their first meeting, the earmarks of primary tension will become a tentative norm. It is not a comfortable norm, however; people do not like such a social climate. They search to release the tension. Someone steps forward to do so. At first, he is unsuccessful. He may try again. If he is again unsuccessful and does not try a third time, the norm of apathy may be established. If he tries again and gains one supporter, he will be encouraged to continue. If one after another joins in, the rest will soon follow. In this case, the dynamics of the small group are illuminated by the pressure for conformity exhibited by large crowds. If a few people in a congregation rise at a certain point in the meeting and no one else does, they soon sit down again. However, if they are joined by a few more people, and then more, until a third or more of the congregation is rising or already standing, a larger number of people will stand. When the majority are on their feet, a flurry of people will rise. The few remaining seated will feel pressure to stand, simply because everyone else is standing. The pressure of the herd for conformity is not as powerful in the intimate setting of the small group, but the same process accounts for the development of some norms.

Some social norms originate with the mannerisms of influential people. This is illustrated by the way in which the kind of joking and humor in a group is influenced by the individual playing the role of tension releaser. Often norms relating to formality or informality of dress, behavior, or language develop because of the styles of behavior exhibited by central persons. For example, every group makes some decisions about the right and wrong ways to express emotions, strong attitudes, and opinions. At some point in the early proceedings, a participant may curse. He may say, "Personally, I say to hell with it." If the discussion proceeds with no one else cursing, this member may insert a "Goddamn" in his next comment. If another and then a third person curse, their example and influence could set the norm.

A number of groups discussed questions relating to the population explosion and birth control. Each set norms to deal with sensitive areas related to these topics. One group discovered early in its first meeting that its members included Protestants, Catholics, and Jews. This group quickly established a norm of not talking about the moral issue relating to birth control. Each group had to decide how to talk about birth-control techniques and the reproductive system. Some groups adopted norms that included very abstract and euphemistic linguistic conventions. Some adopted norms that substituted vague references for explicit language. They used phrases such as, "you know . . . ," "things like that . . . ," and "problems of that sort." One developed the norm of using explicit clinical language to discuss the reproductive process and contraceptive devices. It was a coeducational group, but no one found this norm embarrassing. However, when they presented a symposium discussion to the class, the first speaker continued to use this language norm, which *was not the norm* of the class. As a result, everyone was embarrassed.

Groups may develop norms relating to modes of dress or hair style. They may develop norms relating to ethical conduct, that is, right and wrong behavior *within the group*. Of course, highly cohesive organizations may determine the values of its members when they interact in other, less cohesive groups.

Every task-oriented group has some ostensible goal or goals, which are often clearly indicated. These may be imposed by the external environment. In organizational structure, upper management may set production goals for a unit of workers. The group may discuss and set its own goals. These ostensible goals can become norms to guide behavior. Such norms often increase cohesiveness; those working gain a sense of purpose from a clear and realizable goal. If they know what is required for success, they can work for it and recognize when they have succeeded. Reaching goals contributes to the satisfaction of the individuals; it is tangible evidence of the excellence of the organization. The members can say that the group exceeded the production goal or collected more money for charity than required. The cohesive force of a clear goal is often employed to unify volunteer organizations in charitable fund-raising campaigns. Professional fund raisers commonly use the technique of assigning an overall goal clearly expressed in terms of money and time. They may divide an overall goal into small segments and assign part of the total to a series of subgroups. Clear goals relating to production are frequently established in industry. Each unit has a production goal, and each subunit may have an optimum daily or weekly output as a goal.

The group may have a set of ostensible goals that are not norms for behavior. In that case, the group has hidden goals that govern the members' behavior. Such disparity is more likely to exist when the goals are imposed from outside the group. Industrial psychologists studying production schedules occasionally discover units in which management's attempts to increase production always fail. In these groups, the norms for production are not set by the ostensible goals furnished by upper management, but by the work group itself. Cohesive units can enforce their own norms so effectively that the organization's incentive system cannot shake the worker's tendency to conform to them. Similar findings emerge from the study of the classroom, in which highly cohesive cliques establish norms of classroom behavior that are more effective than those set by the teacher.

pressures for conformity

THE PRESSURE OF GROUP ACTION

One of the most definite conclusions of small-group research is that groups exert great pressures on their members to conform to the group norms. Even perceptions of such phenomena as an illusion of moving light or the comparative lengths of lines may be distorted by social pressure. The discovery that everybody else is doing something puts powerful social pressure to follow suit on the one who is not doing it. The fact that everyone is doing something with a certain style often causes the recruit to do the same thing with the same style. When a pedestrian finds a group in which all are shading their eyes and peering into the sky, he will find himself under strong pressure to do likewise. The tendency of crowds to cause members to stand, cheer, or sing *when everybody is doing it* is a common occurrence.

Once a norm emerges and stabilizes during the course of the shake-down experience, people will tend to conform to it simply because most do so. If the norm is established that participants will not swear, even the person who usually swears will not do so in the group. New persons adopt the norms almost subconsciously simply because of the pressure of being in a group where everyone else is acting and talking in a certain way, *even though the veterans make no conscious effort to change the recruit's behavior.*

THE PRESSURE OF COHESIVENESS

A group with a high level of cohesiveness exerts greater pressure on its personnel to conform than one with only a low level of attractiveness. If a person finds the group attractive, he is willing to work harder and change his behavior more to become and remain a member. He also finds that participating in the group's normative behavior publicly identifies his membership and his commitment to the group. Some norms result in ritualistic behavior which observers may find silly or foolish, although participants may take the behavior very seriously because it serves to structure the cohesiveness of the organization. Idiosyncratic norms that developed accidentally because of the participants' unique experiences during the shakedown cruise often continue because they serve such ritualistic functions.

Members of a highly cohesive group are sensitive to failure to act in accordance with norms. They see deviant behavior as a threat to the cohesiveness of the organization and act to make everyone conform. Personnel in organizations with little cohesiveness find deviant behavior much less disturbing because they do not care very much about its threat to the group's welfare.

OVERT PRESSURE FOR CONFORMITY

People who perceive deviant behavior as a threat to the collective good often take steps to reduce the danger. They may delay action, hoping that the model of all the others doing the right thing will inspire the nonconformist to change. If waiting does not work, they may talk among themselves about his disturbing activities. They will begin to direct more communication to him. This preliminary communication is often light and humorous. They make genial fun of the member because of his nonconformity. The man who grows a beard when the norm is for the shaven look will be kidded about forgetting to shave. Humor in all forms serves as a corrective mechanism. It creates and releases tension at the same time. It tells the deviating member that his behavior does not have group approval in a way that allows a laugh to release the tension.

If the nonconformist does not change his behavior, the others will increase their communication with him. The genial kidding will become a more cutting use of satire or ridicule. The mood changes from laughing with the offender about his foibles to laughing at him because he is ridiculous, not one of them, different. If he remains adamant, the communication pressure increases and changes to serious persuasive efforts. The atmosphere changes from kidding and ridicule to complete seriousness. Is he to be one of them or not? His behavior is damaging to the entire group. All sorts of arguments, reasonable and unreasonable, may be directed to him depending on the level of cohesiveness and the importance of the norm in the group's hierarchy of values.

An example of how others begin to pressure a person to conform is provided by an excerpt from the diary of one subject included in the Minnesota Studies:

> At the start of our meeting we decided each member should report his findings. Unfortunaetely, the first person "didn't find time to look up the subject." The group laughed at him and told him he had better be prepared next time. However, you could tell they were a bit concerned and I thought the group lost some of its cohesiveness then.

If the deviating person does not finally conform to group expectations, the others will reject him and isolate him from the group. Even if he continues to attend the work sessions, they will ignore him and freeze him out. This rather drastic step tends to occur when the others perceive that his behavior cannot be changed. As long as they think that he will conform, they will try to bring him into line.

COMPETING NORMS

If an individual is a member of several groups and discovers contradictory norms, he will have conflicting loyalties. If he conforms to the norms of group A, and group B discovers what he has done, he will be subjected to overt pressures. If the high-school clique adheres to a certain style of haircut, and a boy's family follows a different norm, he will have difficulty with his family or with his friends at school. Many norms, of course, can be adopted and shed more easily than clothing and certainly are less obvious than a haircut. A high-school student could easily change his language, depending on whether he was at home or with his high-school crowd. He might do the same with his eating, smoking, and drinking habits. However, the conflicting demands of highly cohesive groups cause conflict within an individual. He often tries to resolve the conflict by adopting one norm consistently. When this happens, he will adopt the norms of the more attractive of the two groups.

conformity, creativity, and individualism

A common misconception is that conformity to norms must necessarily stifle individual identity or creativity. To be sure, an organization may require every person to think alike. The participants may have common scapegoats, prejudices, and attitudes and may enforce such conformity. Some movements require this unity of purpose in order to be effective. If a crusade requires a totally mobilized fighting power, immediate, unquestioning compliance with orders is required.

Many organizations, however, require the opposite set of norms for efficient functioning. They may expect participants to be creative and individualistic. A graduate student in art at the University of Minnesota developed a modification of the semantic differential test to give to a group composed entirely of abstract painters. The subjects resisted the notion of the test because it implied standardization, and after they finally agreed to it, each attempted to respond in a way that was as unique as possible. This group demanded that everyone respond in a new and unique way to every stimulus. Triteness was perceived as deviant behavior.

fantasy and the formation of a group culture

Although the small task-oriented group participates in the culture of its environment, it also develops a subculture of its own. The groups included in the Minnesota Studies exhibited a wide variety of group subcultures and associated group styles. The styles were essentially a result of a given group's process of acculturation.

Some small groups have an unruly, boisterous style, and others are quiet and reserved. Some use scapegoats and refuse to face difficult internal and external problems. Some are prone to take flight or to fight whenever they face a crisis. Some are warm and emotional and member-oriented, while others are preoccupied with manipulating the external environment. In some groups, concepts are combined and language is used with considerable skill. Members of these groups deal with abstractions and reason fluently and consistently. Participants in other groups typically mobilize their resources largely with gestures and monosyllables and grunts. In yet other groups, members go through long, involved rationalizations before and after making decisions.

One powerful mechanism for group acculturation is the chaining fantasy described in Chapter 7. The small-group-communication seminar at Minnesota has been using the concept of chaining group fantasies as a research rationale since Bales published his work on group fantasy in 1970. Investigators at Minnesota have found the category of dramatizing communication to be a useful one that yields reliable data.

One of the most fruitful areas of interpretation has been the analysis of chaining fantasies to gain insights into a group's culture. Investigators using a fantasy theme analysis have worked with material hitherto often overlooked because it seemed trivial or irrelevant to the task-oriented group. When a fantasy impresses the members of a group to such an extent that they continue to recall it and respond to allusions to it with some of their original excitement, then the drama becomes part of the group's social reality and, therefore, important to their common and unique subculture.

FANTASY AND THE SEARCH FOR COMMON GROUND

When five or six individuals meet together in a zero-history group, they bring to the meeting their value systems, their interests, and their individual psychodynamic makeups. The members have no way of knowing how their commonalities overlap or how their differences complement one another. Of course, they do not know how their individual world views and psychologies will come into conflict either, but the points of difference are not the stuff from which the group's subculture is made.

The members may search for common ground directly by discussing their values and interests. "I really believe that marriage is outmoded, don't you?" a member may say. Another may respond with agreement, and a third person may sit glumly, nonverbally suggesting disagreement, or may actively argue that marriage is not outmoded. Often, however, the primary tension of the early part of a group's history makes it difficult for members to launch into a direct and fruitful consideration of such matters. The tension, also, encourages the members to tell jokes, personal anecdotes, or to dramatize other situations in an effort to relax the atmosphere and break the ice.

Many of the dramas do not chain out. The members find them

dull or threatening or do not like the particular tone or interpretation of the drama. A member may say, "I'm sorry I'm late but my roommate decided to move in with this guy and I was helping her move her stuff." The member who thinks that the excitement and approval suggested by the way the first person presents the fantasy is laudable and that the roommate is doing the "right thing" will tend to chain in with something like, "Is she really? That's neat." The member who feels that the episode is deplorable is not likely to chain into the drama, but is much more likely to change the subject and might well suggest that the group get down to business.

Most important for the consideration of group culture, however, is the fact that some dramas strike common preoccupations of the members, and they become interested, lose themselves in the excitement of participation, and add onto the drama or say something like, "That reminds me," and dramatize another story on a similar theme.

When a fantasy chains through a group, the members discover in an exciting and emotional way a common ground relating to values, actions, and attitudes. When a number of fantasies have chained out, the group develops a common culture composed of heroes, villains, saints, and sinners and the common scenarios in which these characters act out laudable and deplorable behaviors. The common set of dramatic characters and actions, attitudes, and values that they symbolize becomes an important part of the group's social reality and its subculture. The members come to share a common symbolic world. Group members find it easier to grasp and to respond to many of the most vital political, military, economic, and social issues when they are presented dramatically in terms of concrete characters than when they are dealt with in terms of impersonal institutional analysis. The group finds it difficult to respond emotionally to a concept like the executive branch of the government, but the member can easily respond to a flesh-and-blood president in terms of love or hate or disdain or admiration if the character is presented in the suitable dramatic scenario. Often the radical campus groups in the 1960s dramatized their goals in terms of conflicts with some real individual such as the university president and tried to wrest their demands from a direct confrontation with the individual who symbolized the university. Usually the university president did not have the power or authority to deliver on the demands, but the group members found it easier to grasp the issue and mobilize support for their position if the question were presented in dramatic terms.

Against the panorama of large events and the seemingly unchangeable and often impersonal forces of society or of nature, the individual may feel lost and hopeless. One coping mechanism is to dream an individual fantasy, which provides a sense of meaning and significance for the individual and which helps protect the person from the pressures of natural calamity and social disaster. The group culture generated by chaining fantasies serves much the same coping function for those who participate in the group and often with much more force because of the power of group pressure on the individual and because of the supportive warmth of like-minded companions.

THE RHETORICAL FUNCTION OF FANTASY

One of the most intriguing questions that has emerged from the study of group fantasies relates to the extent to which the chaining is inevitable or accidental or the result of a deliberate effort on the part of one or more members to generate a certain kind of symbolic world for the group. Certainly, Bales' work and the studies at Minnesota indicate that the individual predispositions of the members and the group's social and task problems provide a partial account for why some dramas catch on and others fall dead. Perhaps some dramas chain out accidentally. But evidence from the Minnesota case studies suggests that the artistry with which the drama is presented is a factor in whether or not it chains through the group. One can never be sure whether or not a play will be a success; but, if the playwright is talented and knows his craft, the success of the play is more likely than if he is untalented and inexperienced. Something analogous to the playwright's success seems to be operating in the case of the chaining fantasies in a small group.

Timing, too, appears to be a factor in whether or not a fantasy chains out once it is introduced. In much the same way that group decisions cannot be forced on a group before it is ready to make them, so the group members must be predisposed to respond by a common attitude or problem before they chain out a particular fantasy. Fantasies that are unsuccessfully introduced early in a group's life sometimes chain out when reintroduced later. Thus, proper timing, as well as the artistry of the manner of presentation, appears to be a factor in the success or failure of a fantasy to chain through a group.

In one case study, a girl had written up a fantasy for her diary on her group experience which took the form of a fable. She had depicted each member as an animal or bird. She was reading some of her diary to another member in a low voice while the others were going on about the group's business; the other person became intrigued and called the group's attention to the fable. He urged her to read it to the entire group. She was reluctant at first, but with some urging she started. She caught the group's attention, and they began to respond, at first tentatively, then with greater enthusiasm until, finally, all of the others were actively participating, injecting comments, and roaring with laughter. She had not written her diary with an eye to the audience or with the conscious intent to persuade them to adopt a certain position or attitude. In other words, she did not have a rhetorical purpose. She had simply written the sketch for her own amusement. Her skill in writing it, however, the artistry of her introduction, contributed to the chaining of the fantasy. Moreover, the group had reached a state of tension because of interpersonal conflicts that it had not been able to handle in a direct way, and the fantasy personality analysis in her fable was presented to the group when all its members were at least intellectually aware that personality problems were crippling the group's effectiveness in the task area and were ready for her oblique analysis of their conflicts.

The fact that a person has more chance of having a drama chain through the group if it is presented skillfully makes a rhetorical approach to introducing fantasy themes into a new group possible. Indeed, some people do use group methods for persuasive ends, and they often use fantasies for their own purposes. Organizers of consciousness-raising sessions and other groups designed for conversion purposes frequently rely on dramas for their persuasive ends. The planners of groups used for rhetorical purposes usually arrange for a majority of the group to consist of people already committed to the position. Usually the meeting will include only one or two potential converts. A person being rushed for a fraternity or sorority may find himself or herself closeted with four or five "actives." The woman attending a women's liberation consciousness-raising session may find herself in a group in which the vocal and articulate members are committed to the movement.

Once a meeting gets under way, the insiders begin to introduce important dramas from their community's culture, and the committed then chain into them with the appropriate nuances and emotional responses. Under the pressure of the group, the potential convert often begins to participate in appropriate ways in the fantasies. The neophyte is particularly susceptible if his previous experience has been similar to that of those already committed. One of the case studies at Minnesota was of a consciousness-raising group associated with Gay Liberation. The pattern of fantasy themes in the sessions began with dramas that were widely disseminated nationally through underground presses and the Gay Liberation grapevine. Most of the committed knew the national rhetoric, although some of them were not personally acquainted with one another. When they had formed some common ground by participating in the nationally known dramas, they moved to the narration of personal experiences about the repressions they had suffered. All of the dramas, however, were on themes related to the subculture of the Gay Liberation movement.

Although a conscious rhetorical effort to cause fantasies to chain through a group can succeed in igniting a chain reaction, the results are not always what one hopes or intends. The fantasy often begins to take on a life of its own, and the member who first introduced the theme may well lose control of its development. When the fantasy gets out of hand in a rhetorical group, the organizers will judge that it was a bad session. As the others participate, they add new directions and new emphases to the drama. The originator may be astonished and frightened at the way the chain develops. The final fantasy event, viewed in retrospect, is the joint effort of all the members who contributed to it.

Some meanings are in the messages. In the process of participating in the fantasy, in the communication itself, the members may create a new set of symbols, of symbolic characters, or a new set of meanings. The participants may emerge from the meeting having learned connotative and denotative meanings which no single individual brought with him to the meeting.

The conventional wisdom of communication theorists that "meanings are in people not messages" is much too simple for a complete analysis of small-group communication as it relates to the process of group acculturation. In a very important way, meanings *are* in messages. When the members of a group chain out a fantasy, they emerge from the meeting with new meanings, meanings that they did not have before, and, on some occasions, meanings that did not exist before. If the process of communication did not create new meanings, how could novelty arise? How could innovation take place?

A newborn child does not come equipped with meanings. An individual must learn the meanings that are inside of him. If meanings are in people and not in messages, then a community of meanings can only come about by having some people teach the common meanings to those who do not know. Somewhere there must be an individual or a group of individuals who have within them all of the meanings available to the people living at a given period of time, since people who do not have the meanings in them can acquire them only by being taught by someone who does. Certainly, parents and teachers do pass on meanings to children, and a similar process goes on all through life as others teach an individual new meanings; but that process only accounts for part of the learning of meanings. At any given point in time, the meanings available to a community of people are not only in the people but also in the messages—written, spoken, or recorded on tape or film—accumulated from the past and available to the people. An individual comes to have those meanings by participating in a communication process that involves the messages from the past. In the communication process by which the individual learns a meaning, the person is not inert, but may actively change the meaning and add a new nuance in the give-and-take of communication.

Sometimes creative people will dream up new meanings individually and teach them to others, and that accounts to some extent for innovation and novelty. But new meanings also result from group effort. On occasion, people in groups find themselves caught up in a chain of fantasizing similar to the creative moments that an individual experiences. Under the pressure of the fantasy, the constraints that often operate in a group are released, and the members feel free to experiment with ideas, to play with concepts, and to be ridiculous. More and more members are drawn into active involvement in the communication. Like the abstract painting or the ambiguous modern poem, the original drama serves as a stimulus for the others to interpret or read into it additional meanings or feelings of their own. The total creative involvement of the members creates a meeting in which the flow of meaning is no longer from source to receiver as in the case of man talking to machine, but, rather, all participants add to a common reservoir of meaning until the result is greater than any one of them could have produced alone. The members add to and shape the original fantasy until the outcome is more complex and exciting than the original meanings intended by the person who began the chain.

Fantasy and emotion. Not only are meanings to some extent in messages, but the emotions associated with the meanings are partly in the messages as well as in the people participating in the fantasy chain. The group culture, as it evolves, provides the members with an emotional evocation for various symbolic events and for the things that happen to them. Hate, fear, love, laughter, jealousy, pride, and a host of other feelings and emotions are embedded in the stuff of fantasy. Physiological studies of emotions reveal that changes in heart rate, palm sweat, and so on, vary little from emotion to emotion. One way to account for the perception of many different emotions in the face of little evidence of physiological differences is to divide emotions into a physiological side and a psychological one and to argue that a person may interpret internally similar physiological states as different emotions.

An interesting study pointing up the difference between the physiological and psychological sides of emotions is one by Schacter and Singer. The investigators injected some subjects with placebos and some with a synthetic form of adrenalin which caused a state of physiological arousal. The experimenters told all subjects that the injection was a vitamin supplement. They told one part of the group injected with the adrenalin substitute to expect side effects such as heart palpitations. However, the remainder of those with the real drug were told nothing more than that the injection was a vitamin supplement. They divided the latter group into two experimental treatments. In one treatment they placed the deceived subjects with a collaborator who interpreted the feeling as one of euphoria and in another with a collaborator who interpreted the emotion as one of anger. Most subjects interpreted their artificially aroused physiological states in line with the fantasizing of the stooges.

The drama that accompanies an emotional state partly accounts for whether an individual interprets his feelings as hate or fear or anger or joy or love. The dramatic action in which the group participates provides occasion for humor and ridicule, for hatred and jealousy, for tragedy and catharsis. When a prominent and colorful political figure suffers a setback, both his friends and his enemies will probably respond emotionally. Groups of friends will interpret their emotional response as sadness or despair, while groups of enemies will tend to interpret their response as joy and delight. Under group pressures built up during the excitement of a political race, members of both groups may cry at news of the politician's defeat, but his enemies will interpret their tears as tears of joy.

Motives are in messages. Finally, and most importantly, motives are in messages. The group culture contains the members' common drives to action. People who generate, legitimatize, and participate in a fantasy chain are in turn moved to action by that process. In short, participating in a cohesive group with its associated group culture provides a person with impelling motives to action. Motives do not exist to be expressed in communication, but rather arise in the expression itself and come to be embedded in the participants' memory of the fantasy themes that generated and serve to sustain them. The participant and nonparticipant observers of a group can thus use fantasy theme analysis of a group's messages to discover the motives common to a group.

When a person comes to share a small group's culture, he gains with it supporting dramas and constraining forces that impel him to adopt certain norms of behavior and to take certain action. The group's effect on a member's level of motivation may be very small in the case of a group in a communication class. At the other end of the continuum, some group cultures are so powerful that they may catch up an individual until he changes motivation and life style in dramatic fashion. The born-again Christian is baptized and adopts a life style and behavior modeled after the heroes of the dramas that sustain the group's culture. Likewise, the convert to one of the counterculture groups in the 1960s let his hair and beard grow, changed his style of dress, and adopted other life goals and motivations.

Obviously any group's style is the result of a complicated process of acculturation. It includes the role structure, the traditions and rituals, and the common norms developed during the group's life. Groups develop their customs by repeating them. In many respects, the norms of the group function like the habits of an individual: they provide a guide and a sanction for behavior. Thus, the members' attention and energy can be focused on other matters. Norms provide a stable social environment and reduce the shock of interacting with other people. Just as an individual's habits may be good or bad for him, so a group's culture can be facilitating or crippling in terms of its goals and the satisfactions of its members. When the participants perceive norms as damaging, they attempt to change them.

established groups in the process of change

If the external environment suddenly creates unusual pressures for the group, the established culture may prove inadequate. The role structure may crumble, and the basic model of the LGD will be in evidence as roles are reshuffled. In this process, some members may begin to act in ways contrary to the established norms. If they gain support from others who also adopt the *new* ways, the old norm may be replaced with the new one.

New members of an organization may resist certain norms and substitute other behaviors. If a sufficient number of old members are dissatisfied with the original norm, they may adopt the new way of doing things. Even without a change in membership, people may decide that certain norms are undesirable and adopt new ones. If others begin to follow their behavior, the group may change its norm. If high-status and esteemed persons change behavior, the group often adopts a new norm.

Some norms emerge so accidentally that they are unrelated to the task and unsatisfactory in dealing with the environment. The discussants who adopted a norm of rejecting evidence were attacked when they presented a panel discussion to the class. Their pleas that there was no sound evidence available on the subject did not convince their audience, and their program was a failure. Norms have considerable inertia. The group tends to continue a pattern of behavior after the conditions that established the norms have disappeared. A role struggle or crisis may have been resolved for weeks, but the group may still follow a norm established during that crisis. Such norms hinder effectiveness and cohesiveness. Spontaneous corrective action may not develop. Dissatisfied participants may try conscious and direct orientation, evaluation, and control of the group's style. Norms, like habits, can be identified, evaluated, and changed consciously. On occasion, a task-oriented group is so preoccupied with its work that it ignores its role structure and style. It continues to use nonfunctional norms simply because it does not pause to ask whether or not they are useful.

The core of much work in T-groups, sensitivity training, and group dynamics is the discussion of roles and norms. Frequently, a discussion will expose matters that have hindered performance. The intent and interpretation of communication are often different. Discussion will reveal that first impressions were erroneous. Comments made during the early stages that were perceived as attempts to lower status can be put into proper perspective. Often, inadvertent norms develop that can be changed simply by having everyone talk about them.

Some cases included in the Minnesota Studies conducted a series of discussions on their own group after it had completed several tasks in a period of six weeks. In one group of three men and two women, the men were surprised to discover that they had ignored the suggestions and comments of the women. When they replayed the tapes from the first meetings, they found evidence of such response. One woman responded to being ignored by withdrawal, the other by joking and ridicule. When the men discovered this norm, they immediately and consciously changed their behavior. They listened carefully to what the women said, and, if they fell into the old norm, they were reminded. This one modification did much to increase the participation of the two women and to improve the group's cohesiveness.

A student of group methods should recognize the importance of talking about group roles and norms in improving the operations of a group in the pragmatic style. One must remember, however, that indiscriminate use of such self-evaluative sessions can create more tensions and problems for the group than it dissipates. Some people may enjoy postmortems on social relations and try to work out their own neuroses through them. The difference between a healthy discussion of ways to improve a task-oriented group and the use of the task-oriented group for a therapy session or a group in the consummatory style is not always clear. When evaluation sessions become an excuse for gossiping or cattiness about other individuals, they disrupt cohesiveness.

If certain procedural norms have become troublesome or the role structure seems too unstable, the participants should plan to discuss these matters. The group must establish the norm that what is said about roles and norms is honest and dedicated to the good of all. These sessions should emphasize the perspective that the *group* is somewhat responsible for the role behavior of its members. The discussion should center around what the *group* can do. Blame, in most cases, should be placed on the group. If the organization adopts a norm of scapegoating individuals for its problems, the evaluation sessions are less likely to prove helpful. Several people may point to a participant and say, "You are the one who is causing all the trouble. You have been domineering, inflexible, and impossible. If you would just be quiet, we might accomplish something." If blamed in this way, the scapegoat is very likely to fight back in kind, and a new, more destructive norm may be established.

summary

A norm is a shared expectation of right action. Norms are binding on the members of the group. A stable role structure is the result of a complex set of norms that differentiate among the behaviors of the participants. The group also develops other norms—for example, shared behavior norms, procedural norms, and the social norms evolving from the interaction among group members.

The very existence of a group of people exerts some pressure for conformity. If a majority begins to behave in a certain way, this common behavior exerts pressure on the rest to follow. In addition, participants exert some overt pressure on deviants. This pressure consists of additional communication addressed to the nonconformist, until the group decides that he cannot be changed. At this point, they typically close ranks and isolate him from the group.

The subculture of a small, task-oriented group results from a long and complicated process of acculturation. It includes the role structure, the traditions and rituals, and the common norms developed during the group's history. However, *the group employs the same basic process over and over again to create each bit of that culture.* The process is essentially the same as the basic model that accounts for role emergence.

One powerful mechanism for group acculturation is the chaining fantasy. When a fantasy chains through a group, the members discover in an exciting and emotional way a common ground relating to values, actions, and attitudes. A fantasy theme analysis can give insight into the group's symbolic reality including the meanings that are associated with key dramas, the emotional response to action, and the motives the members share in common.

Norms may cripple the group in its task efficiency and in its social dimension. The group may take corrective action spontaneously, or it may place the problem of its normative behavior on an agenda for direct consideration.

QUESTIONS FOR STUDY

1. What elements in the early meetings of a new group affect the development of normative behavior?
2. What is the relationship between the pressures for conformity within a group and the development of group norms?
3. What is the relationship between group norms and group goals?
4. What is the relationship between group goals and group cohesiveness?
5. What mechanisms do groups use to make members conform to group norms?
6. How might conformity to group norms encourage individual creativity?

7. What is meant by the concept of "group style"?
8. How do fantasy chains contribute to the development of a group culture?
9. Under what conditions might group norms continue even though their usefulness is at an end?
10. How might a group change its norms?

EXERCISES

1. Do a case study of one of your class discussion groups. Describe the norms that developed, and account for their emergence.
2. Select a group that you have been working with for several months, and analyze their task behavior. Are the work norms productive and realistic in the group's present circumstances? Are there better norms that could be adopted? How might you initiate change in the group's work norms?
3. Select a group that you have been working with for several months, and analyze their social norms. Are these norms conducive to a socially rewarding group environment? Are there better norms that could be developed? How might you initiate change in the group's social norms?
4. Select a group, and find the fantasies that have chained out in the meetings. Use Bales' "Questions for the Description of Psychodramatic Imagery" (Robert F. Bales, *Personality and Interpersonal Behavior,* New York: Holt, Rinehart and Winston, 1970, pp. 156–159) to analyze the fantasies. Write an analysis of the group's culture based on fantasy analysis.

References and suggested readings

For studies relating to pressures to conformity and group norms, see:

Aiken, Edwin G. "Interaction Process Analysis Changes Accompanying Operant Conditioning of Verbal Frequency in Small Groups," *Perceptual and Motor Skills,* 21 (1965), 52–54.

Carter, Lewis F., Richard J. Hill, and S. Dale McLemore. "Social Conformity and Attitude Change Within Nonlaboratory Groups," *Sociometry,* 30 (1967), 1–13.

Endler, Norman S. "The Effects of Verbal Reinforcement on Conformity and Deviant Behavior," *Journal of Social Psychology,* 66 (1965), 147–154.

Festinger, Leon, Stanley Schachter, and Kurt Back. "Operation of Group Standards." In Dorwin Cartwright and Alvin Zander, eds. *Group Dynamics: Research and Theory,* 3rd ed. New York: Harper & Row, 1968, pp. 152–164.

Garai, Joseph. "Support of Judgmental Independence on Conformity in Situations of Exposure to Strong Group Pressure," *Psychology,* 1 (1964), 21–25.

Goodkin, Robert. "Changes in Conformity Behavior on a Perceptual Task Following Verbal Reinforcement and Punishment," *Journal of Psychology,* 62 (1966), 99–110.

Kiesler, Charles A., and Lee H. Corbin. "Commitment, Attraction, and Conformity," *Journal of Personality and Social Psychology,* 2 (1965), 890–895.

Milgram, Stanley. "Group Pressure and Action Against a Person," *Journal of Abnormal and Social Psychology,* 69 (1964), 137–143.

For studies relating to goals and norms and cohesiveness, see:

Gerard, Harold B. "Some Effects of Status, Role Clarity, and Group Goal Clarity upon the Individual's Relations to Group Process," *Journal of Personality,* 25 (1957), 475–488.

Raven, Bertram H., and Jan Rietsema. "The Effects of Varied Clarity of Group Goal and Group Path upon the Individual and His Relationship to His Group," *Human Relations,* 10 (1957), 29–47.

The material on fantasy theme analysis comes largely from the Minnesota Studies, although the key concepts come from:

Bales, Robert F. *Personality and Interpersonal Behavior.* New York: Holt, Rinehart and Winston, 1970.

For further analyses of fantasy, see:

Klinger, Eric. *The Structure and Functions of Fantasy.* New York: Wiley-Interscience, 1971.

See also:

Sykes, A. J. M. "Myth in Communication," *The Journal of Communication,* 20 (1970), 17–31.

For a representative analysis of the two sides to emotions, see:

Munn, Norman L. *Psychology: The Fundamentals of Human Adjustment.* 5th ed. Boston: Houghton Mifflin, 1966, pp. 189–223.

Schacter, Stanley, and Jerome Singer. "Cognitive, Social, and Physiological Determinants of Emotional State," *Psychological Review,* 69 (1962), 379–399.

The case study of consciousness raising is from:

Chesebro, James, John F. Cragan, and Patricia McCullough. "The Small Group Techniques of the Radical Revolutionary: A Synthetic Study of Consciousness Raising," *Speech Monographs,* 40 (1973), 136–146.

CHAPTER 11

THE ROLE
OF THE LEADER

Of all the roles that emerge in a task-oriented group, none has fascinated the philosophers, novelists, and social scientists more than the top position. The most influential role has been the subject of much fiction, drama, poetry, and conjecture; and, lately, it has been the concern of many systematic empirical investigations.

People discussing this role usually refer to it as the role of the *leader*. Citizens of the United States have a preoccupation with and a cultural ambivalence to leadership. If a member of a class discussion group suggests that another would be a good leader, the typical response of the one suggested is "Oh, no! Not me. Someone else could do a better job." Despite such protestation, most members of groups want to be the leader. In the Minnesota Studies, Geier[1] interviewed 80 students who participated in 16 discussion groups. All but two students reported that they would like to be the leader of their group. One was a coed who acted as though she were disinterested in leading, but the other person was actually very much in contention for leadership.

On the one hand, our democratic traditions suggest that all men are created equal, and that nobody is better than anybody else. The whole mystique of a classless society rejects the phenomenon of status. In the popular culture of this country, there is a strong cult of the "common man," and some rancor against the elite. The candidate for public office often makes a fetish of identifying himself with common activities, goals, and aspirations. Experts in propaganda analysis give this device special consideration under the labels of "just plain folks" and "common ground" appeals. In this tradition, the candidate does not seek the office for fear of appearing immodest. Only an egotist would

---

[1] See the Appendix for the titles of theses and articles by John Geier, Calvin Mortensen, and other contributors to the Minnesota Studies.

publicly assert that he is better than other men. He allows the job of leadership to seek him, and if he is called, he will humbly do his best to live up to the high responsibility and great challenge.

On the other hand, our culture inherited from the rugged individualism of the past a strong tradition of driving for the top. The status positions at the top are the symbols of success. Every young man is expected to be a success. He is educated for leadership and encouraged to become a "leader of men." Activities ranging from the Boy Scouts to delivering newspapers are supposed to prepare one for leadership. In turn, our society gives rewards to leaders. In view of this ambivalence, the American preoccupation with the top role in a group is to be expected.

a frame of reference

THE TRAIT APPROACH

Among the early explanations of leadership was one that attributed it to divine inspiration. God, or the gods, selected a man and guided him to leadership. He led a charmed life and was unlike ordinary mortals. It was futile to challenge his lead since he was the chosen one of God. He had supernatural sanctions and was thus predestined for greatness. The tradition of supernatural inspiration culminated in Western Europe in the divine right of kings. The king, according to this idea, held his throne directly from God. This idea of leadership fell into disrepute, but the *form of the argument* remained; only the content changed.

A man like Napoleon was different from other men. He led a charmed life because he was possessed of some inner quality. Goethe called this the *daemonic* and thought of it as a mystical, inexplicable power. To this day, some political scientists use the concept of *charisma* to explain the power of some political leaders. Charisma is a certain magic power to capture the popular enthusiasm.

One branch of early experimental psychology in this country modified the idea that leadership was inherent. These psychologists were preoccupied with measuring personality traits by means of psychological testing procedures. They assumed that an adequate battery of psychological tests could identify the cluster of personality traits associated with leadership and thus explain it.

Investigators studied the relationship between physical factors such as height and weight and leadership. They correlated intelligence and personality test scores with formal leadership. These investigations were synthesized in the 1940s, but the results were inconclusive. Many critics evaluated the progress of this line of research at that time and concluded that the results were disappointing. Since then, the notion that some individuals have a certain amount of leadership that will cause them to emerge as the top person in any group has been rejected in most literature on the subject.

The trait approach simply reflects the viewpoint of those who hoped to study individual personality by examining personality traits as separate from the social field surrounding a person. Leadership proved too complicated a phenomenon to be explained in this fashion. Yet the fact remains that certain people do become "stars" in almost all the groups they join. Although it is not the complete explanation, the trait approach does explain some everyday experience.

STYLES OF LEADERSHIP

When the trait analysis of leadership proved unsatisfactory, several other perspectives generated considerable research. One of the most important was that kinds of leadership could be distinguished and correlated with evaluations of excellence. The basic assumption was that there was an ideal type or style of leadership. In this view, excellence did not reside in the individual, but rather in an ideal procedure that could be learned. An important study by Lippitt and White distinguished among three kinds of leadership. They named the three leadership styles *authoritarian, democratic,* and *laissez faire.* In the 1950s, various investigators and theorists used different labels in the same enterprise. They compared autocratic with democratic leadership, group-centered with leader-centered leadership, production-oriented management with employee-oriented management. Some theorists distinguished between leaderless and leadershipless groups. A school of industrial psychologists and management experts developed an approach to *participative management* which was essentially the same as democratic management. The first results indicated a clear superiority of the democratic style of leadership. Occasionally, studies revealed that other styles of leadership created productive, cohesive groups. Such cases were explained away by saying that even better results would be obtained in the same situation with democratic leadership.

Nonetheless, in some kinds of group activity the democratic style was inappropriate. The quarterback on the football field was not democratic, nor was the sergeant in a fire fight. Clearly the external environment and the purposes of the group played a part in evaluating leadership styles.

Questioning what style of leadership is best is a more sophisticated approach than asking what qualities in the individual make him a leader. Research into the styles of leadership was conducted by observing groups in action. Investigators went into factories, organizations, and laboratories and learned a good deal about groups and leadership. They developed the idea that if excellence in leadership resided not in a person but in a way of leading, then the style could be taught. Leaders are not born, but trained. Students could learn a *style* of leadership by participating in groups rather than by developing individual traits. One learned the democratic style by taking part in groups and by practicing it in a realistic situation.

The contingency approach. Fiedler and his associates have developed an account that considers individual traits, leadership styles, and several situational factors. The account assumes that leadership effectiveness is contingent on a clearly specified and limited number of factors and is called a *contingency model* or *approach*. Fiedler developed a scale to test for individual traits of leaders such as concern with good inter-personal relations versus interest in task success and desire for self-esteem as opposed to preoccupation with task performance. In addition, his approach uses a sociometric test to scale a group's atmosphere and to estimate the relationship between the leader and the others. Finally, Fiedler developed a way to evaluate group situations in terms of *favor-ability* for the leader. Fiedler argued that a situation might include more or less authority for the leader in that an organization might provide a leader with a formal position that had sanctions to reward or punish subordinates. The more such sanctions a position had, the more favorable the situation. A person might, also, have earned influence with other members because of the excellence of past performance in the group. The more such earned power a person had, the more favorable the situation. Fiedler also developed a technique for the evaluation of the difficulty of the group's task. The more difficult the task, the less favorable the situation for the leader.

Fiedler used four criteria to evaluate task difficulty: (1) the higher the degree to which the correctness of a decision could be verified by feedback or by checking logical procedures, the lower the difficulty of the task; (2) the higher the degree of clarity of the goal, the lower the difficulty; (3) the fewer the number of different paths or procedures to reach the goal, the lower the difficulty; and (4) the fewer the number of different solutions that might be judged as correct, the lower the difficulty. Fiedler argued that the least difficult tasks were those in which decisions were clearly correct or incorrect, in which the goal was clear, in which one or very few paths could lead to a correct solution, and in which only one solution was correct.

Fiedler weighted the criteria for evaluating the favorability of leadership situations by giving the greatest weight to the leader's personal relationships with the others, next greatest to the difficulty of the task, and the least to position authority.

Fiedler's approach assumes that his testing procedure resulted in identifying individuals who were directive or authoritarian as opposed to those who were democratic and less directive. Fiedler argued that leaders preoccupied with task success would tend to be more directive than those preoccupied with social relationships.

Fiedler and his associates conducted a number of studies to test the hypothesis that the right combination of leadership style and situation would result in task efficiency. Although the studies do not provide unequivocal support, they do give some empirical verification for the contingency approach. The studies suggest that, if investigators evaluate a situation as highly favorable or highly unfavorable on the basis of the four criteria described above, then a directive task-oriented leadership style will result in more task effectiveness than the less directive. When investigators evaluate the situation as moderately favorable, a more democratic and member-oriented style of leadership is more effective than the authoritarian.

The argument is that when a situation is extremely favorable, a leader can be authoritarian because the goal is clear, the path is evident, and the group can easily judge its success or failure. In addition, the leader has many sanctions from an external organization to reward or punish the members and has earned the respect and esteem of the others. Thus, in the highly favorable situation, being bossy does not hinder the willing cooperation of the followers. The more democratic style of people-oriented leadership, on the one hand, is likely to waste effort on needless fence building in the social dimension. When the situation is extremely unfavorable, the group is likely to be facing a crisis, and authoritarian leadership is required. When things are moderately favorable, the leader cannot rely on institutional authority or sanctions nor the rewards of task success as much as in the favorable situation and must keep mending interpersonal relationships to keep earning esteem in order to get the willing cooperation of the others.

Although too simple for an adequate account of leadership the contingency approach is an improvement over either the trait or styles of leadership accounts. One virtue of Fiedler's work is that it focuses attention on factors in the task requirements as important to leadership. The criteria for evaluating the difficulty of a group task are insightful and useful for the person participating in work groups. The notion that different tasks require different styles of leadership is an important concept, and anyone who is a group leader for a period of time during which the group changes tasks could profit from the insights furnished by the contingency approach.

The contingency approach seeks to discover testing procedures that scale potential leaders and discriminate among them so the right kind of leadership can be assigned to the proper kind of leadership situation. The approach would have important practical applications if, indeed, some simple paper-and-pencil testing procedures would allow administrators of organizations to appoint people to leadership situations so that no square pegs would be fitted into round holes. For instance, personnel managers could test several candidates for a leadership position as to task-orientation versus people-orientation and appoint the one who best fit the leadership situation, confident that the result would be the most effective leadership for that particular unit of the organization. The difficulty with testing, scaling, and evaluation procedures is that to be useful they must be both reliable and valid. To be reliable, the test must yield essentially the same results when applied to the same individual by several different testers or when given to the same individual on different occasions. To be valid, the test or scale must correlate with actual behaviors in the group or, in the case of the evaluation of task difficulty, with the actual difficulty of the work. The Minnesota case studies contain groups in which the members discussed their leadership difficulties and succeeded in changing the leadership style of an individual so that their leader was structuring the group in a more acceptable way, and the result was an increase in group effectiveness. In other words, task-orientation versus member-orientation is a field-variant feature of the leadership role and a paper-and-pencil test that assumes that it is field-invariant will be misleading. One would not rely on a test for knowledge of an individual's ability in a foreign language if the person were taking a class in the language so that his knowledge was in the process of change. In the same way a paper-and-pencil test for task-orientation is not valid for those situations in which the person who is testing for the leadership role changes his orientation because of what the group teaches him about the kind of leadership style they prefer.

Nonetheless, the contingency approach and its empirical support provide evidence that an adequate account of leadership must be much more complex and detailed than either the trait or the styles-of-leadership approach. The most satisfactory framework to date has been the contextual study of leadership.

The contextual study of leadership. The contextual study adds to the contingency approach the notion of the dynamic interplay of the communication in a group. The contextual account includes all the factors of the contingency explanation and adds to it the emergence of group norms and roles, the chaining fantasies that contribute to a group culture with their implications for leadership, the evolving communication networks with the amount and direction of the flow of messages, and the verbal and nonverbal contents of the communication.

The contextual viewpoint provides a more sophisticated and complete explanation of leadership than any of the other accounts. It incorporates the idea that leaders are, to some extent, born, but it also suggests that potential leaders can achieve skills and improve talents with training. Since some of the leadership behavior will be unique to a particular group because of the communication and interaction which contributed to its development, *a case history of the group is the only way to provide a complete explanation of its leadership.* Thus, the case-study method is one of the most fruitful ways of studying the complexities of leadership. Investigators can take a number of carefully developed and detailed case studies and by comparison and contrast discover similarities and patterns that generalize across many groups. The procedure is analogous to the techniques used by medical doctors and psychiatrists in the study of disease and psychological problems.

Franklyn Haiman warned of dangers in his book, *Group Leadership and Democratic Action.* The contextual view, he suggested, might give the impression that leadership is unique to a given situation and group, that no principles can be discovered, and that nothing can be said in a general way about the matter.

Certainly the contextual view will frustrate the person who wishes a quick and easy formula that will make him a leader in every group. He will also be frustrated, however, by advice and procedures stemming from another perspective that provide him with an easy formula; the easy formula that works in one situation will not work in another. Still, the possibility of generalizing about leadership from the contextual point of view depends to some extent on the level of analysis. If the student of group methods wishes to generalize about the one set of personality variables that will result in an individual's always assuming leadership, or about the likelihood of a given group accepting a leader whose style is autocratic or democratic, the possibility of generalization is limited. At a different level, however, generalizations are possible. This chapter, for example, is written from a contextual perspective and reports general patterns of leadership emergence based on situational and interactional grounds. Chapter 14 modifies these patterns so they can be applied to task-oriented groups in established organizations on a contextual basis.

In addition, the contextual view explains a good many facts that the other positions must rationalize or note as exceptions. The trait approach does not adequately explain why an individual emerges as leader of one group, but does not in a second similar group. It does not account for the change in leadership that often accompanies a marked change in the purpose of the same group. The one-best-style approach cannot fully explain the groups that are equally successful in terms of cohesiveness and productivity; similar in size, composition, and purpose; and yet exhibit different styles of control.

Different explanatory systems may emerge within the same school of thought. Within the contextual view of leadership, two major explanatory systems account for most differences of opinion among theorists.

The first rejects the idea that one leadership role emerges from group interaction and that this role is played by one individual. Instead, leadership functions become part of the roles of all members; it is therefore misleading to refer to one person as the leader of the group. A better explanation would be that leadership functions are distributed through the behavior repertoires of all group members. The members thus share in the leadership of the group. A slightly different variation on this theme suggests that the leadership role is assumed first by one member and then another.

The second explanation asserts that one leadership role emerges from group interaction and that until this role is played by one member, the role structure of the group is not stable. Further, this explanation asserts that the dynamics of group process tend toward such stability. The perspective of this book is, of course, the second version of the contextual approach. The empirical support for the perspective comes from detailed case studies compiled at Minnesota.

leadership explained

In everyday conversation, people talk about a group's lacking sound leadership, or about the need for more leadership in politics, the community, or the fraternity, and they know generally what they have in mind. However, when social scientists study the phenomenon of leadership systematically, they must clarify the common-sense concepts to eliminate as much ambiguity as possible. If they wish to study leadership in experimental groups, they must define terms very carefully so that other investigators can repeat the studies. Early investigators gave widely varying definitions to the concept of leadership. It would require an entire chapter to explain all the conventional definitions that have been established as ground rules for empirical studies of leadership.

In a highly disciplined, authoritarian organization such as a symphony orchestra or a football team, leadership is easy to observe. When the coach maps a play and the quarterback calls the signals, the team follows the orders without question. In general, leadership includes setting goals, making decisions, giving orders, and evaluating performance. Of course, it is implied that the decisions are implemented, and the orders are followed. In everyday conversation, the term *leadership* often implies that the decisions are good in terms of the organization's goals, and that the personnel willingly follow the orders. Fans praise the football coach and his quarterback for leadership when they make wise decisions about the sequence of plays and the players follow through effectively.

Leadership in an authoritarian organization is easily defined, but many groups do not have an authoritarian structure. What of the committee chairman who asks the group what they would like to do? What if the group makes suggestions and then votes on them? What if some person other than the chairman makes the suggestion that is eventually used? What if someone other than the chairman persuades a majority to accept this position? Who is the leader of such a group? Does the group have a leader?

Leadership might be defined as the behavior of the top man in an authoritarian group. But this definition is too limited because of the tradition of democracy and the assumption that authoritarianism is bad. People in our culture do not like bosses, dictators, and domineering people. Many American groups are "democratic" in the sense that *the group* rather than *the leader* is supposed to make decisions. This is true of educational classes, voluntary organizations, political clubs, and some families.

Investigators in the field of leadership have not restricted their studies to authoritarian groups. They needed a definition of leadership broad enough to include groups in which members reach a consensus about decisions. One approach was to define different types or styles of leadership. As stated earlier, Lippitt and White distinguished three types of leadership as authoritarian, democratic, and laissez faire.

Such distinctions solve only part of the problem, since they do not specify the nature of democratic leadership. Some investigators have suggested that the democratic group may not have a leader, but rather that an analogous role is played by a neutral arbiter who keeps the group within procedural bounds. Labels other than "leader" have been used—for example, *chairman, moderator, facilitator,* or *spokesman*—to refer to this person in the democratic organization. The shift of labels does not avoid the problem, for members continue to follow the group tendency to develop a role structure and a status ladder. Participants differ as to talent, commitment, and the roles they assume. Some are more "influential" than others in structuring the group and making decisions. Some theorists have reacted to those facts by defining leadership in terms of the action or behavior that moves a group toward its goal. This broad a definition might sometimes include everyone in the group; and when everyone is participating in leadership, the proper study of leadership then becomes the study of leadership functions as well as the study of leaders per se.

An investigator has a right to restrict his study by means of the operational definitions he uses. He can study leadership functions rather than leaders if he wishes; but in so doing, he misses some important nuances that are part of the ordinary meanings associated with leadership, whether democratic or authoritarian. In one sense, democratic groups and societies have *leaders* who perform similar functions and are perceived in much the same way as the leader of an authoritarian group.

Other investigators have defined leadership in terms of influence. If the group changed its behavior because it was influenced to do so by one of its members, leadership was exercised. This definition is closer to the usual meaning of the term, but it can be questioned. What about the attempt to influence that is resisted? Is this not negative influence? Does not the person who follows really influence the member who leads? Does not every member, by his presence, influence every other member in some way?

The point of this brief review of definitions of leadership is that these definitions have often fallen prey to the philosophical disease of starting with a stipulated definition and then discovering new meanings in the definition until a factual argument emerges which is based purely on assumptions hidden in the definition. The Minnesota Studies also required an operational definition of leadership: A leader was that individual perceived by all participants as the group leader. When all participants including member A reported that they perceived member A to be their leader, then he had emerged as the leader. The Minnesota Studies discovered such consensus in the great majority of groups that developed stable role structures. Subjects had little difficulty responding to questions in interviews and questionnaires using the term in this context. Their observed behavior gave further evidence that they perceived a given individual as their leader. The group members showed deference to this person, looked to him for directions on procedural matters, and often expected him to make unpleasant decisions.

This operational definition raises the question of what objective behaviors relate to the perception of leadership. Mortensen made a content analysis of the communication associated with the perception of leadership and discovered that, although others communicate some of the same things that the perceived leader communicates, his communication differs in a statistically significant way from that of the other members. Mortensen discovered that the perceived leaders specialized in communication that could be reliably coded into such categories as: introducing and formulating goals, tasks, and procedures; eliciting communication; delegating and directing action; and integrating and summarizing group activity.

If all members of a group do and say some of the same things as the perceived leader, why do they pick a leader rather than regard each member as sharing leadership functions? People participating in groups perceive the interactions of others in general terms. They do not tabulate the percentage of member A's directing actions as compared with the total number of orders and directions given. If A performs a high percentage of directing actions, as tabulated by an observer ana-lyzing group interactions, he is eventually perceived as a leader. One suggestion for action made by member A at a time of crisis may impress the group members as forcibly as many directions given at moments of less involvement. The psychological principles of learning provide a partial explanation for the impact of isolated interactions on the percep-tions and recollections of participants. The primacy of an interaction is often an important factor. Early in a group's life when primary tensions are high, a suggestion for action supported by the group can aid the perception that member A is a leader. Some interactions have greater impact because they are more recent. If member A has been active in structuring the group at the last meeting, he may be perceived as leading even though earlier he had not been as active. In the context of a group, intensity of perception, as well as the importance of the leading at a given time, may give the impression that A is the leader.

Members often carry some stereotyped role structures with them to each new group. They strive to make sense and order out of a socially insecure situation. Stereotypes serve to structure the flow of the meeting. One of the major stereotypes is that of the *leader*. Many people would like to be the leader and "run things," and "get their own ideas across." Even when a member perceives that he will not assume the role of leader, his interest in who will become leader is considerable no matter what stereotype he has of the role. Group members want someone they can "follow," a leader they can admire and trust. They do not want to be "dominated to the point of being subjugated," or to be "led around by the nose." These last comments, drawn from diary accounts collected by the Minnesota Studies, indicate the nature of some typical leader stereotypes.

The interactions that are closely correlated to the perception of leadership in the task-oriented groups are those that relate to procedural matters. If a person suggests that the group should get down to business or that the topic should be divided into military, economic, and political aspects, he is perceived as making a leadership move. Early in the LGD an individual who exhibits a great deal of knowledge and authority in the task area is often perceived as a potential leader, but as the group continues, the procedural directions relate more and more directly to leadership. Very early in an LGD, the participants may perceive the person who talks the most as a potential leader. Indeed, some investi-gators were so impressed with this phenomenon that they investigated it and discovered that leadership did correlate positively with talkativeness.

For some groups, the ability of a person to structure the work is closely related to the ability to do the job. A guide for a mountain-climbing expedition must be a good climber. A college president, on the other hand, may administer the college without being an expert in atomic physics, classical rhetoric, or small-group communication.

The role of leader is closely related to the status rankings within the group. Usually the final decision as to status must wait until this role emerges. When a leader emerges, the group can agree about where he fits in the status hierarchy and where other roles will be placed in relation to him.

The basic theoretical model of the LGD discussed in Chapter 9 explains why no two perceived leaders play precisely the same role in two different groups. It also explains why the same individual does not play precisely the same role in two different groups *even though he is perceived as leader of both groups.*

An important principle of role development is that *the role a person takes is worked out by the individual and the group together.* Thus, the observed behavior of a given group leader is to some extent *idiosyncratic.* An investigator can best explain the behavior of a particular leader by understanding the case history of the group and determining how the role was worked out. The idiosyncrasies of expectations associated with the role of leader make it difficult for investigators to discover broad patterns that account for leadership behavior. To some exent, these idiosyncracies explain the puzzling results of much research literature on leadership; for example, why studies that attempted to correlate leadership style with group cohesiveness and productivity were inconclusive. One group and one individual may work out a leadership role that includes an autocratic style, and yet the group may still be cohesive and productive. Another group may, under similar conditions, work out a more democratic style of giving directions. Nevertheless, there are some typical patterns to the process by which leaders emerge in the LGD.

patterns of interaction resulting in the emergence of a leader

STRUGGLE FOR ROLE AND STATUS

Since the internal esteem rewards are closely related to status within the group, they are always awarded unequally. Some individuals receive greater esteem gratification because the others perceive them as more important to the welfare of the group. As a result, people with high esteem needs contend for the top positions and, in this struggle, come into conflict and disagreements. The conflict generates secondary tensions, and much of the group's energy is directed to the question of who will win. When these struggles are protracted and intense, the group becomes split and gets little done.

The groups included in the Minnesota Studies are divided into two categories: groups in which leaders clearly emerged, and groups in which the roles never stabilized. The large majority of cases are in the first category. The groups that developed stable role structures experienced considerable release of secondary tension and a dramatic increase in cohesiveness at the point when a leader clearly emerged. The continual shifting of roles in groups that failed to find a leader created an unstable social field, high levels of secondary tension, reduced member satisfaction, lower levels of cohesiveness, and less effective work.

The basic principle governing the emergence of leadership in the LGD is that *the group selects its leader by the method of residues.* The group does not pick a leader, but instead eliminates members from consideration until only one person is left. The one outstanding impression that people report having in early meetings of the LGD is that there is difficulty in estimating who will emerge as leader, but little disagreement about who will *not* be the leader. People seem to come to the first sessions looking for cues that will eliminate other participants from the struggle for high-status roles. One possible explanation of this tendency is that eliminating some persons is relatively easy and it helps the individual begin to structure the social field. He can then concentrate on those members still in contention. If the individual is personally ambitious, he may find himself eliminating others from leadership in order to remain in contention himself. When he selects a leader, he eliminates himself from the high-status place.

The first phase. The general pattern of role emergence consists of two movements. The first phase is relatively short and often terminates after a matter of minutes. It seldom lasts more than a session. During this phase, the group eliminates people who are perceived as definitely unsuitable for leadership. Case studies indicate that roughly half of the members were eliminated as potential leaders in this early phase. They were eliminated on the basis of very crude and limited evidence. Participants found certain patterns of interaction so impressive that persons who exhibited them were uniformly eliminated from contention. Among those first eliminated were the quiet ones, those who "did not take part." The participant who said nothing or very little during the first meeting was always eliminated. Although silent participants usually reported that they would like to be leaders, they testified that they would not emerge as leaders because they were not taking an active part.

Some active persons were perceived as being uninformed, unintelligent, or unskilled. They did not seem to know much about the task, or what they said "did not seem to make much sense." They irritated the group because they introduced unnecessary distractions. These people were eliminated from contention early.

Another group eliminated in the first phase were those who often took a most active and vociferous part in the discussion. They took strong, unequivocal stands, expressed their position in flat, unqualified assertions, and indicated that no circumstances would change their ideas. They were perceived as "too extreme" or "too inflexible."

Sometimes the others perceived an individual to be extreme and inflexible, but they did not reject him immediately. The members did not recognize his inflexibility because he phrased his position tactfully. On other occasions, the participants found him so articulate, well informed, and intelligent that they did not reject his bid for leadership until later.

The second phase. This phase of role emergence typically found about half of the group still actively contending for leadership and was characterized by intensified competition. Members felt irritated and frustrated by the meetings. The group was "wasting time," and "nothing was accomplished." Animosities developed among some participants, and the group began to avoid questions relating to its social structure. Some ignored the role struggle by pretending it did not exist or by withdrawing from the group. Others began to find scapegoats to account for their failures. Quite often, the participants testified that little could be done to improve the group. They said they were victims of circumstances or at the mercy of some unfortunate, inherent, unchangeable personality traits of one or more members.

The groups that finally eliminated all but one contender used some additional negative evidence as a basis for rejecting a leader contender. If they failed to reject an inflexible person in the first phase, they rejected him in the second. In addition, the group rejected the contender whose "style" of leadership they found disturbing. The rejected styles were perceived as inappropriate to the situation, task, and group. In groups formed in discussion classes, the authoritarian style was often rejected. Contenders who were too "bossy" or too "dictatorial" were eliminated in the second phase. In Geier's study of 16 groups, only one contender with an authoritarian style emerged as the leader.

Although an authoritarian style was perceived as inappropriate to task-oriented groups in discussion class, other groups in other situations might find the authoritarian style necessary. Certain situations demand instant and unquestioning obedience, and the authoritarian style may be appropriate for their purposes.

To some extent, groups formed in discussion classes rejected women contenders for leadership in the second movement. The tendency to reject female contenders is true only in groups with two or more men.

One man may be rejected by the women who form a group in which a female leader emerges and the man is isolated.

People also rejected leader contenders whose personal style they found irritating or disturbing. A contender whose speeches were sententious and who never made a direct point was perceived as "talking all around the subject" and rejected partly on this basis.

If the members were predominantly interested in the task area, they sometimes rejected the contender who was considered unduly interested in the social dimension—that is, too worried about hurt feelings or too busy socializing. On the other hand, members who were preoccupied with social and esteem needs sometimes rejected the contender who seemed too task-oriented. In the final analysis, groups accepted the contender who provided the optimum blend of task efficiency and personal consideration. The leader who emerged was the one that others thought would be of most value to the entire group and whose orders and directions they trusted and could follow. In some instances, members were not too pleased even with the best contender.

About one-third of the groups included in Geier's study did not complete the second phase and after three months were still contending for high-status roles.

Within the second phase of struggle for position, certain archetypal patterns tended to be repeated. The following discussion will describe four of the most important and illustrate each with a case history.

PATTERN I

Groups that have a relatively easy, short, and painless period of role struggle often follow archetypal pattern I. A hypothetical group of five might exhibit this pattern as follows. Member A has emerged as the tension releaser and is thus removed from contention. Members C and D are eliminated because they seem uninvolved or uninformed. Members B and E are left to contend for the top position. During the second phase, A perceives B to be arbitrary and tactless, but he finds E understanding and better organized. A begins to support E. Members C and D also soon perceive B as less desirable and eliminate him. At this point, E clearly emerges as the leader. *He may not maintain the role.* He will be on probation for a while, but if he continues to lead in a satisfactory manner, he solidifies his role and grows in power and esteem. If the others begin to dislike his style, a new contender will arise to challenge his position. A number of leaders in the Minnesota Studies were deposed after several weeks.

Of course, not all role problems are solved by the emergence of a leader. The group may still have serious difficulties. The person who loses in the final clear-cut struggle is a potential source of trouble. He may be upset enough to sabotage the group. He is always one of the more capable people in the group. When he loses his bid for leadership, his esteem needs are unsatisfied, and he will be frustrated and upset. He often perceives the group as unreasonable and disorganized. He reports that in his opinion many of their decisions about how to organize and do their work have been wrong. He usually finds the leader less than capable and personally obnoxious. The others now perceive this individual to be a trouble maker. Everyone else gets along fine, and the group could accomplish something without him. They are often tempted to reject or ostracize him.

The group can fit the unsuccessful contender back into their role structure and find a useful and productive place for him, but this is not an easy task. The newly emerged leader often has just as much animosity toward the individual he defeated as the loser has for him. The greatest mistake the leader can make at this point is to exploit the power of his new role and make life miserable for his antagonist. If the leader punishes the loser, trouble will continue as long as the unsuccessful contender remains with the group. The wise leader, with support from the others, is always especially careful at this crucial point to support the antagonist in his moves to assume a high-status role commensurate with his abilities. The loser seldom becomes completely reconciled to his role, but he usually assumes this place and works for rather than against the group's goals.

Pattern I exhibits the emergence of a role function that is crucial to the structuring of the group. It can be thought of as the *lieutenant*-role function. When member A begins actively to support E, he becomes E's lieutenant. Member A's role then includes, among other things, being the tension releaser, best-liked member, and E's lieutenant. The emergence of a lieutenant is often a key development in determining a leader.

One of the cases included in the Minnesota Studies exemplified pattern I and also illustrated the successful integration of the loser. This group was composed of five discussants, three of whom were men. One woman was poised, vivacious, and smiling. She soon emerged as the tension releaser. Both women were eliminated from leadership contention in the first phase. The second phase settled down to a contention among the men. Two members were most strongly in contention. One of these was soft-spoken but fluent and assertive. He was tactful and serious. The other was intense, fast-talking, and task-oriented. After a short period of work in the second phase, the third man began to withdraw from the discussion. He eventually entered the deliberations by strongly supporting the more soft-spoken and tactful of the two remaining contenders. The women members quickly began to support this same member. Four members, the leader himself, the lieutenant, and both women now perceived the tactful member to be their leader.

The task-oriented member reported only that the group was wasting too much time and that a number of members did not seem well informed. In the next meeting, he began to challenge the leader vigorously on a point of procedure. At this crucial point the *lieutenant stepped forward to meet the challenge and defend the leader's suggestions.* The women members supported the lieutenant, and the leader remained above the battle. When the eliminated contender capitulated to the pressure, the leader stepped in as a noncombatant with many shows of group solidarity. He suggested that they all work together to make their group a good one. He raised the status of the contender by praising his challenge of the procedure and assured him that the group expected and appreciated vigorous questioning. In this way, the group found a high-status and productive role for the considerable talents of the eliminated leader contender.

PATTERN II

Archetypal pattern II is a longer, more frustrating, and tension-producing path to the emergence of a leader and to stable roles in a task-oriented group. Some groups that fell into pattern II never reached completion and remained without a clearly perceived leader. In a group of five, the first phase of this pattern sees the elimination of three members from contention for leadership. During the second phase, each of the remaining contenders gains a lieutenant. Such support encourages each to strive more vigorously and to hold out for a longer time. In a four-person group, such a division may prove disastrous. A number of groups included in the Minnesota Studies did follow pattern II to the conclusion of stable roles and a clearly perceived leader. The following case history describes such a group, composed of five men.

During the first meeting, the group spent its time getting acquainted and dissipating primary tension. The only role to emerge clearly during this hour was that of member E who kidded around and entertained the group.

During the second meeting, member B made a strong and determined effort to "run" the group and get his ideas across. No other member was equipped with the information or speaking skills to challenge his suggestions and ideas at this meeting.

In the interval between the second and third meetings, B met E in the library and discussed "his" solution with E. Member E reported:

> I ran into B today while doing research. He spent fully one hour convincing me of a solution for our assigned task. His arguments were logical enough, and I finally agreed after I became convinced of the feasibility of his plan. In fact, I was so convinced that I was determined that he be given a hearing

by the rest of the group and further, I was determined to help him shove this solution through as the group's document.

Member B came to the third meeting prepared to "shove" his solution through the group with the help of member E. He began the meeting by "instructing" the group about economic principles with the aid of several economics textbooks. In B's own words, "My major is Business Administration so I'm more qualified than others to speak on economics and economics policy . . . I explained many technical terms. . . ." At this point in the group's life, A and C were eliminated as leader contenders because they were uninformed. Member E was eliminated because he was the best liked and was B's lieutenant. This left B in the major position except for D. Member D reported his impressions as follows: "The first phenomenon observable was the attempt of member B toward leadership. He is a business major and with unmitigated gall let us know he had the whole discussion topic under control . . . I clocked him at 15 minutes for one talk." A bit later, member D reported:

> I could see signs that the other members were falling in behind him and I began to fear that the group would accept his proposals without any deliberation or critical analysis on their part. Consequently I began to question his position not because I disagreed with him so much as I disliked the thought of having any one idea go through unopposed and not analyzed.

When D began suggesting alternate modes of procedure, he was immediately supported by A. The meeting continued with B and his lieutenant, E, and D and his lieutenant, A, conflicting on almost every substantive issue. Member B reported in his diary that D's first challenge "was to go on record as favoring rewording the topic. . . . Two were for his motion, and two were against. The two against argued and argued that this procedure was not cricket."

As the discussion grew more acrimonious, E became more and more disillusioned with B. He reported that "D openly challenged the plan [member B's] and I, feeling incompetent about the matter, let B face the challenge alone. . . . I occasionally nodded my head and added a few statements." However, E was publicly on record as supporting B's plan, and he found it difficult to withdraw that support.

The group had a "lively" discussion for most of the third hour even though it often consisted of quibbles about relatively unimportant substantive matters. Secondary tensions rose, and the talk grew louder and louder. Meantime, member C remained neutral. He took little part in the proceedings, and his responses remained noncommittal. Finally, toward the end of the hour, B directly challenged C by asking, "Where do you stand?" Member C responded, "Directly in the middle."

Under these circumstances, groups that fall into pattern II continue the role struggle. Sometimes they fail to find a satisfactory conclusion. In the case of this particular group, C finally suggested a compromise between the positions of B and D. This gave E an opportunity to sever his support of B without losing face, and he gratefully leaped to the support of the compromise. The group released great amounts of secondary tension and made a number of shows of group solidarity. Members C, D, and E were now definitely in agreement and supportive of member D who was their "leader." The highly competent and aggressive member B remained a source of potential disruption. Member D, with the full support of the other three members, skillfully reinforced member B into the high-status role of task expert.

PATTERN III

Archetypal pattern III is also more difficult and complicated than pattern I. However, it typically results in the emergence of a leader. In successful groups that fall into this pattern, the leader who emerges proves satisfactory, and the group follows willingly. Occasionally, the leader who emerges from pattern III is unsatisfactory, and such groups are often unsuccessful.

Groups that fall into pattern III are faced with an external or internal crisis of such magnitude that the group is seriously threatened. Under the stress of this unexpected threat, the group often turns to a member who provides a solution for them. He becomes their leader.

External factors that pose a crisis for the group are usually unexpected and capricious, such as acts of nature that destroy material resources, health problems that withdraw key members when they are needed, and other unusual and unforeseen demands.

Equally important are the crisis situations within the social structure of the group. When the group's drive for a stable social field is disrupted so violently that the members are seriously disturbed, they face a crisis that opens the way for a leader to emerge. If one of the contenders in the second phase solves the internal problem satisfactorily, he will usually survive the eliminations. Groups whose pattern includes internal social crises contain members whose early attempts at finding a role in the group are so impressive that the others focus attention on them. The group may become so fascinated by the behavior of a particular member that their attention is distracted from the normal considerations of role structuring. Such members are *central persons*. Redl developed the concept of *central persons* to aid in his psychoanalytic interpretation of group process. His analysis resulted in the discovery of specific forms of central persons. The concept is used here in a more general and less psychoanalytic way. Central persons may be *stars* in the sense that they are perceived as so good and potentially helpful to the group that they stand out from it. They may be stars in the social area in that they are exceptionally pleasant, charming, and amusing. Such positive central persons seldom raise the kind of internal crisis that precipitates pattern III. Central persons may also be perceived as extremely hostile to the organization and its purposes, a great threat to the success of the group. And when the central person is unusually apathetic or uninvolved, he is very likely to precipitate an internal crisis.

Member B in the case history for pattern II soon became a central person, and member D emerged as leader partly because of his ability to challenge him. Since D was strong enough to stop B's efforts, he gained support from A and, eventually, from C. Other negative central persons included in the case histories reflect the range of behavior that, if extreme enough, can cause the member to become a central person. One member was so apathetic and uncommitted to the group's purposes that he was called "Mr. Negative," and the group turned to a leader who could handle him, even though the leader had a strongly authoritarian style, and the group remained ineffective. Another central person was a voluble and articulate individual, who systematically demolished all values important to the group's success. He belittled the goals of the group, strongly asserted that he would do no more work than necessary, and laughingly admitted that he was irresponsible and lazy.

The groups that follow pattern III to conclusive and stable roles select leaders who demonstrate that they can effectively handle the problems posed by the central person. Often leadership decision results from a dramatic crisis attributed to the central person. Group members testify that they supported the leader because he was "strong" enough to handle an inflexible member or because he found a productive role for "Mr. Negative" and made him part of the group.

PATTERN IV

Groups following the path of archetypal pattern IV do not achieve role specialization and stability. They are fraught with social tensions and frustrations; people find them punishing. Groups that follow pattern IV try to eliminate contenders in the second phase, but falter just before a decision or depose any leader who does emerge.

During the second phase, a particularly disturbing contest often develops between two contenders for leadership. The group is involved in endless bickering over unimportant points. Group decisions are reversed shortly after they are made or are reconsidered in the next meeting. The group seems to be getting nowhere and to be wasting time. Finally, in desperation, participants bring the problem out into the open, saying that the group needs direction and leadership. At this point, in some groups, a member changes the subject and the group gratefully drops the topic. Sometimes a participant argues against the need for leadership. He asserts that the group is doing fine with everybody leading and with nobody leading; they are all equals and working democratically. Sometimes the group decides that it needs leadership and agrees to an election. At this point, the group avoids the issue by electing a leader (moderator, spokesman, chairman) from among those eliminated in the first phase. They might elect a quiet woman, or a man who has been uninvolved and seems uninformed. Subsequently they justify their selection on the basis that they wanted someone who was "neutral," who would not "take sides" between the two warring contenders. Interestingly, the elected leader begins *to behave like a leader* after election. In all the cases in the Minnesota Studies, when groups selected a leader in this fashion, the elected leader *was not followed* and, within a matter of minutes, *stopped trying to lead*. Selecting someone not in contention does not solve the problem of selecting a leader.

In the other variation of pattern IV, a person emerging as leader for a brief period is then challenged and deposed. Another leader emerges, and he in turn is rejected after a short time. A typical group following this variation had the following case history. The panel was composed of two men and two women. At the end of the first movement, a woman, member B, was eliminated from contention because she was perceived as being quiet and shy. The others were all verbal and aggressive. Member A, a man, was particularly task-oriented and driving in his attempt to structure the group. The woman who remained in contention, member D, fought against A's attempts to run the group. The third member, C, was more relaxed in his manner and might have been the leader except that neither A nor D would support him. In short, no one assumed the role of lieutenant. The group members were continually assuming new roles, and the situation was in a constant state of flux. Whenever one of the contenders seemed to be emerging as leader, the other two would combine against him. In the course of successfully rejecting that individual, one of the two others would seem to be left in the leadership role, but at that point, the third member would switch and combine against the one emerging as leader. The three contenders thus assured that no member would become leader.

A group often follows pattern IV when the contenders for leadership in the second phase all have substantial handicaps and there is little basis to choose among them. A typical case history that illustrates this point found three of the five members eliminated in the first phase. Of the two remaining, member A had a strong, aggressive style of structuring the group. He moved to the blackboard and began dividing the work very early in the first meeting. Several of the others perceived him as a manipulator and resisted his efforts to organize the work. Member D began to challenge A. The others began to alternate their support from A to D. D was congenial and showed consideration for the others when structuring the group. The others much preferred his leadership style to that of member A. However, they discovered that D had not prepared very well for the task and was not as well informed as A. He was quite tentative and fuzzy in his thinking and rather indecisive. Member A was more capable of developing a clear, coherent course of action and was clearly most able to lead the group to their task goals. The members perceived the contenders as roughly equal, but both had serious handicaps as leaders. The members did not follow either, and the role structure never stabilized.

special problems

Because leadership is crucial to the establishment of role structure for the group, it is the focus for many secondary tensions that inhibit group efficiency and satisfaction.

THE MANIPULATOR

Groups frequently have difficulty resolving the leadership struggle because of the presence of an individual who, in many regards, is a star. He is fluent, intelligent, and hardworking. However, he plans to exploit the group for his own purposes. He tries to be a *manipulator*. The most acrimonious role conflicts arise when a person comes into the group to "run" it or to get "his" ideas across. Manipulative efforts are first perceived by the others as attempts to assume the role of leader. Eventually the group perceives that the manipulative person is trying to exploit them for his own advantage. At this point, no matter how brilliant or clever at manipulation, he is rejected as the leader.

Member B typifies one sort of manipulator. Member B was a hard-sell manipulator. He reported in his diary, "I have been in many, many discussion groups and I believe I can manipulate most people to predetermined ends." He subsequently reflected this preoccupation with "winning" the discussion when he evaluated his record within the group. "I convinced the group of several things. First of all, I was against limiting the question . . . and I won."

The member who comes into the group to manipulate it is frustrated because of his rejection. He quite often reacts strongly. He feels that he has been unable to run the group because he has not been tough enough. He must bluster more, make more definite plans, argue more—the actions that created the initial trouble become more offensive. He soon becomes the focal point of group attention. The other members see him as bull-headed and domineering; they think that if he would just be silent or leave, the group might be able to accomplish something.

A second type of manipulator is more subtle in his approach. He is congenial, a good listener, persuasive, tactful, and complimentary. He employs all the techniques commonly found in lists of "do's and don'ts" to improve social relations. He phrases his disagreement carefully and asks leading questions with considerable skill. He seizes the appropriate moment to assert group consensus in line with his own desires. For a time, these tactics succeed, but gradually the group becomes aware that they are being led. If he has emerged as leader and is undergoing his probationary period in the role, he is challenged at this point by another member and will be deposed. If this discovery occurs during the second phase of the leader contention, the group will eliminate him.

One case history included in the Minnesota Studies was of a group judged unsuccessful by both participants and observers. It contained both a hard-sell and a soft-sell manipulator. Member B was smooth, a bit older than the others, and congenial. Member D was fast-talking, aggressive, and driving. B emerged as the leader of the group during the first meeting. Member D was absent for the next two meetings. When he returned, he sensed the group's dissatisfaction with B and began a systematic attack on all B's suggestions. He got considerable support, and, within 30 minutes, B was deposed as group leader. B reported of himself that during "The third meeting I deliberately ran the group my own way, rather subtly I thought. I gave suggestions and called on those who I knew would give me support." During the course of this meeting, the other members became aware that B's friendly democratic style of asking for opinions and directions masked an intent to control and manipulate. Another member reported, "B tries to tell us what to do too often. . . . You can only take so much of that." Another recorded in his diary, "B gets a little worse every meeting. It's as though he were the captain of the ship."

D, having deposed B, was not accepted as leader. The top spot was then open, and a number of the others were in contention. D was soon perceived as a hard-sell manipulator. One member said, "I've never worked with anyone who tries like he does to manipulate the entire group. He just won't listen to reason." D expressed his position as follows:

> When I was in the army the guy who won out was the one who spoke the loudest and the fastest. You had to keep up with the other guys. I've been using the same thing ever since I got out.

Member D was as unsuccessful as B in emerging as leader. Indeed, the group resisted his efforts even more vigorously than they had B's leadership. D, however, was less sensitive to the group's resistance, although he did recognize it. He reported, "I can't understand it. I gave suggestions, I called on participants, I volunteered to write the paper but in the end the group just wouldn't listen."

THE INFLEXIBLE MEMBER

Another special problem that delays successful structuring of the LGD is the perception of the participants that another member is inflexible. The member who takes an unequivocal stand and expresses it with flat certainty, indicating by verbal and gestural messages that he will under no circumstances change his position, causes the group trouble. Such a member becomes a central person, and the other members are soon preoccupied with deciding what to do with him.

One group in the Minnesota Studies contained two inflexible members and was judged to be an unsuccessful group. The group was studying medical care for the aged. Member B flatly and unequivocally stated he was against government insurance programs. Member C was equally strong in her commitment to such a program. She reported:

> *Participant A appears to be the diplomat—He seeks to establish compromises between the extremists—Mainly B and me—participant B admits he's one-sided since he sells health insurance . . . I admit B makes me see red the way he throws out statements without proof for the most part . . . I don't see how we'll ever get together.*

A member may be inflexible in the social dimension as well as in the task area. Some participants are insensitive to the cues that small groups use to extinguish behavior. Despite such verbal and nonverbal indications as disagreement, noncompliance, and having their suggestions or evaluations ignored, these rigid participants continue to do and say the things the group dislikes. The participant who does this confuses and frustrates the other members. They do not know how to teach him a suitable role in the group. College and high-school debaters have often been desensitized in this regard because, in their experience, the proper response to disagreement is a tenacious reaffirmation of the debater's position.

Engineers and other specialists whose training and work experience have stressed productivity and the manipulation of machines and materials often exhibit some of this social rigidity. They sometimes feel that other group members should act sensibly and predictably, as materials and machines do. The virtue of sensitivity training for managers in business and industry is that it makes engineers and other production specialists who find themselves in management positions aware of ways in which groups teach members their roles.

The first edition of this book contained a section on the woman who contended for leadership, which was written before the movement for equality for women had gotten well under way. The section reported the results of case studies at Minnesota in which a woman was an active and able contender for leadership. Essentially the section reported that, in the case histories of discussion-class groups, women rarely emerged as leaders in a coeducational group containing two or more men. The Minnesota Studies also contained case histories of all-female groups, all-male groups, and groups containing only one man or one woman. One reason for studying such groups was to compare the process of role emergence to see if all-female groups were different from all-male groups. In the all-female groups included, the two-phase elimination of leader possibilities and the emergence of a leader by the method of residues was similar to that followed by all-male and by coeducational groups.

In groups composed of women and two or more men, the woman who contended for leadership apparently posed some problems simply because she was a woman. Men usually refused to follow directions given by a woman in the presence of other men. Some expressed the opinion in their interviews, questionnaires, and diaries that women should obey and men should lead. In some groups where a woman was in strong contention, the men even expressed doubts as to the advisability of women receiving higher education.

The groups that included a female contender who was considered extremely able had the most difficulty resolving their leadership problems. If the woman who remained in contention demonstrated exceptional brilliance and good sense and seemed best qualified to lead the group, the fact that she was also female caused considerable ambivalence on the part of the men.

No section of the first edition caused as much discussion, argument, resentment, and antagonism in the author's classes in discussion and group methods as that section. Interestingly enough, it was the women in the classes who were, for the most part, upset by the results of the earlier case studies. Very seldom did any of the male students come to discuss the material with the author, raise the issue in their groups, or in the class meetings. Women were upset with the material, not because they felt it was inaccurate, but because they found it all too accurate, and they felt it was unjust. With the rise of women's liberation and the concern with equality for women, the section served as the stimulus for a number of case studies that focused on the question of women as leaders in task-oriented small groups. Several seminars at Minnesota also dealt with the topic.

Case studies from 1969 to the present indicate that the emergence of women as leaders in small groups at Minnesota is not as rare as it was in the 1950s and 1960s. More men report in their diaries and interviews that they would be willing to accept direction from an able female leader, and a considerable number behave as though they mean what they say. In group discussions of role emergence and in class discussions of the question, the male response tends to be one of surprise that there is much of a problem, often followed by a quizzical or humorous reaction. The female response tends to be much more emotional, and more women testify to the frustrations they have experienced when working in a coeducational group and being unable to lead, when they feel certain they are the best qualified to do so, because of the unwillingness of the others to follow. In some case studies after 1969, women raised the question of influence and leadership directly and confronted the males with their concern about making a greater contribution to the group than simply doing routine chores. In many of the cases the issue focused on who would perform the role function of record keeping, the traditional secretarial role. Many women absolutely refused on principle to be a group recorder or secretary.

In short, the material on the female contender contained in the first edition of the book is no longer an accurate description of the problems faced by a female in contention for leadership. Thus, the question of female leadership is clearly a culture-bound feature of small-group communication. It may well also be a geographically bound feature to some extent, even within the United States. Since the larger culture in the United States underwent a considerable change in attitude and approach to women's role in society, the impact of those changes was reflected in the case studies. Much of the earlier laboratory research on the influence of sex on small-group dynamics (reported in Chapter 7) is thus probably more indicative of historical attitudes and roles than of current or future conditions.

Nonetheless, women continue to have difficulty emerging as leaders in groups containing two or more males, and the situation certainly has not come full circle in the case studies at Minnesota. Women continue to emerge in influential roles in small groups largely through avenues other than as recognized and sanctioned leaders.

One avenue of influence often used by women is the path of hard and dedicated effort for the welfare of the group. Often one or two women will provide the group with most of its information and will be a dedicated, responsible, and dependable core of the group. Sometimes a woman will form a coalition with a male and by playing a lieutenant role function will rise to influence. Women who assume such a role often do much more than simply support the male's efforts at structuring the group's work. They often suggest courses of action, administer details of programs and plans, and assure that the group mobilizes its resources. Sometimes several women will form a coalition and, although no one of them is recognized as the group's leader, they form a power base from which to dominate the group's task and social dimensions. No male can lead the group except at their sufferance.

GOOD POLITICIAN, POOR ADMINISTRATOR

In some groups, a member who has been very skillful at emerging as the leader fails to hold the position. This member is preoccupied with the power struggle and explores various avenues to the top position. He is less interested in the group's work than in the social structuring of the group. He is very sensitive to group opinion and watches carefully for indications of approval or disagreement. He gets to "know" the members and shows interest in them as people. He weights the members in terms of their possible alignment in the jockeying for top position. His perceptions of the group are often in terms of who will support him or another contender. An excellent example of this is furnished by the emergence of roles in a group composed of five men and two women.

Between the second and third meetings, member A made an appointment to discuss the group with the instructor. He felt that the group needed direction, that it had floundered about and was not progressing. He revealed that he would like to be the leader of the group. Finally, he asked the instructor's advice as to how he might become the leader. The instructor was nondirective. He suggested that member A knew the group intimately and that there really were no simple formulas. Member A finally decided to do a little "politicking." He was going to call some of the others and discuss the group's problem with them. He might even suggest that they ought to elect a leader.

Between the second and third meeting, member B also made an appointment with the instructor. He explained why he had been absent from the group and promised to attend future meetings. He said that he had talked to some members and that the group was apparently getting nowhere. He had decided that the group needed leadership and that he could provide it.

The third meeting brought the role struggle to a head. B arrived early and took the chair at the head of the table. He introduced himself to the group and explained that he had discussed its progress with the instructor. He misquoted the instructor as saying that the group was "spinning its wheels" and that it was in "trouble." Immediately he aroused a lively response from the other members who came to the defense of the group. The dynamic new member overrode their objections and asserted that in his opinion the group needed a leader. He then outlined the requisites of a good leader and included, among other things, experience in working in groups and an understanding of group dynamics. He told them that he had 20 hours of group theory in sociology.

The new member upset the tentative role structure the group had established. He posed a crisis of the type characteristic of pattern III. Finally, he suggested that the group elect a leader. The suggestion was quickly supported by A, and the two women agreed. B opened the nominations, and one of the women nominated A. In a few moments, a rather surprised B discovered that A had been elected leader by a vote of six to one.

In his diary, member A recorded that, "Meanwhile, back at the ranch I won the election . . . cohesiveness was restored and we were ready for the task." He was wrong. After his election, he became a very fastidious, authoritarian leader. He made no moves to reconcile B to the group. Neither did he perceive the problem posed by two other former contenders. Within two weeks, mutiny was brewing among these three. As B put it in his diary:

> *He performed his role well, although some members have talked among themselves as to how good a leader he was. The conclusion is, had he been leader for a longer period of time, other members may have replaced him.*

Another of the unsuccessful contenders commented:

> *I think at times A was a little too authoritarian in his leadership and that although we recognized him as a leader, we didn't want to assume a position of being subjugated to a complete position of dominated. I think that some of us felt that he was perhaps a little too zealous in his method of attaining leadership.*

THE UNSUITABLE ASSIGNMENT OF LEADERSHIP

A final problem that often occurs in the small task-oriented group is that posed by the formal assignment of a leader who then proves unsuitable, or the group may make a mistake and elect an unsuitable leader. Member A, in the last case, is such a leader. He was formally elected because he had prepared the way and was able to exploit the crisis presented by the new member. The group accepted him, until he showed that he was not a good administrator.

In many other situations, leaders are assigned by the organization. This is quite often the case with ad hoc and standing committees. The organization usually appoints managers, supervisors, foremen, chiefs, or sergeants for the small task-oriented groups within it. In discussion classes, the instructor may assign a chairman, moderator, or leader. Such an assigned leader typically begins by leading the group. He takes charge, gives direction, controls communication, and initiates action. The group does not accept this person as leader without a period of testing. Challenges to the assigned leader's control arise. If the assigned leader proves unsuitable, the group faces the same situation as if they had formally elected the individual and then discovered that he was unsuitable.

The advice on leadership that stems from the contextual perspective relates only to natural or emergent leadership. A distinction must be made between the formal position of leadership and the leadership role that emerges in the LGD. The insights from the contextual theory of leadership relate only to the LGD. A person may come to formal leadership, headship, or a position of status and authority within an organization by a number of routes. Leadership can be attained through birth, seniority, or luck, or it can be earned. It is this latter process of emerging as the leader—through interacting with the members and earning their esteem and allegiance in order to gain the power to structure and mobilize the group's resources—that is the focus for the following advice.

Even when a person has a position of leadership because of election, inheritance, seniority, or luck, actually earning a leadership role within the organization is of great importance. The person in a position of leadership must emerge as the natural leader, or *someone else will.* The dynamics of group process tend inexorably to the emergence of a leader. If there is a vacuum because of lack of leadership, the LGD follows the pattern of the basic model of role emergence.

emerging as the leader of a small task-oriented group

DEVELOPING AN UNDERSTANDING OF GROUP METHOD

Some people have learned sets of opening moves that apply to different kinds of groups and enable them to emerge rather consistently as the leader, if they wish to do so. Such skill represents a kind of unconscious competence or instinct. A good many persons, however, are not competent by instinct. A grasp of group process and method will help both kinds of people understand why they are successful, or why they are not. An understanding of group process helps the competent practitioner to increase his competence and the incompetent to achieve some measure of success. If a person understands the material in Chapters 7 through 11—particularly the operations of the basic model that governs role emergence and the patterns that groups follow in eliminating leader contenders—he is in a much better position to become the natural leader.

The first principle of emergent leadership is that the person who wishes to become the leader *must respect the laws that govern group process.* If he works against them, the group will not only resist him and his attempts at influence, but he will raise the level of secondary tensions.

The natural laws of group process. A person who wishes to lead must recognize that he is not free to lead the group arbitrarily in the direction he wishes or he feels to be the best. The group limits his area of choice to *those leadership moves that they will follow.* It does little good for the leader to march off at the head of a column in what seems to him to be the wisest direction if the members take another path. Studies have indicated that the individual who emerges as leader may be quite influential in setting the group norms during the early period of role struggle; but, once these norms are established, the group will not follow a leader who departs too widely from these expectations (even if he had been influential in establishing them). If he persists, they will depose him. In one study, the person who emerged as leader was removed from a set of experimental groups and then placed back in the groups after the group norms had been changed. When the subjects rejoined the group, they did not again emerge as leader unless their behavior conformed to the new group norms.

A person who wishes to lead must recognize the drive for specialization and role stabilization within the group. Instead of concentrating on resisting and rejecting behavior which he interprets as striving for high-status roles within the group, he should spend some time thinking about the best roles for individuals within the group—*not in terms of his own, but in terms of group, welfare.* He should examine the talents and achievements of each member, including himself. He will wonder, What task functions can member A best perform for the good of the group? Will A accept the status associated with this task role? What social maintenance functions can this person best perform for the good of all? How can A be reinforced to learn this role? How can A be assured shows of solidarity and esteem sufficient to gratify his social and esteem needs? How can this role assure member A an opportunity for self-actualization?

A person who wishes to lead must expect the period of role struggle to be frustrating and difficult. Even a thorough understanding of the laws of group process will not make things easy during this period. He must give the process sufficient time to work to a conclusion. If a leader attempts to force things before the members are ready to accept them, he will simply build up the secondary tensions. With practice he will develop a sensitivity to the importance of timing. A clearly formulated plan of procedure (agenda) may be completely rejected on Monday; however, by Wednesday, the group may be demanding some sense of direction and be ready to accept with enthusiasm essentially the same plan of action that did not suit it on Monday. A group may pointedly ignore the call to elect a leader on Tuesday and welcome an election on Friday. In short, a person with a good understanding of group method, who has participated in groups and learned their rhythm, will know when to push for structure and when to wait. He will know when to step forward with a plan or an interaction to facilitate the stabilization of roles and when to be silent. Several strong shows of group solidarity at the right moment can do much to build the cohesiveness of the group. The transcript on shows of solidarity in Chapter 8 highlights such a moment. Strong agreements interjected at the crucial moment will help to guide an individual into a good role for both the person and the group. A suggestion that the group has reached a decision, when inserted at the appropriate point, can structure the group's work, mobilize resources, and save meeting time.

The best plan for emerging as the natural leader of a group is devised for each particular situation by a person who knows group methods and the history of the group. Such a plan is an artistic enterprise somewhat similar to designing a house. The architect understands the laws governing mechanics. He must design his house so it will not fall down. He also knows some principles of aesthetics and has some theory of art. But to design a particular building, he must study the environment, the uses to which the building will be put, and the personalities and wishes of the people using his services. Similarly, the problem of emerging as the leader of a task-oriented group poses particular problems that are unique to that group, to their purposes, to the interactions they share in their common history, and to the pressures of the environment. There are no easy tactical plans that encompass a wide number of groups.

THE STRATEGY OF LEADER EMERGENCE

Strategy in this sense refers to the overall plan, the big picture, the general attitudes and objectives of the person who emerges as leader. The following is a composite strategy built up from aspects of individuals who emerged as leaders in the Minnesota Studies.

The desire to be leader. The first element in this strategy is that participants who emerged as leaders wanted to be leaders of the group enough to do what was required to achieve the role. Others felt that they really deserved to lead or could do a very good job of leadership, but they did not want to do the required work or make the requisite personal sacrifices; their stereotype of the role included the notion that the *leader did all the work.* One reason that individuals refuse positions of formal leadership in such organizations as the PTA or League of

Women Voters is that they think the rewards of such positions are not commensurate with the time and trouble involved. The person who wants to be leader without effort seldom emerges as the leader. The member who adopts the strategy that he will work hard enough and make whatever sacrifices of time and resources are necessary to achieve leadership is much more likely to be successful.

The manipulative versus the nonmanipulative attitude. Second, the successful leaders adopted a nonmanipulative attitude and set of personal goals. Their basic strategy was to *work for the good of the group.* From the beginning, they were interested in self-transcendence. They wanted the group to succeed; they wanted the members to be happy and to enjoy their roles. The good of the group became the basic criterion against which they judged and selected tactics.

Not every person who used this kind of strategy emerged as a leader, because some accepted a lesser role for the good of the group. However, most people who became leaders in the Minnesota Studies did follow this strategy. The impressive thing about those who adopted the opposite strategy, what has been called the manipulative approach, is that they rarely emerged as leaders. And yet, those with the manipulative strategy were the most willing to work and most preoccupied with achieving leadership, in order to get their way and have their ideas accepted.

THE TACTICS OF LEADER EMERGENCE

Tactics refer to those things members say and do to implement their overall strategy. For the person sincerely dedicated to the good of the entire group, a careful examination of the group's development, its role structure, and its members and their resources precedes the development of a specific strategy. Even if the group has never met before, certain opening moves can be planned if the participant does some investigating before the meeting. He should first ask: What style of leadership is suitable for this group? Would they expect a democratic-moderator style? Does tradition require authoritarian control? What style of leadership is best suited to my background and temperament? Am I particularly skilled in democratic moderating? In authoritarian leadership? Do I have the patience and ability to restrain my own compulsion for organization and efficiency? Am I indecisive in crises? Can I make snap judgments quickly and then implement them with great decisiveness? Am I good at sensing the feelings of a group? Can I judge when members have come to a decision, whether they have verbalized it or not? Can I be an effective administrator?

No matter what style of leadership seems most appropriate, the opening moves of a would-be leader should emphasize his group commitment, his concern for other members, and his willingness to make sacrifices. He should resist the impulse to bring order to what may seem a time-wasting, chaotic meeting. He should not be surprised or disturbed if suggestions that seem eminently logical and wise are resisted or misunderstood at first. He should realize that some of what seems groping and useless in the early meetings is really hard and careful work on the social structuring of the group. This stage might be thought of as the collective preparation stage, and it is absolutely necessary if important work is to be done later.

When the group is deeply involved in the second phase of eliminating potential leaders, the member must watch secondary tensions. When tensions break the tolerance level, he should deal with them, or reinforce and encourage the members who do. The best tactic for dealing with these tensions is to talk about them directly. Two general approaches may be used. The member can talk to individuals outside the group meetings. He can indicate his concern for the welfare of the group, ask their opinions about the personality conflicts, and give his suggestions for solutions. If a number of members in these conferences suggest that he would make the best leader, he should accept the role, making it very clear that his only interest is the success of the group. If these conferences suggest that another member would be a better leader, he should consider assuming the role of lieutenant and supporting this person. If the other members clearly understand that he is sincerely and unselfishly dedicated to the good of the group, they will accept his leadership much more willingly. They will perceive his directions not as evidence that he feels superior or is exploiting or manipulating the group to satisfy his own power and esteem needs, but rather as a necessary structuring of the group's work, which he is doing for the good of all. Some groups, which require a highly authoritarian style of leadership to meet crises with a quick, efficient mobilization of group resources, will accept crudely barked orders without a great deal of resentment.

The second general approach is to devote part of a regular meeting to a direct examination of the secondary tensions and their causes. This approach may bring the whole problem into the open. New courses of action and new roles may emerge, solve the problem, and result in increased cohesiveness. A group that demonstrates that it can survive this approach impresses on its members its importance and durability.

summary

The major perspectives that have guided research into various aspects of leadership include the trait approach, the styles-of-leadership approach, the contingency approach, and the contextual study of leadership. The trait approach assumes that leadership can be studied in individuals by isolating clusters of traits that are required for it. The styles-of-leadership approach searches for an ideal way to lead. The contingency explanation seeks a limited number of factors in the leader's personality, the difficulty of the task, the leadership style, and the relationships among group members on which group success is contingent. The contextual position explains leadership in terms of all the factors considered by other approaches, but adds to them a consideration of the dynamic interplay of communication within the group's processes.

This chapter reports the results of the Minnesota Studies of leadership emergence in leaderless group discussion, which support the variation of the contextual approach that explains leadership in terms of group process driving toward a stable role structure and one of these roles being perceived by the group members as the leadership role. The leader is defined as the member perceived by the participants as their leader and judged by observers to be the member whose directions are followed. The interactions that are closely related to the perception of leadership in the task-oriented discussion group are those related to procedural matters. The role a person takes is worked out by the member and the group together. The principle is true of leadership as well as the other roles. The behaviors associated with the leadership role in any given group is to some extent idiosyncratic and can often be best explained by a case history of how the role was worked out in a given group.

Despite the idiosyncratic nature of role behaviors, there is a general pattern to leadership emergence. The group rejects people as unsuitable for leadership until it is left with one person who emerges in that role. There are two general phases in this pattern. The first early phase ends when the members have perceived all participants who can be quickly and easily eliminated from contention. These include members who seem uninformed, nonparticipative, or inflexible. The second phase is characterized by intensified competition among the remaining contenders.

Within this general pattern of leadership emergence, at a more detailed level of analysis, four archetypal patterns apply to the majority of case histories. Pattern I is a relatively short and easy way to the emergence of stable roles. In the second phase of the role struggle, one of the two remaining contenders gains a strong lieutenant and the other does not. After a period of time, the contender and his lieutenant swing the uncommitted members to their support, and this contender emerges as leader. Pattern II is a more difficult way to the emergence of a leader since both contenders gain a lieutenant. In archetypal pattern III, the group faces some crisis posed by the external environment or by the behavior of a central person within the group. The contender who provides evidence that he could best handle the crisis emerges as the leader. Archetypal pattern IV is typical of groups that never stabilize their role structures. Support is thrown from one contender to another in such a fashion that no one emerges, or the struggle is bypassed by the formal election of a noncontender to the leadership position. Quite often, pattern IV results from the members' inability to discern a difference among the remaining contenders.

Special problems reflected in these four archetypal patterns include those posed by the hard- and soft-sell manipulators, the rigid member, the female contender in a group containing two or more men, the politician who is a poor administrator, and the formally appointed or selected leader who proves unsuitable.

Individuals who wish to emerge as natural leaders should adopt appropriate strategies and tactics. The most successful overall strategy is that of being willing to work hard enough for the group to achieve leadership and of adopting a sincere desire to work for the good of the group even at the expense of a high-status position. Appropriate tactics are dependent on the given situation. They essentially involve communicating this strategy to the other members of the group by word and deed.

QUESTIONS FOR STUDY

1. What are some of the cultural ambivalences toward leadership in the United States?
2. What is the trait approach to leadership?
3. What are the advantages and disadvantages of the contextual explanation of leadership?
4. How would you define "leadership"?
5. What are some of the communications closely related to the perception of leadership in the small group?
6. What are the implications of the discovery that "the group selects its leader by the method of residues"?
7. What are the characteristics of the two major phases of leadership emergence in the leaderless group discussion?
8. What was the first pattern of leadership emergence? the second? the third? the fourth?
9. What is the "lieutenant role function" in a small group?
10. What is meant by a "central person"?
11. In what ways may a group take flight from the leadership problem?
12. What is the difference between a soft-sell and a hard-sell manipulator?
13. Compare and contrast the leadership emergence in women's groups, men's groups, and coeducational groups.
14. What effect does the assignment of leadership have on leadership emergence?
15. What behaviors did members who emerged as leaders in initially leaderless discussion groups commonly exhibit?

EXERCISES

1. Form a leaderless group discussion with a specific task and objective. Tape record the meetings. After the first meeting, guess who will emerge as leader. List the names of those who will not be the leader. Describe the role that you will most likely assume in the group. After the second and subsequent meetings, make a similar evaluation of the leadership. After four meetings, write a short paper in which you describe the way your group handled the question of leadership. Fit your group into the overall pattern and the appropriate specific subpatterns of leadership emergence. Did your group have a lieutenant? A central person? Hold a postmortem, and discuss the leadership emergence in your group with. the rest of the members.

2. Select a group you have been working with for several months. Write a short paper discussing the assigned chairman or leader. Is the assigned leader the natural leader? If not, who is? What is the relationship between the assigned leader and the natural leader? Why did the group accept or reject the assigned leader?

3. Form a group from your class, and work out a role-playing exercise to demonstrate the principles of leadership emergence. Conduct a class meeting as a group in which you use the role-playing exercise to demonstrate and illustrate leadership principles.

4. Work out a case study suitable for a leadership-training session. Divide the class into buzz groups, and have them discuss the case; then reassemble the class for a general discussion of the case.

References and suggested readings

The bulk of the discussion in this chapter is drawn from the results of the Minnesota Studies. The literature on leadership is voluminous. The great majority of it, however, reports studies with populations of subjects drawn from students in psychology, sociology, or education. Other subjects were drafted from general student populations for the purposes of the investigator. In addition, a number of studies used young children and adolescents as the subjects. The Minnesota Studies included a variety of groups, but the results reported are all drawn from the study of groups set up in discussion courses. They are, therefore, most pertinent to the student working in such a class. To be sure, the basic principles developed in this chapter are applicable to most task-oriented groups, but the idiosyncratic dimension of leadership is partially a function of the classroom situation and the expectations set up by a course in discussion and group methods.

For studies reporting and evaluating the trait approach to leadership, see:

Fiedler, Fred E. "Leadership and Leadership Effectiveness Traits: A Reconceptualization of the Leadership Trait Problem." In Luigi Petrullo and Bernard Bass, eds. *Leadership and Interpersonal Behavior*. New York: Holt, Rinehart and Winston, 1961, pp. 179–186.

Geier, John G. "A Trait Approach to the Study of Leadership in Small Groups," *Journal of Communication,* 17 (1967), 316–323.

Nelson, Paul D. "Similarities and Differences Among Leaders and Followers," *Journal of Social Psychology*, **63** (1964), 161–167.

Stogdill, Ralph M. "Personal Factors Associated with Leadership: A Survey of the Literature," *Journal of Psychology*, **25** (1948), 35–71.

For a summary of research relating to styles of leadership, see:

Hare, A. Paul. *Handbook of Small Group Research.* New York: Free Press, 1962, pp. 309–321.

Studies based on the styles of leadership perspective are too voluminous to catalogue. For illustrative works, see:

Berkowitz, L. "Sharing Leadership in Small Decision-Making Groups," *Journal of Abnormal and Social Psychology*, **48** (1953), 231–238.

This study supports the analysis that the members of an ephemeral meeting accept imposed leadership. See also:

Gordon, Thomas. *Group-Centered Leadership: A Way of Releasing the Creative Power of Groups.* Boston: Houghton Mifflin, 1955.

Rubenowitz, Sigvard. "Job-oriented and Person-oriented Leadership," *Personnel Psychology*, **15** (1962), 387–396.

Wischmeier, Richard R. "Group-Centered and Leader-Centered Leadership: An Experimental Study," *Speech Monographs*, **22** (1955), 43–48.

For the contingency approach to leadership effectiveness, see:

Fiedler, Fred E. *A Theory of Leadership Effectiveness.* New York: McGraw-Hill, 1967.

For studies relating to the contextual approach to leadership, see:

Burke, W. Warner. "Leadership Behavior as a Function of the Leader, the Follower, and the Situation," *Journal of Personality*, **33** (1965), 60–81.

Mulder, Mauk, and Ad Stemerding. "Threat, Attraction to Group, and Need for Strong Leadership," *Human Relations*, **16** (1963), 317–334.

Shaw, Marvin E., and Michael J. Blum. "Effects of Leadership Style upon Group Performance as a Function of Task Structure," *Journal of Personality and Social Psychology*, **3** (1966), 238–242.

For general studies and surveys of leadership research, see:

Bass, Bernard M. *Leadership, Psychology, and Organizational Behavior.* New York: Harper & Row, 1960.

Hollander, Edwin P. *Leaders, Groups and Influence.* New York: Oxford University Press, 1964.

Keltner, John W. "Communication in Discussion and Group Process: Some Research Trends of the Decade 1950–1959," *Journal of Communication*, **10** (1960), 195–204.

Petrullo, Luigi, and Bernard M. Bass, eds. *Leadership and Interpersonal Behavior.* New York: Holt, Rinehart and Winston, 1961.

For the study of stars (great men), see:

Borgatta, Edgar F., Arthur S. Couch, and Robert F. Bales. "Some Findings Relevant to the Great Man Theory of Leadership." In A. Paul Hare, Edgar F. Borgatta, and Robert F. Bales, eds. *Small Groups: Studies in Social Interaction.* New York: Knopf, 1955, pp. 568–574.

A critique of the contextual approach to leadership is:

Franklyn Haiman. *Group Leadership and Democratic Action.* Boston: Houghton Mifflin, 1951, pp. 10–11.

The study of central persons is:

Redl, Fritz. "Group Emotion and Leadership," *Psychiatry,* **5** (1942), 573–596.

For studies relating to leadership emergence, see:

Barnlund, Dean C. "Consistency of Emergent Leadership in Groups with Changing Tasks and Members," *Speech Monographs,* **29** (1962), 45–52.
Bass, Bernard M. "Some Aspects of Attempted, Successful, and Effective Leadership," *Journal of Applied Psychology,* **45** (1961), 120–122.
Clifford, Clare, and Thomas S. Cohn. "The Relationship Between Leadership and Personality Attributes Perceived by Followers," *Journal of Social Psychology,* **64** (1964), 57–64.
Dubno, Peter. "Leadership, Group Effectiveness and Speed of Decision," *Journal of Social Psychology,* **65** (1965), 351–360.
Kipnis, David, and William P. Lane. "Self-Confidence and Leadership," *Journal of Applied Psychology,* **46** (1962), 291–295.
Lippitt, Ronald, and Ralph K. White. "Leader Behavior and Member Reaction in Three Social Climates." In Dorwin Cartwright and Alvin Zander, eds. *Group Dynamics: Research and Theory,* 3rd ed. New York: Harper & Row, 1968, pp. 318–335.
McClintock, Charles G. "Group Support and the Behavior of Leaders and Non-Leaders," *Journal of Abnormal and Social Psychology,* **67** (1963), 105–113.

CHAPTER 12
DYNAMICS
OF THE TASK
DIMENSION

the assumption of rationality

The traditional approach to the study of group problem solving is to assume the desirability of a step-by-step "rational" search procedure. Theorists have developed prescriptive models that describe the thought processes and behaviors participants should use to solve a problem. These models are recommended not only as checklists to aid in search procedures but as process models to be followed to improve decision making. Underlying the typical approach is the assumption that the emotional and nonrational features of group deliberations are undesirable. The assumption of rationality often implies that when the social dimension disrupts the orderly tracing of the steps of a problem-solving model, it is unfortunate. Indeed, some writing in public discussion has ignored the relationship between the social and task dimensions by stressing an orderly search procedure and advising that a proper attitude toward reflective thinking would eliminate nonrational social interactions from task deliberations. Even scholars in social psychology, who were well versed in the social and emotional complexities of group interactions, sometimes wrote of the task dimension as though it ought to follow some rational systematic model.

THE PATTERN OF DISCUSSION

The most popular pattern for problem-solving discussion is based on Dewey's analysis of reflective thinking (discussed previously). McBurney and Hance developed a popular variation specifically adapted to the problem-solving discussion; it included five steps: (1) definition of terms and delimitation of problems, (2) analysis of the problem, (3) suggestions of solutions, (4) reasoned development of advantages and disadvantages of solutions, and (5) further verification. The Dewey model for problem solving has several minor variations, but its salient features remain the same. It has enjoyed considerable popularity not only in material on speech and communication, but in such diverse publications as March and Simon, *Organizations,* and Bany and Johnson, *Classroom Group Behavior.* When Bales and Strodtbeck discovered three phases in group problem solving, they called them the orientation, evaluation, and control phases. The three-phase model retains the core of the Dewey model. It includes discovering and evaluating a problem and searching for a solution to control the situation.

Adaptations of the basic model. Computer technology has inspired a number of theorists to construct elaborate and detailed expansions of the basic Dewey model. Two examples will serve to indicate the tendencies to expand the Dewey pattern.

Kepner and Tregoe developed a decision-making procedure that is widely used in business and industrial training programs. They define a problem as a deviation from a standard and identify the nature and extent of the problem by an elaborate set of step-by-step comparisons. They first compare the "should" to "the actual"—that is, the ideal situation to actual conditions. Next, they compare the "is" with the "is not" to find out what factors are clearly part of the problem. The boundaries of the problem are located by repeated applications of the "is" and "is not" to minute features of the environment to discover if a factor "is" part of the problem. The smaller steps are indicated by the questions: What is the deviation? Where is the deviation? When is the deviation? And. what is the extent of the deviation? Kepner and Tregoe advise the person faced with a problem to use the same technique to determine causes, establish objectives, generate alternative actions, and examine the adverse effects of each suggested solution. According to them, such analysis should result in a rational decision.

Even more closely modeled on computer experience is the Program Evaluation and Review Technique. People using PERT, as it is commonly called, have arrived at a major policy decision that sets a goal. They use PERT to aid in solving the technical and practical problems involved in mobilizing resources to reach that goal. The PERT model provides a step-by-step checklist of procedures to establish priorities, estimate time, and allocate men and material. Step 1 is to specify the final event or goal. Steps 2 and 3 are to determine the events that must precede the final outcome, and order them. What events must take place to assure the final outcome, and what is their most sensible order? Step 4 is to determine the activity time for each event. Step

5 is to break up important links between the major sequence of events into sub-PERT events. Thus, the model proceeds in computer-programming fashion to analyze the administration of a project into ever smaller activities and time segments. Step 6 is to allocate priorities to the activities, and step 7 is to determine the personnel, finances, and facilities to be dedicated to the various parts. Following the example of the computer programmer, the Kepner–Tregoe and PERT models break each aspect of the process into smaller and smaller steps to guarantee a very detailed search for the limits and nature of a problem and its causes.

Decision-making models that stress orderly and rational processes as the ideal for problem solving in task-oriented groups have their purposes. Chapters 4, 5, and 6 contain the elements of such a model. However, the assumption of rationality underlying their development often handicaps understanding of the actual problem solving and decision making that occurs in groups. The proponents of such models argue that the task-oriented groups should follow an agenda structured around the phases or steps in the ideal model. They regard deviations from such systematic agendas as essentially handicaps to group efficiency and success. For example, if a task-oriented group begins a consideration of solutions before discussing the problem, their task abilities would be criticized by proponents of the rational assumption. If the group did arrive at a sound decision, it would be attributed to luck or chance.

The student who makes a radical assumption of rationality will often find his work in groups frustrating. Pollsters surveying attitudes toward the business meeting regularly find that managers think there are too many meetings and that too much time is wasted in them. The impression that conferences waste time and accomplish very little is universal in our corporate society. Some of these impressions stem from the participant's expectation that groups will proceed *rationally* as prescribed by the step-by-step models such as the Dewey pattern. *Except under unusual circumstances, groups do not do so.* People trained to evaluate groups with the expectation that groups proceed through a series of ordered, programmed comparisons find themselves frustrated and disappointed when they meet with *people* who ramble, discuss irrelevancies, get into arguments, withdraw from participation, and take flight from touchy personal questions relating to the decision.

The context of justification and the context of discovery. Not all groups can apply rational procedures without incurring dissatisfaction and frustration, but at the proper point in a meeting, rationality can be expected or demanded. Difficulties arise when participants demand rationality from a group throughout its deliberations. Individuals rarely solve problems in a systematic way, and groups are typically much more immature and emotional than individuals. The use of rationality is largely related to the *context of justification,* rather than to the *context of discovery.*

The context of justification is the verification stage of a group's deliberations when the participants systematize and organize their reasons and evidence to support a solution. In terms of the discussion of the creative process presented in Chapter 6, it is the final or verification stage of a problem-solving cycle. Justification tests the wisdom of any decision. It is a critical process and requires criteria to aid evaluation, orderly presentation of results, and clear support. Justification occurs after the solution emerges much as literary criticism occurs after the writing of a poem. In a sense, both take place outside the problem-solving activity. A writer views the *process* of writing differently than the final product. The critic evaluates the work systematically. He may establish categories like plot, characterization, dialogue, theme, and mood to aid him. In the same way, the critic of the outcome of group problem solving might establish categories like analysis of the problem, examination of representative solutions, and so forth.

The context of discovery, on the other hand, relates to the actual problem-solving process as viewed by the participant. The persons trying to work together to solve a common problem are analogous to a writer at work on a novel. The writer works in an emotional, haphazard, and intuitive way. The critical machinery useful in justification is not very helpful to a writer composing a novel. The apprentice writer gains little insight from advice based on such critical categories as plot, characterization, and theme. Frequently a critic finds much more in a novel than the writer intended. One expects such divergencies of evaluation and intent, once justification is distinguished from discovery. The analogy applies to decision making in groups. The nonparticipant observer will often find more in a group meeting than participants perceive at the time. When the participants study the meeting later, as critics, they also find much more. The rational agenda—such as Dewey's reflective thinking, the Kepner–Tregoe procedure, or PERT—is essentially a model for justification, and when applied to the practical problems faced by participants dealing with the external environment, it is no more useful to the discovery of courses of action than the critic's categories are to a novelist. Indeed, people facing relevant problems, not doing classroom exercises, do not follow agendas patterned after the rational thinking models. Once a decision is made, however, the participants may test their solution systematically. When people understand that there is a time to evaluate group process from the context of discovery and another time to evaluate the product from the context of justification, they will be more able to tolerate the groping, withdrawal, quibbling, and haphazard deliberations that occur early in problem-solving deliberations.

Another approach to the decision-making process assumes that problem solving does not follow a rational model, but rather reflects and affects the social and emotional tone and climate of the meeting. Zaleznik and Moment, for example, emphasize the relationship between emotional effect and work. Starting from essentially Freudian psychoanalytic assumptions, they discuss the work meeting as analogous to a psychotherapy session and describe the participants' tendency to vacillate between hostility and affection, aggression and passivity, fight and flight. These swings of mood and reaction relate to such problems as handling external and internal authority. The group may swing from extreme independence to overdependence on an external authority, or from fighting authority to fleeing from it. Zaleznik and Moment regard work as just one of a number of group modalities, the majority of which are emotional. They suggest that each group must develop its own work norms and discover for itself how it can best solve problems.

Bales also establishes an explanatory framework that accounts for both the social–emotional responses and the task dimension of group process. He suggests an equilibrium model in which the group strives to establish an equilibrium of tensions. When social tensions rise to uncomfortable levels, the group attends to them until it reaches a comfortable state of equilibrium, when it turns again to the task. In this way, the group swings from work to establishing social equilibrium and back to work. In a study of 16 experimental groups, Bales discovered that over one-third of the responses were social–emotional in nature. The proponents of a purely rational model of decision making might consider such a high proportion of social activity a waste of time. Those who assume that cohesiveness and social interactions are just as important as productivity might view these social interactions as evidence of group health.

Zaleznik and Moment use a somewhat different explanatory framework to present essentially the same description. They discuss "levels of work." The first level is characterized by personal needs of the individuals. Each participant talks about his personal experience as it relates to the problem at hand. Members react to one another personally, and, when they do offer new information, it is largely unevaluated. Except for providing individuals with information about the personal needs of the members, little constructive work on the problem results.

The second level begins when participants question information. They begin to ask for reasons to support suggestions. At this level, they are satisfied with conventional answers. They rely on common knowledge and common sense. The testing and analysis are still ego-involved and do not help them to relate to the external environment. The contributions serve mainly to justify the views of each individual.

The third level finds participants raising basic questions. They consider a point for a longer period of time. Participants learn about each other's real position on the important questions and the possible alternatives open to the group.

The fourth level finds participants becoming members of a group. Feedback is increased; people relax and do not hide things from each other. Members say what they think, and misunderstandings are clarified. They stimulate one another to generate new ideas, and these ideas are tested openly and bluntly. The first three stages are preparation for this final level of work. In the first level, individuals get to know one another and confine themselves to safe, conventional behavior. In the second level, ideas are suggested, with the covert understanding that no one will get hurt. In the third stage, members start to disagree. They are getting ready to begin the real work.

For a number of years, Tavistock Psychiatric Institute in London has been conducting human-relations-training workshops based on the work of Bion as expanded and applied by Rice. The analysis of the dynamics of a work group that emerged from the Tavistock group is analogous to those described by Zaleznik and Moment. According to Bion, groups face socioemotional and work problems. The tendency for newly formed groups is to go through stages of immaturity and neurotic behavior before achieving the level of work. Bion outlined three basic neurotic conditions for groups: (1) dependency, (2) pairing, and (3) fight or flight. Bion refers to the neurotic conditions as basic-assumption groups. When the group is making the basic assumption of dependency, it is neurotically preoccupied with power and comes to depend on a strong leader or a strong force external to it. The group expects its strong leader to serve a savior function. When the basic assumption is pairing, the members tend to form coalitions based on compatible needs. The third assumption group is one of flight or fight in which the group tries to preserve itself by avoiding or attacking things it finds threatening. The emphasis is, however, on group survival. Finally, groups that mature move from the basic assumptions to work groups able to focus their energies on a common task.

Zaleznik and Moment as well as Bion and Rice are describing in somewhat more psychoanalytic terms the same dynamics that emerged in the Minnesota Studies. The period of tension in which people are quiet and polite is what Zaleznik and Moment call the first level of work. The period in which participants test one another and find a role structure is equivalent to the second level. The stabilizing of a role structure and the development of a common group culture is the third level. The final level describes the work of successful, highly cohesive groups with stable role structures such as has been evident in the cases included in the Minnesota Studies.

The basic assumptions outlined by Bion and Rice also appeared at Minnesota. The second pattern of leadership emergence in which two leader contenders each gain a lieutenant and thus continue the struggle is much the same as the pairing-assumption group described by Bion. Occasionally a strong, assertive person seemed to be running the groups in the Minnesota Studies because no one challenged him immediately, although the members were very dissatisfied with his leadership. The group always challenged the strong assertive person and rejected his leadership sooner or later, but during the portion of the group's history when that individual seemed to be in charge, the group would behave as though they were making the dependency assumption. Of course, many observers in addition to Bion have reported the tendency of small groups to take flight or to vent aggression. The fight-or-flight behavior has also been a prominent feature in the Minnesota Studies, as has the analysis of role emergence and stability which parallels the basic-assumption groups described by Bion. When several research groups, working quite independently, arrive at descriptive conclusions that parallel and support one another, the assumptions gain credence, and, when the results appear in two somewhat separate cultures as well, the empirical support for the analysis is strengthened.

The following description of the dynamics of the group's task dimension is drawn from the case studies conducted at Minnesota, but it is supported by the analysis of Zaleznik and Moment and by the experience of the Tavistock workshops.

the problem-solving agenda and the task dimension

Empirical evidence indicates that groups do not follow a linear path through the recommended steps of a problem-solving model. For example, Scheidel and Crowell developed a set of categories to study the development of ideas in discussion groups. They discovered that discussions do not follow a linear path through the testing of ideas, but rather that ideas are introduced spontaneously. Someone may extend an idea by changing the emphasis or suggesting a modification. Someone else may simply affirm or reject the idea. Scheidel and Crowell characterize the process as an "idea-in-the-making" in which the original idea is changed through oral modification until it represents the discussants' cumulative, developing, mutual point of view. They discovered that discussions drawn from a course on the principles of group discussion devoted only 22 percent of their thought units to the initiation, extension, modification, and synthesis of ideas. About one-fourth of the group effort was used to clarify and substantiate ideas already displayed before the group. These workers decided that group thought moves forward in a reach–test cycle rather than in a straight line; that is, one discussant reaches forward with a new idea which is then tested by elaboration and acceptance or rejection. When this thought is "anchored" in group acceptance, a procedure that occupied almost half of the time of the discussions, a participant will reach forward with another idea, and the cycle will be repeated. Scheidel and Crowell suggest that the typical linear development of group problem solving should be replaced with a spiraling model.

Taylor and Faust justify their use of the game of Twenty Questions in a study of the relationship between problem-solving efficiency and group size on the basis that the game is a realistic approximation of everyday problem solving. In this game, players are told that they must find an object by asking a series of yes–no questions. Taylor and Faust maintain that solutions to everyday problems are seldom reached by a linear pattern of rigorous, well-defined steps, but that individuals often begin with a vague problem about which they ask a series of vague questions. When these questions are answered, they have a clearer impression of the problem and can ask a series of sharper questions. The same authors discovered that groups of people were more efficient than individuals at playing the game of Twenty Questions. They suggested that this occurs because a group has more relevant information and is more flexible than an individual in its approach to a solution. Individuals who played the game were sometimes unable to stop an unproductive line of questioning.

GROUP ATTENTION SPAN

One striking feature of groups is their relatively short attention span. Berg studied over 100 discussions by student, faculty, religious, political, and professional groups. He made a content analysis of the themes introduced and measured with a stop watch the length of time a particular theme was discussed without interruption. In all, he coded 5079 themes and discovered that the mean time per theme (group attention span) was 58 seconds. The range, on a group basis, was from 28 to 118 seconds; the small amount of variance is indicated by a standard deviation of 18 seconds. He further coded the themes into categories and discovered that substantive themes were attended to on the average for 76 seconds and that procedural topics were attended to for 47 seconds. The groups' attention span for topics irrelevant to the task was 29 seconds. The most interesting feature of these data was their uniformity. When groups composed of three to five members were compared with groups of five to eight, and when class discussions used as training exercises were compared with groups dealing with "real" problems, the attention span remained very stable.

Larson refined Berg's category system and gathered further normative data that essentially supported Berg's findings. Faffler used Berg's categories in a cross-cultural study of American and Middle Eastern students in Beirut and found similar results, as did Ryberg in a study of bilingual North and South Americans discussing in both Spanish and English.

GROUP RISK TAKING

A number of investigators of small-group process have been preoccupied with the discovery by Stoner that groups tend to make riskier decisions than individuals. Stoner's notion, which came to be called the "risky shift," was intriguing because one widely held stereotype of groups prior to that time was that they were essentially average or even conservative in their decisions. A number of subsequent studies investigated the risky shift usually by giving subjects descriptions of hypothetical situations and asking them how sure they would have to be of success before they would risk a course of action. The subjects first responded to the questionnaire individually and then took part in a group discussion until there was consensus on the same list of hypothetical situations. Investigators using the technique of hypothetical situations replicated the results of the original research so that the phenomenon was, for a time, generally accepted as having been demonstrated, at least for the hypothetical situations.

Subsequent research was directed to discovering the process that accounts for the increased risk taking by groups. Among the hypotheses put forward was the notion that risk taking is a cultural value and that most North Americans see themselves as above average risk takers, and, when they discover in a discussion that they are average or below average, they shift to a riskier decision. Another hypothesis was that risky individuals are more influential in groups than cautious ones. A final hypothesis was that a group decision diffuses responsibility and thus makes it easier to take a risky position with the support of like-minded group members.

Several studies have reported historical examples of groups making risky decisions. Chapter 3 described Janis' work on important foreign-policy decisions in the United States in the 1950s and 1960s such as the Bay of Pigs invasion and the escalation of the Vietnam war. Raack applied behavioral theory to historical materials relating to the anti-French conspiracy in Prussia in 1808 and discovered that forces within the small radical groups heightened the influence of the risk takers and stifled that of the moderates. In addition, he judged that the plot developed a momentum of its own which seemed to force the leaders to act more precipitously than they wished and to take action counter to their original plans.

Clearly, groups often make riskier decisions than the individuals composing the groups might make singly; however, recent research into the risky-shift phenomenon demonstrates that groups vary as to conservatism or risk taking depending on their norms and culture. Studies by Dion, Miller, and Magnan, and Kroger and Briedis, for example, demonstrated cautious decisions by groups in which cautious norms were experimentally induced. Although groups may develop either a cautious or risk-taking culture, the research into the risky-shift phenomenon demonstrates that the stereotype of groups as more mediocre, average, or cautious than individuals in decision making is not adequate. Rather, the group culture, the motivations generated by the group's chaining fantasies, and the group's norms provide a better account for risky or cautious decisions than the hypothesis that groups invariably make either cautious or risky decisions.

APPROACH–WITHDRAWAL BEHAVIOR

Another feature of group discussion is the participants' tendency to explore a topic until they discover that it is related to a role struggle or has other status implications. They deal with the topic until the secondary tension becomes uncomfortable and then typically withdraw. They approach the problem by getting a quick and superficial survey of the ground. They find the areas of easy agreement and the points of difficulty. When they feel that the rise of tension is a threat to cohesiveness, they withdraw and introduce a different theme. They must, of course, return to the difficult questions in order to succeed. After a time, they try another probe of the difficult area. If it seems less difficult than they first suspected, they may make a decision. The really crucial and divisive themes are withdrawn from and approached several more times until the external pressures and deadlines force them to a decision.

A BASIC MODEL OF GROUP DECISION MAKING

Work by Fisher in the small-group seminar at Minnesota suggests a hypothesis that explains much of the data relating to group decision making. When the Dewey model or some variant of it is used, it is assumed that a group uses one process in establishing roles and norms (the model developed in Chapter 9) and another (Dewey's reflective-thinking model) in solving problems related to the task. The research results outlined above can better be explained by a simpler hypothesis:

Decisions emerge from group interactions in the same way that roles emerge and normative behavior develops.

Bales' equilibrium model reflects this tendency in decision making. His discovery of a swing from task to social responses supports the basic model. The Zaleznik and Moment suggestion that groups probe deeper and deeper into the entire problem as they proceed through levels of work also is accounted for by the hypothesis that decisions emerge as do roles and norms.

The basic model of decision emergence in the small task-oriented group is as follows. Participants attack a problem in a cyclical fashion rather than in a linear way. They approach the entire problem several times. Someone submits an idea. Others contribute statements of fact, advice, and opinion. A number of ideas are displayed. Some information is rejected quickly and easily, just as some leader contenders are eliminated in the first phase of role emergence. The members accept some ideas just as quickly because of their source or because all find them clearly meritorious. As people discuss the idea, they sharpen their questions and discover areas of disagreement. Some significant ideas are not acceptable to all. Discussants do not follow a rational step-by-step model at this point because they cannot do so. They must find the areas of consensus and of difference, the touchy points and the safe ones. The participants approach the problem in its entirety at a rather superficial level, then return to the problem again and dig into a deeper analysis, swing away and return again to probe deeper.

Early in their deliberations, participants may display a number of solutions and discover that several are clearly unsuitable, but one has strong support from several members. Participants may drop consideration of the solution at that point to discuss the problem. The proponent of the solution may introduce his plan again and relate it to the discussion. Others may now disagree with the solution, and tensions will grow. At this point, an irrelevant tension-releasing theme is introduced. After a time spent in releasing tension, someone may ask what they are trying to do. The members respond by considering goals, which enables the proponent of the solution to suggest its usefulness again. If the solution is again rejected, another participant may be encouraged to display a solution. The group swings from problem to solution to goals to problem to goals to solution to solution, with tension release and group solidarity comments inserted at points throughout their deliberations.

At some point during this process, the group will discover that a decision has emerged, a decision to which they are committed and which they are willing to implement. Often the decision is reached without a vote or a formal show of consensus. On occasion, the discussion does not result in the clear emergence of a decision; and the participants may then vote and settle the question on the basis of majority rule.

Such a situation is analogous to the problem faced by a group that is unable to structure its roles and perceive that a leader has clearly emerged. Problem solving is similar to peeling an onion, layer by layer. The group removes the superficial layers of the problem until the participants become uncomfortable. They withdraw for a time and then return to it. This process occurs many times until they are forced to return to the task by the pressure of the problem, and they must reach the core and make a decision.

Task decisions that emerge by accident. Just as some norms develop as a result of chance happenings during the course of a discussion, so some decisions emerge accidentally. Early in one group's first meeting, for example, a participant asked if they should elect a chairman. As might be expected, posing a status issue so early flustered the others. Finally another discussant broke the tense silence by asking if they should vote by a secret ballot or by a show of hands. Still flustered, several others suggested that a show of hands would be better than a secret ballot. Member A then turned to member B and said that in his estimation, B was the best person to be chairman. Member B protested modestly that someone else would be better. When the others urged him to be chairman, however, he capitulated and said that he would do his best. The decision to elect a chairman was made by accident. The group withdrew from the issue through a question on procedure that *assumed they would elect a chairman.* No one questioned this assumption.

Task decisions that emerge because of role struggles. In the second phase of the leadership contention, a substantive decision may be a by-product of role struggles. For example, in one discussion, a leader emerged, but his style of leadership proved unsatisfactory. The showdown came during the course of a work meeting devoted to writing a committee report. The leader arrived for the meeting with the preamble to the resolution already drafted. He had an agenda to guide the group's deliberations on the substantive sections of the report, but he felt he would facilitate matters by writing the introduction. After explaining this to the others, he began to read the preamble. He started with considerable enthusiasm. Perhaps he expected the group to reward him for his extra time and effort in preparing for the meeting. He received no compliments; instead, he was interrupted by a participant who asked that a certain phrase be read again. The leader was puzzled, but he read the phrase again. The other participant then challenged the wording of that section. The leader tried to brush off the challenge by reminding the committee that the introductory material was relatively unimportant and that they should begin work on the substance of the report. The

challenger repeated his demand that the phrase be reworded and suggested new language to be substituted. The leader was now aroused
to defend his language. For some minutes the leader and the challenger
quibbled about the wording of the innocuous phrase. Finally the challenger received support from a lieutenant; and, after a few more minutes,
the remaining members supported the changed wording. The leader
held out a little longer and then capitulated. The phrase was changed;
and, from that point, the challenger assumed the role of leader. The
group had deposed an unsatisfactory leader and selected a new one
without formal election. An observer with a rational bias would criticize
the session because most of it was devoted to an argument over an
essentially trivial point. Yet the group made an important decision in
regard to its social structure. As a by-product of that social structuring,
they also made a task decision about the wording of their report.

Another committee drafted a proposal heavily influenced by fantasy
chains relating to the social–emotional problems the discussants faced.
In the first meeting, one individual complained about being placed in
an all-female group. She felt such a committee could not make an intelligent study and report. Immediately, she became a negative central person. The others found themselves working to integrate her into the group.
Subsequently, she missed several meetings. When she returned, the group
was in the middle of a study of the problem posed by police brutality.
She expressed her opinion in strong terms and argued that local police
forces were hampered by unrealistic restrictions on their ability to question suspects and obtain confessions. After some discussion, the others
perceived that she would not change her position. The group withdrew
from a decision until the deadline for their report forced them to act.
They approached the topic again, and, when secondary tension rose,
they went into a period of prolonged group fantasizing. Using the Supreme Court—whose decisions, they said, made the job of the police
untenable—as a scapegoat, they argued that nothing could be done
about the Court. Obviously, their analysis had taken them to a dead
end. They responded with loud satirical attacks on the Court. The leader
dramatized, "Let's all march on Washington!" Another participant suggested a mayors' conference to which the committee would "present
a huge, long document." They were now laughing and speaking loudly.
"Citizens to overthrow the Supreme Court!" the leader fantasized. After
a moment, they began to consider somewhat seriously the possibility
of public opinion's changing the Court's decisions. "What can one mayor
do about it? That's the problem!" "So what can four college kids do
about it?" Clearly, they were in an untenable position. The leader started
to laugh again and said, "We'll have everyone meet. And we'll deputize
everybody!"

After a prolonged period of near-hysterical fantasy chains which had the theme of attacks on the Court, they proceeded to write a report. It was a one-sided analysis in which they suggested that police brutality was nonexistent and that policemen were unable to function effectively because of the Supreme Court decision that allows suspects to have legal counsel and does not allow confessions obtained without counsel to be admitted as evidence. Their report concluded that the main problem was the philosophy of the Court, which they admitted could not be changed. They then suggested that better training for police officers, more money, and more personnel would enable the police to do a better job despite the restrictions imposed by the Court. Their final decision was made partly in response to the information about the group's external environment and partly as a response to the needs of the group's internal social structure. The shape of their decision was heavily influenced by fantasies which stemmed from the problems posed by the negative central person.

Task decisions based on authority. The highest level of efficient work takes place in organizations with stable role structures. One feature of such work is the tendency for task decisions to be made on the basis of role expectations. Participants make many procedural decisions largely on the basis of the source of the recommendation. Thus, minor decisions concerning the structuring of the work are quickly made because the leader suggests them. A group may follow any one of five or six different agendas, for example, and achieve their task goals with equal efficiency. During the process of achieving a role structure, people discuss these procedural plans at great length because they furnish the battleground for the leadership struggle. After a leader emerges, he will make frequent procedural suggestions, and many will be accepted because he makes them.

Other kinds of decisions are made on the basis of authority. If an influential person suggests or agrees with information about the external reality or a suitable solution, the others often accept the information or solution. Chapter 4 outlined, in general terms, the mechanism by which authoritative advice based on specialization is accepted by the nonspecialist. The same mechanism operates within the organization with stable role structures.

Task decisions based on factual analysis. A good group, in which members work efficiently as a team, will make significant decisions on the basis of a thorough and accurate examination of the facts and will make plans with a clear perception of the problems posed by the external environment. At those moments when a good group reaches the highest level of work, it is an exciting thing to watch. It is just as exciting when one is participating. Ken Kesey, in his novel *Sometimes a Great*

Notion, is describing three men cutting timber, but he captures the spirit common to all task-oriented small groups when they are functioning at peak efficiency.

> *Until the three of them meshed, dovetailed . . . into one of the rare and beautiful units of effort sometimes seen when a jazz group is making it completely, swinging together completely, or when a home town basketball squad, already playing over its head, begins to rally to overtake a superior opponent in a game's last minute . . . and the home boys can't miss; because everything—the passing, the dribbling, the plays— every tiny piece is clicking perfectly. When this happens everyone watching knows . . . that, be it five guys playing basketball, or four blowing jazz, or three cutting timber, that this bunch—right now, right this moment—is the best of its kind in the world! But to become this kind of perfect group a team must use all its components, and use them in the slots best suited, and use them all with the pitiless dedication to victory that drives them up to their absolute peak, and past it.[1]*

Of course, even highly cohesive groups working efficiently achieve such moments only rarely, but they do achieve them, and they are among the most gratifying experiences of people who work with and participate in groups. Some groups in the Minnesota Studies made detailed analyses of their own dynamics. One of the more successful case studies contained the following description of the group's work norms:

> *Cooperatively we arrived at an illustration or hypothesis of how the group frequently works when we all meet. It is obviously a great oversimplification, but we still feel that it has some validity and also somewhat clarified the role structure; Stig throws out an idea for consideration. Pam—"the first filter"—picks up the idea, feels out the consensus of the group and attempts to establish the attitude. If it is positive, Jim as "the second filter" in his turn picks it up, twists it about, jokes about it, and ends up by reinforcing or rejecting it. Barb then questions the idea, adds some comments of her own, and occasionally seriously criticizes it—if so, it will normally be dropped right away. Finally Mark, who has remained silent up to this point, usually summarizes, crystallizes and explains the revamped idea by adding another dimension to it; he then throws it back to Stig for final approval.*

Clearly a group that processes ideas in a relatively orderly and specialized fashion requires a stable role structure. The members of this group perceived the role structure in this way: Stig was the leader;

[1] Ken Kesey. *Sometimes a Great Notion.* New York: Bantam, 1965, p. 476.

Jim was the tension releaser; Pam gathered information, questioned ideas, and initiated certain kinds of action; Mark was summarizer, a clarifier of ideas, a philosopher; Barb was a questioner of ideas and "a (not too frequent, and consequently all the more powerful!) critic."

Of course, the group did not process all ideas in the same way. When they dealt with an important decision on which there was disagreement, they did not run it through an assembly line as the above description might suggest. They, too, followed the general model of a cyclical or spiral path through the superficial layers to the basic issues of a problem. Yet various people did specialize in task functions, and a particular individual did influence the group in certain ways. They were using their components in the "slots best suited." They had achieved a level of cohesiveness such that each member felt free to respond to an idea with an honest opinion. Stig was the leader, but his ideas were criticized as thoroughly as everyone else's. When the group rejected Stig's ideas, he did not lose status or esteem. The same stability protected people playing the other roles. Stig was realistic and generally made a sound analysis of the requirements of the task. Pam was more sensitive to the internal stresses a course of action might evoke. She was alert to the meshing of the work modality with the social affects within the group. In Barb, the group had an intercollegiate debater thoroughly trained in argumentation, who was able to do a superior job of testing evidence and reasoning. Mark was a capable philosopher who saw the ramifications of a course of action as they related to both immediate and long-range goals.

With stable roles and healthy work norms, the group dealt with the demands placed on it by the external environment in superior fashion. They did not go through the steps of the Dewey pattern, but they did work out their own normative pattern. The group's task norms were tailored to the skills of its personnel, and they enabled the group to make sound decisions.

Although the case studies do not reveal groups going through the Dewey pattern of reflective thinking, work by Ferguson in the small-group-communication seminar suggests that small groups sometimes deal with problems creatively in a way that is analogous to the creative process in an individual.

Chapter 6 outlined the creative process in individuals as consisting of a preparation phase, an incubation phase, an illumination phase, and a verification phase. After a period of studying the problem, a creative individual is often stumped and will lay the problem aside. While the person's conscious attention is directed elsewhere, he will sometimes find his mind wandering in a daydreaming sort of way. The problem is incubating. At some point during such daydreaming, a moment of illumination may strike when the person suddenly sees the direct application of the daydreaming to his problem. Such moments are highly emotional and an exciting part of creative work. After the moment of illumination, the individual tries the solution and tests it for workability and desirability.

Ferguson was making a case study of the fantasy themes in a group of teenagers working on a "tot lot," which was to be a playground for small children. The teenagers were to help plan details of the playground and would work as volunteer supervisors when it was set up. She felt that some of the fantasies of the group were very analogous to the period of incubation in individual problem solving. For example, at one point the group was considering the problem of rules for the children, and they broke off their direct analysis of the problem to fantasize about how teenagers did not obey their parents.

Thus, a group might begin a problem by direct discussion of the information relating to the difficulty as developed in Chapters 4 to 6. After failing to find a suitable answer, the tensions might stimulate a fantasy chain that seems ostensibly unrelated to the work at hand but that contains a double meaning applicable to the problem. Suddenly the group experiences a moment of illumination and sees a good solution to their here-and-now problem, and with great excitement the members discover that a decision has emerged.

In such a way, some fantasy chains may contribute to solutions in a productive way because they stem from problems relating to the group's task dimension even though other fantasies may contribute to solutions that are not very good because they stem from internal conflicts in the social dimension.

Some other practitioners of group methods have stumbled onto the importance of fantasizing to creative problem solving. For example, Prince suggests that, when a group bogs down, the members take a fantasy vacation and agree to think and talk of something completely removed from the problem.

improving the task dimension of group interaction

ASSURING THAT WORK NORMS ARE EFFICIENT

The student who wishes to improve the productivity of a small group should first observe and describe the way it goes about its work. What are the task roles? What are the work norms? Group norms are analogous to individual habits. Just as habits may be good or bad for an individual's physical health, so norms may be good or bad for the organization's productivity.

Bad habits are not easy to change, and neither are unproductive norms. Both habits and norms, however, can be evaluated and modified by conscious effort. One group discovered that they had developed a norm of withdrawing into socializing and tension release whenever they had a business meeting. They were, in many respects, congenial and cohesive as long as their interactions remained on a social level. However, they did not achieve a high level of work. The group was divided, two against three, on a basic question about the kind of information required to do a good job. Three members felt that secondary sources from popular magazines would furnish adequate information if supplemented by interesting personal experience. Two participants felt that, for a public discussion, more information from primary sources was required and that group members should do much more intense library research. To some extent, the alignment represented cliques that developed during the second phase of leadership contention. Member A and his lieutenant were clearly task oriented. Member B and his supporters were more interested in social cohesion. The clique led by B was composed of people who felt inadequate either because of lack of time or training to gather information from the library. When the group failed to get a good grade on their class discussion, they talked over the reasons for the poor performance. They discovered the norm of fleeing into socializing and discussed the best way to find information. They determined to change the norm for future assignments and largely succeeded.

Another common norm that develops out of the social structuring of a group, which often inhibits the quality of work, is the use of a sensible division of labor for gathering information as an excuse to withdraw from the tensions of group work. People often approach a new committee with the stereotype that the others will be lazy. The myth of minimal effort is widespread in our society. Douglas McGregor, in his book *The Human Side of Enterprise,* suggests that the traditional perspective for business management assumes that the average human being has an inherent dislike for work and will avoid it if he can and that he must be coerced, controlled, and threatened to put forth effort for the organization. McGregor argues that work is as natural as play or rest and that the average person will not only accept responsibility, but will seek it out under proper conditions. People who have the stereotype that human beings are lazy typically approach any suggestion that would require work from any or all committee members with great reluctance. They would prefer to have someone volunteer to work rather than face the decision of directing or appointing someone to do a job. Quite often an appointed or elected chairman will, in the early meetings of a task-oriented group, ask for volunteers. If no one steps forward, he will do the work himself rather than ask or order another person to do it. Task-oriented groups often establish experts to deal with the division of labor in a fair and just fashion. If it is an intellectual task such as studying a question of public policy, they may "divide the topic" so that each member will be responsible for one area. The following transcript is typical.

MEMBER A: Should we break it up into magazines? We should each be responsible for like—*Time, Newsweek, America, Nation*—rather than all going over the same . . .

MEMBER C: But you know you are still going to have a lot of overlapping if . . . and to prevent that, so that we won't take up quite so much time getting out extraneous material . . . maybe if we decided to take various separate things, either divide up according to country, or divide up according to areas, political, economic, . . .

MEMBER A: Yes . . .

MEMBER C: We cut down on this overlapping . . .

MEMBER A: Yeah. That's all right with him, isn't it? If we do it that way?

MEMBER D: He mentioned in class that if we do that more than one person is bringing in one kind of information and then no one else really knows.

> [*This comment refers to the instructor's warning, while explaining the assignment, that dividing the work into content areas was likely to result in a lack of thorough testing of information.*]

MEMBER A: Yeah. But if we break it up into areas I think . . . in order for the paper to be complete, we are going to have to . . . otherwise we are going to have this mish-mash of junk sitting there and we are going to have to painstakingly take each thing out and that would be awfully hard . . .

MEMBER C: Yes, I don't see how we really . . .

MEMBER A: Let's see, economic would be important . . . political, social . . . what does social include? Sort of conditions?

At this point, the group has decided that they will divide the topic according to sets of categories including political, social, and economic. Notice how this decision emerges. Member A makes the suggestion and is supported by C's immediate consideration of how the division might best be accomplished. Member D suggests that the instructor might not approve, but her disagreement is quickly drowned out by A and C. By the time A begins trying to find a suitable set of categories along the lines suggested by C, the group has decided to divide the work. The next thing they do is volunteer to take certain sections.

Committees that divide the work in this way develop specialists in content areas. In this instance, one participant became a specialist in economic conditions, and another a specialist in political affairs. When the group began its work, a norm was established in which economic problems were referred to the economic specialist and her word was never challenged by the other members. In return, when the political specialist offered ideas involving political affairs, her information was not challenged or tested by the others. They referred all questions to the appropriate authority and accepted the expert's information without question.

If each person in a small task-oriented group becomes a specialist in some content areas, information can be processed with a minimum of social tension. The others simply turn to the appropriate authority and accept his testimony. Disagreements about the truth of statements of fact are largely ruled out by this procedure. Participants can also avoid the questioning of advice in this fashion. The committee's productivity is thus dependent on the skill of its experts. The work may suffer because some of the experts are not competent. In addition, content specialists reduce group interaction, cohesiveness, and commitment.

In groups with such division of labor, a typical information-processing session proceeds as follows. The committee meets and the economic authority delivers a 15-minute lecture while the others take notes. Next the expert on political affairs reports, and so forth, until all have given their speeches. On the other hand, a group that has each person specializing in a task function, such as testing the truth or falsity of statements of fact, is not handicapped in the same way. If, in addition, the task roles emerged during the shakedown cruise and are performed by the most capable people, the job is done effectively.

Channels of communication. A considerable body of research literature reports the relationships among artificial channels of communication—restricting feedback and who can talk to whom—and task effectiveness and the social dimension. The research is usually referred to as studies of *communication networks.* The investigators used research designs that differed as to details, but usually the channels of communication were experimentally manipulated, and the effect of various channels was estimated by scaling or testing variables such as task efficiency and member satisfaction. Researchers controlled the flow and direction of messages by such devices as having subjects separated by partitions and then allowing them to communicate only by written messages, telephone connections, and so forth. For instance, an investigator might use three-person groups in which he allowed member A to talk to B, and B to C, and C to A, but he did not allow the subjects to talk freely to one another. In another experimental treatment, the researcher might allow all three subjects to speak to one another as much as they wished. In another, the design might include five-person groups arranged so one member was the center of the network in that the other four could talk to him, and he could talk to all of the others, but they could not talk with one another. Investigators used considerable ingenuity in working out variations of networks. In a survey of the research, Shaw noted that the literature contained as many as five variations for three-person groups, six for four-person groups, seven for five-person groups, and five for six-person groups.

The main finding of the research that is useful for the student of the small task-oriented group in the natural setting is that feedback (the ability to reach back and forth and to change messages in order to aid interpretation of their intent) increases task efficiency in the experimental groups. In addition, the unrestricted flow of communication tends to improve member satisfaction. Some research evidence suggests, however, that unrestricted communication *takes more time* under conditions of free, unlimited feedback than it does without feedback. In other words, to facilitate maximum understanding on the part of all, the meetings must take considerable time. Too frequently, the planners of a conference try to do too much in the time allotted. They often cut off feedback by nonverbal communications such as looking at the clock, talking rapidly, growing restless when questions are raised, and in other ways indicating that everyone is in a hurry and, if people will be quiet, the meeting will end on time.

The main lesson to be learned from the study of communication networks in the laboratory is that norms that restrict the flow of information tend to reduce the productivity of the group.

Often the communication flow that actually takes place in a discussion is restricted by the role structure and the norms. Observers who chart the flow of communication within a meeting discover that there is a wide variance in the amount of participation. Bales and his associates have compiled a large amount of normative data that demonstrate this variability. One study by Stephan and Mishler presented data that in 17 groups of six persons each, the leaders contributed, on the average, 43 percent of the communication; the next most active participant, about 24 percent; and the next, 15 percent; with the least active people contributing only 2 percent. Empirical investigations demonstrate that participation in discussion groups is seldom balanced. People are often unhappy with the lack of equal participation. They hold the stereotype that in good discussion everyone should participate equally and are disturbed if one person monopolizes the discussion or some people do not participate. Balanced participation is a virtue in a discussion *program* because of the common audience expectation that all experts should have equal time. It can be approximated by careful planning and rehearsal by following the suggestions in Chapter 13; but in task-oriented groups, unequal distribution is the inevitable concomitant of specialization and structure. Bales, for example, discovered that the leaders generally participated more than the best-liked person.

The communication within a group is not only distributed unevenly among the participants, but is often restricted in other ways by the norms that develop to form the communication network. One person may seldom receive any direct verbal communication from any other member. Two people may talk to one another more than they talk to anyone else or to the entire group. Norms of this sort usually develop during the early stages of role emergence or the periodic status struggles. Often they reflect the pattern of those struggles. The leader and his lieutenant may talk things over frequently. The leader and the loser in the status struggle may seldom speak directly to one another.

The status ladder influences the flow of messages. People tend to direct more talk upward on the status ladder. They talk more with peers than they do to those on a lower status level. The participants with the highest status tend to direct more communication to the whole group than to the individual members. As the size of the group increases, the communication tends to focus on one individual.

Investigators have accounted for patterns of who-talks-to-whom by member choices on a sociometric index. The sociometric index is a simple questionnaire in which the subject is asked to select other people on the basis of social attraction or rejection. Participants may be asked such questions as: Who would you most like to have serve on another committee with you? Who would you least like to have serve on another committee with you? Stemming from the pioneering work of Moreno, the sociometric technique has been used often to investigate and explain such phenomena as communication flowcharts.

Informal channels of communication are inevitable and may serve to increase task efficiency. Certain people will assume roles that require them to talk more than others. The job may demand that certain workers communicate more with one another than with other personnel. However, an organization may have norms governing the flow of communication that grew up during the status struggle. The resultant network may be inefficient for the present demands placed on the organization, and it may persist only because it is habitual. The participants can discuss, evaluate, and change norms in order to increase their group's productivity. In general, the communication network should be such that each person has access to the information he requires to do his job successfully. He should also have channels to social and esteem rewards so he will be committed to the successful completion of the work. The network needs to be diverse enough to assure a free flow of messages back and forth among the members. The level of cohesiveness must be high enough so that the listener furnishes the speaker with sufficient feedback to assure a high fidelity of communication.

Cohesiveness. The highly cohesive group provides a social climate that encourages feedback and thus assures efficient communication. Bales and his associates developed normative data comparing the ratio of questions to answers in a wide variety of discussions. Their content analysis of the communication revealed a *much higher proportion of answers than of questions.* Discussions are characterized by a large number of answers looking for questions. The Minnesota Studies corroborate these findings, particularly in the period of group structuring and role struggle. People do not ask many questions in the period of searching for a role and for status, because they do not wish to appear ignorant or stupid. They may, therefore, act as though they understand much more than they do and have considerably more knowledge than they have. People are very polite at this point, and they often do not ask questions for fear of insulting the person who is making the comment. Asking a question might imply that the speaker is not able to express himself clearly or even that his reasoning is not cogent or logical. Finally, participants often cannot ask a question because they have not listened to the previous comment. During the period of role testing, people are eager to demonstrate their talents. They wait for a cue from the discussion that makes them "think of something to say." They then plan how they will say it, and they watch impatiently for an opportunity to gain the floor. When they do get the floor, they say as much as they can as effectively as possible, and, when they must relinquish the floor, they try to think of another good comment. When one occurs to them, they look for another opportunity to get the floor. Often the person who has not done well in demonstrating skill by active participation will be disturbed enough to review the proceedings and "replay" the meeting, this time mentally providing the good comments he could have made. The "quiet listener" may be so busy mentally that he is not listening well at all. People generally feel that they should participate. If they do not, they fear that they have not made a good impression and are disturbed.

Since people do not listen well during the early discussion, they often say something unrelated to the topic discussed by the previous speaker. They say what they have on their mind when they get the chance to speak, even if the comment is no longer pertinent. They often say as much as they can even if they introduce several ideas within one speech. Berg's discovery that the group has a very short attention span is somewhat accounted for by these facts.

When a group achieves a stable role structure and a high level of cohesiveness, the need to "show off" is largely eliminated. A participant is secure in his position and does not worry about appearing ignorant when he asks a question. He is confident that another person will not take offense if he asks him for clarification or tests his information. Participants begin to listen and, when confused, will ask for clarification.

A person who is strongly attracted to a group and wishes the group well will want to maximize the communication efficiency. He knows that the group will do a better job if he is thoroughly briefed and if he clearly understands what he is to do. Therefore, if he does not know, he asks. The knowledgeable person will search for feedback and welcome it in the highly cohesive group. He may even ask for it. He is alert to nonverbal cues that others are confused or unsure about.

Displaying knowledge and demonstrating expertise are different from communicating knowledge or explaining technical matters. The person who is primarily interested in making a good impression may talk rapidly and introduce complicated concepts in technical jargon. By using language to confuse and obscure, he can impress people with his understanding and knowledge without becoming subject to embarrassing questions. Most professions have developed a tradition of protecting the expertise of their members from the questions of the layman by means of a complicated technical vocabulary. Medical doctors, for example, describe common ailments in technical terms. When one's nose is running, one may be told one has *allergic rhinitis; contact dermatitis* may simply mean that the doctor does not know what is causing a skin rash. Lawyers use Latin words and phrases for the same purpose. Small-group specialists may use terms like *syntality* and talk of *vectorial measurement of group synergy.* The layman is thus often reduced to relying on the expert's judgment. If the others are untrained in statistics, they may request the statistician to interpret the statistics. Technical terms can serve a useful function in naming clearly defined concepts. The expert may change his purpose from defending his status to explaining technical matters to his listeners. When he does so, he may still use the technical vocabulary; however, the change in attitude should result in a change in presentation. Generally, when trying to inform, the expert will introduce the technical concepts more slowly, define them carefully, and encourage questions and feedback.

The personnel in an organization will vary as to their skills in the art of communicating. Some may have difficulty listening carefully, others may have trouble expressing their ideas clearly, and others may be unable to hold a chain of inferences in mind to see if they relate in a consistent or inconsistent fashion. Achieving communication appropriate to the group's task under such circumstances often takes considerable time and tension-producing effort. Communication is hard work. The group should develop norms that encourage such effort at feedback and communication. It should establish the norm that sufficient time will be spent (not wasted) to assure the proper level of understanding.

the processing of information

The group relates to its external environment. Too often the group is provided with undigested and unevaluated information. If the internal data-processing structure is inefficient, the group may waste time with irrelevancies and falsehoods. It may also find itself unable to deal with the external environment and achieve its task goals. Participants should work to develop the presentational skills necessary to convey their knowledge to the group with efficiency. Presentations require preparation, analysis, and structure. The resource person should examine the data and discover the central issues. He should estimate the importance of the information and decide how much time the group should devote to processing the data. He should then prepare suitable messages to disseminate the information. As modern reproduction facilities are at the disposal of most important task-oriented groups, he should consider using both written and spoken messages. Too often, a student will come to a meeting with notes jotted in a notebook, which he reads or refers to while making a series of disjointed comments about his discoveries. The bulk of such information can be provided in a duplicated memorandum, brief, or outline distributed before the meeting. The participant can use his time in the session to clarify ambiguous points, and the others can devote their efforts to testing the soundness of the information.

The group processes information. A sound and healthy social dimension is necessary, but it does not guarantee that a group will process information in such a way that it will do a good job. The first skill that the participant must have is the ability to describe the facts in clear report language. He must have the basic expository skills required to draft specific topic sentences and to support these topic sentences with sufficient illustrations and materials to make them clear to the others. Presentational skills require that the resource person provide interpretations of statements of fact. He should provide background information and draw out the implications of the facts for his group. The student of group methods can apply the material in Chapter 4 as a guide in developing the requisite presentational skills.

The presentation of information requires dialectical skills as well as expository techniques. The knowledgeable member must cultivate the art of fitting the information into the flow of the group's deliberations. Good groups usually have at least one philosopher or big-picture person, who can relate the information to the project at hand. All participants should use transitions that relate their comments to a major theme under discussion. Periodic summaries and stock-taking comments help the participants to remember the theme. Summaries often become part of the role functions of one or two persons, but if each participant works to develop a sense of the overall pattern used by the group to process information, he can help eliminate those moments of aimless confusion when members stop and wonder where they are and what has happened.

The group must develop work norms that include careful testing of information. The art of asking questions is crucial to this process. If one member, as part of his role function, asks, How do you know? with monotonous regularity, the ability of the group to work effectively would be increased. The art of asking questions involves skill in thinking of and posing questions, as well as a certain attitude toward communication. One cannot ask good questions unless he listens carefully to the speaker.

Part II has described and explained in great detail the reasons for a participant's initial tendency to interpret the flow of verbal and non-verbal messages in these terms: What does this message imply for me as a person? Does it raise or lower my status? Does it show agreement or antagonism to me? Participants also tend at first to interpret messages in terms of the person who sends them: Is he leadership material? Is he ignorant? intelligent? quick tempered? humorous? Once the role structure is stable, the discussant can focus on ideas rather than status.

The presentation and testing of information assault the emotional health of the group. The knowledgeable person, even if he is primarily concerned with the job at hand and has little desire for status, will cause secondary tensions. He is immediately perceived as potentially a high-status person. The ambitious member who is not so well informed finds it difficult to compete with him. In his desire to participate, the ambitious individual may make some false statements. The knowledgeable member may prove with specific information that the statements are false and thereby anger the ambitious person. He may try to save face by belittling statistics or questioning the relevance of library research or scholarship to "real life." He may ignore or misunderstand the information. Thus, the informed member who has no motive other than to help the group may nonetheless find the others misunderstanding, rejecting, or resenting his contributions, simply because he gives his presentation with great eagerness and is not aware of the resentment he arouses.

Testing information by asking a speaker how he knows that something is true or false also causes secondary tensions. The speaker may view the question as a threat to his authority or integrity. If people have developed norms during the period of role struggle that cause them to resist the questioning of their information, the group should, after it reaches the level of real work, discuss these norms.

One of the most interesting factors controlling the communication within an organization is the status structure. As noted, status arrangements are closely related to the channels of communication and to the flow of messages through those networks. Status differences determine the quality of the messages as well as their quantity and direction. Frequently, status differences inhibit the free flow of information and restrict feedback. High-status people often do not know of the discontent and grievances of low-status people. They think the morale of the organization is higher than it is. Although they think their talk is clear and straightforward, the low-status listener searches for hidden meanings and interprets much that was not intended. Often, unpleasant information is not revealed to high-status levels until such a crisis occurs that it can no longer be withheld. A subordinate frequently tells his supervisor only the good news. He does not tell the boss upsetting things or information that makes him look bad.

Efficiency in group discussion may be increased if the members discover that they can say, "I do not know," without losing status. Units within an organization often work better if participants discover that their status is not jeopardized by having others test their information. The engineer who discovers that having his blueprints criticized by a machinist does not hurt his standing within the project or within the company will tolerate such testing, and the efficiency of the unit will increase.

The group tests solutions. Solutions need to be thoroughly questioned. Testing courses of action creates more tension than testing factual information. Examining a solution requires estimates of probable outcomes if the plan is adopted, and opinions as to right and wrong come under discussion. The group must not only predict outcomes, but must agree on goals. Often each course of action entails costs as well as rewards; the gaining of time may cost wasted effort and materials, or a short-term gain in efficiency may exact a toll in cohesiveness. The organization often must balance production goals against the morale of employees. A hierarchy of value statements will aid in the selection of solutions, but hierarchy is difficult to shape; there are often disagreements. Courses of action always raise questions of ethics. Discussants must not only ask if the plan will work, but also if the plan is right. Questions of ethics often generate secondary tensions.

The group mobilizes resources. When the unit mobilizes its resources, it assigns tasks to various people and sets a schedule of completion dates. It assigns resources such as equipment, money, and materials to the various workers responsible for particular parts of the plan. The division and integration of work require the giving of directions to others. Few features of a task place a greater strain on the group's social ties than the giving and taking of orders. People who control and divide the material resources and give directions and orders inevitably grow in importance. The workers who need the resources find themselves dependent on the one who controls them. The administrator who sets salaries and distributes new machines grows in importance. Participants are often sensitive to perceived injustices in the distribution of work loads and material resources. They resent someone who is not ordered to do his share. They are dissatisfied if they feel they do not have the equipment they deserve and need. Group resources must sometimes be distributed unequally in order to meet external pressures. Usually the leader is forced to make the unpopular decisions. Former President Harry Truman is often quoted as saying of the presidency, "The buck stops here." If members are forced as a unit to make a decision, they may withdraw from the problem by dividing the resources equally. If, for example, the decision of how to divide salary increases is forced on the members as a group, they may raise all wages an equal percentage, even though there are important reasons to give individual merit raises.

Directions are hard to take. They often imply that the person giving them is better than the persons receiving them. The worker may perceive nonverbal communications in his supervisor's orders that imply that the boss thinks he knows more and is better than the worker. Yet, if the group is to do its job, members must take and follow orders or directions. Good groups develop norms that encourage the facing of emotional effects directly. Ignoring, repressing, or avoiding the open expression of emotions is often damaging. Participants should respond directly and not dodge shows of either antagonism or liking. Often an honest, antagonistic response will clear the air just as a sincere acceptance of a show of affection will preclude embarrassment.

The group makes decisions. When the student of group methods understands the way decisions emerge, he can be alert to the ways in which the process goes astray. Frequently, a committee will act as though it has made a decision only to have the participants begin to question the action. They may find the solution untenable and ask to reconsider the decision. Hasty decisions usually occur because the group has pushed too hard. Often people need time to mull over the various solutions. Participants should develop a sense of timing and watch for the cues that indicate the group is ready to act. Also, they should guard against acquiescence that occurs without everyone knowing what the decision is or why it has been made.

Quite often, a consensus should be explicitly stated. Getting direct expression of support, neutrality, or nonacceptance will often avoid drifting decisions. Consensus may come quite naturally through nonverbal agreements such as vigorous nods of approval or verbal assertions of "right" or "I agree." Some members may ask for a vote. If the timing for the request is right, the direct show of support may aid the group in making a decision.

Bales discovered that many groups experienced the highest levels of disagreement just before moments of decision. When courses of action are decided on, secondary tensions often reach their high points. Decisions about solving group problems relating to the control of the external environment are often those that groups approach, withdraw from, and approach again and again before finalizing. They are the most damaging to the group's social dimension. If group members are not careful, they may select a solution that eases the internal social strain, but does not solve the real problems. In other words, the reality of the external environment will punish the group. Decisions should be made with a clear understanding of their implications: Are the internal tensions more important than the external environment? Is the present social reward sufficient to justify a loss in task efficiency? Obviously, these are difficult questions, and it is to be expected that decisions about dealing with the external conditions lead to the highest levels of disagreement and secondary tension.

summary

The traditional approach to the study of group thinking is to assume the desirability of a step-by-step rational search procedure. Such an approach is more suitable to the context of justification than it is to the context of discovery. Empirical research indicates that groups do not follow a linear path through the recommended steps of a problem-solving model, because problems of group maintenance continually intrude into such patterns. In addition, participants approach the problem several times in order to find areas of consensus and difference. Decisions emerge from group interaction in the same way that roles emerge and normative behavior develops.

Some decisions emerge by accident. Others are a by-product of status struggles. In groups with stable role structures, some decisions are made on the basis of esteem for the individual making the suggestion. Important decisions, however, ought to be made on the evidence of a thorough and accurate examination of the facts.

The group's work norms should be periodically evaluated to see if they still meet the demands of the external environment in realistic fashion. Norms can often be changed if the group discusses and evaluates them. Communication patterns that encourage feedback and insure the distribution of information are important to success.

Even under ideal conditions, discussants must have speaking skills that enable them to prepare and report on factual conditions and listening skills that enable them to understand others and ask sensible questions.

The processing of information causes social strain because the person who presents knowledge may be resented and the probing question frequently seems to be a personal attack. The status hierarchy often presents a barrier to effective communication. If the group establishes the norm that a member can admit ignorance without loss of status and that one's ideas and plans can be questioned without threatening one's position, communicative effectiveness is enhanced.

The control phase of group operations, when plans are implemented, resources allocated, and work orders distributed, frequently generates secondary tensions. Good groups develop norms that devote some time after a difficult decision to repairing cohesiveness.

QUESTIONS FOR STUDY

1. What are the advantages and the disadvantages of evaluating the task-oriented small group on exclusively rational criteria?
2. What is the difference between the context of discovery and the context of justification?
3. What is the relationship between the social dimension and the task dimension in terms of group decision making?
4. What is the difference between a linear problem-solving model and a spiral problem-solving model?
5. What is the difference between the decision-emergence model developed in this chapter and the steps in the discussional pattern as adapted from John Dewey's reflective-thinking analysis?
6. In what ways might task decisions emerge from group interaction on nonrational grounds?
7. What are the advantages and the disadvantages of a group that bases its task decisions on external reality?
8. In what ways can specialization and the development of task experts hinder a group's task effectiveness?
9. What is the relationship between feedback and cohesiveness?
10. What informal restrictions may inhibit the free flow of communication within the small group?

EXERCISES

1. Form a problem-solving group in your class, and work out a careful agenda based on the Dewey reflective-thinking process. Hold a meeting in which the group attempts to follow the agenda carefully. Allow for no digressions. Tape record the meeting. Analyze the tape to discover how closely the group stayed with the agenda. Did the group do a good job? Was the agenda an aid or an impediment to the work of the group?
2. Form a problem-solving group in your class, and begin with a period of "kicking the topic around" without any agenda to restrict the deliberations. Let the members free associate if they wish. After a time, if the group feels the need for a plan of procedure, work one out. Let the group decide what topics to take up and in what order. Use the outline as a guide, but allow digressions. Tape record the meeting. Analyze the tape to see how the group went about its task. Did the group do a

good job? Hold an evaluative session in which the entire group discusses its work norms and possible ways of improving task efficiency. Hold another work session. Tape record and evaluate the second meeting.

3. Select a group that you have been working with for several months that in your judgment is cohesive and productive. Write a short paper analyzing the group's fantasy chains as they relate to group problem solving.

References and suggested readings

The variation of the problem-solving discussion pattern is from:

McBurney, James H., and Kenneth G. Hance. *Discussion in Human Affairs.* New York: Harper & Row, 1950.

See also:

Bany, Mary A., and Lois V. Johnson. *Classroom Group Behavior: Group Dynamics in Education.* New York: Macmillan, 1964.

March, James G., and Herbert A. Simon. *Organizations.* New York: Wiley, 1958.

For expansions of the Dewey pattern, see:

Kepner, Charles H., and Benjamin B. Tregoe. *The Rational Manager: A Systematic Approach to Problem Solving and Decision Making.* New York: McGraw-Hill, 1965.

A discussion of PERT will be found in:

Phillips, Gerald M. *Communication and the Small Group.* Indianapolis: Bobbs-Merrill, 1966.

The three-phase pattern is discussed in:

Bales, Robert F., and F. L. Strodtbeck. "Phases in Group Problem-Solving," *Journal of Abnormal and Social Psychology,* **46** (1951), 485–495.

On the relationship between affect and work and the levels of work, see:

Zaleznik, Abraham, and David Moment. *The Dynamics of Interpersonal Behavior.* New York: Wiley, 1964.

The discussion of Bales' equilibrium model and the data on percentage of social interactions is to be found in:

Bales, Robert F. "The Equilibrium Problem in Small Groups." In T. Parsons, R. F. Bales, and E. A. Shils, eds. *Working Papers in the Theory of Action.* New York: Free Press, 1953, pp. 111–161.

The percentages of communication are from:

Stephan, F. F., and E. Mishler. "The Distribution of Participation in Small Groups: An Exponential Approximation," *American Sociological Review,* **17** (1952), 598–606.

On the levels of work, see:

Bennis, Warren G., and Herbert A. Shepard. "Group Observation." In W. Bennis, K. Benne, and R. Chin, eds. *The Planning of Change*. New York: Holt, Rinehart and Winston, 1961.

An excellent survey of research relating to the development of work patterns is to be found in:

Tuckman, Bruce W. "Developmental Sequence in Small Groups," *Psychological Bulletin*, **63** (1965), 384–399.

The Tavistock approach is described in:

Rice, A. E. *Learning for Leadership: Interpersonal and Intergroup Relations*. London: Tavistock, 1965.
Rioch, Margaret J. "Group Relations: Rationale and Technique," *International Journal of Group Psychotherapy*, **10** (1970), 340–355.

Bion's basic analysis is to be found in:

Bion, Wilfred R. *Experience in Groups*. New York: Basic Books, 1959.

The spiraling model is from:

Scheidel, Thomas M., and Laura Crowell. "Idea Development in Small Discussion Groups," *Quarterly Journal of Speech*, **50** (1964), 140–145.

The game of Twenty Questions was used in:

Taylor, Donald W., and William L. Faust. "Twenty Questions: Efficiency in Problem Solving as a Function of Size of Group," *Journal of Experimental Psychology*, **44** (1952), 360–368.

The studies of group attention span are by:

Berg, David M. "A Descriptive Analysis of the Distribution and Duration of Themes Discussed by the Task-oriented Small Group." Ph.D. dissertation, University of Minnesota, 1963.
Faffler, Irene. "A Cross-Cultural Study of the Task-oriented Small Group in the Middle East." Ph.D. dissertation, University of Minnesota, 1971.

Larson, Charles U. "Leadership Emergence and Attention Span: A Content Analysis of the Time Devoted to Themes Discussed in the Task-oriented Small Group." Ph.D. dissertation, University of Minnesota, 1968.

For a survey of research relating to the risky-shift phenomenon, see:

Shaw, Marvin E. *Group Dynamics: The Psychology of Small Group Behavior*. New York: McGraw-Hill, 1971, pp. 73–79.

Stoner's work on the risky shift was originally a master's thesis at Massachusetts Institute of Technology. It is cited in:

Wallach, Michael A., Nathan Kogan, and Daryl J. Bem. "Group Influence on Individual Risk Taking," *Journal of Abnormal and Social Psychology,* **65** (1962), 75–86.

For some studies that discovered cautious as well as risky decisions, see:

Cecil, Earl A., Jerome M. Chertkoff, and Larry L. Cummings. "Risk Taking in Groups as a Function of Group Pressure," *Journal of Social Psychology,* **81** (1970), 273–274.
Dion, Kenneth L., Norman Miller, and Mary Ann Magnan. "Cohesiveness and Social Responsibility as Determinants of Group Risk Taking," *Proceedings of the Annual Convention of the American Psychological Association,* **5** (1970), 335–336.
Kroger, Rolf O., and Irene Briedis. "Effects of Risk and Caution Norms on Group Decision Making," *Human Relations,* **23** (1970), 181–190.

In addition to these studies summarized by Shaw, above, a study by Kee provides some support for cultural influence on risk taking. Kee compared the group dynamics of North American graduate students in business administration playing a computerized business game with Indian foreign students. Using a modified form of the Berg categories, Kee discovered that the North Americans developed norms that were much more risk taking than the Indians'. The study is:

Kee, Yong Tan. "Business Across Boundaries: A Laboratory Experiment to Analyze the Decision-Making Behavior of Groups from Different Cultures." Ph.D. dissertation, University of Minnesota, 1970.

The historical examples of important group decision making and the level of group risk are by:

Janis, Irving L. *Victims of Groupthink.* Boston: Houghton Mifflin, 1972.
Raack, R. C. "When Plans Fail: Small Group Behavior and Decision-Making in the Conspiracy of 1808 in Germany," *Journal of Conflict Resolution,* **14** (1970), 3–19.

The study of decision emergence is by:

Fisher, B. Aubrey. "Decision Emergence: A Process Model of Verbal Task Behavior for Decision-Making Groups." Ph.D. dissertation, University of Minnesota, 1968.

See also:

Fisher, B. Aubrey. "Decision Emergence: Phases in Group Decision-Making," *Speech Monographs,* **37** (1970), 53–66.
Fisher, B. Aubrey. "The Process of Decision Modification in Small Discussion Groups," *Journal of Communication,* **20** (1970), 51–64.

The relation of fantasy to creativity in the small group is from:

Ferguson, Beverly. "The Relation of Fantasy Themes to the Function of a Small Group." Unpublished seminar paper, University of Minnesota, 1970.
Prince, George M. "How to Be a Better Meeting Chairman," *Harvard Business Review,* **47** (1969), 98–109.

The discussion of the inherent laziness or lack of it in human beings is from:

McGregor, Douglas. *The Human Side of Enterprise.* New York: McGraw-Hill, 1960.

For a survey of research on communication networks, see Shaw, above, pp. 137–148.

For some typical studies of communication networks, see:

Bavelas, Alex. "Communication Patterns in Task-oriented Groups." In Dorwin Cartwright and Alvin Zander, eds. *Group Dynamics: Research and Theory,* 3rd ed. New York: Harper & Row, 1968, pp. 503–511.
David, James H., and John Hornseth. "Discussion Patterns and World Problems," *Sociometry,* **30** (1967), 91–103.
Lana, Robert E., Willard Vaughan, and Elliot McGinnies. "Leadership and Friendship Status as Factors in Discussion Group Interaction," *Journal of Social Psychology,* **52** (1960), 127–134.
Lawson, Edwin D. "Changes in Communication Nets, Performance, and Morale," *Human Relations,* **28** (1965), 139–147.
Miraglia, Joseph P. "Communication Network Research and Group Discussion," *Today's Speech,* **12** (1964), 11–14.
Watson, David, and Barbara Bromberg. "Power, Communication, and Position Satisfaction in Task-oriented Groups," *Journal of Personality and Social Psychology,* **2** (1965), 859–864.

For studies of feedback and its relationship to small-group communication, see:

Leathers, Dale G. "The Feedback Rating Instrument: A New Means of Evaluating Discussion," *Central States Speech Journal,* **22** (1971), 32–42.
Leathers, Dale G. "Process Disruption and Measurement in Small Group Communication," *Quarterly Journal of Speech,* **55** (1969), 287–300.
Leathers, Dale G. "The Process Effects of Trust-Destroying Behavior in the Small Group," *Speech Monographs,* **37** (1970), 180–187.
Leathers, Dale G. "Quality of Group Communication as a Determinant of Group Product," *Speech Monographs,* **39** (1972), 166–173.
Leathers, Dale G. "Testing for Determinate Interactions in the Small Group Communication Process," *Speech Monographs,* **38** (1971), 177–181.
Scheidel, Thomas M., and Laura Crowell. "Feedback in Small Group Communication," *Quarterly Journal of Speech,* **52** (1966), 273–278.
Zajonc, Robert B. "The Effects of Feedback and Probability of Group Success on Individual and Group Performance," *Human Relations,* **15** (1962), 149–161.

The conclusions of a number of studies on status and communication patterns are summarized in:

Collins, Barry, and Harold Guetzkow. *A Social Psychology of Group Processes for Decision-Making.* New York: Wiley, 1964, Chap. 9.

For more detailed treatment of sociometric indexes and analysis, see:

Jennings, Helen Hall. *Leadership and Isolation.* New York: Longmans, Green, 1943.

Moreno, J. L. *Who Shall Survive?* Washington, D.C.: Nervous and Mental Disease Publishing, 1934.

For further studies of the task dimension of group interaction, the work of Gouran and his associates at Indiana University is particularly useful. The Indiana Studies have been concerned with the process analysis of communication, particularly of leadership and the orientation of the group, as it effects such decision variables as consensus. See:

Gouran, Dennis S. "Conceptual and Methodological Approaches to the Study of Leadership," *Central States Speech Journal*, **21** (1970), 217–223.

Gouran, Dennis S. "Correlates of Member Satisfaction in Group Decision-Making Discussion," *Central States Speech Journal*, **24** (1973), 91–96.

Gouran, Dennis S. "Evaluating Discussion: Toward an Empirically Based System," *Today's Speech*, **18** (1970), 26–29.

Gouran, Dennis S., and John E. Baird, Jr. "An Analysis of Distributional and Sequential Structure in Problem-Solving and Informal Group Discussions," *Speech Monographs*, **39** (1972), 16–22.

Hellman, Connie. "An Investigation of the Communication Behavior of Emergent and Appointed Leaders of Small Group Discussion." Ph.D. dissertation, Indiana University, 1970.

Hill, Timothy A. "An Experimental Study of the Relationship Between the Opinionatedness of a Leader and Consensus in Group Discussions of Policy." Ph.D. dissertation, Indiana University, 1973.

Knutson, Thomas J. "An Experimental Study of the Effects of Orientation Behavior on Small Group Consensus," *Speech Monographs*, **39** (1972), 159–165.

Lumsden, Gay. "An Experimental Study of the Effects of Verbal Agreement on Leadership Maintenance in Problem Solving Discussions." Ph.D. dissertation, Indiana University, 1972.

Russell, Hugh C. "An Investigation of Leadership Maintenance Behavior." Ph.D. dissertation, Indiana University, 1970.

See also:

Bochner, Arthur P., and Brenda Bochner. "A Multivariate Investigation of Machiavellianism and Task Structure in Four-Man Groups," *Speech Monographs*, **39** (1972), 277–285.

Bower, Joseph L. "Group Decision-Making: A Report of an Experimental Study," *Behavioral Science*, **19** (1965), 277–289.

Burgoon, Michael. "Amount of Conflicting Information in a Group Discussion and Tolerance for Ambiguity as Predictors of Task Attractiveness," *Speech Monographs*, **38** (1971), 121–124.

Clarkson, Geoffrey P., and Francis D. Tuggle. "Toward a Theory of Group Decision Behavior," *Behavioral Science*, **11** (1966), 33–42.

Fisher, B. Aubrey, and Leonard Hawes. "An Interact System Model: Generating a Grounded Theory of Small Groups," *Quarterly Journal of Speech*, **52** (1971), 444–453.

Geier, John G., Robert F. Forston, and Charles Urban Larson, "Small Group Discussion Versus the Lecture Method: A Study in Individual Decision Making," *Western Speech*, **34** (1970), 38–45.

Hall, Jay, and Martha S. Williams. "A Comparison of Decision-Making Performances in Established and Ad Hoc Groups," *Journal of Personality and Social Psychology,* 3 (1966), 213–222.

Kline, John A. "Orientation and Group Consensus," *Central States Speech Journal,* 23 (1972), 44–47.

Kline, John A., and James L. Hullinger. "Redundancy, Self Orientation, and Group Consensus," *Speech Monographs,* 40 (1973), 72–74.

Larson, Carl E. "Forms of Analysis and Small Group Problem-Solving," *Speech Monographs,* 36 (1969), 452–455.

Pyron, H. Charles. "An Experimental Study of the Role of Reflective Thinking in Business and Professional Conferences and Discussions," *Speech Monographs,* 31 (1964), 157–161.

Ryberg, Lillian. "A Comparative Study of Small Group Discussion in the Native and Target Languages." Ph.D. dissertation, University of Minnesota, 1974.

Saine, Thomas J., and Douglas G. Bock. "A Comparison of the Distributional and Sequential Structures of Interaction in High and Low Consensus Groups," *Central States Speech Journal,* 24 (1973), 125–130.

Sharp, Harry, Jr., and Joyce Milliken. "Reflective Thinking Ability and the Product of Problem-Solving Discussion," *Speech Monographs,* 31 (1964), 124–127.

Stech, Ernest L. "An Analysis of Interaction Structure in the Discussion of a Ranking Task," *Speech Monographs,* 37 (1970), 249–256.

Utterback, William. "Majority Influences and Cogency of Argument in Discussion," *Quarterly Journal of Speech,* 48 (1962), 412–414.

Zagona, Salvatore V., Joe E. Willis, and William J. MacKinnon. "Group Effectiveness in Creative Problem-Solving Tasks: An Examination of Relevant Variables," *Journal of Psychology,* 62 (1966), 111–137.

PART III
APPLICATIONS

CHAPTER 13

DISCUSSIONS AND CONFERENCES

the nature of the ad hoc meeting

The Latin term *ad hoc* means "for this special purpose." Thus, an ad hoc meeting is one set up for a special purpose for which the participants have not met before and are not likely to meet again. Some of the members may have participated with one another in other ad hoc meetings, and some may be acquainted from social contacts or other business meetings; but the composition of an ad hoc meeting is unique and temporary.

The ad hoc meeting differs from an ad hoc committee. Some organizations, such as universities, may have ad hoc committees formed for a special purpose that is significant enough that the committee may meet a number of times and continue for a period of weeks or even months. In an organization, an ad hoc committee differs from the standing (permanent) committees. Some organizations also create project teams to work on a given task. A computer firm, for instance, may set up a special project team to develop a new information-processing system. In contrast, the planners of an ad hoc meeting anticipate achieving their purpose in a single session.

Since the people in an ad hoc meeting have not met before, they form a zero-history group. The fact that the group has no history means that the members have no experience on which to base future expectations of roles, norms, goals, or culture. In short, both the social field and the task objectives are unstructured and ambiguous.

The leaderless group discussions in the Minnesota Studies were also zero-history groups; but, in contrast with the ad hoc meeting, they had a *future*. A group's future plays an important part in the dynamics of even the first session and results in the process described in Chapters 7 to 12.

The zero-history LGD is under pressure to test potential leaders and other influential members, to develop norms and other features of their group culture carefully, to take nothing at face value, and to check reputations, formal status, and assigned structure before accepting them. Much is at stake; hence, the members search and evaluate the social realities of the group with more rigor in the first session of the ongoing group than they do in the ad hoc meeting. Much of the primary tension in the first meeting of the LGD with a future stems from the fact that much more is at stake.

One of the most important tendencies in the ad hoc meeting, on the other hand, is to accept leadership. The members are likely to accept and appreciate guidance from the chairman whether he is self-appointed or has been assigned by some organizational unit to lead the meeting. The group needs to get to work quickly without a lot of the leadership contention and role-testing, which characterize groups with a future. Members realize that they have little time and tend to accept arbitrarily stipulated goals and procedures with little challenge.

The members of an ad hoc meeting tend to take shortcuts to structure the group into a "pecking order," so they can get on with the business at hand. They are willing to risk substantial mistakes because of the shortage of time and because they often perceive the task as less important than the assignments characteristic of longer-term groups. They tend to use organizational status, professional standing, or community reputation as ways of assigning leadership and influence. Thus, if seven people attend an ad hoc meeting and one is known to be the dean of the college, another as the student body president, and a third as editor of the student newspaper, that information will help structure a hierarchy of influence and importance. Once the discussion is under way, members use quick stereotypes to find a role for those members who do not have societal positions or community reputations to help assign them slots in the group.

Members of ad hoc meetings also tend to accept a stereotyped picture of how a meeting ought to be run. The zero-history group that will meet for many sessions will work out its own roles, norms, and culture according to the dynamics described in Chapters 7 to 12. Time limitations, however, force the members of the ad hoc meeting to use some other tactic. The culture of a given society or region will tend to develop a general stereotype of how an ad hoc meeting should be organized and conducted. In North America, the culturally accepted picture of how a group discussion should proceed includes the assigned role functions of moderator, leader, or chairman, and, often, of a secretary or recorder.

The moderator, leader, or chairman is expected to tend to the administrative details of setting up the meeting place. In addition, the chairman typically plans the agenda, sends out preliminary information, and schedules the meeting. During the course of the session, the assigned chairman is expected to "lead" the discussion. Much of the following advice on how to plan, moderate, and participate in a one-time meeting reflects the cultural expectations for such sessions in the United States.

Of course, the picture of how a good ad hoc meeting should proceed varies from what actually takes place in a typical meeting. All participants do not willingly follow the assigned moderator even when they know they should. They are, however, much more likely to do so in an ad hoc meeting than in a group with a longer life. Even in a short meeting, role differentiation does take place. A few people talk more than others despite the best efforts of the moderator. Some people are silent. Some are friendly, humorous, and likeable. Others are well organized and insightful and contribute to the success of the group's work. The general cultural expectations that the discussion is composed of one leader and a group of indistinguishable "participants" soon evaporates under the natural dynamics of group pressure.

This chapter applies the theory of small-group communication developed in Part II to the ad hoc meetings that characterize the cultural setting of the United States. Generally, ad hoc meetings are held in three contexts: (1) a group of people who have come together in private to discuss a topic; (2) a group of people who have come together to discuss a topic for an audience that observes the discussion live or over television or hears it on radio; and (3) a group of people who have come together for a conference or workshop in which they listen to lectures, audio-visual presentations such as films, and who alternate these sessions with ad hoc meetings with other participants.

The ad hoc meeting is an important and widespread communication situation. The student of small-group communication is well advised to learn how to participate in ad hoc meetings both because of their intrinsic importance and because the communication skills useful in such sessions transfer to the more complicated task-force and business meetings in which the dynamics of role emergence and norm development come into play. The fundamentals of communication that one learns and practices in the ad hoc meeting are useful when combined with an understanding of small-group-communication theory to other, more important group settings.

uses of ad hoc meetings

USING THE MEETING TO INFORM

A person developing or planning a short course, symposium, seminar, or retreat might well consider one or more of the many forms of discussion. He could use discussion to give the participants information. Public discussion encourages audience participation, thus assuring that the available time is used to answer questions the audience wants and needs to have answered. In addition, when several experts are free to challenge one another, information will not be accepted simply because it comes from an authority.

The business meeting is often a briefing session, for it can be a guard against the charge that important people within the organization have not been informed or consulted.

USING MEETINGS TO STIMULATE INTEREST

Participants often use the public discussion program to stimulate interest in important questions. If experts present relevant information about an important problem and discuss representative solutions, even though they do not reach a solution, listeners become more aware of the problem and may begin to investigate it.

Discussion is prevalent in educational settings. The short course, symposium, seminar, or retreat seldom sustains itself entirely with a series of lectures. Most conference planners try to pack a great amount of material into a short time. Conferees, however, seldom will tolerate 8 to 10 hours a day of concentrated lectures, no matter how dynamic, entertaining, and informative the lecturers may be. One way to change pace is to alternate lectures with discussions. An audience has a tendency to sit back and relax when an instructor begins to lecture. He may hold their interest, but the audience is not actively involved in the learning process. When the program of the conference moves from a lecture to a discussion, the participants are under considerable social pressure to take part; thus, participation fosters interest.

USING MEETINGS TO SOLVE PROBLEMS

Discussion programs can be used not only to stimulate public interest in a problem but also to bring people together in a common solution to a problem. A series of discussion programs might present relevant information and various solutions. The participants will then agree on a course of action. A neighborhood improvement association might, after a series of public discussions, agree to raise money, hire a lawyer, and protest spot zoning in their area.

USING MEETINGS TO STIMULATE CREATIVITY

Discussion programs are sometimes used to stimulate creativity and new ideas. The dramatic form of such discussion is the one developed and popularized by the advertising executive Alex Osborn under the label of "brainstorming." Osborn used the informality and spontaneity that characterizes discussion programs to stimulate people to dream up "wild" ideas and solutions to specified problems.

An interesting variation of brainstorming is the *nominal group*. Investigators studying the brainstorming group and comparing its ability to generate ideas to the efforts of the same subjects working individually discovered that people sitting together and working silently generated more ideas than they did when participating in a brainstorming session. Conference planners applied the research discovery to encourage creativity by using the nominal-group technique. The participants are divided into groups and given a period of time in which to think up ideas and write them down while sitting with the others. After a period of listing ideas in the nominal group, the members begin to communicate and form an interacting group. They select a recorder, and each member reads his list. The recorder puts the list of ideas on a blackboard or flip chart, combining similar ideas, until all suggestions are before the group. The members then begin to evaluate the list critically, culling out the unsatisfactory ideas until a solution emerges.

types of discussion formats

Planners of discussion programs can choose from a wide variety of formats. There is so much diversity that considering all the details or even most of the modifications is pointless. The student who is planning a discussion program may want to introduce some novelty in the format he uses by modifying current practice. However, some general features of discussion programs cut across the many different specific formats.

FORUM DISCUSSIONS

If there is a special time set aside during the program for audience participation, the program is a *forum discussion*. If the discussion program is presented on radio and television, the audience may ask questions by letter or telephone. Regardless of the form of the discussion proper, the producers may aim for audience participation if one of their purposes is to involve the audience and thus stimulate their interest. A forum period is sometimes not used because of time limitations or the explosive nature of the subject and the occasion.

PANEL DISCUSSIONS

In panel discussions, a small group of discussants talk, much as in a conversation, about the topic. Informality is the keynote, and the members of the group can interrupt one another. A *moderator* may be assigned the role of cutting off verbose members and encouraging quiet ones. The panel discussion is often organized around an outline of topics or questions, and the participants extemporize their comments much as a speaker might outline and deliver a speech extemporaneously. The panel using an outline can adapt to the audience situation and to the unfolding discussion. If participants get "going" and depart to some extent from the planned outline, the group may prefer to continue on a tangent for a time because they find it rewarding. In like manner, if a topic is covered more quickly than expected, the group may modify its time allotment. This freedom to maneuver is one of the virtues of the panel discussion. It allows a panel of experienced public discussants to present a lively, extemporaneous program that gives the illusion of being a spontaneous working session and at the same time offering an organized program that covers the topic concisely and efficiently. The good panel-discussion program appears to be a natural and spontaneous conference. The illusion is the result of careful planning and considerable artistry on the part of the participants.

The flexibility of structure can also be a liability. The participants must keep a balance between improvisations and planning. They may assume that there is no need for preparation since the panel discussion is informal and consists of just "kicking the topic around." The result is that they may flounder about and fail to cover the topic. This is a distinct danger in classroom panel discussions. Students should not be misled by the deceptively simple format of the panel. On the other hand, a group must also guard against the other extreme: If planned too carefully, the program may proceed with dispatch and be well organized, but seem like a "canned" performance.

The panel discussion is well adapted to public discussion programs on radio and television. Radio is preeminently an informal and intimate medium. The radio panel discussion is one of the most popular formats and is widely used for public-affairs broadcasting and political campaigning. The panel discussion also exploits the visual potentialities of television. The television camera can convey the facial gestures that highlight verbal intonations as the individual participants speak. The extemporaneous nature of the panel discussion projects a naturalness that allows viewers to get a clear impression of the personalities of the participants.

The panel discussion is also well suited to presenting programs to relatively small audiences in informal surroundings. The 40-seat classroom that is filled to capacity is a good setting.

SYMPOSIUM DISCUSSIONS

Another widespread form of public discussion is the *symposium discussion*. In the symposium, a group of experts divides up the topic. Each is allotted a certain amount of uninterrupted time in which to make a brief statement. After the prepared speeches, the experts may participate in a panel discussion, they may question one another, another group of interrogators may question them, or the audience may be invited to participate.

The symposium is less spontaneous and more formal than the panel discussion; however, audience participation and questions and answers from other participants may add a measure of spontaneity. It does have the advantage of not requiring extensive planning. Care must be taken that the symposium does not become simply a program of speeches. There must be an attempt at give-and-take. Symposiums also require participation by all discussants. Panel discussions are sometimes dominated by the more extroverted, voluble members, with the result that some positions are not represented adequately.

The symposium is suited to programs presented from a stage to a relatively large audience in an auditorium. It is also useful when the occasion calls for more formality and for greater emphasis on the authoritative nature of the participants than can be furnished by a variation of the panel discussion.

INTERROGATIONS

Broadcasters have popularized another version of the discussion program—a format that, essentially, involves the questioning of experts. In the dialogues of Plato, Socrates plays a game in which one party to the dialogue agrees to answer all of the other person's questions. In this fashion, the questioner is given a chance to test the adequacy of the other person's ideas. The oral examining committee that questions a graduate student operates in a similar way. The questioning is probing and is designed to catch inconsistencies or inadequacies of thinking. Questions can also be used to elicit further information or to gain greater understanding. Many radio and television programs have had formats in which an expert or a group of experts answers the questions posed by another group of people. According to the rules, the questioners are not to make statements and speeches, and the experts are not to ask questions. Such programs as *Meet the Press* and *Face the Nation* are examples.

Interrogation is a popular technique in broadcasting, for it often results in conflict, and conflict is inherently interesting. The audience likes a dogfight, and, if the questioner can pin down the expert or make him angry, the program is likely to be more interesting. Conflict also allows the members of the audience to identify with one or more of the personalities involved. Programs of this sort are dramatic and have much appeal. Interrogation formats that force participants into conflict are often used because public-affairs programs must compete with entertainment programs for audiences. As a result, the number of interrogation formats that exemplify the spirit of inquiry is very small.

A prevalent use of interrogation is as a modification of another form of public discussion. For example, at some point in a panel discussion the audience is invited to ask questions, or the members of a symposium discussion are given a chance to question one another. The interrogation period is useful in testing ideas and gaining audience involvement and participation. And it is perhaps most worthwhile as a device to assure that information is understood. Questions from the audience indicate what is grasped and what is not.

Students planning a discussion program for an audience will find that asking questions for information and clarification will be the least troublesome and most useful type of inquiry. Questioning to test ideas requires considerable skill in the art of interrogation. Too often, the questioner who tries to test the authority ends by making speeches in the form of questions.

techniques for the conference

Conferences in which a large number of people actively participate, as compared to the small-group program, are also usually organized around a central theme, although they may continue for several days, or even a week or longer. Conferences that use discussion as a main procedural tool may have groups meeting in private, or the groups may meet in a large room.

Conference sessions tend to be intensive, and many participants are not accustomed to working in such a setting. Conference planners must bear in mind the importance of holding the audience's attention. In addition to a wide range of audio-visual devices such as films, film strips, tape recordings, flannel-board presentations, they often use special techniques to stimulate participation.

BUZZ SESSIONS

One of the more popular techniques for involving an audience in a training situation is the buzz session. The audience is divided into small groups, each of which briefly discusses an aspect of the topic of the meeting. For example, after an hour of lecture, the audience is divided into groups of six, and each group is asked to discuss a specific topic for six minutes. After the brief buzz session, the audience reassembles, and the groups report on what they have talked about.

STANDING COMMITTEES

Somewhat like a carefully planned, extended, and organized buzz session is the conference patterned after a legislative session in which the participants are divided into standing committees to exist for the duration of the conference. The committees report to the entire assembly, where their reports are discussed and acted on by a committee of the whole. Selected members of the graduate faculty of the University of Minnesota used this procedure for a weekend conference on the topic, "How can the testing procedures of the graduate school be improved?" This general topic was divided into such subtopics as: How can we improve the oral examination for the master's degree? How can we improve the oral examination for the Ph.D. degree? How can we improve the written preliminary examination for the Ph.D. degree? A standing committee was assigned to discuss each of these subtopics, and the entire group assembled from time to time to hear reports.

In such conferences, the committee might meet for six to eight hours or for several days, and the sessions of the committee of the whole might run for several hours to a day or more. Standing committees are useful for sharing information and are well adapted to the discussion of problem situations with a view to changing policy.

THE CASE STUDY

The case-study method of instruction is widely used in law schools. The basis of such study is a real or imaginary situation exemplifying certain principles of law. The class discusses the legal precedents and makes a finding on the facts of a specific situation or case. The use of cases for instructional purposes is popular in those disciplines where scientific laws do not apply. The equivalent teaching device in the sciences is the problem, which allows the group to apply general scientific laws to a specific instance. In the sciences, a problem always has a correct solution. In disciplines where the answers are not clear, but are dependent upon various factors—as, for example, many of the problems in human relations—the case-study discussion is often helpful. Teachers in business administration, in social studies, and in group methods often use case studies as instructional aids.

The success or failure of the case-study method often depends on the quality of the cases developed for the discussions. Good case studies are works of art and are not easy to write. They should be adapted to the level of skill and knowledge of the participants and to the time to be devoted to them. They should be brief enough to be covered in the time allotted and yet contain enough detail so that lack of information does not hinder the discussion. If participants continually inquire about matters of fact, probably not enough information has been included. In building a case for study, the student should try to include several important issues or points and make them so clear that most participants will understand them. He may wish to include several subtle points to check the skill of the better participants; he can then coincidentally make the point that the problem is considerably more complex than it appears at first.

The case study provides a concrete basis for the application of theory. A public discussion of a case gives participants a chance to apply principles and to demonstrate understanding and skill. The good case brings theory to bear on a concrete situation in which people are involved. The case humanizes the principles being studied. If the participants do not prepare before the conference, the case study provides them with a common situation and a minimum level of information at the meeting.

ROLE-PLAYING

Role-playing was first widely used by clinical psychologists and psychiatrists in the diagnosis and treatment of personality disorders. Planners of discussions and conferences have adapted the technique of role-playing to their needs. In a conference setting, certain participants are assigned roles relevant to application of the theory under study. They are then given a situation and proceed to *act out* in impromptu fashion the implications of the situation. For example, the instructor of a discussion class might have six students prepare a panel–forum discussion program to present to the speech class. He could then assign each member of the group a role to play during the discussion. One fellow could be told to be aggressive, talkative, and a poor listener; another could be silent; a third could agree to everything and smile a great deal. One could be told that he desperately wants a good grade at the exclusion of all else and believes that to impress the instructor he must become the group leader. Another could be told that he has just had a fight with his girl friend and he can think of little else right now. Another could be taking the course only because it is required and resents the whole idea.

The drama inherent in role-playing makes it an excellent device to heighten audience interest and involvement. People playing the roles can relax and act out the part, because the group members and the audience know that they are not playing themselves. Conflict situations can arise that otherwise might be masked by social pressures. A word of caution: Role-playing can be dangerous. If the participants do not enter into the spirit of the game, the general climate of the conference can be severely damaged. Role-playing can be even more dangerous when the participants play their roles with enthusiasm. It often reveals personality quirks damaging to the participant's self-image and, unless carefully used, may be a punishing rather than a learning situation.

THE USE OF GAMES, EXERCISES, AND PROBLEMS

The popularity of groups in the consummatory style in the 1960s resulted in the widespread development and use of sensitivity or encounter games and exercises. Trainers and facilitators of consummatory groups designed, traded, and borrowed many different projects, games, and exercises designed to speed up the dynamics of such group phenomena as norm development, leadership contention, role conflict, the breaking of primary tension, and the establishment of like–dislike bonds among members.

One of the earmarks of the consummatory style was the development of interpersonal trust, of honest self-disclosure, of congruency (being authentic). Trainers developed the technique of self-disclosing communication for achieving trust among the members. In order to encourage self-disclosing communication, trainers developed a number of games that require members to tell one another intimate details about themselves. Given the power of group pressures for conformity, even a brief exercise that succeeds in creating norms of self-disclosure can elicit a great deal of personal and intimate information. A rather extreme example of a game designed to elicit self-disclosure is "truth hearts" which is played with an ordinary deck of cards. A dealer gives each member of the group a card until someone gets a heart. The person who receives a heart must then truthfully answer any question put to him by the others. Each of the others gets to ask one question for each heart.

Trainers also developed exercises and games to increase or illustrate the concept of interpersonal trust. One popular exercise was the "trust walk" in which the members of the workshop were divided into pairs and one member of the pair was blindfolded while the other led him about. The blindfolded member had to trust the other person to lead him in a protective way.

Leaders of workshops developed a host of exercises to break the primary tensions in a zero-history group. Often these "icebreakers" were get-acquainted kinds of games that encouraged self-disclosure.

Facilitators also created a number of games and exercises to encourage conflict and secondary tension. Confrontation exercises in which group members focus on one individual and tell him what he is doing in the group or how they feel about him usually will speed up the rise of secondary tensions and often create a group culture that emphasizes high levels of emotion. The opposite effect is achieved by games and exercises designed to elicit shows of solidarity and create a positive social climate. A strength-bombardment session, for example, has the group focusing on an individual; but, instead of confronting the negative features of the person's role in the group, the members are required to point out only the positive features and to raise the individual's status in the group.

Another class of group games aims to achieve cooperation or competition either within groups or among them. The prisoner's-dilemma game, for example, is one that groups and individuals may play cooperatively or competitively. The new-equipment dilemma is an exercise in which one member of a hypothetical work group is to get a piece of new equipment and thus arouse intergroup competition.

Teachers of small-group communication have also developed a number of tasks including puzzles, brain teasers, and logic problems that illustrate various features of the task dimension of group process.

Games and exercises can generate some of the powerful social forces inherent in group process under hothouse conditions so they may be experienced and discussed in relatively brief instructional sessions. In the hands of a wise and skillful teacher, such games, exercises, and problems can be useful teaching devices. An able trainer can use them to achieve good groups in the consummatory style. At their worst, inept or unscrupulous individuals can use these devices as a bag of tricks to exploit people by creating powerful, exciting, and dangerous social forces. Once a game or exercise starts fantasies chaining through a group, the inept leader will often find the dynamics of the group getting out of his control.

A student of small-group communication would be well advised to use games, exercises, and problems carefully with much preparation and forethought. One should also be most careful about participating in a laboratory or workshop designed to create groups in the consummatory style that employs such devices. A person should always investigate the integrity and skill of the trainers and facilitators to make sure that the styles of the groups created in the laboratory provide the desired experience. *Under no circumstances* should a person be required by an organization to participate in a consummatory group against his will.

A number of the games and exercises are innocuous, however, and can be used much as one would use buzz sessions, panel discussions, and symposiums as pedagogical techniques to increase learning.

For a number of years, a relatively active grapevine has been disseminating group games to facilitators and trainers. As a result, the literature describing a number of collections of such games, exercises, and problems is growing. A number of published collections of such projects is to be found in the references and suggested readings for this chapter.

combining and modifying forms of discussion

Freshness of format is achieved through combining and modifying the basic forms of discussion to serve the needs of a specific program or conference. A panel discussion might be combined with a forum period, making a panel–forum discussion. A symposium discussion can also be combined with a forum period. The symposium may be followed by a panel discussion by the members of the symposium, and this, in turn, may be followed by an audience forum. The program might begin with an opening set of statements by the participants (symposium), followed by an interrogation period to test ideas and to examine the experts, and finally by a closing set of statements (another symposium). Or the program might begin with a panel and end with a closing summary by each member. A symposium presentation could be followed by a buzz session of everyone in the audience, and this could be followed by a forum. The conference could begin with a lecture followed by buzz sessions on a case study, followed by a symposium composed of a spokesman from each discussion group, followed by a forum under the direction of the lecturer.

Obviously, the possibilities for innovation and modification are numerous; and, when students plan a discussion program, they should ask themselves which forms in what combinations will help them best to achieve their objectives for the given program or conference.

planning the ad hoc meeting

SELECTING THE TOPIC

Discussion programs are often organized around general themes or topics. Selection of a topic should be influenced by an analysis of the participants and the audience that will view the program if the discussion is public. Will attendance be compulsory? Will the audience be well informed? What attitudes and interests will the audience represent?

The purpose of the discussion determines to some extent the suitable topics. Often, the occasion will help formulate the purpose. Some occasions are created by the planners in order to achieve their purposes; other occasions call forth the program, and the purposes must be adapted to the occasion.

Frequently, the general theme of a program should be phrased so as to arouse interest and promote attendance. The working topic, however, should be a question, and a clear definite one. A vaguely worded question such as "What About Civil Rights?" is like the label "Civil Rights"; it does not limit or structure the program.

Better wordings for discussion questions regarding civil rights would be limited and specific ones such as: What policy should our City Council adopt in regard to civil rights? or, What should the policy of the federal government be in regard to civil rights in northern cities? A good question limits the topic to enable adequate discussion in the time allotted and yet allows for some range of inquiry into the alternative solutions. The question can also facilitate the purposes of the program.

Questions of fact. A factual question furthers the aim of informing the participants. Examples of factual questions are: Is communism growing in influence in Latin America? To what extent is drinking related to automobile accidents? Has there been an increase in premarital sexual relations on the part of American coeds?

Questions of value. A group may wish to prod members of the audience to examine their value systems. For example, Is euthanasia justified? Should capital punishment be abolished? Should single girls have affairs? Questions of value are best adapted to audiences composed of people who are still unsure of their position. The group can expect considerable difference of opinion in a discussion of value, and these differences will end in the ultimate argument of "I believe it is" versus "I believe it isn't."

Questions of conjecture. Sometimes groups phrase questions in terms of conjecture about future events. Examples of such questions are: Can the United States avoid another major depression? Is World War III inevitable? Can Germany be reunified? Such questions are often used as attention-getting devices. They can be helpful to participants drafting speeches for a symposium presentation, but have less utility for seriously exploring a problem.

Questions of policy. An excellent question is one that asks for a clear statement of policy. A question of policy implicitly asks, What should we do? It directs the group's attention to a problem and asks for the best solution. Examples are: What should Tri Zeta's rush program be for the next quarter? How can the student body best express its displeasure with the university's speaker policy? What should the federal government's policy be with regard to atomic energy?

SELECTING A SUITABLE FORMAT FOR DISCUSSION

An analysis of the purpose, the audience, and the occasion aids the planners in picking a format. An informal discussion designed to stimulate audience interest could take some form of the panel–forum–interrogation. When the purpose is to furnish information to large audiences, the group might select an adaptation of the symposium.

A group producing a discussion show for radio or television will want to exploit the intimacy of these media by using innovations in the panel–interrogation format.

An instructional conference might include case-study, role-playing, or buzz-session discussions. If the organization is interested in advice regarding policy, it might select the standing-committee approach with a legislative session or a committee of the whole following the individual committee meetings.

SELECTING THE PHYSICAL SETTING

The planners muste select a suitably sized room, arrange furniture, and attend to such matters as seeing to the public-address system and being sure that the doors are open on time and that the room is clean and adequately ventilated.

Program planners will find careful attention to details of room selection and arrangement to be worthwhile. Investigations of the effect of spatial relationships on communication in small groups indicate that the physical setting and proximity of members are of considerable significance.

Individuals and groups tend to select a territory and then defend their proprietary rights to the area. Seating arrangements tend to increase or decrease the members' feeling of ease or discomfort as to where they are sitting. Individuals also have boundaries of personal space that they do not like to have invaded, and the arrangement of tables and chairs should take this fact into account. The distances that separate members will also influence the flow of communication. The members will have preferences for what they consider comfortable distances for talking with one another depending on the degree of intimacy among them and on the content of the communication.

Most important for the planners of a meeting to consider is the fact that the spacial arrangements in terms of table shape, size, and location in the room and the placement of chairs around the table will affect the flow and direction of messages. When the group is placed at a round or square table, the situation will encourage the flow of communication across the table. Members will tend to talk to others facing them rather than to the persons adjacent to them. If the table is rectangular, the members tend to perceive one end of it as the head position, and they will tend to look to the person sitting there for direction. Often the chairman of an ad hoc meeting will arrange to have a rectangular table so that he can sit at the head and encourage the group to accept his moderating of the meeting.

A relatively bare meeting room is better than a lavishly furnished conference room. Overstuffed chairs and mahogany conference tables are comfortable, but they separate members of the group from each other. Also, such a setting distracts the group's attention away from the meeting.

Auditoriums are not always suitable for presenting speeches or discussion programs. The wise planner will shun the large, spacious auditorium with a high stage or platform, an elaborate speaker's stand, and a complicated public-address system. Experienced public speakers who wish to talk to their audiences, judge their response, and perhaps encourage their participation will often speak from *in front of the stage*, rather than from the speaker's stand up on the stage. Raised platforms and stages establish a distance between the audience and speakers that inhibits informality and spontaneity.

In general, planners should check the facilities before scheduling the program. Sometimes the best available is far from ideal, and they should then exploit the room's possibilities. For example, even if the program is held in a large auditorium with a stage, all the seats can be roped off except for a few in the front rows. The participants can then use chairs in front of the stage immediately before the audience, at its level.

The settings for after-luncheon or dinner programs are often particularly poor. The audience may be scattered around the room, facing different directions, with waitresses clearing tables. One solution to this problem is to set up chairs in rows in a separate section of the dining room, to which the audience can move for the program. If this cannot be done, the audience may be requested, after the meal, to move their chairs around and arrange themselves.

ARRANGING THE PARTICIPANTS

Arranging the participants for a public discussion program. It is most important that the participants be able to talk easily to the audience and to each other. One good arrangement is to seat them along one side of a table, with the more active participants at each end. Another is to seat members in a semicircle with the moderator in the middle and the talkative members at the ends. Another common arrangement is to place several tables in the shape of a U, with the panel at the head table and the audience seated at the other tables. If a meal is to be served first, the audience seated around U-shaped tables is in a better position to listen and participate than when scattered at smaller tables throughout the room. Members of such an audience are sometimes more willing to participate, and they are all part of the same group. However, these advantages do not apply to a large group; with more than 30 people, this arrangement is unwieldy. For larger audiences, the planners should rearrange the room so that the audience sits in rows. Even if they need tables to write on, rows of tables are more conducive to audience participation than the U-shaped arrangement.

Arranging the participants at a conference. In planning a conference, the facilities for each discussion group should be carefully arranged. A table is helpful, as it furnishes a focal point for the deliberations. It allows members to lean forward and to write more easily. Everyone at the table, in a sense, is invited to participate. However, the table can become a problem. If the table is not large enough, members with a reluctance to speak up may use the lack of space as an excuse to withdraw from the discussion. If the table is rectangular, role struggles may be accentuated because early in the discussion considerable significance is attached to sitting at the "head" of the table. If the table is too large, it may serve as a mental barrier to the flow of discussion. When an oversized central table is used, conference planners are wise to place chairs away from the table and have the groups huddle together for discussion.

PREPARING FOR PUBLIC DISCUSSION

In the classroom, the instructor may expect all students preparing a discussion to hold planning meetings. The importance of joint planning cannot be overemphasized. The process of working together on the plan will provide clues about interactions that may develop during the program. Even a short planning period will accomplish some of the necessary social structuring of the group. The entire group should, when possible, work out the outline that will serve to organize the program.

Planners of discussion programs for community organizations may find that it is impossible to assemble all the experts for a planning session. If the program is for radio or television, a preliminary meeting might be held just prior to air time. A 30-minute or 1-hour warm-up discussion over coffee before taping or air time will break the primary tension of the members and create a livelier program from the beginning.

Preparing the outline. The discussion program has much in common with the extemporaneous speech, and, when possible, the group should outline its performance in a similar way. First, the participants should clarify the purpose of the program. If the discussants disagree about purpose, this should be the first item on the agenda of their planning meeting. Then the group should select and arrange the material and decide how time should be apportioned, considering the importance of the items on the outline and the interests, informational background, and understanding of the audience. An agenda for the discussion group's planning session is the following:

1. What should be the purpose of our program?
   a. Is our primary purpose presenting information?
   b. Is our primary purpose to arouse interest in the question?
   c. Is our primary purpose to stimulate the audience to make further study and make up their own minds?
   d. Is our primary purpose to encourage creativity and new ideas?
   e. Is our primary purpose to go through the process of inquiry, seeking a solution to the problem?
2. What materials should be included in the program?
   a. What problems should we discuss?
   b. What evidence should be presented?
   c. What points of view should be included?
   d. What solutions should be considered?
   e. What devices to interest the audience should be included? examples? analogies? personal experiences? narrative materials?
3. How should the material be arranged?
   a. Should we follow the steps of the discussional pattern? definitions, problems, solutions, testing of solutions, selection of best solutions?
   b. Should the material be organized topically?
   c. Should the material be organized chronologically?
   d. Should the material be organized spatially?
4. How should we apportion discussion time?
   a. What is the most important section? the next most important? Can some of the material be dropped? Have we forgotten anything?
   b. How much time should we allot the most important section? to the next most important?
   c. How much time should we provide for introduction and conclusion?

Individuals may keep detailed outlines containing examples, statistics, personal experiences, or positions to be included under each major division. Just as an extemporaneous speaker may modify his speech, so the discussion group can depart from their outline because of changing conditions. The group members may find it impossible to include certain material, or they may forget to do so. Nonetheless, the program will have greater unity, clarity, and impact if the discussion group develops an outline to use as a basis for their program.

Here is a sample of an outline suitable for a 30-minute panel discussion:

intro. 1 min.	PURPOSE: To obtain audience involvement and participation in an important problem. QUESTION: What policy should the United States follow to halt the spread of communism in Latin America?

definition
2 min.
	1. What terms need to be defined?
	    a. What do we mean by communism?
	    b. What do we mean by Latin America?

5 min.	2. How widespread is communism in Latin America?
3 min.	3. Is it likely to spread further?
5 min.	4. Why is communism gaining influence in Latin America?
12 min.	5. What might our government do to stop the spread of communism in Latin America?
conclusion 2 min.	

The symposium discussion is somewhat easier to plan, since each member has a definite responsibility and a certain amount of time. The group should draw an outline similar to the one for the panel discussion and then assign the major topics to individual members. Here is a sample of an outline suitable for a 30-minute symposium discussion:

3 min.	Introduction of topic and speakers by moderator. PURPOSE: To obtain audience involvement and participation in an important problem. QUESTION: What policy should the United States follow to halt the spread of communism in Latin America?
6 min. each speaker	FIRST SPEAKER: The present situation. 1. Definition of terms. 2. Current state of communism in Latin America. 3. Evidence for future growth. SECOND SPEAKER: Factors encouraging the growth of communism in Latin America. THIRD SPEAKER: Economic solutions to the problem. FOURTH SPEAKER: Political and diplomatic solutions to the problem.

(additional minutes to allow a cushion for changing speakers)

Rehearsal of the panel discussion. A good program stops when audience interest and involvement are high. A rehearsal of the program helps to attain this objective. Since panel-discussion groups have a tendency to try to cover too much ground, a rehearsal will indicate whether the group has too much material. Of course, it will also reveal too little material on the agenda. The audience should leave the program feeling that they would have liked more time, but not that they needed more time to understand the material.

A rehearsal will also enable members to be more fluent during the program. Having expressed their ideas, participants will be able to find the words to express them again more readily. The pace of the program can then increase. In general, the faster people join in with comments, the greater sense of pace and tempo the program will project; also, pauses and gropings for expression that slow the pace will be reduced.

The discussion group must be careful not to rehearse so thoroughly that their program seems "canned" or mechanical. It is a mistake to destroy the illusion that the program is a spontaneous and informal discussion, and the overrehearsed group may sound like an amateur drama in which the cast has not learned its lines.

participating in an ad hoc meeting

CHARACTERISTICS OF A GOOD PARTICIPANT

The proper attitude for discussion. The participant should adopt an open-minded, objective, and unbiased attitude. He should listen to all points of view and describe problems as the observation of the facts indicates they are, rather than as he wishes they were. This ideal is often beyond reach of the participants, but it is a goal worth striving to approximate.

Balanced participation. A good participant contributes to the program with his full ability. His comments are short and to the point. He gears his contribution exactly to the topic and develops only one point at a time.

Good manners. Participants in ad hoc meetings do not have time to develop appropriate idiosyncratic group norms. Instead, certain culturally approved norms govern social interactions for strangers meeting for a brief discussion program. These norms are simply *good manners*— the regulation of conduct so that disagreements are tactfully phrased, other members of the panel and the audience are treated with courtesy, and others have an equal opportunity to participate. Breaches of good manners disturb the participants because they violate expectations. Tactless comments and impolite behavior suggest that some members of the group are not willing to abide by the generally accepted rules of behavior. The members, aware that working out a new set of standard operating procedures would require considerable time and energy, often become irritated by such behavior. For these reasons, the good discussant conforms to the expectations of tact, good manners, politeness, and courtesy. The discussant should not sacrifice relevant information or refrain from asking questions to test information for fear of embarrassing someone. The good participant manages to test information by suggesting with his language and manner that he is concerned with the *content* of what is being said, not the *person* who says it.

CHARACTERISTICS OF A GOOD MODERATOR

The participant expects one person to be responsible for procedural and administrative decisions relating to the meeting, just as one expects good manners among the discussants. The person who assumes this role is usually called a moderator, chairman, or leader. Since the term *leader* is defined in a somewhat different way in Part II, the label *moderator* will be used for the role in this chapter.

A moderator must have a commitment to the meeting and a desire to produce a good discussion. He should have enough time and energy to devote to the task. He should enjoy participation in discussions and in the give-and-take and frustrations sometimes associated with the process of inquiry. He should be a good speaker. Above all, he should be knowledgeable in the skills and principles of public discussion. He must know how to use discussion groups for various purposes and be familiar with the formats most suitable to his needs. He should understand the nature of inquiry and advocacy and the advantages and disadvantages of each kind of public program.

moderating the ad hoc meeting

DUTIES OF A MODERATOR

The moderator usually introduces the members to one another, and to the audience if it is a public meeting. He also introduces the topic and concludes the session. More important, he supervises the channels of communication and tries to involve a member who is not participating and to allow the person who has not spoken to have the floor before someone else has a second chance. He tries to keep one or two members from talking too much and keeps an eye on the time and the agenda. He tries to keep the group on the subject and on schedule. If the program is a public forum, he calls on members of the audience and controls the discussion much as the chairman of a parliamentary meeting does.

The moderator has many less well-defined duties pertaining to the social climate of the meeting. For example, the general social tone will be set early, and the moderator is largely responsible for establishing the mood that allows people to relax and to participate.

Since the role of moderator is so complex, the question of his substantive participation often arises. A case can be made for restricting the moderator to the special functions of administration and procedural control. If the panel contains an adequate representation of authorities and the moderator can serve little useful function by taking substantive part in the discussion, the meeting is better served if he confines himself to that role. But if the panel is small and the moderator is an authority or a person whose opinion the audience wants to hear, he may be both a procedural organizer and a contributor. If he chooses the latter course, he should announce his role early in the session so that the members will know what to expect.

The moderator has three basic tools to use in conducting procedural leadership during the discussion: the question, the summary statement, and the direction.

Asking questions. Many ad hoc meetings take place in a voluntary context and arouse expectations that democratic procedures will be used; that is, the audience assumes that all points of view will be presented, that everyone will be allowed to speak, and that majority opinion will prevail. They expect the moderator to be democratic and to ask people what they *want* to do rather than tell them what they *will* do. The question is one of the most important devices available to the moderator.

The moderator may phrase questions in such a way that they suggest a response of a certain kind. In one phrasing, the proper response is either *yes* or *no*. For example, the moderator may ask a panel member, "Dr. Homberg, are you a member of the American Medical Association?" Such questions are useful in getting a considerable amount of factual information quickly. Several skillful questions of this sort can reveal a great deal of information. However, such questions do not encourage participation. The aggressive participant may go on to a statement. Dr. Homberg might respond, "No, I do not belong to the AMA," and then interrupt the moderator's next question to say, "Just let me explain for a minute why I do not." But a participant who is reluctant to enter the discussion may simply respond with a "no."

Another kind of phrasing, characterized as either–or questions, suggests that *either* answer A *or* answer B is appropriate. "Do we want to explore this point further or should we move on to the next problem?" The form of the question makes it difficult to supply a third answer. An aggressive participant may respond, "Neither. I suggest we take a five-minute break," but participants are more likely to accept the implications of the question and select one of the suggested answers. The moderator can use questions of this type to suggest procedure and to structure the group's response without appearing autocratic. This sort of question is also useful in eliciting information quickly, but tends to restrict the range of responses.

A third kind of question is one that seeks a wide range of responses and is called the open-ended question. The moderator may ask, "Where should we begin?" or "How do you react to this suggestion?" Asked early, such questions are likely to be met with silence because they provide little suggestion as to the appropriate response. The participants must do too much of the structuring. In addition, the nervous tension present in the first minutes of a meeting often inhibits quick responses. Both of these factors can produce embarrassing silence. If the moderator senses that his panel is tense and unsure, he might begin with the more structured questions, moving to the open-ended type only after tensions have eased and the panel has warmed up. Open-ended questions suggest an atmosphere of respect for the group's opinion and suggestion. They emphasize the moderator's role as gatekeeper for group opinions and decisions rather than as a giver of directives. Open-ended questions are, therefore, democratic; but they can invite anarchy and confusion. Because they do little to structure the response, they may stimulate discussion far removed from the point under consideration.

On occasion, the moderator may wish to participate in the discussion without seeming to do so, and he may then use assertions framed in question form to present his ideas. Sometimes these questions are characterized as leading questions, loaded questions, or argumentative questions. However, the group will find it less confusing to think of these as *propositions* asserted in the grammatical form of questions rather than as interrogations or inquiries. The following are propositions asserted in question form:

> When will the AMA cease being a reactionary force and recognize the needs of the American people for medical security? (*Translation: The AMA is a reactionary force that does not recognize the needs of the American people for medical security.*)
>
> How do you explain the inconsistency in your position when you advocate freedom and in the next breath deny freedom of speech? (*Translation: You are inconsistent, for you both advocate freedom and deny certain individuals the right to speak.*)
>
> Don't you think that it is simple justice to give the man in a divorce proceeding equal rights before the law in regard to the custody of the children? (*Translation: Men do not now have equal rights before the law in regard to the custody of children, and this is unjust.*)

Generally, use of this technique is dangerous in public discussion. If the moderator uses many such assertions he will inject himself into the discussion in an indirect way that often confuses both the participants and the audience. If the participants are unaware of what he is doing, they become confused. They realize that something about the question prevents them from answering it as they would like to. The grammatical form of the statement tricks them into regarding it as an interrogation.

If they realize what is going on, they will treat it as an assertion and begin by answering that they do not agree with its assumptions or implications. This reaction involves the moderator as a debater. Thus, if the participant responds with violent disagreement to the assertion that the AMA is a force of reaction, the moderator is forced out of his role as moderator into a role as debater. He can retreat and resume his role as moderator or accept the challenge and continue the debate either with further assertions phrased as questions (which becomes quite a tax on his ingenuity) or with argumentative statements. If he does this, however, he places himself at some disadvantage, since he can no longer assume the role of a moderator objectively and dispassionately steering the discussion. Also, if he loses the argument, he will also lose considerable status and thus be less effective as a moderator. Finally, once the moderator enters a debate he may monopolize the proceedings, as his role includes the control of the channels of communication. A moderator needs much self-discipline to let a participant have the floor when he, himself, has a winning argument on his lips. Nonetheless, the moderator keeps this technique of propositions in question form in his repertoire so that when he thinks certain positions of importance are being slighted, he can express them. Sometimes he will use this technique simply to enliven a program that threatens to become very dull.

A discussion program often begins by orienting the audience to the facts in the case. Fact-finding questions are generally phrased as *what* questions: What is the case at Roosevelt High School? What are the current income tax rates in this state? By confining himself to questions that ask for factual information early in the program, the moderator is more likely to keep the group on topics that orient the audience. Factual information tends to be less controversial and thus is a good place to begin the discussion. The moderator may use yes–no, either–or, or open-ended questions. After the audience has been oriented, he often asks questions designed to isolate factors or causes that explain the facts. These can be thought of as *why* questions: Why has the United Nations failed to keep the peace in Southeast Asia? Why is there anti-American feeling in Latin America? After the audience has been oriented to the "why" of the case, the program may consider possible courses of action. Questions that emphasize *how* will then be useful. How might we overcome this anti-American feeling? How can we deal with drug problems at Roosevelt High School? How can we improve our divorce laws? As the group proceeds with the program, the moderator may periodically ask various participants to evaluate the accumulating facts and suggestions. Questions that imply the *what* form are most useful to get evaluations. The moderator may use yes–no, either–or, or open-ended questions to determine the *what*, the *why*, and the *how* of the topic. For example, he may ask "Do you think drug taking is immoral?"

"Do you think we should treat narcotics addicts as criminals or as mentally ill people?" "What do you think about the way drug addiction is treated in England?"

Making summaries. The second major device available to a moderator is the summary statement. Moderators often keep brief notes on the discussion to remind the group of what has been said, which may include direct quotations and condensed outlines of what has been covered. The summary statements can be brief or elaborate and may include some direct quotations in restating or outlining the proceedings. They may be expressed in terms of a familiar quotation or maxim. The moderator may say, "Well, then, we seem to be saying that we ought to do unto others as we would have them do unto us in the United Nations. Is that a fair statement of our position?"

Summaries are used primarily to organize the discussion program. Keeping both the time and the agenda in mind, the moderator can interrupt the discussion with a summary and lead the group from one topic to the next. If the group has drifted from the agenda, the moderator can bring them back by summarizing without including the digression. He can also use summaries to remind the audience of the program's overall structure. By emphasizing the main topics and their relationship, the skillful moderator furnishes a pattern that enables the audience to see the relevance of the details being discussed.

The summary can serve as a diversionary tactic when difficult social situations arise. The moderator can use a summary to stop a participant who talks too much without arousing social tensions, since the group generally accepts a summary as an important procedural function. Also, the moderator can interrupt any conflicts for a summary and prevent a situation from becoming painful.

Summaries will become less effective if overused and can irritate the participants. The moderator should not interrupt useful and heated discussions to summarize points that most of the audience has in mind anyway. If, however, he does not provide needed summaries, some other member may begin to do so.

Giving directions. The third tool of the moderator is the direction. If he gives directions tactfully and they seem useful to the group's purposes, they are generally obeyed and facilitate the procedure. The following examples indicate the nature of such directions:

> *Let's have each panel member make a very brief statement of where he stands on this question.*
>
> *Let's start with Roosevelt High School.*
>
> *Please raise your hands in the audience and I will give everyone a chance, but we must take one at a time.*

> *At this point I must stop the discussion of this topic so that we can consider some of the suggestions for improvement.*
>
> *Just a minute, Joe; you've talked on this before and some members haven't. Let's hear what they have to say.*

Skillfully given directions are willingly followed and help structure a program and enable brisk, logical progress. If the moderator is alert for cues, he can give directions the group will follow, because they feel the need for such structure and welcome the guidance. However, the moderator must avoid being dictatorial. If his directions seem to shut off discussion, or if he does not seem to give all sides a fair hearing, his directions may not be followed; instead of facilitating the procedure, he may cause conflict and confusion.

LEADING THE DISCUSSION

Getting the discussion started. Because a new social situation always creates some tension, the moderator faces a difficult task at the start of the meeting. Questions are among the useful techniques to get the program under way. The moderator should direct open-ended questions to the members most likely to respond with poise and fluency early in the session. Later on, he may wish to cut them off, but a talkative member is a big help at the beginning. Questions such as the following are useful in opening the discussion:

> *George, do you think we are in serious trouble in Southeast Asia today?*
>
> *Bill, what has been your experience in dealing with this problem?*
>
> *Joe, what is the situation as you understand it?*

The moderator should establish early that comments should be short and to the point. He can do this if he interrupts the first speaker and asks a direct question of another participant. The first few contributions should not sound memorized, but it can be useful to designate particular members to respond to his first two or three questions.

The discussion drifts off the topic. Among the most common problems facing the moderator is the natural tendency of a group to drift from topic to topic. When such tangents lead to important matters of interest, the skillful moderator recognizes their worth and lets the discussion proceed. More frequently, however, digressions are wasteful, and the moderator should end the digression by using questions, summaries, and assertions. Questions such as the following can focus the discussion once more:

> *Can we tie this in with the point about broken homes?*
>
> *Are we getting out in left field?*
>
> *Just a moment; how does this relate to the problem of who gets the custody of the children?*
>
> *Let's see now. I'm a bit confused. Where are we now in relation to our goals for this discussion?*

To assert that the group is off the subject and suggest that they return to the topic, the moderator may say:

> *We seem to be getting off the subject. Let's get back to what Bill said about the main problem.*
>
> *This is interesting, but it really doesn't help us much in regard to the question of responsibility.*
>
> *I've been listening to the last few minutes here and wondering how it ties in. We must return to the basic question that Helen mentioned earlier.*

Moving the program along. The group often expects the moderator to apportion the time they devote to each topic. The skillful moderator looks for cues from the audience and panelists that indicate the item under discussion has been adequately treated, and he then moves to the next point. He looks for a slackening of interest, drifting from the subject, and repetitions.

The group might be able to discuss the main question for hours, but they have to apportion their time so that all important points are raised and discussed briefly. The moderator must decide how much time the discussants can profitably spend on each major division of the outline and then move them from point to point even if he must interrupt a lively and pertinent discussion. He must balance the member's interest in the point under discussion with its importance in the overall discussion pattern. If he breaks in at a point that leaves both discussants and audience with a feeling of frustration and incompleteness, he may damage the effect of the entire program. On the other hand, if too much time is spent on one topic, other equally important or more important matters may be slighted. The moderator can try to foresee possible decisions of this sort *before* the program begins and work out some tentative plans to handle them. Even so, the situations that develop during the discussion may require improvisation.

The most useful technique for moving discussion to another topic is the summary, which concludes one section of the program and furnishes a transition for the next. The moderator may ask the group if they would like to move on, or he may state that they have spent enough time on a given point and direct them to change.

Helping the group reach a decision. From time to time, the group may feel the need of a consensus. The moderator can help if he steps in at such points and explains the consensus or decision for the participants. He may use such questions as the following:

> *Are we in substantial agreement then on this point?*
>
> *What have we done up to this point?*
>
> *Can we all agree that the problem is concentrated in the core of the city?*

The moderator may also assert that he senses agreement on certain issues and summarize the points of agreement. He may help the group to reach a majority decision by stating the issue and asking for a vote. A small group may vote by a nodding of heads, or, if no one disagrees, the moderator may simply assume a group decision. The unscrupulous moderator may manipulate a discussion at these decision points. He may use the evidence of silence to assert a group consensus when he does not really have majority support for his position. Members of ad hoc meetings should be alert for this tactic and object when it is used.

Even if the group fails to reach a decision, the moderator must bring the discussion to a satisfactory conclusion. The summary is the most useful device for this purpose. He can summarize any definite conclusions the group has reached. If the group has reached very few conclusions, he may make a "progress" report in which he indicates how much they have accomplished. If the group remains divided at the end of the meeting, the moderator may ask each member to summarize his individual position in place of his own customary summary.

HANDLING DIFFICULT SITUATIONS

Participants who monopolize the discussion. Perhaps no problem is more widespread and awkward for the moderator than the member who dominates the discussion. If the moderator is blunt in approaching the talkative member, he may embarrass the others. He can ask a yes–no question, and, when the talkative member answers, he can quickly direct an open-ended question to another participant. The following dialogue is illustrative:

MODERATOR: (*breaking in*) Just a minute, Joe; would you be willing to vote for a candidate who advocated a termination of all our foreign-aid programs?

JOE: Now I didn't say . . .

MODERATOR: I just want to clear this up. Would you vote for such a candidate?

JOE: Well, no, but . . .

MODERATOR: (*interrupting*) Bill, I wonder how you feel about this matter?

Sometimes, if the person who is monopolizing the discussion is speaking at an abstract level, he can be stopped with a question asking for specific information and examples.

JOE: Altogether too many people are going into bankruptcy because it is the easy way out. After all, why shouldn't someone go into bankruptcy when all you have to do is . . .

MODERATOR: (*interrupting*) Excuse me, Joe, but how many people in our state declared bankruptcy last year?

JOE: I don't have the figures right with me, but I know that there were way too many . . .

MODERATOR: (*interrupting again*) Just a moment. Does anyone have information on the rate of bankruptcy?

A summary interrupts and terminates a long-winded contribution. If his summary concludes with a direct question to a different member, the moderator can tactfully limit a talkative participant.

The moderator may have to use assertions about procedure to limit participation. He might use some of the following:

> *This is an extremely important point. Let's get the reactions of the rest of the group.*
>
> *Just a minute. You have raised three or four important points. Before you go on, I would like to spend a little more time on this question of responsibility. Let's hear what some of the rest of us think about it.*
>
> *You have made some very interesting and provocative statements. I notice several other members are eager to get into the discussion.*
>
> *I'm going to ask you to stop there for a minute and hold your next comment; everyone has not yet been heard on this point. Then we will come back to you.*
>
> *Let me interrupt here. We have so many people eager for the floor that I think the best way to proceed is to limit our comments to about one minute and give everyone a chance to speak once before anybody has a second turn.*

Participants who do not take part. A less spectacular, but almost as difficult, situation for the moderator occurs when a participant will not talk. The moderator should direct questions to the reticent member by name and should use open-ended questions rather than a yes–no or either–or type of inquiry. When he is drawing out a reluctant participant, he should ask relatively easy questions to avoid embarrassing the reluctant member. Thus, if the moderator is in doubt about the factual information available to the member, he should ask for his opinion instead. Questions such as the following are designed to draw out the reticent:

> *Bill, what do you think about this proposal to limit the university's enrollment?*
>
> *Jim, where do you stand on the moral issue involved in helping India use birth-control techniques to limit their population?*
>
> *Helen, we haven't heard from you about this yet. What do you think?*

Participants come in conflict. The moderator should not take sides in a conflict. If questioned about his opinion, he can relay the question to the group. "That is a tough one. Can someone on the panel answer?" Or he may return the question to the questioner. "Let me ask you: How would you answer the same question?" If he answers questions about substantive matters, the moderator will be drawn into the conflict, and becoming part of the discussion proper damages his ability to make procedural decisions.

If several participants come into conflict, the moderator should interrupt to focus attention on the group process rather than on the individuals in conflict. He can remind the *group* of the areas of agreement and admit that intelligent people differ, but that different opinions should be expressed calmly and rationally. He should emphasize the importance of the ideas rather than the personalities in the conflict and suggest that one of the virtues of a discussion is the opportunity it presents to understand all points of view. If the moderator can use humor (not sarcasm or irony) to relieve tensions, he should do so.

summary

The ad hoc meeting is a communication event composed of a group of people drawn together for a purpose that is to be achieved in one meeting. The composition of the group is unique to the single situation.

Because of its transitory nature, the ad hoc meeting accepts prescribed structures and uses stereotyping devices to provide procedures for doing its work.

Ad hoc meetings include the private discussion, the public discussion, and the conference or workshop.

The ad hoc meeting may be used to inform participants, to stimulate interest in a topic, to encourage participants to form their own opinions, or to aid in solving problems. The basic formats for public discussion include the forum, the panel, the symposium, and the interrogation. Forum discussions are those in which the audience is encouraged to participate; panels are organized around a topic in ways that encourage a free flow of communication; symposiums are set speeches by the participants, and the interrogation is a period devoted to questions and answers.

Certain special techniques of discussion are widely used in conferences. These include the buzz session, the standing committee, the case study, role-playing, and group games, exercises, and problems. These are often used as interest devices to encourage understanding of group pressures, to gain participant involvement, and to add interest to a conference.

A discussion is often organized around a general theme. Even so, a good meeting requires a working topic formulated as a question to limit and structure the program. The questions may be ones of fact, of value, of conjecture, or of policy.

The discussion program has much in common with the extemporaneous speech, and the group should have some planning sessions in which they develop an outline of their program. The outline consists of a series of questions that lead to the major points to be covered and often indicates the proportion of time allotted to each major division.

A skillful participant in a discussion exhibits an inquiring attitude, contributes in a balanced way, speaks to the point with short comments, and follows the accepted norms of tact and good manners common to ad hoc meetings.

The duties of the moderator include introducing the program and the participants, keeping the channels of communication open, drawing out the silent member, and discouraging the talkative participant. He checks the time and the agenda and holds the group to its plan and purpose. In addition to these procedural tasks, the moderator supervises the social climate of the meeting. He often relieves the stiffness typical of the beginning of a program. If conflict develops, he must minimize its disruptive influence.

The moderator has three basic techniques to perform his duties. These are: the question, the summary, and the direction. The question is most useful for the moderator using the democratic style of leadership. The summary helps to keep the program on the agenda. The directive is most helpful for a moderator using a more authoritarian style.

While leading the discussion, the most difficult tasks involve starting the meeting in a lively and spontaneous way, keeping the discussion on the outline, moving the discussion along, and helping the group reach a decision.

1. What is the difference between an ad hoc meeting and an ad hoc committee?
2. What are the cultural expectations for an ad hoc meeting in the United States?
3. What are some typical techniques for the conference?
4. What are some things to keep in mind when selecting a room for a discussion program?
5. In what ways are discussion programs different from and similar to committee meetings in which no audience is present?
6. What are the duties of a moderator?
7. What is the difference between a rhetorical question and an open–ended question?
8. For what purposes may a moderator use summaries?
9. How might a moderator get members to increase their participation in a group discussion?
10. How might a moderator deal with the member who talks too much in a group discussion?

EXERCISES

1. List 20 topics that you would like to discuss in class. There should be five questions of fact, five questions of value, five questions of conjecture, and five questions of policy. Take particular care to word the questions properly.
2. With four or five of your classmates, prepare a radio panel discussion. Appoint someone to introduce the panel and sign off the program. Prepare an outline for a 30-minute program. Tape record your discussion, and play it for the class.
3. With five or six of your classmates, prepare a symposium discussion. Prepare an outline for a 30-minute program, and allow the remainder of the hour for an audience forum period. Present the program for your class.
4. With five or six of your classmates, prepare a television interrogation program. Plan the program for 30 minutes. Allow the remainder of the period for class evaluation.
5. Evaluate the moderator in one of the panel discussions performed in class (or on radio or television), and discuss his ability to use questions, summarize, and give directions. How well did he handle the difficult situations?
6. Evaluate the participants in one of the panel discussions in class.
7. Attend a discussion program, and write a 500-word paper discussing the physical arrangements for the meeting. Suggest ways in which they might have been improved.
8. Listen to the tape recording of your panel discussion, and write a short evaluation of your participation.

References and suggested readings

For more information on brainstorming, see:

Osborn, Alex. *Applied Imagination*. rev. ed. New York: Scribner, 1957 (rev. 3rd ed., 1963).

Osborn suggests that the four main features of the brainstorming (group creativity) technique are: (1) criticism is ruled out; (2) freewheeling of ideas is welcomed—the wilder the ideas, the better; (3) quantity of ideas rather than quality is emphasized; and (4) hitchhiking or modification of ideas is encouraged.

For a description of the nominal group and suggestions on how to use it, see:

Huber, George P., and André Delbecq. "Guidelines for Combining the Judgments of Individual Members in Decision Conferences," *Academy of Management Journal*, **15** (1972), 161–174.

For more on planning public discussions, see:

Gulley, Halbert E. *Discussion, Conference, and Group Process*. 2nd ed. New York: Holt, Rinehart and Winston, 1968.
Wagner, Russell H., and Carroll C. Arnold. *Handbook of Group Discussion*. 2nd ed. Boston: Houghton Mifflin, 1965.

The buzz-session technique is often attributed to:

Phillips, J. Donald. "Report on Discussion 66," *Adult Education Journal*, **7** (1948), 181–182.

For role-playing, see:

Kane, Peter E. "Role Playing for Educational Use," *Speech Teacher*, **13** (1964), 320–323.

For more detail on the case-study technique, see:

Sattler, William M. "The Use of the Case Method in College Discussion Classes," *Speech Teacher*, **7** (1958), 216–225.

For aid in planning a conference, see:

Beckhard, Richard. *How to Plan and Conduct Workshops and Conferences*. New York: Association Press, 1956.
Kindler, Herbert S. *Organizing the Technical Conference*. New York: Reinhold, 1960.

For a compilation of games, exercises, and problems, see:

Pfeiffer, J. William, and John E. Jones. *A Handbook of Structured Experiences for Human Relations Training*. 4 vols. San Diego, Calif.: University Associates, 1969 (annually thereafter).

See also:

Gazda, George M., et al. *Human Relations Development*. Boston: Allyn and Bacon, 1973.

Johnson, David W. *Reaching Out.* Englewood Cliffs, N.J.: Prentice-Hall, 1972.

Otto, Herbert A. *Fantasy Encounter Games.* Los Angeles: Nash, 1972.

For a discussion of the use and impact of human-relations exercises, see:

Dunnette, Marvin D., and John P. Campbell. "Laboratory Education: Impact on People and Organizations," *Industrial Relations,* **8** (1968), 1–27.

For a survey of research in territoriality, personal space, and group spacial arrangements, see:

Shaw, Marvin E. *Group Dynamics: The Psychology of Small Group Behavior.* New York: McGraw-Hill, 1971, pp. 117–136.

See also:

Hare, A. Paul, and Robert F. Bales. "Seating Position and Small Group Interaction," *Sociometry,* **26** (1963), 480–486.

Howells, Lloyd T., and Selwyn W. Becker. "Seating Arrangement and Leadership Emergence," *Journal of Abnormal and Social Psychology,* **64** (1962), 148–150.

Sommer, Robert, *Personal Space: The Behavioral Basis of Design.* Englewood Cliffs, N.J.: Prentice-Hall, 1969.

Strodtbeck, Fred L., and L. Harmon Hook. "The Social Dimensions of a Twelve-Man Jury Table," *Sociometry,* **24** (1961), 397–415.

CHAPTER 14

THE TASK-ORIENTED SMALL GROUP AND THE ORGANIZATION

Some groups are short-lived and transitory, like those in discussion and small-group-communication classes. The basic model of role emergence in an LGD serves as an adequate explanation for the dynamics of such groups in general. Other groups are part of larger, well-established organizations. Organizations typically have formal structures and an organizational culture composed of a mythology analogous to the culture of the small group.

Often students wonder about the applicability of the theoretical material in Part II to the ongoing work groups that are part of a larger organization. Does the small-group-communication analysis that grows out of case studies of leaderless group discussions relate to the staff of an office for a large corporation, or to the faculty of a department in a college or university, or to the team of doctors, nurses, and paramedical assistants in a hospital? The answer to such questions, based on a survey of relevant research, observations of organizations, and the case studies of simulated organizations, is that the material in Part II does explain group process in the organizational context when the influence of other groups and the organizational mythology is taken into account.

The plan of this chapter is to apply the theory of group process and communication to the organizational context using information from both observation of organizations and from case studies of simulated organizations.

The University of Minnesota is a large urban university. Although the majority of students in the classes come from high school directly into the College of Liberal Arts, there are always numbers of students, particularly in upper-level courses, who are older, who have worked, or are working at the time they attend class. The range of ages and experience outside school is thus admittedly more varied than for the more homogeneous populations of some colleges and universities. One of the things that has been apparent to the investigators at Minnesota from the beginning of these simulations is the fact that most students who have continued their education uninterrupted to the junior year of college have little or no experience in self-structuring of a learning experience. These students complain the most about the "artificiality" of an organizational simulation and about the relevance of classroom group dynamics to the "real world." Trained so many years as competitive consumers–reproducers of information, they are uncomfortable when told that there will be a valuable learning experience when they go through an actual organization-building process which stresses cooperative effort rather than individual excellence.

Because the world of work and business is still unknown to these students for the most part, they appear to have assumptions that, once graduated and working, the "petty problems" that arise in a class simulation will be irrelevant, something they will put aside when joining the working world of adults. Often older students in the class point out that things are the same "out there," bringing to the class insightful applications of material in the simulations to the problems in which they are currently involved in some office or organization.

Since 1968, the small-group-communication class at Minnesota has been taught as a simulated organization. The instructor places the students in small task-oriented groups that are, in turn, made to form divisions of an organization called Group Dynamics, Incorporated. In Group Dynamics, Inc., as in most organizations, the larger group is divided into smaller task-oriented groups by a *formal* structure.

Because the class is taught in a laboratory setting, the meetings of all divisions of Group Dynamics, Inc., as well as the sessions of the Executive Committee and the large group meetings, are tape recorded, and a number of them are recorded on videotape. Members of the small-group-communication seminar, graduate students, as well as the instructor and teaching assistants, make nonparticipant observations that contribute to the case study of a given simulation. The members of the class spend several sessions making participant-observer studies of the organization. Most of the discussion in this chapter is drawn from 10 case studies of simulated organization. The Appendix describes the case-study procedure in greater detail.

The following discussion of the small task-oriented group in a larger social context is based primarily on the case studies of simulated organizations at Minnesota, to some extent on the Tavistock Workshop experiences, and on the work of Bales in observing self-analytic groups at Harvard.[1]

creating a formal structure to aid organizing

Among the more prominent and visible features of contemporary organizations are the formal aspects which include structures such as the table of organization, job descriptions, position titles, lines of authority, and formal channels of communication.

Often a student of small-group communication views the formal aspects of an organization as so influential and controlling on the dynamics of the small work groups within its context as to make the knowledge in Part II inapplicable. Thus, one of the first important questions relating small-group communication theory to the organizational context is the nature and effect of formal structure.

Figure 9 indicates the formal organization of a hypothetical firm called Invention, Incorporated. The table of organization is arranged in a status ladder. The manager is placed in a position above the first-line supervisor, the vice-president is placed in a higher position than the manager, and so forth. Associated with this formal status is a commensurate amount of *prestige*. Organizations attach clear evidences of status to each formal position. This evidence may be idiosyncratic, but the members of the organization can easily see and interpret it. Even an outsider will soon discover the marks of formal status. Material trappings often indicate status. How desks are arranged may be indicative. Does everyone have a desk? What sort of desk does he have: metal, wood, small, large? Where is it located? Is it in a "bull pen" with many other desks, or in a large, separate, carpeted office? What secretarial help is associated with the position—a private secretary, an executive secretary with several assistants? Movies and stage plays satirizing business have poked fun at the fact that possessing a key to the executive washroom is often an important evidence of status in such organizations.

Prestige is thus a function of formal position. A certain amount of prestige is accorded the person who occupies the position. As new people fill the positions, they are given the same amount of prestige.

[1] Since 1972, Professor William S. Howell has taught a section of the small-group-communication course at Minnesota in which he modifies the simulated organization by using some of the exercises of the Tavistock Workshops. The Tavistock approach grew out of the human-relations training program developed by the Tavistock Institute of Psychiatry in London. Essentially, the Tavistock approach is to take participants in a workshop numbering 30 or 40 and in an intensive week-long or 10-day program alternate small group meetings with intergroup exercises and large group meetings. The staff and participants in the Tavistock Workshops study the way power is earned and awarded among groups of people. Thus, the Tavistock experience is a way to study leadership contention and emergence not only in the small groups but in larger collections of individuals.

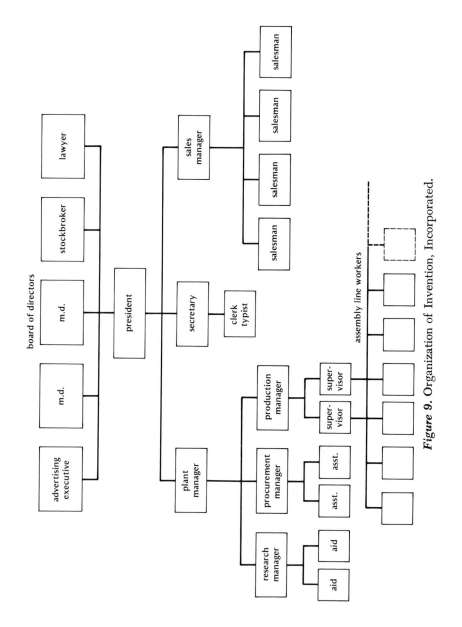

Figure 9. Organization of Invention, Incorporated.

RESPONSIBILITY AND AUTHORITY

Each position in the organization has certain tasks associated with it. These may include such things as dividing and assigning the work, determining and awarding salary increases, hiring and firing personnel. The formal position restricts the behavior of its occupant to some extent. The tasks associated with a particular formal position are the *responsibilities* of that position, and the individual who holds that position is held responsible for their successful performance.

The organization seldom spells out all the do's and don'ts. The occupant of an office may choose to do some things and not to do others. Because of this flexibility, the natural tendency of the small task-oriented group to develop roles for its members can operate along the lines of the basic model. Organizations differ in the amount of development their structure will allow. If the list of responsibilities is long and clearly specified, it will hinder the operation of the model more than if the job descriptions are quite short and vague. In addition, organizations that restrict the flow of communication to rigidly specified formal channels will inhibit the natural drive for roles to a greater extent than the organization that uses a complex network of informal communication.

Associated with the responsibilities and sanctions of each formal position is a commensurate amount of *authority*. Statements such as, "He has the authority to fire him," or "He is the only one in a position to make that decision," indicate the way organizations provide authority. Authority, like prestige, goes with the formal position regardless of the skills, talents, and achievements of the person in the position. The formal structure provides a context of authority and prestige in which the actual workings of the organization take place.

POWER AND ESTEEM

Authority may be exercised without effect, or it may be neglected. Authority is not the same as *power*. Power is the effective exercise of authority. Power is a function of the role a particular individual develops within the work groups to which he belongs. In the formal structure, each position of leadership entails the authority to sanction the actions of others. A position requires this authority to enforce its responsibilities. The informal role has the sanction of group acceptance. The leader who emerges during the group interaction has the willing cooperation of the others when he gives directions. The sanctions of group acceptance compose the power of the informal role. Since every person in a formal position also earns a role in the informal work groups, his responsibilities may differ from the group's expectations, and his authority may differ from his power.

During his work in a group, the man in a formal position will earn a certain amount of esteem. As power is to authority, so esteem is to prestige. The deference and other shows of esteem accorded *to the person* playing a role in the informal groups are associated with him whatever his formal position may be. Every individual in the formal organization has the prestige of his position plus the esteem he has earned in working out a role in the informal group.

The differences between authority and power and between prestige and esteem are illustrated by the difficulties the instructors encountered in trying to impose an organizational structure on a large, zero-history group. One of the major differences between the Tavistock Workshops and the Harvard self-analytic groups, on the one hand, and the simulations of an organization at Minnesota, on the other, is that the latter provides a formal organization to structure the larger group, which gives insight into the entire question of the relationship of organizational structure to the dynamics of small-group communication. The realities of difficulties arising constantly in real-world organizations can be demonstrated sufficiently in a classroom simulation to give some insight and understanding of highly complex organizational dynamics to a student.

Over the years, the instructors have revised the syllabus describing the structure of Group Dynamics, Inc., again and again. The first class periods are devoted to explaining the organizational structure and the duties of each division, the nature of the Executive Committee and its duties and responsibilities, and the composition and function of the Board of Directors. Despite the best efforts of the instructors, their attempts to set boundaries for divisions and to specify tasks and goals resulted in confusion in each simulation. The investigators first interpreted this as indicating that the explanation of the principles of the organizational structure was inadequate, but, after many case studies and many attempts at clarification, it became apparent that *organizational structure could not be imposed on the larger group any more than it could on the smaller ones.*

Earlier studies of the LGD had indicated that assigned roles did not serve to structure a zero-history small group, and the same principle applies to larger collections of individuals. Because a prospectus spelled out the structure in detail, it did not follow that the groups would understand and follow the structure. The people in the organization had to develop an understanding and perception of the organization, its goals, the relationships among the groups, the boundaries that separated the groups, and the channels of communication that tied them together *by actually trying to work together.* A common question once the small groups began to meet was: "What are we supposed to be doing?" Often the group would call the instructor or a teaching assistant in to a meeting to ask the same question. Even after elaborate explanations, the same question would continue to crop up for weeks.

After several weeks of working in the simulation, students would often suggest some minor change in the structure or some reorganization of the syllabus as a way to overcome the problems they had experienced or to encourage the easy and rapid imposition of a facilitating structure on the members of the organization. Some of the suggested adjustments sounded sensible to the investigators, and they adopted them in subsequent simulations only to find future suggestions sending them back to methods employed earlier; in other words, eventually, nearly all of the possibilities of structuring turned up again and again, none reducing the problem appreciably. In spite of the best efforts of instructors, investigators, and participants over the years, no "better way" to shortcut the process of organizing behavior of the individuals was found.

The informal structuring thus becomes the more important feature of the organizational context. That does not mean that the formal structure does not play an important part in the way a group works or in the satisfaction of its members, but simply that the visible elements of structure are not as important as they might at first seem.

If a formal structure cannot be imposed on a collection of individuals to form an organization, is there a general process or dynamic that characterizes the organizing efforts of a large, zero-history group? There appears to be.

intergroup competition

When groups are set in competition, as in athletic conferences, the teams tend to develop similar patterns of internal communication and similar fantasies to explain victory and defeat. In the Minnesota Studies, groups were put into competition by having them do a task force investigation and write up the results of their work in a comprehensive report which was then ranked against the efforts of the other groups in the class. Thus, if there were five groups, one was ranked first, one second, and so forth.

Schein summarized the results of research in intergroup competition in the field of social psychology, and his findings agree with the discoveries of what happened when the LGDs were put in competition at Minnesota. The following description characterizes groups in competition.

Generally, the result of competition among groups is an increase in intragroup cohesiveness, and the group climate moves from casual and playful to more work-oriented. Each group becomes more highly structured and organized, and members demand more loyalty and conformity so that they may present a united front against opponents.

The content of internal communication is characterized by dramatizing the insiders as heroes and the members of the opposing groups as villains. The communication presents only the good part of the in-group and denies the group's weaknesses. Conversely, the group's internal messages tend to present only the worst aspects of the other groups and to deny their strengths. The groups develop negative characterizations in their fantasy chains of the others: "They do not play fair like we do." The emotional tone of the fantasies encourages hostility and hatred toward the other groups, and communication among the groups decreases, thus making it easier to maintain the negative characterizations and more difficult to correct perceptual distortions.

When the results begin to come in, and one group is clearly the victor in the rankings, the winners tend to become more cohesive, to release tension, and to enjoy intragroup cooperation. Sometimes the winners may begin to neglect the task because of the rewards of cohesiveness and the social status afforded winners. The winning group may now fall prey to a "fat and complacent" stage. The group becomes overconfident and lazy. The members may become self-satisfied and sure that their group is the best (as they had always thought) and that the enemy groups are bad, so there is no need to keep up their task skills or to reevaluate the reality of their perceptions.

The losers often begin to chain into fantasies that deny or distort the reality of their losing. They did not really lose. The judge's evaluation was wrong, or, in a close game, a technicality went against them, or one fluke play caused the score to fail to reflect the relative value of the competing teams. They did not really lose, the game was stolen by blind luck or a bad judge. If the group reevaluates its fantasies and accepts the loss, the members may splinter into hostile cliques; conflicts may come to the surface; blame for the loss is assigned. Having first fantasized a scapegoat external to the group to account for why they did not really lose, the group, once coming to accept the reality of losing, tends to search for an internal scapegoat to account for their failure. The group becomes more tense, but may be ready to work harder. The leader tends to have low cooperation from members and may begin to drop concern for member needs and emphasize task matters. The spiral may continue with greater resentment of the new tougher leadership style, greater fantasizing, and a tradition of losing or a loser's culture may come to characterize the group.

Very much the converse can happen, of course, if the members of the losing group come to learn a lot about the group because the positive characterization of itself and the negative view of the enemy have been challenged by the fact of the upset by the competition. The group may reexamine the situation and may, if the members utilize the loss as a way to improve their social and task dimensions, become more cohesive and effective.

Interestingly enough, many of the characteristics of competitive group communication were illustrated in the groups staffing the simulated organization, even though the instructors made every effort to create a cooperative orientation toward intergroup effort.

A TERRITORIAL EXPLANATION FOR COMPETITION

Research is accumulating that suggests that many animals have a sense of territoriality. A fox, for example, will stake out a certain geographical region as its "territory," and, when another fox invades its region, it will fight viciously to defend what it considers its borders. Some research indicates that human beings have a similar sense of territory. People are generally more comfortable with the known rather than the unknown, with the familiar rather than with change. Certainly, most young children demonstrate great anxiety when something new and different threatens a comfortably familiar situation. Students tend to sit in the same place in the classroom and tend to be disturbed if someone else sits in their place. People save seats in a public auditorium by placing a personal object such as a coat on the chair and are disturbed if their "squatter's rights" are invaded. Although it is undoubtedly going to become an increasingly valuable skill for people to learn to adapt to rapid changes, as Toffler argues in *Future Shock*, it is nonetheless a skill to be acquired, not one normally present in most people. The human desire to surround oneself with the familiar and stable seems to coincide with the animals' more vocal and obvious demand that "this spot is mine." The case studies of the organizing behavior of individuals in larger groups suggest that a similar mechanism of territoriality is operating at the rhetorical level of social reality.

The members of Group Dynamics, Inc., did exhibit the feeling for geographical place suggested by the research. Often a group would come to feel very early that a certain room or meeting place was "theirs" and would become angry if another group met in their room. But, in a much more important way, the case studies of the organizing behavior of individuals suggest that something like the sense of territoriality was operating at a level of social reality in which the territories were not geographical but jurisdictional and were related not to tangibles alone but also to duties, responsibilities, status, power, and authority.

After their first confusion, the groups began to stake out organizational functions and responsibilities for themselves rhetorically, that is, they did some things and watched what the other groups were doing and drew a verbal boundary around their place in the organization. When they perceived that another group was doing something that they felt was their prerogative, they attacked the other group angrily with the charge that it had done "our job." The other group quite typically responded with outraged innocence, arguing that the task they had performed was, indeed, their prerogative. Then the "legal experts" in both groups were likely to search the prospectus for the organization for supporting words and phrases which they used in arguments, or the more antagonistic group members might engage in a shouting match. Sometimes the group that was charged with overstepping its bounds agreed that it had done the other group's work, but maintained that the other group was not doing its task and that, since someone had to do it, they had picked up the slack.

STRUGGLE FOR ORGANIZATIONAL TERRITORY

As the groups defined their territory, they came into competition, and some of the groups began to drive for larger territories in terms of jurisdiction and organizational power. The mechanism of empire building in an organization which is sometimes apparent in long-standing organizations came into play early in the simulations.

In one of the simulations, the executive group made few efforts to administer the organization, and a stronger-than-usual power vacuum resulted. One of the five groups comprising the organization had done exceptionally well with the task force reports and had developed a group culture with strong motivation for achievement. In their fantasy chains, they saw the other groups as inferior to themselves. They happened to have the responsibility for developing the class syllabus and instruction. Before long, it became apparent that the group was, in fact, running the entire organization. They were not only planning and implementing the instructional program, but were also scheduling events and using equipment without the help of the other units.

Soon the other members of the organization began to resent the efforts of this top group. After a time, a revolt erupted, and the powerful group was charged with unauthorized exercise of power. When the class interrupted the organization in order to make a participant case study of what had happened, they discovered that by simply viewing each group as analogous to an individual in the model of role emergence (Chapter 9), they could also account for the way the groups organized themselves into the larger unit. The five groups faced an unorganized and unstructured situation. Various groups tried to perform organizational functions and were rewarded or punished by the other groups. In the presence of a power vacuum the group that was highly cohesive and efficient stepped in and began to run the entire organization. The others, however, were not pleased with the group's manner of leadership, nor were they certain that the group should have so much unchallenged power; the result was a showdown.

intergroup communication

One difference between the jockeying for position in the simulated organization and in the small group is the nature of the communicative distances involved. Usually the channels of communication within a group are relatively available to all members in a face-to-face setting. (Even so, of course, as discussed in Chapter 12, the free flow of communication is often impeded by status differences, coalitions, and other crippling norms.) When people are members of small groups trying to work together in a larger organizational context, however, the availability of communication channels is restricted, and, at the same time, the distance between source and receiver is often increased. Communication often travels through other people, as when a representative to the Executive Committee returns to his group and reports what happened or, in turn, goes to the Executive Committee and reports what is going on in his group. Informal channels often consist of networks of people, so a group may get a message from a member who got it from a member of another group while standing in the hall, and the member of another group may have received the information from still a third party.

Because the distances and the availability of communication channels within an organization make high-fidelity communication in the pragmatic style more difficult, the frustrations and unhappiness of organizational members tend either to be pent up and unexpressed in sanctioned ways, or to explode in a crisis situation. Often members express frustration in small informal groups of three or four or to the instructors, or even to their fellow group members, but take no formal action on the rationalization that it would not help, or that the structure is too difficult to change, or that the power system is too entrenched, or because it is only a class and not worth all the effort required. Thus, problems may fester longer in the organization without corrective action than they do in the LGD. When these pent-up difficulties surface, however, the confrontations tend to be more violent and emotional.

the power explanation of conflict

The discoveries of the Tavistock Workshops as described by Rice corroborate the insights from the case studies at Minnesota with regard to the importance of power and its assumption in the organizational context. The Tavistock Workshops have evolved to the point where the staff emphasizes the study of power and how it is earned and awarded in social groups. The Tavistock approach is thus much different from that of the groups in the consummatory style such as T-groups, encounter groups, or strength groups.

Rice maintained that an unstructured large group was a terrifying experience for the members because it was potentially unreasonable and violent. The Tavistock analysis is psychiatric in its basic assumptions, and the account suggests that subconscious and violent forces may be unleashed easily by a large group of human beings unrestrained by norms, formal structure, or established power and authority. Since the members instinctively feel the threat of the unstructured group, they search desperately and early for an authority figure and tend to find it in the leader and staff of the workshop. One of the Tavistock exercises consists of assembling the large group of participants and then having the staff leave the room without explanation, thus throwing the group on its own resources.

The case studies of simulated organizations discovered similar forces at work among the members of the larger groups at Minnesota. The members often turned to the instructors for salvation. Frequently, they expressed disbelief that they could now plan and implement the syllabus for the course. Repeatedly, they would test the limits of their power, often by suggesting that they would eliminate a scheduled examination, and then, when they became convinced that, indeed, they did have the authority to take control of the class, they became frustrated and angry as though the instructors had let them down. The members' ambivalence to power and authority was thus a major feature of their early organizing effort. They did, as Rice argued from the Tavistock experience, seem to fear the unstructured group. They wanted the security of norms and limits and clear jurisdictional boundaries and, on occasion, seemed willing to take orders from a strong authority figure. At the same time, however, whenever anyone or any group in the organization began to take power, the other members would rise up and challenge and often depose the individual or the group.

the authority and power of the executive committee

The syllabus gave the Executive Committee the authority to set goals, allocate resources, and coordinate the work of the various units—the typical functions of management. When they began the simulations, the instructors assumed that, once a leader emerged in the small groups, the members would select that person again to represent them on the Executive Committee. However, the groups did not always, or even a majority of the time, send their emerged leaders to the management group. Often the groups sent one of their negative central persons to the Executive Committee, or they sent a disgruntled leader contender or a talkative inflexible person who was the focus of negative attention. These groups saw the Executive Committee as a convenient way to find some role function for a troublesome member although, in actuality, the member continued to meet with his original group as well as meeting with the Executive Committee.

Some groups saw the Executive Committee duties as a different set of role functions from those of internal group leadership. They appeared to fear that if they sent their leader to the Executive Committee, he would cease to continue to play the desired leadership functions within the group. When the members discussed the role functions required for their Executive Committee representative, they would often talk in terms of the group's parochial interests. The group might see the Executive Committee as a sort of battleground for the conflicts among the groups, and, thus, they would chain into a fantasy in which "their" representative had to battle the others for their group's rights and prerogatives. The kinds of aggressive skills and toughness required for such organizational infighting, which they perceived as necessary, might not be the sorts of skills they preferred in their own leader.

The following transcript is of a group meeting after the members had selected their representative to the executive group, and he is preparing to go to the first meeting where the Executive Committee is to assign the groups to the various divisions of the organization. The group fantasy chain emphasizes pugnacity and fighting. Indeed, the Mafia becomes one of the heroic institutions in their fantasy chains, although, to be sure, in a joking and satirical style. The group came to talk much of shooting, rubbing out, and fighting.

MEMBER A: (*Now assigned to the Executive Committee and explaining his strategy*) I'll just go up there and say . . . I don't . . . You know I'm, I'm pretty much for P & F. [The initials for the division of the organization then called Plant and Facilities.] Our group said that if you don't come back with it they're going to . . . you know . . . they're going to go off by themselves, they, they don't . . . you know . . . we're going to sell our stock.

[*Group laughing, chorus of "That's right."*]

MEMBER A: (*continues*) We're getting out.

[*Group now chaining into fantasy and background murmurs of agreement and encouragement.*]

MEMBER A: (*continues*) Yeah, we quit . . .
MEMBER B: (*talking over member A*) If you don't give us what we want, I mean, we've got the money . . .

[*All are talking and giggling at once.*]

MEMBER A: We'll start our own corporation!
MEMBER C: I want to fight.
MEMBER A: (*dramatizing, addressing the "corporation"*) Listen, I know a prospective buyer. Er, he's a . . .

[*Group laughing and giggling.*]

MEMBER A: (*continues*) I hear you haven't been doing too good a job lately.

MEMBER B: (*joining in the dramatizing*) I hear this other speech class
wants to buy this class out. You better . . .
MEMBER A: . . . form a conglomerate . . .
MEMBER C: That's right. Get the Mafia going . . .

Another group held the following discussion when they picked their
representative to the Executive Committee. Member A noted that it
would be a "dog-eat-dog type of thing—everyone's out for themselves."
Member B said that she thought of Member D for the job, but felt
he was too quiet for such "dog-eat-doggers." Member C added that
Member D's work schedule was also a problem. Member D agreed
that his work schedule was a problem, but, in regard to the point about
his quietness, he stated that he could be a "bastard" if he had to, "I
mean, if I need to, I could play that role pretty good."

The members of the two groups were clearly preoccupied with
jurisdictional boundaries and their prerogatives, and they saw the organization as a battleground in which they needed a strong fighter for their
rights and position representing them on the Executive Committee.
Under such circumstances, a group would often send someone other
than their leader to the committee.

Usually, despite the way the groups selected representatives for
the Executive Committee, that group would begin to structure itself
in much the same manner the original groups had and, once organized,
would begin to try to manage the organizational effort. Once the Executive Committee began to function, its members supposedly being repre-
sentational, the groups and members began to question its authority
and to resist its efforts. One prominent feature of every simulation has
been an authority crisis that has precipitated the calling of a showdown
meeting of the entire class.

THE CRISIS MEETING

Whatever behind-the-scenes activity led up to the calling of the crisis
meeting, the session was always ostensibly called by the Executive Committee. The Committee canceled regular work in the organization and
explained that the session was to be devoted to problems of the organization and its function. The Executive Committee usually sat in front
of the others and faced them in a climate of drama. On one occasion,
only two members of the Executive Committee were in the front of
the room, but, before the end of the meeting, the other class members
had urged the rest of the Executive Committee to move to the front
of the room as well.

In a majority of instances, the crisis meeting clearly either legiti-
mized or denied the authority of the Executive Committee. In order
for leadership to emerge in the larger group, there seems to be a need

for several "devil figures" to emerge in the large group sessions. So far, only one class has failed to produce its devil figures in one guise or another. The devil figures tend to be vociferous talkers, usually express themselves in strong and emotional language, and tend to fantasize rather than reason. They typically attack the values of the majority of the members and the actions required to make the organization a success. They often assert that the organization is trivial, childish, unimportant, or silly. They accuse the others of self-aggrandizement and assert that they will not be bound by group decisions. One such individual gleefully reported to the instructors that she was going to sabotage the entire organization. Devil figures are seldom as candid as this; more often, they are people genuinely frustrated by various factors during the tense period of organizational formation. Somehow, they want things changed.

The devil figures resemble the negative central persons of small groups except that they seem magnified in the fantasy themes of the small groups and, in the informal grapevine of rumor and gossip that grows up within an organization, they become larger-than-life symbolic figures in the rhetoric of the members. The magnification results from the emotional tone of their rhetoric in the large group meetings, from their ability to dramatize in a way that disturbs the majority of the members, and by the way they are characterized as villains in the fantasy chains of the small groups.

When the Executive Committee opens up the crisis meeting for discussion of the organizational problems, one of the devil figures typically rises and makes an impassioned attack on the Committee and on the way the organization has been going. As the emotional tone of the meeting rises, more members are drawn into the discussion, and the devil figures use every opportunity to get the floor to continue the attack. After a time of airing of grievances, another central negative type of individual usually responds to the devil figures. Someone usually makes an impassioned speech to the effect that much time is being wasted in silly bickering, and he, for one, is fed up with it and with the immature way people are acting. Why not decide on what has to be done and give the Executive Committee the authority to do it and then the class can get on with its work and the organization can get something done? Often, if the devil figures have created sufficient animosity, the impassioned call for law-and-order and efficiency will cause some others to chain into their vision, and the spokesman for the position may well gain the floor again. The more he talks, however, the more apparent it becomes that he sees himself as the logical person to take over the controls of the organization, and, if he has his way, the lines of authority will be clear, the orders will be unequivocal, and the others will have to do as they are told.

In some simulations, the Executive Committee picks up on the enthusiasm generated by the call to legitimatize its authority. The spokesmen for the Committee, after the harangues from the extremists, begin to make suggestions for constructive effort. When moderate members attempt to modify the suggestions, the Executive Committee seems open-minded and flexible. The meeting then ends with a formal vote of support for the Executive Committee. The management of the corporation having been legitimatized, the members of the Executive Committee then serve the important organizational function of transcending the boundaries of the individual cohesive groups and generating commitment to the entire organizational effort. Once the members see themselves as part of the total effort—as well as members of the smaller groups—they find it easier to work cooperatively with other groups and the competitive, conflict-ridden early stages of organizing give way to a more cooperative mode of procedure.

In some simulations, at the crucial point in the meeting where skillful leadership from the Executive Committee would coalesce the center into support and a vote for legitimatization, the spokesmen for the Committee have, instead, responded in an emotional, tactless, dictatorial, or inept fashion. The meeting then would continue on in an acrimonious and emotional fashion, and, although no actual call for a vote to legitimatize the Committee was made, the Executive Committee would in fact be discredited in the minds of the members, and the power vacuum that remained had to be filled by some other group.

Bales discovered a similar phenomenon to the dynamic interplay of devil figures, those who challenge the basic assumptions and values of the organization, and those, on the other hand, who call for strong measures of authority and power. He reported that the members of the 25-person self-analytic groups expressed values that could be distributed through group space in a spiral fashion.[2] The spiral resembled the distribution of opinion in the stereotype of the political spectrum. Bales found members ranging from the far left, to the liberal parties, on through the center parties, through the conservative center parties, to the far right. Bales characterized the members of the far left as completely rejecting traditional values of religion, economics, and politics. The far left does not feel part of the traditions of the local community and does not feel bound by the values and rules associated with it.

---

[2] Bales reported in 1970 (*Personality and Interpersonal Behavior,* New York: Holt, Rinehart and Winston) that because of lack of space and resources he and his associates have been teaching a human-relations course composed of 25 members in a laboratory setting rather than the smaller groups he had used in prior research studies. Bales reports the results of several year-long case studies of such larger groups. As a result of participant and nonparticipant observation of naturally formed groups in the classroom, data are accumulating about the way people go about organizing themselves in larger groups.

The far left in Bales' case studies of self-analytic groups resembles the devil figures who trigger the mechanism by which power and authority came to be legitimatized in Group Dynamics, Inc. The far right, according to Bales' study of value profiles, identifies with power and authority and tends to view itself as the legitimate source of authority. The member in the far-right position in group space is a strong proponent of autocratic leadership and discipline.

In the one simulation when the crisis meeting took place without the emergence of the devil figures, the Executive Committee opened the meeting and suggested the presence of grievances, but no one rose to ventilate the problems, and the meeting limped along in anticlimactic fashion. The Executive Committee, having presided over an unsatisfactory session in which nothing was settled, did not pursue the matter further. The grievances festered, and the Executive Committee withdrew further and further into fantasy chains about past mistakes and who was to blame for failures rather than taking action to meet current problems. The effect of the crisis meeting was that the Executive Committee drifted along in an ineffective manner. What happened then in this particular simulation will be discussed later in the chapter. What the investigators learned, however, was that the need for disagreements for the airing of differences of opinion in small groups clearly parallels a need for devil figures in larger groups to voice grievances and to force the larger group to face up to the problem of power and authority.

formal and informal structures

The attempts to impose the structure of Group Dynamics, Inc., in its entirety on the members of the organization as blueprinted in the syllabus always failed. The formal hierarchy of status, authority, and responsibility as well as the specializations and jurisdictional lines for the various divisions were reinforced, discounted, and changed by the informal groupings, communications, and interactions that developed among the members as they worked together. On the other hand, in only one simulation was the formal structure completely overthrown. In all the others, elements of the formal structure continued to exercise an influence on the group. For some simulations in which the Executive Committee was legitimatized, the prospectus of Group Dynamics described the evolving organization quite well. The formal and informal structures of the organization were similar. In other simulations, particularly those in which the Executive Committee failed to achieve authority and power, the informal structure that evolved was quite different from the organization described in the prospectus.

In one sense, the informal departures from formal structures in an organization represent a blurring of the lines of control, of the communication channels, and of the specializations established to increase the efficiency of the institution. Usually, the students assumed that the organization would be much more efficient if the formal map matched the actual operations. Some members of the organization usually viewed departures from the formal structure with alarm. Actually, in the simulations, whether or not the organizational structure that evolved was similar to the structure described in the prospectus seemed relatively unrelated to the efficiency of the final organization. The satisfaction, morale, and commitment of the members seemed relatively unrelated as well.

However, the simulations differed in one important respect from most ongoing institutions such as business companies, educational institutions, governmental agencies, cooperatives, and voluntary associations in that they were relatively closed systems in terms of membership. Most long-term, large-scale organizations are open systems in the sense that a portion of the membership is constantly changing. Old members leave, new members take their places, or the expansion and contraction of the organization cause new members to be added or old members to be discharged. In the classroom simulations, every member participated in the creation of the informal structure of the organization and understood it quite well. New members of established organizations must learn the informal as well as the formal structure.

Informal departures from formal structure make it more difficult for newcomers to become acculturated and productive. When power and authority coincide, when prestige and esteem approximate each other, then those unfamiliar with the informal structure and dynamics of the organization will be able to work together with less tension and wasted motion. Learning all the ins and outs—including skeletons in the closets, feuds, and attachments—requires time, effort, and tact. The energy devoted to such study could be invested in other activities if the organizational map fits the territory. On the other hand, formal structures tend to be static. In only one simulation did the group draft and adopt a new formal structure. The demands on an organization are dynamic, and, thus, the static formal structure cannot meet all of them successfully. The more rapid changes facing any organization must be accommodated by the informal structure.

Changing membership in an organization gives the formal structure a greater influence on new members because of the sanctions involved in formal positions with fate control over subordinates. In addition, established informal structures influence new members because of the pressures for conformity to old established organizational norms.

WHEN THE EXECUTIVE COMMITTEE IS AWARDED AUTHORITY

The following interplay of formal and informal structures is illustrative of what happened when the Executive Committee was legitimatized as the authority group for the organization.

In one simulation, the Executive Committee emerged from the crisis meeting with a vote of confidence. They moved with dispatch to take action to manage the organization, and soon their directives were being followed willingly. They had earned the power that goes with the authority conferred by the vote of confidence. A general feeling of commitment to the organization and the class spread throughout the membership with the exception of three or four alienated or isolated persons. The groups began to cooperate and communicate more with each other. The distortions of insider heroes versus outsider villains began to disappear from their internal communication. The formal structure of the syllabus came to describe the organization rather well. The various divisions functioned as specialists in roughly the areas staked out in the prospectus. The group members developed some feeling of kinship with members in the other groups and expressed a desire to "get to know" other class members. They organized informal meetings, parties, and get-togethers to facilitate the social bonds throughout the organization. (Interestingly enough, the organizational party cropped up in all the simulations as regularly as the big crisis or showdown meeting. Usually, however, the successful organizational party came later in the organization's life than the big blow-up did.)

In another simulation, the Executive Committee was legitimatized by the major confrontation meeting, but as the organization continued, although the Executive Committee functioned as the overall power group, spontaneous groupings of individuals arose to perform various projects related to the organization's work. The organization functioned like what Toffler called an *ad hocracy*. Three or four members would get together and develop a project which they then would take to the Executive Committee and ask for organizational resources to implement their effort. As these spontaneous groupings came to characterize the work norms, the formal groups ceased to do much on tasks, although they continued to meet and to perform some social functions. In this simulation, then, the formal structure no longer provided much of a description of the task specialization and coordination of the members, although the participants continued to use the names of groups provided by the prospectus to discuss the organization.

WHEN THE EXECUTIVE COMMITTEE IS NOT AWARDED AUTHORITY

In one simulation, the Executive Committee never took decisive action and essentially abdicated from any effort at achieving power in the group. The organization was thus left with a stronger-than-usual power vacuum. One of the groups had responsibility for the development of a class syllabus and its implementation. This was the group mentioned earlier that soon appeared to be, in fact, running the entire organization, not only planning the instructional program but also scheduling events, using equipment, and evaluating work without the help of the other units. The major confrontation meeting in this simulation was not with the Executive Committee but with the group that had taken control. The group members defended themselves vigorously and maintained they had been unjustly attacked. They in turn expressed grievances with the organization including their perception that they had tried to do a good job, had worked hard, and had received for their efforts on behalf of the organization only attacks, resentments, and unwarranted charges of power grabbing. In the course of talking out the conflict, the other members of the organization recognized the contribution of the group and explained that they did not want the powerful group to cease all activity, but simply to cease monopolizing all of the "interesting" work. The group accepted the criticisms, and its position was legitimatized as the top group. The Executive Committee continued to meet, but it became an ineffectual figurehead group. As the organization continued to evolve, spontaneous groupings formed, and the structure of Group Dynamics, Inc., no longer related to much of the organizing behavior of the class. Interestingly enough, however, in this simulation, too, the terminology of the various divisions continued.

In still another simulation, the confrontation meeting with the Executive Committee was unsatisfactory and did not resolve the grievances. As difficulties continued, another confrontation meeting was called late in the term and found a group of rebels presenting a completely new plan of organization that involved rescinding the structure imposed by the syllabus and setting up a troika to organize and manage a large final project and to establish a whole new set of divisions to which members were assigned. In a stormy session, a majority supported the new plan, and it was quickly and efficiently put into operation. An interesting feature of the proposal was that members of the troika were to be elected, but, in order to be considered, one would have to nominate himself and be willing to testify to the desire to serve and to put in the extra time and effort to make the new plan work. Once elected and legitimatized in this fashion, the members of the troika were able to manage the setting of goals, the assignment of tasks, and the integration of effort without the pulling, hauling, and quibbling over jurisdiction, prerogatives, and authority that had characterized the organization for weeks up to that point. The dynamic interweaving of group demands and allowable styles of leadership was clearly demonstrated in this simulation. Also, the importance of timing was illustrated by the fact that the earlier confrontation did not work. Had the exact same suggestion for a new structure come earlier, it probably would have been rejected.

communication and power

The communication within and among groups tended to follow the typical patterns of groups in competition and conflict until the problem of power and authority had been settled. Once a group of individuals had been legitimatized as having authority and once these people assumed the power to structure the organization, the scapegoating for failure, the paranoia about territory, and the fantasy themes that presented the organization as the battleground for group conflict were transcended. The rhetoric of the membership began to include celebrations of the entire organization, and their fantasies began dramatizing other groups as allies and colleagues rather than as competitors and enemies. With the transcending rhetoric came more cooperative effort and more efficient work patterns.

The dynamic of larger groups is apparently analogous to the process of small groups in many interesting ways. In addition, the model of the LGD explains the process of the small groups in the organizational context when the influence of the other groups and the organizational power struggle, jurisdictional disputes, and mythology are all taken into account.

applications to established organizations

Much of the theoretical material in Part II can now be applied to the operation of small groups in the context of established organizations with changing membership and an established formal structure that includes powerful sanctions relating to monetary rewards, work opportunities, and status satisfactions.

WHEN NEW MEMBERS JOIN THE GROUP

Assume that a task-oriented group with a clear and stable role structure and a high level of cohesiveness find it advisable to add a new person. If the new member could be assigned duties other than those jobs being done by the original personnel, the old role structure could continue. However, the new participant must be integrated into the existing role structure. He brings a unique complement of skills and talents to the group, and these must be utilized. The group must decide which functions now being performed by old members will be assumed in whole or in part by the new person. Assume that he is a star who can perform leadership functions with great skill. He meets with the group for only a short period before he begins to challenge the leadership moves of the established leader. If the leader is popular, the new man will be rejected, and the group will close ranks around the established person. The new member will feel the rebuff and resent it. Secondary tension will arise, and the others will perceive the new man as a troublemaker, remembering that no trouble existed before he arrived. If possible, the new man will leave the group. If he cannot, he may be frustrated enough to try to form a clique of antileader sentiment. Often he will retreat into inactivity and become "dead wood."

Many leaders are not popular enough to ward off a challenge so quickly. Leaders must make decisions for the welfare of the group that may be contrary to the ideas or desires of certain people. In addition, low-status people typically harbor some resentment and envy of high-status individuals. The new person will probably get support for a challenge of the old leader, at least for a time. If the old leader is weakened or deposed, the established group will be in a situation very much like that of an LGD just beginning its work. All the roles will be reshuffled into new clusters of functions. Even if the new man does not challenge the leader for his role, he may challenge others for their roles. The addition of a new member results in a situation reminiscent of the game of musical chairs. Six people must fit into five places.

Absorbing a new recruit is painful, and veterans often fail to understand what is going on. Things were going smoothly; but, when the new person joined, everything changed. An easy way to release their frustrations is to blame the new man.

Most established organizations experience a turnover of personnel. They may establish formal procedures to minimize the strain on old employees when new people join. The new person is often forced to begin on the lowest level of group work and is assigned less attractive duties. The organization may use seniority to protect the older workers, as it arbitrarily limits the amount of participation of new people. The freshman senator is often given a few unimportant committee assignments. He is expected to wait until he is accepted before he takes an active role. If he speaks too soon or too brashly, he is chastised by those senators having seniority. New employees in industry often must build up seniority before they are given attractive work assignments. The principle of seniority enables an organization to limit a new person in assuming duties that challenge high-status roles in the group.

The formal restrictions as well as the informal cultural traditions of the organization affect the operations of the basic model. Even when restrictions are rigid and severe, however, the recruit has some area of freedom to work out a role in the group. Restrictions serve to concentrate role struggle in the region of the organization where the new worker competes for a role. In this region the role realignment will follow the model of the LGD.

WHEN THE GROUP LOSES PERSONNEL

When a person leaves a group with a stable role structure, his duties must be assumed by the remaining personnel. If he had an important role, people with less status will be tempted to fight for his place. The basic model explains the resultant struggle. Participants who stand to gain by climbing upward leave their old roles and create what is essentially an LGD. These members, formerly happy and content, become restless and striving. Often the level of cohesiveness drops during this period. If members are naïve about the effects of the removal of a person from a stable role structure, they are surprised by the resulting conflict and tensions. They cannot understand what went wrong. Last year they were a highly cohesive and successful group; this year nothing seems to get done, and Joe and Bill have had a falling out. Things are going badly. We need good old Harry, they will say, to hold things together.

WHEN NEW MEMBERS REPLACE OLD MEMBERS

Occasionally in old, established organizations, an individual will leave a formal position, and a new person will be appointed or hired for this place. In this case, the protections afforded by the seniority system or other restrictions on the activity of new people are bypassed. The formal position may be one with top authority and responsibility in the group—that is, the head of the group. If the departmental manager is transferred or promoted, a new manager may be hired from another group. The new manager has certain built-in levers to assure at least token compliance with his directives, but he *must go through a period of testing* until he establishes a role for himself. The way in which he finally assumes a role is by the mechanism developed in the basic model. In the Minnesota Studies, a number of groups had leaders assigned, and the effect of such structures was compared with the basic leaderless discussion group. Mortensen did a content analysis of the leadership communication in three such groups and compared it with the leadership communication in three LGDs. In two of the three groups, the assigned leaders did not emerge as the leaders. In the remaining group, the assigned leader emerged during the first hour of meeting. The basic model of the LGD was modified by assigning a leader. In the two groups that first deposed the assigned leader and then started the process of choosing another contender, the role struggle was lengthened and intensified when compared to the typical LGD. In the group that accepted the assigned leader after brief testing, the process of role emergence was shorter and less difficult than in any other group studied. When the formal leader proved to be the natural leader, the productivity and cohesiveness of the group were increased.

Some organizations have a policy of never promoting a man from within a work group because doing so may cause bad feelings. Sometimes this policy is based on the assumption that a man who is known well would be unable to lead his friends when he is promoted over them.

Often, promotions are made into different departments or divisions in other cities for these reasons; however, the new employee must still find his role in the informal structure. Promoting from within the group also upsets the role structure and requires a period of reshuffling.

The dynamics of the task-oriented groups that comprise an organization do not furnish a complete explanation of its structure and operation. Group methods do not give a complete account; however, the dynamics of the task-oriented small group furnish considerable insight into the operations of such groups, even when they are tightly integrated into larger formal organizations.

handling the problem posed by role emergence and change

Students are sometimes disturbed by the way roles are fought for and assigned in discussion groups. They feel that the struggle for power and position is not quite nice and wish to avoid it. They suggest two main expedients. First, they sometimes agree that all members will share equally in all the duties. Second, they sometimes work out an arbitrary structure for the group before the discussion.

The notion that all members of the discussion group will be equals seems sensible. Yet groups attempting to maintain equality fail. The members inevitably perceive that some person is doing more for the group and is a better thinker or worker than another member. The second line of attack is more intriguing. The idea of removing certain roles from contention by assigning them does recognize the group's need for specialization. A number of studies have distributed various functions among the members and then evaluated the effect of such a structure on productivity and cohesiveness. In general, this research does not support the idea that structures can be imposed on a group to increase its efficiency and cohesiveness. Structures must be tested and accepted. In the process of testing, the group usually grows away from the formal, arbitrary structure.

Groups and organizations develop in a way that is more analogous to a plant than to a machine. Engineers can draw up blueprints for a machine that will function as predicted. The parts of the machine do not change in shape or function from day to day. A gardener can prune and try to shape a plant in a certain way, but its roots continually seek water, and the leaves turn toward the sun. The roots often break the pot containing the plant, and a more "realistic" vessel must be found to hold it. Using a plan or blueprint to assign a formal structure to a group creates a similar result. The roles continually break out of the formal restrictions, and the face-to-face communication does not follow the blueprint. Nonetheless, the gardener who understands the laws that govern plant growth can work with plants to develop strong, healthy, and beautiful specimens. In a somewhat similar way, knowledgeable group members can work with the natural tendencies of the group to create stable and suitable role structures and efficient, cohesive groups.

The first rule is to recognize and understand the process by which roles emerge in the LGD. Individuals who pretend the process does not exist or that their group can avoid or short circuit the role struggle can do little consciously to improve their organizations. When a student of group methods understands the basic model and its modifications, he has a new perspective of the group. When the inevitable periods of role conflict arise, he will not be surprised. One of the most disturbing features for members who do not understand these matters is the development of unexpected disagreements and antagonisms. They come as a shock, particularly early in the life of a new group or after stable roles have been disturbed. Suddenly a member begins to act in unexpected ways, or the group becomes punishing to its members. The naïve participant reacts with behavior that is also uncharacteristic. He may blame individuals for what has happened. Joe has become unreasonable or uncooperative. The members of the group are stupid or cannot understand plain English. When problems arise without warning, there is less possibility of dealing with them. In a sense, the most potent antidote for the stresses and strains of role emergence and change in any group is the understanding of what is happening and why.

A participant starts with the insight that each member's role is worked out by the member and the group together. Thus, the group is partly responsible for the way each member acts. Blaming the group's problems on one or more of the members is a manifestation of group neurosis. The problem usually is with the group's behavior and a member's reaction to it. It is true sometimes that the basis of the problem lies outside the group. A member may be having trouble in another group, which makes him unable to function in any group. He may be fighting with his family or his girl friend. In this case, discovering the facts can help the group members understand and excuse his behavior. An understanding of group method serves to prepare a member for the stresses of role emergence. Some groups in the Minnesota Studies were instructed in the tasks to be performed and told nothing more. Other groups were given the same instructions, as well as a short series of lectures on the material covered in Chapters 7 to 12. Each group went through the same process of specialization and role struggle. Knowledge about group process did not keep that process from developing. However, the groups given lectures on group methods had less virulent struggles and lower tensions than the others.

Attitudes are important in handling the problems of role emergence. Much has been said about the problem posed by individuals who plan to exploit the group for their own purposes. Members do not work willingly in a group if the benefits go largely to one or two members. The sum of group interactions always tends to benefit everyone. Each member should decide if he wishes to belong or not. If he does, he should adopt the attitude that he is willing to work for the group's welfare. He will then be more receptive to the rewards a group can bestow on its members. If he feels that membership is not worthwhile, he should withdraw from the group.

Assuming that a member is sincerely dedicated to the group's welfare, he can take an active part in evaluating the skills and abilities of the other members and reinforce those that seem most beneficial to the group, *even if such reinforcement would sacrifice his personal standing within the group.* When a role conflict is resolved, he should be alert to the social and esteem needs of the loser. What role can this member best play and how can he be encouraged to assume it? How can he be reassured that, although the other members have chosen someone else, they still consider him a valuable member and want and need his help? A group often loses part of its talent because the unsuccessful contenders for important roles become unproductive. The good groups in the Minnesota Studies found roles for the losers that drew them back into the group.

A constant problem that results from role emergence is the person who finds himself playing a role with little status. He is just a worker, just a member, just a follower. As one person said in an interview, "Nobody in the group knows I exist as a person. I don't believe they would say 'hello' to me if they met me on campus." Status implies that if there are high-ranking positions, there must be low ones. Every group has a certain number of participants in the low positions. These people are the least active. Often referred to as dead wood, these people do not work very hard, do not attend meetings regularly, and dampen the enthusiasm and cohesiveness of the group. The low-status member often gets few social or esteem awards from membership. His opinions are often ignored; he is given little attention and consideration as a person. If a group wants a person to become involved, they should give him a job. But this is not enough. The job is only rewarding if it gives the person an opportunity to improve his status. If the work brings him to the attention of the others and he is recognized as being more important and worthwhile, be becomes more committed. If the job reinforces his low status, he will not be drawn into the group. If the task is menial, he probably will not do it.

The successful groups and organizations included in the Minnesota Studies developed ways to assure low-status members that they were highly important. Although they were not as important as others, they received definite assurances of respect. Many groups have difficulty because they devote so much time and energy to the high-status roles that they ignore the low-status positions. Thus, they encourage nonparticipation, inactivity, and disinterest.

Formal leaders often complain about dead wood in their organizations. They regard the problem as lack of interest among low-status personnel and offer solutions such as the use of interesting programs and social functions to encourage member commitment. It is better in these cases to examine the status structure and then plan a program to improve the standing of the nonparticipants. If his standing cannot be improved, can the organization make the low-status member feel the importance of his position in the group? More attention to the social and esteem needs of these people often creates increased interest and participation.

summary

Among the more prominent and visible features of contemporary organizations are the formal aspects which include structures such as the table of organization, job descriptions, position titles, lines of authority, and formal channels of communication.

Each position in a formal organization has certain tasks associated with it. These can be thought of as responsibilities. Authority is associated with responsibility. The authority is inherent in the position and accrues to any person who occupies that position. Each place in the table of organization has a certain amount of status in relation to the other positions, and, thus, each has a certain amount of prestige attached to it.

Studies of the LGD indicate that assigned roles do not serve to structure a zero-history small group and the same principle applies to larger collections of individuals. Studies of zero-history organizations in which structure was provided indicate that people in the organizations could not work within the framework of a blueprinted and imposed structure. They had to develop an understanding and perception of the organization, its goals, the relationships among the groups, and the channels of communication that connected them by actually trying to work together.

The informal structuring thus becomes the more important feature of the organizational context. This does not mean that the formal structure does not play an important part in the way the group works or in the satisfaction of its members, but simply that the visible elements of structure are not as important as they might at first seem.

Various members earn a certain amount of power and esteem within the organization. Power and esteem are unique to the individual who achieves them. Therefore, the power of a person holding a position of authority may be the same, more, or less than his authority. That same person may have esteem that is equal to, more, or less than the prestige of his office.

When groups come into competition within an organization, the result tends to be an increase in cohesiveness within each group, an increase in structure, and an increase in conformity. The content of internal communication tends to emphasize the worth and goodness of members and the villainous nature of other groups. Intergroup communication tends to be defensive and serves to increase antagonism rather than overcome it. Often groups ostensibly working cooperatively in an organization fall into competition because of a drive for organizational territory, empire building, and jurisdictional disputes. In addition, the earning and awarding of power within the organization bring individuals and groups into conflict.

The formal organization is static. The actual work of the organization is carried on by a series of interlocking and overlapping small task-oriented groups that may reflect the formal groups or may not. The role structure of these small task-oriented groups is influenced by the rigidity built into the formal structure and the communication channels, but it tends to fluctuate and change. The informal roles often depart from their formal counterparts.

The basic model of the dynamics of role emergence in a leaderless group discussion accounts for much of what happens in the task-oriented work groups that compose an organization on those occasions when the stable role structures are disrupted. These are often associated with a turnover of personnel.

A basic understanding of the process of role emergence is the best antidote to the problems posed by the disruption of stable role structure. No general formulas are available to apply to each new situation that arises in all groups. Participants who understand the tendencies of group dynamics can develop courses of action to meet specific problems if they understand the past history of their group.

QUESTIONS FOR STUDY

1. What is the difference between the formal and informal structures of an organization?
2. What is the difference between power and authority?
3. What is the effect of competition on intragroup and intergroup communication?
4. In what way can a drive for organizational territory account for intergroup competition?
5. What are the dynamics of the crisis meeting in the simulated organization, and what is its effect on the earning and awarding of power and authority?

6. What is the effect of a new member's joining the group?
7. How may seniority be used to inhibit the development of the informal group structures within an organization?
8. What is the effect of replacing a person in a position of prestige and authority within a work group?
9. How may low-status members of an organization gain esteem rewards?
10. What effect does the organizational restriction on the flow of communication have on the development of informal group structures?

EXERCISES

1. Form a field-study group with some members of your class. Select an organization within your community for study. Discover its table of organization. Observe the channels of communication, both formal and informal, as the people go about their work. Present a symposium discussion to your class in which you discuss the formation and operation of small task-oriented groups within the restrictions of the organization.
2. Form a group with some members of your class, and prepare a bibliography of works on organization. Have several work meetings in which you share information about organizations, and then develop a case study designed to present issues relevant to small groups within organizations. Present your case study to the class.
3. Work out a role-playing exercise with some members of your class that will illustrate some of the troublesome situations that arise because of the divergence of informal structure from formal structure within an organization. Present your role-playing exercise to the class, and conduct an educational conference on the problem.
4. Form a group with others in your class, and plan an alter-ego demonstration of status barriers to organizational conferences. Behind each person in the meeting, place a second person who expresses the real ideas and feelings of the members after each comment in the meeting. For example, the member might say, "I really don't mind . . ." but the alter ego says, "I sure hope you aren't going to pull that old trick . . . ," and so on. If there are not enough members in the group to use alter egos, the same effect can be obtained by the use of stage asides by the members themselves. After making a comment, everyone else freezes, and the member reveals his real feelings in an aside to the audience.

References and suggested readings

The basic analysis describing group process in the organizational context and the intragroup and intergroup communication as they relate to formal and informal structures is drawn largely from the case studies of simulated organizations at Minnesota. The results are in substantial agreement with the discoveries of other investigators, particularly those associated with the Tavistock Workshops in human relations. Professor William S. Howell of Minnesota is a trained staff member of the Tavistock approach and has compared and contrasted the results of the Minnesota simulations of Group Dynamics, Inc., with the Tavistock discoveries. The best sources for the Tavistock work with large groups are:

Rice, A. E. *The Enterprise and Its Environment*. London: Tavistock, 1963.
Rice, A. E. *Learning for Leadership: Interpersonal and Intergroup Relations*. London: Tavistock, 1965.

Bales reported his case studies in:

Bales, Robert F. *Personality and Interpersonal Behavior*. New York: Holt, Rinehart and Winston, 1970.

For detailed analysis of the relationship between small task-oriented groups and organizational context, see:

Bass, Bernard M. *Leadership, Psychology and Organizational Behavior*. New York: Harper & Row, 1960.
Zaleznik, Abraham, and David Moment. *The Dynamics of Interpersonal Behavior*. New York: Wiley, 1964.

For further discussion of leadership, communication, and organizational structure, see:

Blau, Peter M., and W. Richard Scott. *Formal Organizations*. San Francisco: Chandler, 1962.
Bormann, Ernest G., William S. Howell, Ralph G. Nichols, and George L. Shapiro. *Interpersonal Communication in the Modern Organization*. Englewood Cliffs, N.J.: Prentice-Hall, 1969.
Etzioni, Amitai. *Modern Organizations*. Englewood Cliffs, N.J.: Prentice-Hall, 1964.
Weick, Karl E. *The Social Psychology of Organizing*. Reading, Mass.: Addison-Wesley, 1969.

The survey of the effect of competition on groups is from:

Schein, Edgar H. *Organizational Psychology*. 2nd ed. Englewood Cliffs, N.J.: Prentice-Hall, 1970, pp. 80–82.

For a survey of research on territoriality and small groups, see:

Ardrey, Robert. *The Territorial Imperative*. New York: Atheneum, 1966.
Shaw, Marvin E. *Group Dynamics: The Psychology of Small Group Behavior*. New York: McGraw-Hill, 1971, pp. 118–122.

See also:

DeLong, Alton J. "Dominance-Territorial Relations in a Small Group," *Environment and Behavior*, **2** (1970), 170–191.
Sommer, Robert. *Personal Space*. Englewood Cliffs, N.J.: Prentice-Hall, 1969.

For the discussion of ad hocracy, see:

Toffler, Alvin. *Future Shock*. New York: Random House, 1970.

For a study of the effect of assigning chairmen to class discussion groups, see:

Mortensen, Calvin D. "Should the Discussion Group Have an Assigned Leader?" *Speech Teacher*, **15** (1966), 34–41.

APPENDIX
THE MINNESOTA STUDIES

The studies of the author and his associates in the Small-Group Communication Seminar at the University of Minnesota furnish the empirical amplification as well as the key concepts of much of the material in Part II of *Discussion and Group Methods*. The Minnesota Studies consist of the research of the author over the past 14 years and the work of his students reported in seminar papers, master's theses, and doctoral dissertations. The seminar's basic approach has been clinical. The backbone of the program is the collection of exhaustive case studies of small task-oriented groups. The author and his associates made about 200 case studies at the University of Minnesota from 1959 to 1974. Before that time, the author collected case studies of classroom discussion groups at Eastern Illinois University and Florida State University.

The controlling assumption of the Small-Group Communication Seminar is that a group's role structure (including leadership), norms, and culture are to some extent idiosyncratic and that a given group's process can be completely explained only if one knows the history of the group. Thus, an intensive case study provides the best explanation of a group's dynamics. To implement the group histories, students have used a number of different observational techniques to collect data. In the early years of the research program, investigators relied largely on rating blanks, attitude scales, and content-analysis procedures. Among the more well-known techniques, they used the Bales system of content analysis of the interaction process, sociometric indexes, and whom-to-whom communication matrixes. The typical case history supplemented qualitative data with information from interviews with the participants, tape recordings of the meetings, and anecdotal descriptions of direct observations.

As the clinical observations produced more specific hypotheses for investigation, members of the seminar have relied more heavily on content-analysis procedures designed to investigate specific research problems and on diaries, interviews, and questionnaires.

The Small-Group Communication Seminar is taught in conjunction with an upper-division course in discussion in the College of Liberal Arts. Members of the seminar select a group either from the course or from some other setting for study. Each student prepares a case history as the core of his seminar work. As a result, many of the case studies are of groups set up in discussion classes, which makes their histories pertinent to the work of such classes. The majority of the groups from the discussion course were leaderless group discussions (LGDs). Some investigations, however, required a comparison of structured and unstructured groups; in those instances, the instructor assigned chairmen for some of the groups. Other investigations required a comparison among groups composed of men, of women, and of both men and women.

The groups varied in size from three to seven, and most met for the entire quarter. Some investigations, however, required a comparison between a given subject's role in two different groups, and, in those instances, the groups met for half a term. In the latter case, the class of 25 was randomly divided into five LGDs of five each at the start of the term, and each subject was then assigned to a new LGD at mid-term in such a way that no two individuals remained together in the second group. Observers could then compare the role a subject assumed in the first LGD with the one that developed in the second.

Members of the seminar, on occasion, selected groups from the field. Some of these were student government groups; others were drawn from business, education, and religion.

Since 1968, the author has taught the upper-division course in small-group communication as a simulated organization called Group Dynamics, Inc. The author and his associates and members of the Small-Group Communication Seminar have made extensive studies of 10 simulated organizations. Eight of the simulations have been of organizations composed of five task-oriented small groups, and two have been composed of seven divisions. Each study of a simulation includes case studies of each of the component small groups. In addition to the basic divisions of the organization, the structure of the corporation includes a management group called the Executive Committee. Investigators have made case studies of the Executive Committee to compare and contrast its dynamics with those of the LGD in isolation and in the organizational context. The case studies of the organization include investigations of the informal communication networks, the communication flow and content from the Executive Committee to the other divisions, and the nature and influence of rumors and fantasy themes on the organization.

Since 1970, a new line of investigation which is essentially a rhetorical analysis of the communication of the small groups has provided the rationale for much of the research by members of the Small-Group Communication Seminar.

For a more detailed explanation of the methodology of fantasy theme analysis for rhetorical criticism, see:

Bormann, Ernest B. "Fantasy and Rhetorical Vision: The Rhetorical Criticism of Social Reality," *Quarterly Journal of Speech*, **58** (1972), 396–407.

In addition to case studies of classroom simulations, a seminar in organizational communication taught by Professor David Smith in 1972 analyzed fantasy themes and organizational myths in four organizations in the Twin Cities. Included in the study were a religious organization, a division of a major computer facility, a small family-owned business-supply company, and a station of the University of Minnesota hospitals.

THESES

The following theses have contributed to the Minnesota Studies:

Berg, David M. "A Descriptive Analysis of the Distribution and Duration of Themes Discussed by the Task-oriented, Small Group." Ph.D. dissertation, University of Minnesota, 1963.

Berg's category system is being used to explore several new questions in a doctoral dissertation now in progress by Irene Faffler.

Fisher, B. Aubrey. "Decision Emergence: A Process Model of Verbal Task Behavior for Decision-Making Groups." Ph.D. dissertation, University of Minnesota, 1968.

Forston, Robert. "The Decision-Making Process in the American Civil Jury: A Comparative Methodological Investigation." Ph.D. dissertation, University of Minnesota, 1968.

Geier, John. "A Descriptive Analysis of an Interaction Pattern Resulting in Leadership Emergence in Leaderless Group Discussion." Ph.D. dissertation, University of Minnesota, 1963.

Larson, Charles U. "Leadership Emergence and Attention Span: A Content Analysis of the Time Devoted to Themes in the Task-oriented Small Group." Ph.D. dissertation, University of Minnesota, 1968.

Mortensen, Calvin. "A Content Analysis of Leadership Communication in Small, Task-oriented Discussion Groups." Master's thesis, University of Minnesota, 1964.

Runkel, Judy. "A Survey of the Small Group Techniques Used in College Beginning Speech Classes." Ph.D. dissertation, University of Minnesota, 1972.

Although one doctoral candidate submitted a dissertation in another department, Business Administration, he used modifications of the Berg category system and the author's computer program for the analysis of time devoted to themes, and the author served on the graduate committee of that study. See:

Kee, Yong Tan. "Business Across Boundaries: A Laboratory Experiment to Analyze the Decision-Making Behavior of Groups from Different Cultures." Ph.D. dissertation, University of Minnesota, 1970.

Some of the results of these studies have been published in the following articles:

Berg, David M. "A Descriptive Analysis of the Distribution and Duration of Themes Discussed by Task-oriented Small Groups," *Speech Monographs,* **34** (1967), 172–175.

Berg, David M. "A Thematic Approach to the Analysis of the Task-oriented Small Group," *Central States Speech Journal,* **18** (1967), 285–291.

Chesebro, James W., John F. Cragan, and Patricia McCullough. "The Small Group Techniques of the Radical Revolutionary: A Synthesis of Consciousness Raising," *Speech Monographs,* **40** (1973), 136–146.

Fisher, B. Aubrey. "Decision Emergence: Phases in Group Decision-Making," *Speech Monographs,* **37** (1970), 53–66.

Geier, John. "A Trait Approach in the Study of Leadership in Small Groups," *Journal of Communication,* **17** (1967), 316–323.

Larson, Charles U. "The Verbal Response of Groups to the Absence or Presence of Leadership," *Speech Monographs,* **38** (1971), 177–181.

Mortensen, Calvin. "Should the Discussion Group Have an Assigned Leader?" *Speech Teacher,* **15** (1966), 34–41.

The following unpublished seminar papers and master's B papers written by students at Minnesota are included here because they are illustrative of the nature of the more recent, focused case studies or because materials from the papers were used in the text.

Bargen, Don. "Role Definition and Fantasy," 1970.

Berman, Theresa. "A Thematic Analysis of Two Community Task-oriented Discussion Groups," [n.d].

Brooks, David A. "The Dyad Within the Triad," 1972.

Bjornson, Janice. "A Study of Group Problem-Solving Techniques," 1966.

Chartrand, Bill. "An Interactional Analysis of an Intercultural Communications Workshop Group," 1972.

Cragan, John. "Organizational Myths: A Possible Methodology," 1971.

De Ranitz, Richard. "The Role of Fantasy in Group Decision Making," 1970.

Dugas, Charmagne. "Time Orientation and Group Roles," 1973.

Ferguson, Beverly. "The Relation of Fantasy Themes to the Function of a Small Group," 1970.

Forston, Robert F. "A Study of the Use of Three Types of Questions and Their Effect on Group Understanding," 1965.

Franzmeier, Wesley. "A Description and Criticism of the Use of Arguments in Two Radio, Round-Table Discussion Programs Prepared for Speech 106," 1963.

Hawes, Leonard. "The Interactive Effects of Choice, Participation, and Ambivalence on Small Group Productivity," 1969.

Henderson, Bill. "Analysis of an On-going Task-oriented Small Group: The Macalester Speech and Theater Arts Department Staff Meetings," 1972.

Hensley, Carl Wayne. "A Study of Factors by Which a Small Group Confers Status upon Its Members," 1969.

Hoffman, Barbara, and Greg May. "Last Tango in Minneapolis: Fantasy Theme and Burkean Analysis of Two Small Groups," 1973.

Ilkka, Richard J. "Case Studies of Two Task-oriented Small Groups to Discover Relation of Fantasy Themes to Group Problems," 1970.

Johnson, Fern L., and Virginia V. Kidd. " 'Oh fang oh ga do dang: Simple as a Pimple in a Dimple': Small Group Research with the Four and Six Year Old," 1972.

Johnson, Lyle K. "Expression of Hostility in a Small Group," 1965.

Johnson, Suzanne. "Myth as Method: A Study of a Forty-Member Unitarian Fellowship," 1972.

Krawczyk, Doris. "An Examination of the Relationship Between the Quality and Quantity of Leader Communication to the Quantity of Staff Communication in a Mental Health Team," 1973.

Kroll, Phillip R. "Talkative Members in Small Groups," 1972.

Lee, David G. "Observed Patterns of Interaction During Crisis Situations with Emergency Medical Care Ambulance Teams: A Study in Small Group Communication," 1971.

McCullough, Patricia. "Myths and Communication in a Technical Organization," 1972.

McDonald, Jean A. "The Relationship of Fantasy Events to Role Emergence in the Leaderless, Task-oriented Small Group," 1970.

McGlaughlin, Dorothy. "The Woman Contender for Leadership: A Study of the Roles of Women in Leaderless Discussion Groups," 1973.

Mortensen, Calvin. "Leadership Decision Moments in the Leaderless Group," 1963.

Mosvick, Roger. "Group Dynamics: Reflections Concerning Some Characteristics of Small Groups and Leader Emergence in Relatively Unstructured Groups," 1965 (based on observations of engineering conferences at Minneapolis Honeywell).

Nishiyama, Kazuo. "Selection of Steering Committee Representatives in Leaderless, Task Oriented Groups and the Roles the Representatives Played in Their Own Task Groups," 1968.

Nishiyama, Kazuo. "The Study of Japanese Task-oriented Small Groups," 1969.

Paik, Penelope. "Studying Intercultural Communication: A Fantasy Theme Approach," 1971.

Putnam, Linda. "Dramatistic Themes in the Analysis of an Office-Supply Firm," 1972.

Ramsperger, Frank S. J. "Elements Which Influence Decision Making in Unstructured Small Groups," 1968.

Rousselow, Jesse. "A Case Study of the Manifest Personality of Members Compared to Cohesiveness, Structure, and Tension in an All-Woman Group," 1963.

Schaffer, Philip A. "Stage-Related Development and Participation in a Moral Dilemmas Discussion Group," 1972.

Seibel, Roy. "A Descriptive Study of Statements Made by an Individual in Small Group Discussion Which Are Interpreted as Attempts to Build His Ethos Within the Group," 1964.

Shields, Don. "The Public Character of the Fire Fighter," 1973.

Sjodin, Richard B. "Fantasy in the Task-oriented Small Group," 1971.

Thomas, Patricia. "Case Study of Fantasy in a Task-oriented Small Group," 1970.

Veninga, Robert. "A Study of Discussant Dissatisfaction in Group Problem Solving," [n.d.].

Wallen, Sue. "Group and Individual Fantasy in a GDI Group," 1970.

Watson, Robert. "Hollywood and the Politician: A Case Study of the Effects of Leadership on Small Group Decision Making," 1966.

Weisser, Margaret M. "A Study of Some Cohesive Characteristics of Alcoholics Anonymous Small Group Meetings," 1973.

Witte, Barbara J. "Studies in Leadership: An Analysis of Fischer's 'Interaction Analysis System,'" 1972.

Zimmerman, Alan R. "The Rehabilitation of Juvenile Delinquents Through Positive-Peer-Culture Groups: An Investigation into the Problem-Solving Dynamics of One Such Group," 1972.

INDEXES

AUTHOR INDEX

Aristotle, 66

Bales, Robert F., 18, 115, 163, 164, 177, 199, 200, 284, 290, 300–301, 307, 355, 368, 369
Bane, Laverne, 12
Bany, Mary A., 281
Berg, David, 287, 288, 302
Berlo, David M., 32, 287, 288
Bernays, Edward, 14
Bion, Wilfred R., 285
Bormann, Ernest G., 203
Briedis, Irene, 289
Buber, Martin, 45

Cartwright, Dorwin, 18
Crowell, Laura, 286, 287

Darwin, Charles R., 9
Deutsch, Morton, 18, 151
Dewey, John, 9, 13, 16, 280, 281, 282, 283, 289, 295
Dion, Kenneth L., 289

Faffler, Irene, 288
Faust, William L., 287
Ferguson, Beverly, 295, 296
Fiedler, Fred E., 245, 246
Fisher, B. Aubrey, 289
Freud, Sigmund, 44, 213

Galbraith, John Kenneth, 2, 8, 9
Gandhi, Mahatma, 67
Geier, John, 255
Goethe, von, Johanne Wolfgang, 243
Goodrich, Chauncey, 10
Gunderson, Robert, 18

Haiman, Franklyn S., 248
Hance, Kenneth G., 280
Hare, A. Paul, 17
Hellman, Hugo, 12
Howell, William S., 355

Janis, Irving, 66, 288
Johnson, Lois V., 281

Kant, Immanuel, 66
Kelley, H. H., 150

Kelman, Herbert, 18
Kepner, Charles H., 281, 282, 283
Kesey, Ken, 293
Kierkegaard, Sören A., 45
Kinsey, Alfred Charles, 105
Kroger, Rolf O., 289

Larson, Charles, 288
Lewin, Kurt, 18, 44
Likert, Rensis, 1, 2, 147
Lincoln, Abraham, 58
Lippitt, Ronald, 244, 250
Long, Huey, 67

McBurney, James H., 280
McCarthy, Joseph, 67
McGregor, Douglas M., 297
Magnan, Mary Ann, 289
Maier, Norman, 146
March, James G., 281
Meade, Margaret, 46
Menninger, Karl, 63
Mill, John Stuart, 13
Miller, Norman, 289
Mishler, E., 300
Moment, David, 284, 285, 286, 290
Moreno, J. L., 44, 301
Mortensen, Calvin D., 251, 375
Mosvick, Roger, 203

Osborn, Alex T., 190, 322, 323

Quintilian, 66

Raack, R. C., 288
Rice, A. E., 285, 363, 364
Riesman, David, 8, 9
Rogers, Carl, 44
Ryberg, Lillian, 288

Sartre, John Paul, 45
Schacter, Stanley, 235
Scheidel, Thomas M., 286, 287
Schramm, Wilbur, 32
Schutz, William G., 159, 160, 200
Shannon, Claude E., 32
Shaw, Marvin E., 148

SUBJECT INDEX

Stereotypes, 209–210, 252, 320
Structure, 160–162, 355, 358–359,
    369–370, 376
Surveys, 107–108
Symposium discussion, 324–325

Tavistock, 285, 363–364
Tension releaser, 206–207. *See also* Role

Territoriality, 361–362
T-Groups, 44. *See also* Encounter Groups
    games and exercises for, 19, 329–330
Topic, wording of, 332
Transitions, 304

Women, role of in groups, 148–149,
    255–256, 266–268